Social Security in the Balkans
Volume 3

Studies in Critical Social Sciences Book Series

Haymarket Books is proud to be working with Brill Academic Publishers (www.brill.nl) to republish the *Studies in Critical Social Sciences* book series in paperback editions. This peer-reviewed book series offers insights into our current reality by exploring the content and consequences of power relationships under capitalism, and by considering the spaces of opposition and resistance to these changes that have been defining our new age. Our full catalog of *SCSS* volumes can be viewed at https://www.haymarketbooks.org/series_collections/4-studies-in-critical-social-sciences.

Series Editor
David Fasenfest (Wayne State University)

Editorial Board
Eduardo Bonilla-Silva (Duke University)
Chris Chase-Dunn (University of California–Riverside)
William Carroll (University of Victoria)
Raewyn Connell (University of Sydney)
Kimberlé W. Crenshaw (University of California–LA and Columbia University)
Heidi Gottfried (Wayne State University)
Karin Gottschall (University of Bremen)
Alfredo Saad Filho (King's College London)
Chizuko Ueno (University of Tokyo)
Sylvia Walby (Lancaster University)
Raju Das (York University)

Social Security in the Balkans

Volume 3

An Overview of Social Policy in Serbia and Kosovo

Edited by
Marzena Żakowska

Haymarket Books
Chicago, IL

First published in 2021 by Brill Academic Publishers, The Netherlands
© 2021 Koninklijke Brill NV, Leiden, The Netherlands

Published in paperback in 2023 by
Haymarket Books
P.O. Box 180165
Chicago, IL 60618
773-583-7884
www.haymarketbooks.org

ISBN: 978-1-64259-811-7

Distributed to the trade in the US through Consortium Book Sales and Distribution (www.cbsd.com) and internationally through Ingram Publisher Services International (www.ingramcontent.com).

This book was published with the generous support of Lannan Foundation and Wallace Action Fund.

Special discounts are available for bulk purchases by organizations and institutions. Please call 773-583-7884 or email info@haymarketbooks.org for more information.

Cover design by Jamie Kerry and Ragina Johnson.

Printed in the United States.

10 9 8 7 6 5 4 3 2 1

Library of Congress Cataloging-in-Publication data is available.

Contents

Acknowledgements VII
List of Figures and Tables VIII
Abbreviations XI
Notes on Contributors XIV
Abstracts XX

Serbia and Kosovo: EU Integration and the Development of the Social Security Systems 1
 Marzena Żakowska

PART 1
Social Security in Serbia

1 Overview of Social Protection in Serbia: Current Perspectives and Challenges 27
 Katarina Stanić and Gordana Matković

2 The Pension System in Serbia: Developments, Current State and Challenges 50
 Katarina Stanić

3 Decentralization of Social Care Services in Serbia 72
 Gordana Matković

4 Unemployment in Serbia: Characteristics and Challenges 89
 Maja Jandrić and Marzena Żakowska

PART 2
Social Security in Kosovo

5 The Renegotiation of Social Policy in Kosovo: Gradual Institutional Change since Independence 127
 Artan Mustafa and Pëllumb Çollaku

6 Developments and Challenges in the Kosovo Pension System   162
   Remzije Istrefi and Ruzhdi Morina

7 Buying Social Peace: Lessons from Kosovo   188
   Besnik Fetahu and Marzena Żakowska

8 Kosovo Society: Coexistence, Challenges and Opportunities   224
   Dritero Arifi and Ngadhnjim Brovina

PART 3
Conclusion

9 Social Security in the Balkans: Lessons and Recommendations   257
   Marzena Żakowska and Dorota Domalewska

Index   265

Acknowledgements

The inspiration for writing this three-volume book was the experience gained during research begun by Marzena Żakowska in the Balkans in 2014. However, it could not have been written without the help of many people whom I wish to thank profusely.

My gratitude goes to Professor Cezary Smuniewski for his encouragement to start the project and his guidance and constructive comments during the development process. I would like to thank Professor Jarosław Gryz and Professor Mark Juszczak for their insightful discussions during the research. I acknowledge the funding received from the War Studies University, Warsaw, Poland. I am also thankful for the support I received from Professor Col. Tadeusz Zieliński, Professor Col. Andrzej Soboń, and Professor Jarosław Solarz, who authorized the project and offered thoughtful advice. I owe thanks to Tomasz Żornaczuk from the Polish Institute of International Affairs and Marta Szpala from the Center for Eastern Studies for their valuable counsel.

I am thankful to Professor Ilona Urych, Col (res) Doctor Lech Drab, Doctor Adam Szynal and Shkëlzen Macukulli for believing in my work. I would like to thank the authors of all the individual chapters – without their expertise, patience, and dedication, this book would not have been completed.

I extend my gratitude to Katarzyna Tarasewicz, Richard Koss, Małgorzata Zeniuk, Debbie de Wit, and Judy Pereira, who supported forming the final shape of the book.

I am grateful to my Family, Friends, and all of my Colleagues in the Balkan states. Without their support this endeavour would not have been possible.

A special word of thanks goes to the Editor of the *Studies in Critical Social Sciences* Series, Professor David Fasenfest, who offered constructive remarks and coordinated the study.

Figures and Tables

Figures

1.1	Social protection benefits (% of GDP) in 2015	28
1.2	System of social protection in Serbia	30
1.3	Absolute poverty line and minimum pension	34
1.4	Amounts of FSA and CA for different family types vs. the poverty line and minimum wage, 2016	41
2.1	Number of pensioners by type of pension, 2002–2018 (end of year)	57
2.2	Net replacement rate in Serbia, 2003–2019 (in%)	57
2.3	Net replacement rate in EU and Serbia, 2016	58
2.4	Aggregate replacement ratio (ARR) and relative median income of the elderly (RMI 65 and above) in EU and Serbia, 2018	59
2.5	Minimum pension and the absolute poverty line (in %)	61
2.6	Absolute poverty rate, 2006–2017	62
2.7	At-risk-of-poverty rate, total and by gender (in %, income in 2018)	62
2.8	Pension expenditures in the EU and Serbia (% of GDP)	63
2.9	Budgetary transfers to PDI fund and pension deficit (% of GDP), 2009–2018	65
3.1	Social care services within the mandate of LGs	75
3.2	Sources of CBS financing 2018	78
4.1	Employment in Serbia (15+), 2004–2010	92
4.2	Employment rate, unemployment rate and activity in Serbia in 2014–2019	93
4.3	Unemployment rate in age groups 15+, 15–24 and 15–64	94
4.4	Youth unemployment rate (15–24) in European countries in 2019	95
4.5	Unemployment rates from age and gender perspective	96
4.6	Unemployment rates (15–74, total in %) in European countries in 2019	97
4.7	Employment and activity rates in European countries in 2019	98
4.8	Length of job seeking time in 2019	100
4.9	Median age of population in 2019	102
4.10	First permits for persons with citizenship of RS in EU 28	103
4.11	Employment elasticity during the recession 2008/2009	105
4.12	EPL index	111
4.13	Countries with greater de facto relative flexibility: EPRC	113
4.14	Countries with greater de facto relative flexibility: EPR	113
4.15	Share of unemployment benefit recipients in total registered unemployment (in %)	115
4.16	Public expenditure on active labor market policies (% of GDP in 2017)	118

5.1   Number of left-wing MPs, GDP, and government revenue, expenditure, and debt, 2001–2017   142
5.2   Current structure (2008–2016) of social protection expenditure as % of GDP and the prognosis of social protection expenditure   143
5.3   Consumption and income poverty rate, 2009–2015 (in %)   146
5.4   Employment and unemployment rate, 2002–2019   150
6.1   Annual changes to unit price 2002–2018 (in %)   172
7.1   Social security system in Kosovo   199
7.2   Beneficiaries of social assistance in Kosovo, 2003–2019   206
7.3   Kosovo average net wages in the budget sector, 2003–2019 (in euro)   212
9.1   Factors affecting social security system   262

Tables

1.1   Social protection expenditure in Serbia (% of GDP), 2010–2015   29
2.1   Pension coverage of elderly people (65+ years of age)   56
2.2   Perspective net replacement rate (1st & 2nd pillars), EU and Serbia   60
3.1   LG social care services, Serbia, 2018   76
3.2   Distribution of LGs by share of expenditures on social care services in local budgets, 2018   77
3.3   Distribution of LGs by share of earmarked transfers, 2018   79
3.4   Expenditures for CBS, Serbia, 2012–2018   80
3.5   Eligible LGs, type of services, structure of funds and criteria, according to type of transfers   82
3.6   Criteria and weights for the allocation of earmarked transfers   83
4.1   Employment, unemployment, and activity rate in the period 2004–2013   91
4.2   Regional differences in key labor market indicators in 2019   100
4.3   Changes in the share of the working-age population in the total population in Serbia in the period 2010–2050   102
4.4   Employment rates and GDP growth in 2008–2019   105
4.5   Changes in the EPL index in Serbia   112
4.6   Classification of the transition countries according to the strictness and the level of EPL application in 2005   112
4.7   Key changes in the unemployment benefit system in Serbia – the rate of benefits   116
6.1   Pension systems in the region   169
6.2   Kosovo population according to age groups and year   175
6.3   Pension system model recommended to be applied in Kosovo   176
7.1   Forms of social policy in the European Union   193

7.2	Impact of European integration on social expenditure of Member States	195
7.3	Macroeconomic indicators in Kosovo 197	
7.4	Kosovo budget funds for social expenditures (in euro) 202	
7.5	Pension scheme for families of martyrs disabled veterans by categories (in number) 203	
7.6	Distribution of funds within social welfare in Kosovo (in euro) 204	
7.7	The distribution of pensions in Kosovo (in euro) 205	
7.8	Macroeconomic indicators and social expenditure in Kosovo and selected EU countries 209	
8.1	Structural change of the ethnic population in Kosovo 1981–1999 235	
8.2	Population by ethnicity in Kosovo, according to the last census from 2011 239	

Abbreviations

AAK	Alliance for the Future of Kosovo
ABF	Household Budget Survey
ARR	aggregate replacement ratio
CA	child allowance
CBK	Central Bank of Kosovo
CBS	Community-based services
CPI	Consumer Price Index
CSOs	Civil society organizations
CSW	Centers for Social Work
CWD	Children with disabilities
DB	Defined benefit
DC	Defined contribution
DFID	The United Kingdom Department for International Development
EAS	Employment Agency Service
ECJ	European Court of Justice
EMU	European Monetary Union
EPC	an index showing the strictness of additional provisions related to collective redundancies
EPL	employment protection legislation
EPR	an index for standard contracts
EPRC	a sub-index which refers to the protection of permanent workers against individual and collective dismissals it represents the weighted average of EPR and EPC sub-indices
EPT	indices for temporary contracts
ESPN	European Social Policy Network
ESS	Social Survey
EUROSTAT	European Statistical Office
EUSILC	European Union Statistics on Income and Living Conditions
FRY	Federal Republic of Yugoslavia
FSA	financial social assistance
HBS	Household Budget Survey
HI Fund	Health Insurance Fund
HPI	Human Poverty Indicators
ICO	International Civilian Office
IDPs	Internally Displaced Persons
ILO	International Labor Organization

IMF	International Monetary Fund
KAS	Kosovo Agency of Statistics
KFOR	The Kosovo Force
KLA	Kosovo Liberation Army
KPC	Kosovo Protection Corpus
KPST	Kosovo Pension Saving Trust
KS	Kosovo
KSAK	The Socialist Autonomous Province of Kosovo
KSF	Kosovo Security Force
LB	Unification Movement, a political party in Kosovo
LDK	Democratic League of Kosovo
LFS	Labor Force Survey
LGS	local governments
LPSFS	Law for Pension Schemes Financed by the State
LSMS	Living Standard Measurement Study
LTC	long-term care
MLSW	Labor and Social Welfare in Kosovo
NDC	National Defined Contribution
NEET	Not in Education, Employment, or Training
NES	National Employment Service
NISMA	Social Democratic Initiative
NRU	natural rate of unemployment
OECD	Organisation for Economic Cooperation and Development
OSCE	Organization for Security and Co-operation in Europe
PAYG	Pay-as-You-Go system
PDI Fund	Pension and Disability Insurance Fund
PDK	Democratic Party of Kosovo
PIO	Pension and Disability Fund
PP	power standard
PSD	Social Democratic Party
PSK	Socialist Party of Kosovo
PWD	persons with disabilities
RMI	relative median income
RR	replacement rate
RSD	Serbian dinar
RTK 2	Radio Television of Kosovo 2
SAA	Stabilization and Association Agreement
SAS	Social Assistance Scheme
SFRY	Socialist Federal Republic of Yugoslavia

SIF	Social Innovation Fund
SILC	Survey on Income and Living Conditions
SKPF	Slovenian-Kosovan Pension Fund
SORS	Statistical Office of the Republic of Serbia
SP	social protection
SRSG	Special Representative of the Secretary General
STM	Stabilization and Association Tracking Mechanism
SWOT	Strengths – Weaknesses – Opportunities – Threats
TSS	Transitional Support Strategy
UNDP	United Nations Development Program
UNHCR	United Nations Commissioner for Refugees
UNMIK	United Nations Interim Administration Mission in Kosovo
UNSCR 1244	United Nations Security Council Resolution 1244
USAID	United States Agency for International Development
VV	Vetëvendosje, a social-democratic Albanian nationalistic political party in Kosovo

Notes on Contributors

Dritero Arifi
is a professor at the Faculty of Political Science at the University for Business and Technology, Kosovo. His areas of research are political parties, security issues, and European foreign policy. He has published a number of articles, including "The concept of comprehensive security, as a draft for reconstructing security in a system of international relations" (ILIRIA International Review, 1(1), 2016); "Kosovo Political Party Attitudes Towards European Integration" (co-authored with Fjolle Nuhiu, European Journal of Social Science Education and Research, 5(1), 2018); "Roma community in Kosovo: between reality and the European dream" (co-author with Dashamir Berxulli and Ngadhnjim Brovina, Journal of Identity and Migration Studies, 12(2), 2018). His ORCID is https://orcid.org/0000-0002-0523-2412 and e-mail address: dritero.arifi@ubt-uni.net.

Ngadhnjim Brovina
is a professor at the Faculty of Political Science at the University for Business and Technology, Kosovo. He has written a number of publications in the field of foreign policy, public diplomacy, public policy, international relations, and international law including "European Union Public Diplomacy – case study – The Intervention in Bosnia and Herzegovina" (co-authored with Fjollë Nuhiu & Ngadhnjim Brovina, European Journal of Social Science, Education and Research, 10(2), 2017); "Peacebuilding in Kosovo" (ILIRIA International Review, 7(1), 2017); "The role of international organizations in the policy-making process in Kosovo" (co-author with Jonuz Abdullai, Institute of Knowledge Management, 17(2), 2017); "Roma Community in Kosovo: between reality and the European dream" (co-author with Dashamir Berxulli, and Dritero Arifi, Journal of Identity and Migration Studies, 12(2), 2018). His ORCID is https://orcid.org/0000-0002-9895-2397 and e-mail address: ngadhnjim.brovina@ubt-uni.net.

Pëllumb Çollaku
is a lecturer at the Riinvest College and a Senior Research Associate at the Riinvest Institute for Development Research, Kosovo. He received Civil Society Scholar Award (2016/17) from Open Society international Foundation; a research Grant from Scholarships for Post-Graduates from the Republic of Austria (2016); Erasmus+ Traineeship Scholarship from Sapienza University of Rome and EU Commission (2016). He did several economic consultancies among others for Social Development Investment (Tirana, Albania, 2019), Kosovo Democratic

Institute (KDI) (Pristina, Kosovo, 2020). He received Erasmus Mundus Basileus IV Programme Scholarship for doctoral studies from the European Commission (2013). His recent publications include "Pushing on a string? An evaluation of regional economic cooperation in the Western Balkans" (co-authored with Richard Grieveson, Vladimir Gligorov, I. Mara, M. Pichler, Bertelsmann Stiftung, 2020); "Socio-economic implications of Covid-19: Kosovo and Western Balkans" (Riinvest Institute, 2020); and "Living with COVID-19: Three pillars of recovery" (co-authored with Muhamet Mustafa and Visar Vokrri, Riinvest Institute, Kosovo, 2020). His ORCID is https://orcid.org/0000-0003-2400-0294 and e-mail address: pellumb.collaku@riinvestinstitute.org.

Dorota Domalewska
is an assistant professor at the National Security Faculty, War Studies University, Warsaw, Poland. She is the Head of the Department of Security Education. During the years 2012–2015, she was a lecturer at Stamford International University and Rangsit University in Thailand and, in 2019, a research fellow at Rangsit University, Thailand. She carries out interdisciplinary research blending the field of security, communication, and education. She is the author of "Multidimensional communication from a security perspective. Communication in crisis situations and strategic communication" (Warsaw: War Studies University, 2020, in Polish), and "Determinants of the modern security environment" (co-editor with Radosław Bielawski, Warsaw: War Studies University, 2020, in Polish). She has published numerous articles on security education, immigrant integration processes, strategic communication in social media, and societal security. Since 2016, she has been an Associate Editor and, since 2020, Editor-in-Chief of Security and Defence Quarterly, ISSN 2300-8741. Her ORCID is https://orcid.org/0000-0002-1788-1591 and e-mail address: d.domalewska@akademia.mil.pl.

Besnik Fetahu
is an assistant professor at the Faculty of Public Safety, the Kosovo Academy for Public Safety and Lecturer at the Faculty of Philosophy at the University of Pristina, Kosovo. He is Head of Institute for Research and Development, the Kosovo Academy for Public Safety and Political Adviser at the Prime minister's office. He was a Taiwan Fellow at the University of Taipei (2016), an Austrian Fellow at the University of Graz (2015), a Visiting Professor at the University of Applied Science of Brandenburg Germany (2019), a Visiting Professor at the University College of Police in Tampere Finland (2018), and a Visiting Professor at the Estonian Academy for Security Science (2017). His publications include "Applying Esping-Andersen Typology of Welfare State in Western Balkan

Countries" (International Journal of Interdisciplinary Civic and Political Studies, 12(2), 2017); "Challenges with Poverty and Unemployment: Comparison of Austria with Western Balkan Countries" (Czech and Slovak Social Worker, Reviewed Scientific Journal for Fields of Social Work, 16(1), 2016); "International RnD Cooperation versus National RnD Cooperation" (Annual of Institute for Sociological, Political and Juridical Research, 41(1), 2017); "Child beggars in Kosovo" (Journal of Social Policy, 13, 2017); "Causes and Consequences of domestic violence, socio-cultural differences in Kosovo" (Methodological Horizons, 10(2), 2015). His ORCID is https://orcid.org/0000-0002-1495-306X and e-mail address: besnik.fetahu@uni-pr.edu.

Remzije Istrefi
is an associate professor at the Faculty of Law, University of Pristina, Kosovo. She was a researcher at the Hague Academy for International Law Online Centre for Studies and Research (2020–2021) and a Fulbright scholar at the Duke University NC USA (2008). She has written numerous articles including "Public Administration in an Atypical Transition and the Need for the Agents of Europeanisation in Kosovo" (co-author Arben Hajrullahu, Croatian and Comparative Public Administration, 20(2), 2020); "Consolidation of Statehood through Membership in the UN: Some Remarks on Kosovo, Democracy and International Law" (co-author Iliriana Islami, Review of Central and East European Law, 43(3), 2018), "International Security Presence in Kosovo and its Human Rights Implications" (Croatian International Relations Review, 23(80), 2017), "European Union Support and Transitional Justice Processes in Kosovo" (Europolity – Continuity and Change in European Governance, 14(1), 2020); "Incorporation of international human rights into national legislation: The case of Kosovo" (co-author Iliriana Islami, SEER Journal for Labour and Social Affairs in Eastern Europe, 20(1), 2017). Her ORCID is https://orcid.org/0000-0003-4503-7918.

Maja Jandrić
is an associate professor at the Faculty of Economics, University of Belgrade, where she teaches courses in Principles of Macroeconomics and Theory and Analysis of Economic Policy. Her main scientific interests are economic policy and, specifically, labor market issues, with a focus on flexibility and security issues in the labor market. Some of her most important publications are "Convergence clubs in different regions of Serbia" (co-author with Maria Candelaria Barrios, Dejan Molnar, Svetozar Tanasković, Applied Economics Letters, 2020), "Multiple criteria decision aiding as a prediction tool for migration potential of regions" (co-author with Mihail Arandarenko, Salvatore

Corrente, Mladen Stamenković, European Journal of Operational Research, 284(3), 2020), "Adaptability of the workforce in Europe changing skills in the digital era" (co-author with Saša Ranđelović, Zbornik radova Ekonomskog fakulteta u Rijeci: časopis za ekonomsku teoriju i praksu, 36(2), 2018). Her ORCID is https://orcid.org/0000-0002-7817-919X.

Gordana Matković
is a professor at the Metropolitan University FEFA Faculty and Program Director of Centre for Social Policy. She holds a B.A. and M.A. degree from the University of Belgrade, Faculty of Economics and a Ph.D. from the Faculty of Philosophy, Sociology Department. Gordana Matković is a high-profile expert with extensive experience in the area of social policy. Over the past years, she has worked as an international consultant for the World Bank, UNICEF, and UNDP. She served as the Minister of Social Affairs in the first democratically elected Government of Serbia (2000–2004). Her professional interests cover different fields such as social welfare and social insurance, demography, and human development. Professor Matković is the author of numerous studies and papers including "The Welfare State in Western Balkan Countries: Challenges and Options" (Stanovništvo, 57(1), 2019); "The Development of Private Pensions in Serbia: Caught Between a Generic Blueprint and an Unconducive Local Environment" (co-author with Nikola Altiparmakov, Transfer: European Review of Labour and Research, 24(1), 2018); "Policies Reducing the Economic Cost of Parenthood in Serbia" (co-author with Boško Mijatović, and Katarina Stanić, Towards Better Demographic Future of Serbia, edited by Vladimir S. Kostić, Slavica Đukić Dejanović, and Mirjana Rašević, Serbian Academy of Science and Institute of Social Sciences, 2018); "Understanding the Increase in the Number of Childbirth – related Leave Beneficiaries in Serbia" (co-author with Katarina Stanić, Stanovništvo, 55(1), 2017).

Ruzhdi Morina
is a doctor at the Faculty of Law, University of Prishtina, Kosovo. He is also the Chairman of the Board of the Kosovo Pension Saving Trust. His main research interests are pension funds, European Union standards, and economic development. His most important publications include "The role of the European Union in the area of supplementary pension funds: The case of Kosovo" (EUROPOLITY, 12(11) 2018); "Development of Kosovo Pension Saving Trust Fund" (co-authored with Ymer Havolli, Eurasian Journal of Business and Management, 4(4), 2016); "Diplomacia e Kongresittë Vjenës" (VIZIONE, 18, 2012, Shkup); "Opsionetsiletra me vlerë" (VIZIONE, 18, 2012, Shkup).

Artan Mustafa
is a lecturer at the University for Business and Technology (UBT), Kosovo and Country expert on pensions and social inclusion at the European Social Policy Network (ESPN). He received a Civil Society Scholar Award from Open Society Foundations (2014/15). He did social policy consultancies for: UNDP, Kosovo Democratic Institute (KDI), Kosovo Government and Kosovo Parliament (2017–2019). He was awarded a scholarship at the University of Vienna in 2015 (Kurzfristige wissenschaftliche Auslandsstipendien). In 2015–17, he worked as university assistant/lecturer (pre-doc position) at the University of Vienna, Department of Political Science. His recent publications include "Kosovo's social policy during self-management, UNMIK and independence: Persisting high inequality and social exclusion" (International Journal of Social Welfare, 29, 2020); "The politics of citizenship, social policy, and statebuilding in Kosovo" (Unravelling liberal interventionism: Local critiques of statebuilding in Kosovo, edited by Gëzim Visoka and Vjosa Musliu, Routledge, 2019) "ESPN Thematic Report on Financing social protection – Kosovo, European Social Policy Network (ESPN)" (co-author with Amir Haxhikadrija, Brussels: European Commission, 2019); "ESPN Thematic Report on In–work poverty–Kosovo, European Social Policy Network (ESPN)" (co-author with Amir Haxhikadrija and Artan Loxha, Brussels: European Commission, 2019). His ORCID is https://orcid.org/0000-0003-4042-6658.

Katarina Stanić
is an assistant professor of Welfare Economics at the Faculty of Economics, Finance and Administration (FEFA), Belgrade Metropolitan University, Serbia. She holds a BSc in economics from the University of Belgrade and an MSc and PhD in economics from the University of Nottingham, UK. She is a Chevening and a Nottingham University scholar. Katarina is one of the founders of the Center for Social Policy in Belgrade where she works as a pension and social policy researcher. She began her career in 2001 as a researcher at the Economics Institute in Belgrade. From 2005 to 2010, she worked as an economist and pension expert on USAID funded projects in Serbia. In the period end-2010 until mid-2012 she was working as a short-term pension expert on the Pension and Labor Market (PALM) project in Armenia. She is continuously engaged as a short-term expert by the WB, UNICEF, and other international organizations. Her academic and policy interests include many aspects of social policy in its widest sense – pension systems, long-term care, social welfare services, child and family protection, poverty and social assistance, and inclusive education.

Marzena Żakowska
is an assistant professor at the National Security Faculty, War Studies University, Warsaw, Poland. She is Director of the Global Affairs and Diplomacy Studies and Chair of War Studies Working Group at International Society of Military Sciences. Her main field of expertise includes war and armed conflicts, Balkan states' security, migrations and social security. She is the author of such publications as "The roots of armed conflicts – multilevel security perspective" (Security and Defence Quarterly, 3 (30), 2020), "Strategic challenges for Serbia's integration with the European Union" (Security and Defence Quarterly, 2(11), 2016); "Mediation in armed conflict" (Security and Defence Quarterly, 4(17), 2017); "Determining Polish parliamentarians' tweets on migration: A case study of Poland" (co-author with Dorota Domalewska, Czech Journal of Political Science 3, 2019); "Migration from war-torn countries – an analysis of parliamentarians' tweets" (co-author with Dorota Domalewska, Przegląd Europejski, no. 2 (2019), in Polish). Her ORCID is https://orcid.org/0000-0002-32457684 and e-mail address: m.zakowska@akademia.mil.pl.

Abstracts

Chapter 1

Serbia is an upper-middle-income Western Balkan country characterized by depopulation and pronounced aging of the population, trends which have been perceived as a major challenge for the welfare state and for society as a whole. The unemployment rate is high, while the standard of living is low, and poverty is widespread. The aim of this chapter is to depict the overall social protection system in Serbia, assess its adequacy, and identify the main challenges and areas for improvement. The study is explanatory in nature, using desk research to provide a comprehensive literature review and regulatory framework that defines the social protection system in Serbia and an analysis of national and EU statistics. The Serbian social protection system is Bismarckian in origin, where the upper layers of protection are organized through social insurance and employment-related benefits. In addition, there are various cash and in-kind benefits within the system of social welfare, child and veteran protection, the most important being means-tested financial social assistance (FSA) and child allowance; both are aimed at reducing poverty. Consequently, there are certain vulnerable groups who are not covered by the insurance system, yet simultaneously not poor enough according to the administrative criteria to be eligible for the last-resort benefits aimed at poverty reduction. There is major scope for improvement and further development of the social protection system in Serbia by adding coverage of that part of the population which is in some way excluded from social protection. When it comes to welfare services, community-based services are insufficiently available, especially in less-developed municipalities and in rural areas, while cash benefits are not linked to services; this is primarily an issue in the area of long-term care and activation policies. These are the most important areas for further development and improvement.

Chapter 2

The pension system in Serbia is public, insurance-based and financed on a pay-as-you-go basis. During the deep political and economic crises of the 90s, the pension system faced serious financing problems creating huge debts for pensioners. In the period 2001–2003 the system underwent bold reforms but nevertheless it started to face significant financial pressure. As a response, instead of a coherent set of measures, what followed has been a long period of frequent changes in pension policy particularly ad hoc indexation. Pension policy has been vacillating between different approaches and the absence of a clear strategic vision resulted in "patchwork reforms". This chapter describes the reforms of the last 20 years and portrays the main characteristics of the pension system in Serbia. The aim of this chapter is to depict the developments and the state of the Serbian pension system and to identify the key challenges and areas for its improvement. Developments are analyzed with a number of most important pension system indicators showing an increasing trend in pension coverage and improvement of financial stability of the system while at the same time endangered relative adequacy of benefits. In order to prevent further decline of the replacement rate, the general point value should be uprated by the real wage growth rate which further raises an issue of separating the indexation method for the general point and pension in payment. When it comes to safeguarding the absolute standard of living in old age, the role of the pension system is essential. Nevertheless, there are still around 150–160 thousand or some 10% of the 65+ population not covered and for whom some form of social pension is desirable. A special "module" for the elderly within the financial social assistance program is a possible solution.

Chapter 3

The decentralization of social welfare in Serbia has mainly materialized through the expansion of community-based social care services within the jurisdiction of local governments. The aim of this chapter is to analyze the availability of community-based services in Serbia and the adequacy of earmarked transfers from the national level that have been introduced to boost the development of these services. The study relies on the mapping of social care services within the jurisdiction of local governments and analysis of legal and public documents. In Serbia, community-based services remain underdeveloped and insufficiently available. In 2018, most LGs provide only two to three services and more diverse and complex services are present only in some larger cities. Services for independent living, targeted at persons with disabilities, are the least developed, which is a major obstacle to deinstitutionalization. It was found that earmarked transfers from the central level, introduced in 2016, are critical for the further development of services within the mandate of local authorities, but there is a need to redefine the criteria for their distribution in order to make them more efficient. Due to poorly defined criteria, many

LGs did not have the capacity to effectively absorb the allocated transfers. The research also shows that improved criteria, publication of data on the distribution of transfers, monitoring and evaluation and the exchange of LG's experiences are essential for further development of community-based services and the process of decentralization and deinstitutionalization in Serbia.

Chapter 4

Unemployment has been one of the main economic problems for Serbia in recent decades. A proper assessment of the link between labor market performance, macroeconomic factors and labor market institutions is crucial in order to address this issue adequately. This chapter aims to examine unemployment in Serbia through a comprehensive analysis of the major factors influencing the labor market, including the correlation between economic growth, labor market institutions and (un)employment in the period from 2001 to 2019. Moreover, the study explores employment protection legislation, the unemployment benefit system and active labor market policy. This research shows that proper estimation of the effects of flexibilization on labor market performance requires further and more sophisticated empirical study, which would allow these effects to be distinguished from the influence of other institutional and macroeconomic factors. Three specific areas should be targeted – econometric analysis of the effects of reforming specific labor market institutions on key labor market indicators; evaluation of the skills mismatch; and examination of the main factors that affect migration flows taking into account both internal and external migrations. The current knowledgebase indicates that caution is advised about how optimistically one can regard the degree of positive effects achievable from legislative reforms seeking to reduce employment protections. Furthermore, labor market flexibilization was not accompanied by strengthening security networks provided by labor market institutions, which had negative consequences on the balance between labor market flexibility and security.

Chapter 5

This chapter explores institutional change in Kosovo since its declaration of independence by focusing on three main social policy sectors: social insurance, poverty protection, and employment and wage protection. The methodological framework for this study is based on two branches of institutional change theory: the first emphasizes the role of political parties and coalitions in influencing change, while the second points to incremental endogenous and multifactored change. Data for this study were collected from public policy reform documents, social indicators, and public events in order to theorize about the directionality and meaning of the observed changes. Existing research on postsocialist trajectories in south-eastern Europe shows that international organizations such as the World Bank played a leading role in social policy formation during the United Nations Mission in Kosovo (UNMIK, from 1999), which fully administered the territory following NATO's military intervention that ended the war (1998–1999) between the Albanian majority population and the Government of Yugoslavia. Due to this foreign influence, Kosovo established the most radical pro-market social policy among the former entities of socialist Yugoslavia. However, since Kosovo's declaration of independence, two forms of active institutional change have taken place: (i) significant short-term layering in the form of categorical rights, and recently (ii) changes that have a longer-term relevance oriented towards installing social insurance, strengthening employment and wage protection, and poverty protection. The research has indicated that, in addition to other factors, these changes were influenced crucially by state institutional characteristics, political parties that were created by the former Kosovo Liberation Army leadership, and recently the left leaning parties. Cumulatively, the changes amount to a significant transformation from a 'caricature' of residual, liberal policy to a government-finance dominated social protection with clientelistic features, and potentially to a mixture of government financed redistribution, social insurance and private market solutions.

Chapter 6

This chapter critically examines peculiarities of Kosovo's pension system and the main challenges in its implementation. The actual state of the pension system in Kosovo was determined in the period 2001–2003, whereby the international and domestic authorities made a distinct move away from the solidarity system to a defined contribution system. Although, the newly established multi-pillar pension system in post-war Kosovo is based on the principles of modern pension funds, the post-war environment and high unemployment rate affects the enjoyment of the benefits that the pension schemes are supposed to provide. The analyses in this study are primarily based on comparative review of the theoretical and legal framework governing the pension schemes, EU standards related to the pension schemes, information, and data available in institutional reports, various published books and articles, and documents from organizations. The performance of the Kosovo Pension Savings Trust (KPST) to date is evaluated in order to follow long-term trends in return on investment, and maintaining the liquidity of pension assets, as well as the impact of financial crises and movements in financial markets. The main conclusion of the study is that the current multi-pillar pension system is not adequate for Kosovo's post-war society since it does not address the needs of all categories of pensioners. In particular, it has negatively affected citizens who were already pensioners when the new pension system was established. We recommend a new pension system that picks up the tradition of PAYG with new elements of the National Defined Contribution (NDC) in the first pillar, continuation of the Defined Contribution (DC) market-based second pillar as a strong mandatory pension scheme with more guarantees on investment returns in the long run; and promotion of the third pillar accompanied with policy incentives, and an awareness raising campaign with Trade Unions and workers on pension literacy.

Chapter 7

This chapter aims to analyze the process of building social security in Kosovo and to examine the factors that influenced this process after the period of war in 1999. The use of shock therapy (without any feasibility plan) to stimulate the post-communist transition was very challenging for Kosovo. Today, the country is facing numerous social problems, high levels of unemployment, poverty, corruption, and difficulties in the process of European integration. The social security system in Kosovo is analyzed through two different theoretical approaches: the left (Marxism) and the right perspective (liberalism). The Kosovar social system used to be regulated through the left perspective, but now it is making an effort to build the system largely from the right perspective. This dualistic effort has caused more social turmoil in society. The study employs secondary legal documents, international reports, macro indicators, social expenditures, and government policies that regulate social security in Kosovo. Comparative analysis and cluster analysis show the differences and failures in building the social security system through the application of this dualistic approach. The study also employs cross-sectorial survey data through which micro- and macro-level social model analysis is conducted in selected EU countries and Kosovo. The data reflects citizens' perceptions of worker mobility, income levels and social inequalities, as well as the efficiency of social services and various social protection schemes in Kosovo. The research indicates that social expenditure, unemployment, poverty and corruption significantly influence the development of security policy and social security in Kosovo, all of which provide valuable lessons for policymakers in transition countries.

Chapter 8

This chapter aims to examine inter-ethnic relations, social integration, and their impact on societal security in Kosovo institutional identity. It analyzes and discusses the level of integration of all society with Kosovo's institutions. Qualitative content analysis was carried out to perform an in-depth analysis of relevant literature and documents. The main contribution of this research is to show that despite the challenges Kosovo society currently faces, Kosovars are developing a sense of national identity. Most citizens of Kosovo have already established "light civilian institutionalization", i.e., a common Kosovar community. Regardless of ethnicities and religions, the majority of the communities identify with the Kosovo state, although it remains polarized on several social issues, such as the system of education. Most public education institutions are separate for different minority ethnic communities (especially for the Serb community which often resists participation in public Kosovo institutions). Therefore, society in Kosovo remains identified only at the state (political) institutional level. It is recommended that a more cohesive society should be created especially through the education system. Furthermore, a new agreement is required between the northern Serbs and the Kosovo government to promote more active engagement with Kosovo institutions and the mediation of the southern Serbs is essential in this process.

Serbia and Kosovo: EU Integration and the Development of the Social Security Systems

Marzena Żakowska

Serbia and Kosovo[1] both have challenging paths to sustainable growth and social stability. Firstly, the breakup of Yugoslavia led to armed conflicts resulting in a profound political and economic crisis, massive unemployment, poverty, and the disintegration of the social security system. Secondly, the onset of the democratization process in 2000, with the accompanying transition from socialism to capitalism, enforced the implementation of radical reforms that have put the social and economic sectors under severe strain. Finally, the integration process of Serbia and Kosovo with the EU has generated numerous challenges in implementing the EU's recommendations, especially those regarding social policy development.

This third of the three-volume publication on social security in the Balkans is dedicated to presenting a multifaceted analysis of a vast spectrum of issues related to the social security systems of Serbia and Kosovo, particularly the social protection, pension system, and social care service sectors. The book also provides a comprehensive overview of the drivers and nature of unemployment, and poverty. Finally, policy recommendations to increase the efficiency and effectiveness of the social security system have been explored.

This introductory chapter briefly outlines the EU integration process of Serbia and Kosovo highlighting significant impediments, along with the main

---

1 The status of Kosovo, a territory in South-East Europe with an ongoing territorial dispute with the Republic of Serbia, remains unresolved, as the state only has not yet been fully recognised internationally. From 1945–1999 Kosovo was an autonomous region of the Socialist Republic of Serbia within the Socialist Federal Republic of Yugoslavia (commonly referred to as Yugoslavia, SFRY). From 1992, following the breakup of Yugoslavia, Kosovo was part of the Federal Republic of Yugoslavia (FR Yugoslavia, FRY) with the official name of Kosovo and Metohija Autonomous Province within Serbia. After the end of the war, in 1999, Kosovo came under the administration of the United Nations Interim Administration Mission in Kosovo (UNMIK) based on United Nations Security Council Resolution 1244 (1999), which included the presence of an international peacekeeping force, the Kosovo Force (KFOR). On 17 February 2008 Kosovo unilaterally declared independence from Serbia. For more information see Marc Weller, Contested Statehood. Kosovo's Struggle for Independence (Oxford: Oxford University Press, 2009); Douglas Hamilton, Kosovo Declares Independence from Serbia, www.reuters.com/article/us-kosovo-serbia-idUSHAM53437920080217 (accessed November 15, 2020).

features of their social security systems emphasizing recent developments, challenges, and risks for social policy implementation.

1   The EU Integration Process – Road and Impediments

For both Serbia and Kosovo, EU accession represents an important step towards social stability and economic prosperity. The road to EU membership for the two countries is long and rocky, with progress regularly and closely evaluated by the European Commission.[2] The integration process for Serbia began in 2003, when the country was identified as a potential EU membership candidate during the Thessaloniki European Council Summit.[3] In March 2012 Serbia was granted EU candidate status and in the following year the Stabilization and Association Agreement (SAA) with the EU entered into force which opened the door to starting accession negotiations.[4] Significant progress in the negotiations has made Serbia one of the most advanced EU membership candidates and it is expected to join the European Union by 2026 at the latest.

The integration process of Kosovo with the EU is more complex. Kosovo began the process in 2002 through the Stabilisation and Association Tracking Mechanism (STM)[5] and is officially considered a potential candidate for EU membership. In February 2008, Kosovo unilaterally declared independence from Serbia; this was also a clear sign of its readiness to join the EU and international community. However, the declared independence was not approved by the government of Serbia and only received partial recognition from EU states and the international community.[6] Nevertheless, Kosovo has

---

[2] For more information regarding the evaluation by the EU of Serbia's European integration in period 2005–2020, see reports at Ministry of European Integration Government of the Republic of Serbia, Annual Progress Reports of the European Commission for Serbia, https://www.mei.gov.rs/eng/documents/eu-documents/annual-progress-reports-of-the-european-commission-for-serbia/ (accessed November 15, 2020); regarding Kosovo's progress toward EU membership see Kosovo Reports at European Commission, Strategy and Reports – Previous Documents, https://tinyurl.com/yt6b9638 (accessed November 15, 2020).

[3] European Commission, EU-Western Balkans Summit Thessaloniki, 21 June 2003, https://ec.europa.eu/commission/presscorner/detail/en/PRES_03_163 (accessed November 15, 2020).

[4] Regarding outline of Serbia Status of Membership Negotiation with EU see European Council and Council of the European Union, Serbia. Status of Negotiations, https://www.consilium.europa.eu/en/policies/enlargement/serbia/ (accessed November 15, 2020).

[5] Elton Tota, EU Enlargement and its Impact to the Western Balkans (Berlin: Logos Verlag, 2019), 129.

[6] Serbian government refuses to recognise Kosovo's independence because this declaration constitutes an action in flagrant violation of UNSCR Resolution 1244 (1999). Five, of the 27 members of the EU, namely Spain, Slovakia, Cyprus, Romania, and Greece have

continuously enjoyed EU support for continuing its STM program and signed the Stabilization and Association Agreement in October 2015.[7] Progress made by the Kosovo government towards adopting and harmonizing with European criteria and standards resulted in the country being included in the latest European Commission enlargement perspective for the Western Balkans, thus giving Kosovo the green light for EU membership.[8]

The ongoing dispute between the governments in Belgrade and Pristina regarding Kosovo's political status is one of the main obstacles to EU accession which undermines socio-economic stability, future development of social reforms and policies as well as impacting social cohesion (most essential at the local level). According to the EU Commission, Serbia and Kosovo must comply with the Brussels Agreement and normalize their bilateral relations to join the EU.[9] Despite Serbia's firm contention that the status of Kosovo should

    not recognised the Republic of Kosovo as an independent state, despite the European Parliament adopting a resolution on 8 July 2010 calling on all its member states to recognize the independence of Kosovo. One of the main concerns of these states is that Kosovo's independence would set a precedent strengthening the positions of their own intra-state separatist movements and affect their national politics. Internationally, Kosovo has gained diplomatic recognition as a sovereign state from 97 out of the 193 (51%) United Nations member states, 22 out of 27 (81%) EU member states, 26 out of 30 (87%) NATO member states, and 31 out of 57 (54%) Organisation of Islamic Cooperation (OIC). See Security Council, Security Council Meets in Emergency Session following Kosovo's Declaration, SC/9252, 18 February 2008, https://www.un.org/press/en/2008/sc9252.doc.htm (accessed November 16, 2020); Craig Turp-Balazs, The Explainer: The EU's Kosovo Awkward Squad, https://emerging-europe.com/news/the-explainer-the-eus-kosovo-refuseniks/ (accessed February 10, 2021); World Population Review, Countries that Recognize Kosovo 2021, https://worldpopulationreview.com/country-rankings/countries-that-recognize-kosovo (accessed February 10, 2021).

7   Commission of the European Communities, Kosovo – Fulfilling its European Perspective, COM (2009) 534 final, Brussels, October 14, 2009, 2, https://eur-lex.europa.eu/LexUriServ/LexUriServ.do?uri=COM:2009:0534:FIN:EN:PDF (accessed November 16, 2020); European Council, Stabilisation and Association Agreement (SAA) between the European Union and Kosovo signed, https://www.consilium.europa.eu/en/press/press-releases/2015/10/27/kosovo-eu-stabilisation-association-agreement/ (accessed November 18, 2020).

8   European Commission, A Credible Enlargement Perspective for and Enhanced EU Engagement with the Western Balkans, COM(2018) 65 final, Strasbourg, 2 June 2018, 2, https://ec.europa.eu/info/sites/default/files/communication-credible-enlargement-perspective-western-balkans_en.pdf (accessed November 18, 2020).

9   For a detailed analysis regarding the dialogue process between Serbia and Kosovo facilitated by the European Union see Krenar Gashi, Vjosa Musliu, Jan Orbie, "Mediation Through Recontextualization: The European Union and The Dialogue Between Kosovo and Serbia", European Foreign Affairs Review 22, no. 4 (2017): 533–550; Marzena Żakowska, "Strategic challenges for Serbia's Integration with the European Union", Security and Defence Quarterly 11, no. 2 (2016): 3–29, https://doi.org/10.5604/01.3001.0010.5631; Marta

not be tied with the EU membership negotiations, progress was made in talks mediated by the US in September 2020, which positively influenced both parties and led to the establishment of economic relations between Serbia and Kosovo.[10] Perhaps, this is a good sign for the future development of the ongoing negotiation process to resolve the Kosovo political status issue in a sustainable way and promote the process of building social wellbeing, social cohesion and lasting peace.

2 The Social Security System – Scheme and Reforms

The social security system in Serbia consists of social insurance, social protection, and family benefit schemes. Three basic types of insurance cover are included in the social insurance scheme – health, pension and invalidity, and unemployment. They are financed mainly by social insurance contributions and, to some extent, public budget.[11] The main role of the social protection system, including social insurance, social welfare and child protection, and veteran protection, is preventing social risks, covering basic social needs and reducing poverty. A wide range of material benefits and social protection services are delivered in accordance with the needs and best interests of the beneficiaries.[12] Since 2000 the social protection system has undergone a range of reforms ensuring a minimum subsistence level and improving service standards.[13] Despite these reforms, some problems still require attention, such as

---

Szpala, Serbia-Kosovo Negotiations – Playing for Time under Pressure from the West, https://www.osw.waw.pl/en/publikacje/osw-commentary/2018-08-21/serbia-kosovo-negotiations-playing-time-under-pressure-west-0 (accessed November 18, 2020).

10 Security Council, Economic Agreement, Resumed Talks between Belgrade, Pristina, Mark Important Steps towards Reconciliation in Kosovo, Mission Head Tells Security Council, Press Release, SC14334, https://www.un.org/press/en/2020/sc14334.doc.htm (accessed November 18, 2020).

11 Senad Jasarevic, Social Security Law in Serbia, Second edition (Wolters Kluwer, 2020).

12 For details of material benefits and social services provided under the Law on Social Welfare see The Government of the Republic of Serbia, Social Benefits, https://www.srbija.gov.rs/tekst/en/129940/social-benefits.php (accessed November 20, 2020).

13 Senad Jasarevic, Social Security Law in Serbia, Second edition. For detailed information see Zakon o penzijsko invalidskom osiguranju, "Sl. glasnik RS", br. 34/2003, 64/2004 – odluka USRS, 84/2004 – dr. zakon, 85/2005, 101/2005 – dr. zakon, 63/2006 – odluka USRS, 5/2009, 107/2009, 101/2010, 93/2012, 62/2013, 108/2013, 75/2014, 142/2014, 73/2018, 46/2019 – odluka US i 86/2019; Zakon o zapošljavanju i osiguranju u slučaju nezaposlenosti, "Sl. glasnik RS", br. 36/2009, 88/2010, 38/2015, 113/2017; Zakon o finansijskoj podršci porodica sa decom, Sl. glasnik RS, br. 113/2017 i 50/2018; Zakon o pravima boraca, vojnih invalida i članova njihovih porodica, "Službeni glasnik RS", br. 137 od 24. decembra 2004, 69 od 20.

providing insurance cover to vulnerable groups and increasing the availability of community-based service, particularly in less-developed municipalities and in rural areas in order to reduce poverty. There is a multiplicity and diversity of social programs with different aims resulting in a lack of comprehensive coordination of services. Overly complex bureaucratic procedures hinder the implementation of social programs, and the majority of welfare programs are not means-tested.[14]

In Kosovo, the Social Assistance Scheme (SAS), is a fundamental social protection instrument originally introduced in 2000 by UNMIK and ratified in 2003 with Law No. 2003/15.[15] SAS aims to protect against poverty, and also against other risks like disability, unemployment, and caregiving responsibilities, including for children. It rests on three main pillars: social insurance, social assistance, and labor market programs.[16] The system has been reformed several times with significant changes being introduced in 2012 - revisions to the benefit base, introduction of a flat-rate benefit, a child allowance, and further tightening of eligibility criteria of decentralized social protection services.[17] Continuing, in 2019 the Kosovo government approved the Concept Document on Social and Family Services aimed at reorganizing SAS by updating eligibility criteria by introducing a new poverty test based on the income of all household members, revising category-based filters to reduce poverty, increasing the child allowance, allowing people to engage in public employment programs,

---

jula 2012 – us, 50 od 29; Zakon o doprinosima za obavezno socijalno osiguranje, "Službeni glasnik RS", br. 84/2004, 61/2005, 62/2006, 5/2009, 52/2011, 101/2011, 7/2012 – usklađeni din. izn., 8/2013 – usklađeni din. izn., 47/2013, 108/2013, 6/2014 – usklađeni din. izn., 57/2014, 68/2014 – dr. zakon, 5/2015 – usklađeni din. izn., 112/2015, 5/2016 – usklađeni din. izn., 7/2017 – usklađeni din. izn., 113/2017, 7/2018 – usklađeni din. izn., 95/2018, 4/2019 – usklađeni din. izn., 86/2019 i 5/2020 – usklađeni din. Izn; Zakon o socijalnoj zaštiti, "Sl. glasnik RS", br. 24/2011.

14 Bertelsmann Stiftung, BTI 2020 Country Report – Serbia (Gütersloh: Bertelsmann Stiftung, 2020), 25.
15 UNMIK, Law No. 2003/15 on The Social Assistance Scheme in Kosovo, http://old.kuvendikosoves.org/common/docs/ligjet/2003_15_en.pdf (accessed November 20, 2020).
16 While social insurance is contributions based – providing pensions, disability, survivors and unemployment payments; social assistance is non-contributary and means tested supporting social pensions and family and child benefits. The labor market programs are designed to support market functioning (employment services) and ensuring a well-trained workforce to meet labor demand stimulated by subsidies and public works. See Stefanie Brodmann, Boryana Gotcheva, Florentin Kerschbaumer, and Erëblina Elezaj, Kosovo Social Assistance Scheme Study. Assessment and Reform Options, Report No. AUS0000628 (Washington: World Bank Group, 2019), 11.
17 For detailed information see Law No. 04/L-096 on Amending and Supplementing the Law No. 2003/15 on Social Assistance Scheme in Kosovo.

and vocational training.[18] The European Commission stresses the necessity to improve the targeting of groups in need and to allocate sustainable long-term financing for social services to municipalities. Child poverty, child labor, and organization of efficient social support for ethnic groups (e.g., Roma, Ashkali and Egyptians) which receive limited social welfare benefits are all crucial problems requiring attention.[19]

3 The Pension System – A Short Comparison

Although the pension systems in Serbia and Kosovo are based on the PAYG principle, predominantly public and insurance-based, they differ in the structure of their respective schemes. The Serbian system is organized in a scheme with two main pillars and the system safeguards against three main types of risk: old age, disability, and spousal survivor risks. The first pillar, referred to as the mandatory system, covers all three types of pensions (old-age, disability, and survivors) and is financed by contributions (both employee and employer, and with state interventions in case of deficits). The scheme's efficiency is low due to a remarkably small ratio of workers to retirees (2.3 mln to 1.7 mln). This trend may persist in the future because of the high rate at which the population of Serbia is aging. The third pillar functions as a voluntary pension insurance scheme. Although still underdeveloped, this pillar is based on privately managed fund schemes. The Serbian pension system lacks a second pillar because of high deferred transition costs, an underdeveloped capital market and deficits in compulsory insurance.[20]

In 2002 UNMIK created, a fundamentally new pension system in Kosovo, independent from the old Yugoslav system.[21] The first pillar of Kosovo's

---

18 Amir Haxhikadrija, Kosovo Moves Towards a Strengthening of the Social Assistance Scheme, European Social Policy Network Flash Report 62, 2020.

19 European Commission, Kosovo 2020 Report, SWD (2020) 356 final, Brussels, 6 October 2020, 80, https://ec.europa.eu/neighbourhood-enlargement/system/files/2020-10/kosovo_report_2020.pdf (accessed November 21, 2020).

20 Drenka Vuković, Natalija Perisić, "Social Security in Serbia – Twenty Years Later", in Welfare States in Transition – 20 Years after Yugoslav Welfare Model, ed. Marija Stambolieva and Stefan Dehnert (Bulgaria: Friedrich Ebert Foundation, 2011), 230. For detailed information regarding the pension system, including benefit calculation, indexation formula and structure of pensioners see Katarina Stanic, Pension System in Serbia – Design, Characteristics, and Policy Recommendation (Beograd: USAID SEGA projekat, Center for Liberal-Democratic Study, 2010), 35–97.

21 UNMIK, On Pensions in Kosovo, Regulation No. 2001/35, 22 December 2001, https://www.atk-ks.org/wp-content/uploads/2017/11/Regulation_2001_35.pdf (accessed November 22, 2020).

three-pillar pension system consists of the public old-age pension (paid to all citizens of Kosovo and permanent residents from the age of 65), disability pension, contributory pension, family pension, work invalidity pension, and early pensions for former miners (Trepca Pension). The second pillar is a statutory funded scheme that is a mandatory individual pension savings scheme financed by up to 10% of gross salaries paid equally from employer and employee contributions and managed by the Kosovo Pension Savings Trust (KPST) autonomous body. Finally, the third pillar, the so-called personal pension scheme, is built on voluntary contributions and provides a supplemental individual or employer-sponsored pension or both at the same time. This pillar is still underdeveloped.[22]

In Serbia since the transition to democracy (2000), the pension system has been reformed several times. Its primary aims are to eradicate poverty and pay off overdue benefits from the mid-1980s and '90s. Significant reforms to the system include increasing the retirement age (from 55 to 58 for women and from 60 to 63 for men); introducing the so-called Swiss formula for pension indexation; calculating pensions based on salaries earned; and tightening the rules governing rights to a disability pension.[23] Future measures towards a more sustainable pension system would benefit from an informed decision to guide the formation of a clear strategy on which the development path for the pension system should follow – a Bismarckian or Beveridge-type system or perhaps a hybrid model. An instrument securing a minimum income in old age to prevent elderly poverty should be part of any new pension scheme development.[24]

In turn, Kosovo implemented pension system reforms to produce the following outcomes: avoiding high payroll taxes by having no wage-based social contribution and maintaining low personal income taxes. Universal coverage

---

22 Selatin Kllokoqi, Pensions in Kosovo – Challenges and Opportunities, Kosovo: Institute for Development Policy, Swiss Cooperation Office, 11, https://indep.info/wp-content/uploads/2018/09/INDEP_Pension-system-reform.pdf (accessed November 22, 2020).

23 Drenka Vuković, Natalija Perisić, "Social Security in Serbia – Twenty Years Later", in Welfare States in Transition – 20 years after Yugoslav Welfare Model, 229–230. For detailed analysis about the reform process in pension system see Gordana Matković, Katarina Stanić, "The Serbian Pension System in Transition: A Silent Break with Bismarck", Economic Annals 65, no. 225 (2020): 111–113.

24 Government of the Republic of Serbia, Third National Report for Social Inclusion and Poverty Reduction in the Republic of Serbia: The Status of Social Exclusion and Poverty Trends in the Period 2014–2017 and Future Priorities, (Belgrade 2018), 234–236, https://media.srbija.gov.rs/medeng/documents/third-national-report-on-social-inclusion-and-poverty-reduction2014-17_eng.pdf (accessed November 24, 2020).

ensured by Pillar I aims at poverty eradication whereas Pillar II takes the role of a savings vehicle. These mandatory and voluntary funded pensions are complementary with a solid foundation and effective transparency requirements.[25] However, reform efforts continue, especially of special pension schemes designed for specific groups (e.g., war veterans, police officers, visually impaired, paraplegics and tetraplegics) and operating within the first pillar. A large number of schemes, which in the period 2008–2018 amounted to thirteen apart from the flat-rate basic pension, cause difficulty in sustaining funding from the state budget, when more than 95% of all pension spending is financed through general taxation whereas only around 85% of government revenues are collected from consumption taxation.[26] In 2018 the Ministry of Labor and Social Welfare proposed a reform package emphasizing the abolition of various benefits for interest groups and establishing an equitable system of rules to increase the income of pensioners in general. The proposition, which affects the interests of many social groups, brought wider public discussion; unsurprisingly it is consequently still under evaluation.[27]

4 Health System: Stressing Development Factors

In Serbia, the health care system was inherited from the former Yugoslavia where it was known as the Swedish model in the Balkans. This system, which provides almost complete coverage of the entire population (98%), is predominantly funded by mandatory contributions (employers and employees).[28] Despite a decrease in total health care expenditures in the last few years,[29] the

---

25   John Gubbels, David Snelbecker, Lena Zezulin, The Kosovo Pension Reform: Achievements and Lessons, SP Discussion Paper No. 0707, (2007), http://documents1.worldbank.org/curated/en/523821468264528122/pdf/394060XK0070701PUBLIC1.pdf (accessed November 26, 2020).
26   Artan Mustafa, Kosovo Plans Significant Pension Policy Shift, European Social Policy Network, ESPN Flash Report 2018/77, December 2018.
27   Ibid.
28   Vesna Bjegovic-Mikanovic, Milena Vasic, Dejana Vukovic, Janko Jankovic, Aleksandra Jovic-Vranes, Milena Santric-Milicevic, Zorica Terzic-Supic, Cristina Hernandez-Quevedo, "Serbia: Health System Review", Health Systems in Transition 21, no. 3 (2019): 13–16, 61–62.
29   The expenditure went to from 9.3% of GDP in 2012 to 8.5% of GDP in 2018, which is above the UE average (9.8% of GDP in 2018) see The World Bank, Health Expenditure (% of GDP) – Serbia, https://data.worldbank.org/indicator/SH.XPD.CHEX.GD.ZS?locations=RS (accessed November 28, 2020); The World Bank, Currant Health Expenditure (% of GDP) – European Union, https://data.worldbank.org/indicator/%20SH.XPD.CHEX.GD.ZS?locations=EU (accessed November 28, 2020).

performance of the Serbian health care system has considerably improved as evaluated by the European Health Consumer Index.[30]

In Kosovo, the development of the health care system combines the experience of health care in the former Yugoslavia as well as the experience of the 'parallel health care system' established after 1989 and run by the humanitarian association "Mother Teresa" for ten years. Currently, the system is financed from mandatory contributions with the central government functioning as the purchaser and provider of health care services.[31] Total health care expenditure is low (in 2017 was 4.5% of GDP), which means that residents directly fund their own care. This amounts to about 40% of total healthcare spending.[32]

The Serbian and Kosovar systems share a similar scheme of organization: primary, secondary and tertiary services, with a stable expansion of the private health care sector.[33] Since 2000, there have been a number of reforms, in both countries, aiming to improve the organization, governance, financing, and provision of healthcare to enhance efficiency, service quality, and equity.[34] In spite of this, in Serbia, a particular exemption mechanism is an issue that requires attention due to ineffective targeting of exempted groups, which greatly reduces the financial sustainability of the health care system. On the one hand, low-income groups of exempted individuals report being charged

---

30 Based on data from 2018 Serbia is ranked 18th. place, with 699 points from 1000 due to greatly improved waiting times, partially due to heavy investment in radiation therapy and MRI scanners, and the introduction of e-Prescriptions, see Arne Björnberg, Ann Yung Phang, Euro Health Consumer Index 2018. Report no. 8, 14, https://healthpowerhouse.com/media/EHCI-2018/EHCI-2018-report.pdf (accessed November 28, 2020).

31 Mybera Mustafa, Merita Berisha, and Basri Lenjani, "Reforms and Challenges of Post-conflict Kosovo Health System", Mater Sociomed 26, no. 2, (2014): 126, doi: https://doi.org/10.5455/msm.2014.26.125-128.

32 Ministry of Health Republic of Kosovo, National Health Accounts Report for 2017, Prishtina 2019, 11, https://msh.rks-gov.net/wp-content/uploads/2019/10/Raporti-p%C3%ABr-NHA-ENG.pdf (accessed December 2, 2020).

33 For more information see Vesna Bjegovic-Mikanovic, Milena Vasic, Dejana Vukovic, Janko Jankovic, Aleksandra Jovic-Vranes, Milena Santric-Milicevic, Zorica Terzic-Supic, Cristina Hernandez-Quevedo, "Serbia: Health System Review": 147–154; Mybera Mustafa, Merita Berisha, and Basri Lenjani, "Reforms and Challenges of Post-conflict Kosovo Health System": 126.

34 Vesna Bjegovic-Mikanovic, Milena Vasic, Dejana Vukovic, Janko Jankovic, Aleksandra Jovic-Vranes, Milena Santric-Milicevic, Zorica Terzic-Supic, Cristina Hernandez-Quevedo, "Serbia: Health System Review, Health Systems in Transition": 18–19; Mybera Mustafa, Merita Berisha, and Basri Lenjani, "Reforms and Challenges of Post-conflict Kosovo Health System": 126–127; Valerie Percival, Egbert Sondorp, "A Case Study of Health Sector Reform in Kosovo", Conflict and Health 4, no. 7 (2010): 5–13, doi: https://doi.org/10.1186/1752-1505-4-7.

for healthcare and on the other hand, several groups who are not needy have been exempted. The situation is confusing for both healthcare providers and patients because no comprehensible instructions to determine patient eligibility for exemption have been provided. These regulations result in vulnerable population groups being left unprotected.[35]

In Kosovo, a significant drop in the quality of health care services (e.g., long waiting lists mean that some procedures are not available in a timely fashion) has been observed which has pushed the population towards accessing the private health sector and making out-of-pocket payments. This situation encourages unofficial, informal, and quasi-informal patient payments, which makes corruption a worrying phenomenon.[36] This problem is also present in Serbia's health care system due to lack of clarity regarding payments for healthcare (definition of standard and non-standard procedures) and incomplete reforms.[37]

There is still room for improvement in both the Serbian and Kosovar health care systems so that the needs of the population and in particular the vulnerable groups (including ethnic minorities, refugees, and internally displaced persons [IDPs]), are adequately met. The development of an integrated master plan for healthcare needs would enable a coordinated response to present challenges, including management and information systems, health care affordability and accessibility, improvement of organizational capacities by reorganization and completion of the existing infrastructure. Furthermore, professional human resources development tailored to actual health services and the introduction of innovative medical technologies – medicines and equipment, is required.[38] Taking everything into consideration, successful

---

35   The exemption mechanism in Serbia included population groups such as children younger than 15 years old, pregnant women, persons older than 65, disabled persons, HIV-infected persons, monks, people with low-family income, unemployed, chronically ill people, military service servants, people registered as refugees, and the Roma population. For more details see Jelena Arsenijevic, Milena Pavolva, Wim Groot, "Social Protection in Health Care and Vulnerable Population Groups in Serbia", Frontiers in Public Health 3, no. 194 (2015): 1–2, doi: 10.3389/fpubh.2015.00194.

36   Taryn Vian, Corruption Risk Assessment in the Health Sector in Kosovo. Findings and Recommendations (Pristina: United Nations Development Programme, 2014), 13–24; Levizja FOL, Corruption in Public Health Care Institutions in Kosovo, Public Opinion Survey, February 2016, http://levizjafol.org/wp-content/uploads/2016/02/Health-Corrup -Scan-En.pdf (accessed December 4, 2020).

37   Drenka Vuković, Natalija Perisić, "Social Security in Serbia – Twenty Years Later", in Welfare States in Transition – 20 years after Yugoslav Welfare Model, 238.

38   Government of the Republic of Serbia, Third National Report for Social Inclusion and Poverty Reduction in the Republic of Serbia: The Status of Social Exclusion and Poverty Trends in the Period 2014–2017 and Future Priorities, 259–260; Mybera Mustafa, Merita

strategy development and implementation are dependent on increasing state budget investments in healthcare and more targeted coordinating activities in both the public and private healthcare sectors.

5 The Challenges for Future Social Policy Development

The significant challenges to social policy that impact social wellbeing in both Serbia and Kosovo are poverty, unemployment, demographic change, and corruption. It should be noted that after 2012, Serbia witnessed continued economic growth and labor market recovery following earlier years of recession.[39] These changes led to a decline in the unemployment rate (from 24% in 2012 to 10.4% in 2019).[40] However, this is still high compared to the EU (EU28 at 6.2% in 2019),[41] and likewise unemployment among young people (in 2012 rate was 50.58% and dropped to 27.12% in 2019),[42] remains high in comparison to the EU28 (14.1% in 2019).[43] Poverty had significantly reduced[44] but was still much higher than the EU expects from candidate countries. In the latest data (2018), 7.1% of the population of Serbia was considered to be living in absolute poverty, the at-risk-of-poverty rate was 24.3% (EU-28 17.1%) and the

---

Berisha, and Basri Lenjani, "Reforms and Challenges of Post-conflict Kosovo Health System": 126.

39 Labor market performance improved, which boosted the employment rate from 35.5% in 2012 to 49.0% in 2019 and the labor force participation rate from 61.6% in 2012 and increased to 67.57% in 2019. See Statistical Office of The Republic of Serbia, Labour Force Survey 2013, Bulletin 578, Belgrade 2014, 10, https://publikacije.stat.gov.rs/G2014/PdfE/G20145578.pdf (accessed December 10, 2020); Statistical Office of The Republic of Serbia, Labour Force Survey in the Republic of Serbia, 2019, Bulletin 658, Belgrade 2020, 7, https://publikacije.stat.gov.rs/G2020/PdfE/G20205658.pdf (accessed December 10, 2020); Statista, Serbia: Labor Force Participation Rate from 2009–2019, https://www.statista.com/statistics/993701/labor-force-participation-rate-in-serbia/ (accessed April 7, 2021).

40 Statista, Serbia: Unemployment rate from 1999 to 2020, https://www.statista.com/statistics/440532/unemployment-rate-in-serbia/ (accessed April 7, 2021).

41 Eurostat, Euroindicators: Unemployment, https://ec.europa.eu/eurostat/documents/portlet_file_entry/2995521/3-30012020-AP-EN.pdf/b9a98100-6917-c3ea-a544-ce288ac09675 (accessed January 7, 2021).

42 Statista, Serbia: Youth Unemployment Rate from 1999 to 2020, https://www.statista.com/statistics/812963/youth-unemployment-rate-in-serbia/ (accessed April 7, 2021).

43 Eurostat, Euro Area: Unemployment at 7.4%, https://ec.europa.eu/eurostat/documents/portlet_file_entry/%202995521/3-30012020-AP-EN.pdf/b9a98100-6917-c3ea-a544-ce288ac09675 (accessed January 7, 2021).

44 Macrotrends, Serbia Poverty Rate 2012–2021, https://www.macrotrends.net/countries/SRB/serbia/poverty-rate (accessed January 7, 2021).

at-risk-of-poverty or social exclusion rate was 34.3% (EU-28 21.8%).[45] As in previous years poverty dominated in rural areas rather than in urban areas (10.4% vs. 4.8%). Some 10% of employed people are at risk of poverty, which means that they cannot fulfil their basic needs, despite working.[46]

In turn, in Kosovo the employment rate increased from 25.5% in 2012 to 30.1% in 2019.[47] The unemployment rate has dropped but still remains high (from 30.9% in 2012 to 25.7% in 2019), predominantly among young people (55.3% in 2012 and dropped to 49.4% in 2019).[48] Nearly one in three young Kosovans is considered 'NEET' (not in education, employment, or training).[49] The poverty rate decreased (from 23.7% in 2012 to 21.4% in 2019),[50] primarily due to strong economic performance (per capita growth averaged 3.4 percent annually). However, the rate of poverty is still high especially in rural areas

---

45 Statistical Office of the Republic of Serbia, Assessment of Absolute Poverty in Serbia in 2018, http://socijalnoukljucivanje.gov.rs/wp-content/uploads/2019/10/Assessment_of_Absolute_Poverty_in_2018.pdf (accessed December 5, 2020); Statistical Office of the Republic of Serbia, Poverty and Social Inequality, 2018, https://www.stat.gov.rs/en-us/vesti/20191015-siromastvo-i-socijalna-nejednakost-2018/ (accessed December 5, 2020); Eurostat, At-risk-of-poverty Rate by Poverty Threshold, Age and Sex – EU-SILC and ECHP Surveys, https://appsso.eurostat.ec.europa.eu/nui/show.do?dataset=ilc_li02&lang=en (accessed December 5, 2020); Eurostat, People at Risk of Poverty or Social Exclusion, https://ec.europa.eu/eurostat/databrowser/view/t2020_50/default/table?lang=en (accessed December 5, 2020).

46 Statistical Office of the Republic of Serbia, Assessment of Absolute Poverty in Serbia in 2018, http://socijalnoukljucivanje.gov.rs/wp-content/uploads/2019/10/Assessment_of_Absolute_Poverty_in_2018.pdf (accessed December 5, 2020). For more information see European Commission, Serbia 2020 Report, SWD(2020) 352 final, Brussels, October 6, 2020, 96, https://ec.europa.eu/neighbourhood-enlargement/system/files/2020-10/serbia_report_2020.pdf (accessed December 5, 2020).

47 The World Bank and Kosovo Agency of Statistics, Results of the Kosovo 2012 Labor Force Survey, September 2013, 10, https://ask.rks-gov.net/media/1671/results-of-the-kosovo-2012-labour-force-survey.pdf (accessed December 12, 2020); Kosovo Agency of Statistics, Labor Force Survey in Kosovo, 2019, 12, https://ask.rks-gov.net/media/5412/labour-force-survey-2019.pdf (accessed December 12, 2020).

48 Ibid.

49 In 2015 NEET in Kosovo was 31.4% and remained still high in 2019 – 32.7%, see European Training Foundation, Kosovo Education, Training and Employment Developments, 2020, 16, https://www.etf.europa.eu/sites/default/files/document/Country%20Fiche%202020%20Kosovo%20Education%20Training%20and%20Employment%20Developments.pdf (accessed May 4, 2021).

50 The World Bank and Statistics Office of Kosovo, Consumption Poverty in the Republic of Kosovo May 2019, 5, https://ask.rks-gov.net/media/4901/poverty-statistics-2012-2017.pdf (accessed December 15, 2020); The Word Bank Group, Kosovo. Poverty & Equity Brief, April 2021, https://databank.worldbank.org/data/download/poverty/987B9C90-CB9F-4D93-AE8C-750588BF00QA/SM2021/Global_POVEQ_XKX.pdf (accessed April 7, 2021).

and among families with multiple children. 18% of Kosovars live below the poverty line and 5.1% – below the extreme poverty line.[51] This socio-economic situation produces a high out-migration rate and contributes to the growth of both the informal economy and informal employment. Intergenerational poverty persists amongst informal workers and their families, a large vulnerable group, stripped of social protection. On the other hand, informal employment becomes the source of additional income, which helps to decrease income disparities.

In addition, the COVID-19 pandemic challenged economic development, pushed Serbia into mild-recession and confirmed the fragility of Kosovo's consumption-based growth model, which has had a negative impact on continued reform progress in poverty reduction in both countries. Pandemic-related lockdowns have shocked the job market leading to some permanent business closures, job losses and reduced the number of job opportunities. This situation has increased the likelihood of higher unemployment and poverty rates.[52] Even with the adoption of the offered UN recovery plan[53] by the governments of Serbia and Kosovo, the economy is expected to recover more slowly. Hence, the recovery process of the labor market and social welfare system will be extended. Prioritization is needed to effectively target social protection spending onto the poorest; this is crucial both for faster poverty reduction and as an automatic stabilizer to prevent steep decreases in consumption. The current socio-economic situation presents a potential opportunity for reform of the education systems to enable retraining of the workforce and supplying the labor demand which will come with recovery following the trauma of COVID-19 pandemic job losses and economic set back. Recovery will demand a workforce with the appropriate professional knowledge and skills for a rapidly changing and competitive market.

To enable the education systems to address the challenges of recovery both governments will have to provide funding and direction to adapt their education systems building institutional capacity, strengthening school leadership, modernizing the teaching profession, preventing discrimination, ensuring

---

51 The World Bank and Statistics Office of Kosovo, Consumption Poverty in the Republic of Kosovo, May 2019, 4, https://ask.rks-gov.net/media/4901/poverty-statistics-2012-2017.pdf (accessed December 15, 2020).

52 The World Bank Group, An Uncertain Recovery, Western Balkans Regular Economic Report No. 18, Fall 2020, 57–63, 76–81, https://openknowledge.worldbank.org/bitstream/handle/10986/34644/153774.pdf?sequence%20=1&isAllowed=y (accessed December 17, 2020).

53 UNDP Serbia, COVID 19 Socio Economic Response Plan, October 2020; UN Kosovo Team, Socio-Economic Response Plan to COVID-19, August 2020.

quality education at all levels (especially for children and students from disadvantaged backgrounds) and organizing relevant vocational training, linking education with labor market demands. All these measures are a prerequisite to building social capacity.[54] Otherwise, challenging employment conditions will make it difficult for people with low qualifications to keep or find employment. This situation has created a high risk of labor-migration. Elevated levels of emigration have negative consequences for the development of human capital, competitiveness, growth and economic convergence in the long run, and threaten the sustainability of the social protection and health care systems.

Furthermore, demographic trends in Serbia and Kosovo affect the long-term labor force and labor-market, and in a fundamental way long-term social security financing. In the Serbian population, which has already been classified as old, aging will intensify in the coming years.[55] This trend, combined with accompanying and persistent high emigration, will reduce the potential workforce, which is a serious challenge to the welfare state due to inevitable rising health care and pension costs. In stark contrast, Kosovo has the youngest population in Europe with around 50% of its population under the age of 25. Because of a persistent high youth unemployment rate, around 50–60% of youth has declared an intent to emigrate in the near future to look for job opportunities abroad, thus exacerbating the brain drain.[56] To provide jobs for youth entering the job market and hold unemployment steady, the economy would have to grow by 8% per annum,[57] which is a great challenge to overcome due to the unpredictability of economic growth and job market evolution.

54　For information regarding the need for education reform recommendations see European Commission, Serbia 2020 Report, SWD (2020) 352 final, Brussels, 6 October 2020, 102–103; European Commission, Kosovo 2020 Report, SWD (2020) 356 final, Brussels, 6 October 2020, 83–85.

55　Goran Penev, "Population Ageing Trends in Serbia from the Beginning of the 21st Century and Prospects until 2061: Regional aspect", Zbornik Matice srpske za drustvene nauke, no. 148 (2014): 687–700, doi: 10.2298/ZMSDN1448687P.

56　Mihail Arandarenko and Stefanie Brodmann, Job Opportunities for Youth in Kosovo: Two Steps Forward, One Step Back?, https://www.worldbank.org/en/news/opinion/2019/03/15/job-opportunities-for-youth-in-kosovo-two-steps-forward-one-step-back (accessed December 17, 2020). For more information on the factors causing youth migration see UNDP Kosovo – Public Pulse Project Team, Challenges and Perspectives of Youth in Kosovo, Pristina August 2018, 16–18; Katerina Veljanovska Blazhevska, "Factors that Influence the Process of Migration of Youth: A Case Study of Kosovo", Security and Defence Quarterly 17, no. 4 (2017): 48–73, doi: https://doi.org/10.5604/01.3001.0011.7846.

57　Bertelsmann Stiftung, BTI 2020 Country Report. Kosovo (Gütersloh: Bertelsmann Stiftung, 2020), 26.

The level of corruption, which remains high in Serbia and Kosovo,[58] also deeply affects the well-being of their citizens. Corruption is prevalent in many areas and exacerbated by the overall weak rule of law and political situation. Corruption has a corrosive effect on the trust of citizens in democratic state institutions, particularly in the case of younger citizens who are disenchanted with public services and disengaged from institutions. Both Serbia and Kosovo are in the process of developing effective mechanisms for fighting corruption. What remains to be demonstrated is a strong political commitment to tackling corruption, establishing more efficient institutional systems for the prevention and suppression of corruption, with an emphasis on strengthening transparency in the justice system (robust criminal justice response to high-level corruption).[59]

The challenging factors mentioned above have a negative impact on social cohesion decreasing the ability of society to ensure the well-being of all its members and its ability to reduce differences and avoid divisions.[60] Growing societal frustration is compounded by the failure to provide adequate social services (poor social welfare system); to develop economic conditions to stimulate employment (continuing high unemployment); to make progress with social justice issues, education, the empowerment of youth, and the protection of minority rights. Another societal challenge resulting from increased polarization is the distribution of wealth (low wages, high living costs) especially when it comes to social responsibility and low living standards. This situation widens the social distance between ethnic groups, heightens crime and emigration levels. It is also exacerbated by the activities of the political elites (polarized by disputes such as the status of Kosovo), political parties (particularly the ideology of radical ones), propaganda, and the exclusion of ethnic minorities from political, socioeconomic, and educational life.[61] Preserving

---

58 The 2020 Corruption Perception Index shows that Serbia is considered a country with a high level of corruption, since it has a score 38 points out 100, which ranks it the 94th place out of 180 countries; similarly Kosovo – has a score 36 points out 100, which ranks it the 104 place (n.b.: 100 points means very clean, 0 – means highly corrupt), see Transparency International, Corruption Perceptions Index 2020, https://www.transparency.org/en/cpi/2020/index/nzl (accessed January 7, 2021).

59 European Commission, Serbia 2020 Report, SWD (2020) 352 final, 6 October 2020, 5, 25–29; European Commission, Kosovo 2020 Report, SWD (2020) 356 final, 6 October 2020, 5, 24–26.

60 For more information on the approach to social cohesion see Council of Europe – European Committee for Social Cohesion, A New Strategy for Social Cohesion, 2004, https://www.coe.int/t/dg3/socialpolicies/socialcohesiondev/source/RevisedStrategy_en.pdf (accessed January 7, 2021).

61 Government of the Republic of Serbia, Third National Report for Social Inclusion and Poverty Reduction in the Republic of Serbia: The Status of Social Exclusion and

social cohesion requires the strengthening of good governance mechanisms, reforms and the development of social assistance programs, job creation, and wider and equal access to education and the job market.

6 Overview of Chapters

This book is the outcome of a four-year project realized between 2016–2020, funded by the Faculty of National Security at the War Studies University, Warsaw, Poland, co-ordinated by Marzena Żakowska and carried out by an appointed international team of scientists and experts. The first part of the book is dedicated to social security problems in Serbia. In the chapter "Overview of Social Protection in Serbia: Current Perspective and Challenges", Katarina Stanić and Gordana Matković examine the social protection system in Serbia, assess its adequacy, and identify the main challenges. As the authors argue, the most important area for improvement in the social protection system is the addition of coverage for certain vulnerable groups in the population which are currently excluded. In the case of welfare services, there is a need to increase the range and availability of community-based services particularly in less-developed municipalities and in rural areas, focusing on improving long-term care and activation policies. Additionally, Stanić's study, "The Pension System in Serbia: Developments, Current State and Challenges", provides a detailed analysis of reforms in the last 20 years and portrays the main characteristics of the pension system in Serbia. Several important pension system indicators were employed to illustrate recent developments and to show an increasing trend in pension coverage and improvement in the financial stability of the system. However, the author points out that at the same time the relative adequacy of benefits is under threat. This raises the issue of separating the indexation method for the general point and pension in payment. Gordana Matković in the chapter "Decentralization of Social Care Services in Serbia" examines the social care services provided by local governments and the adequacy of earmarked transfers from the national level. She notes that community-based services in Serbia are still underdeveloped and insufficiently available because most local authorities provide merely

---

Poverty Trends in the Period 2014–2017 and Future Priorities, 98–101; United Nations Development Programme in Kosovo and Folke Bernadotte Academy, Social Cohesion in Kosovo: Context Review and Entry-Points, Kosovo 2019, 16–17, https://www.ks.undp.org/content/kosovo/en/home/library/democratic_governance/social-cohesion-in-kosovo--context-review-and-entry-points.html (accessed January 7, 2021).

two or three services and more diverse and complex services are present only in some larger cities. Services for independent living, targeted at individuals with disabilities are the least developed, which is a major obstacle to deinstitutionalization. Finally, Maja Jandrić and Marzena Żakowska in the chapter, "Unemployment in Serbia: Characteristics and Challenges" examine the unemployment trends in the period 2001–2019, pointing out the relationship between economic growth and (un)employment, as well as labor market institutions and unemployment. Despite the significant recovery in recent years, the unemployment rate is still above observable levels in most EU countries. Other key labor market indicators, such as employment and activity rates also show that there is still room for improvement to catch up with EU levels. The authors explore employment protection legislation, the unemployment benefit system, and active labor market policy, as well as the position of some of the most vulnerable groups – youth and women.

The second part of the volume reviews social policies in Kosovo. Artan Mustafa and Pëllumb Çollaku in their chapter "The Renegotiation of Social Policy in Kosovo: Gradual Institutional Change since Independence" provide an assessment of the direction of social policy reform since Kosovo's declaration of independence. The study not only compares recent reforms in the field of social insurance, employment and wage protection, as well as poverty protection but also identifies measures that can be taken to enhance their effectiveness. Remzije Istrefi and Ruzhdi Morina in the chapter "Developments and Challenges in the Kosovo Pension System" analyze the Kosovar pension reforms and explore key challenges to the pension system. Despite a series of reforms, the system still faces some structural problems related to intergenerational equity. A three-pronged strategy is recommended to improve the pension system: supplementing the traditional pay-as-you-go system with new elements of a National Defined Contribution (NDC) in the first pillar, continuation of the Defined Contribution (DC) market-based second pillar as a strong mandatory pension scheme with more guarantees on investment returns in the long run; and promoting the third pillar with accompanying policy incentives, and an awareness raising campaign with Trade Unions and workers on pension literacy. Besnik Fetahu in the chapter "Buying Social Peace: Lessons from Kosovo" explores socio-economic and political determinants of social changes in post-war Kosovo. The author analyzes the effects of political regime and aspiration to join the EU on social welfare. He also enquires into the key challenges to the Kosovar social security system both on the revenue and the expenditure side and offers broad recommendations that can be implemented to respond to them. Finally, Dritero Arifi and Nhadhnjim Brovina in their paper "Kosovo Society: Coexistence, Challenges and Opportunities" analyze the extent to which inter-ethnic relations in multi-ethnic Kosovo affect societal security. The authors examine the process of national identity formation for the Kosovars, who, despite experiencing the atrocities of the 1998–99 civil war, are currently forming a common national identity.

This collection of case studies takes a broad, socio-economic approach to provide a comprehensive overview of the social security systems in Serbia and Kosovo. As proved across the chapters in this book, social security is a prerequisite to social cohesion and social peace, which are fundamental components ensuring the security of states. Therefore, I trust that this book will facilitate a wide-ranging discussion regarding the social and economic challenges to attain sustainable growth, stability and security in Serbia and Kosovo. Finally, I hope that policy makers and other experts in the fields of social policy and security will find valuable lessons to guide their decision-making in building stability and increased prosperity in the region.

Bibliography

Arandarenko, Mihail, Stefanie Brodmann. Job Opportunities for Youth in Kosovo: Two Steps Forward, One Step Back? Accessed December 17, 2020. https://www.worldbank.org/en/news/opinion/2019/03/15/job-opportunities-for-youth-in-kosovo-two-steps-forward-one-step-back.

Arsenijevic, Jelena, Milena Pavolva, Wim Groot. "Social Protection in Health Care and Vulnerable Population Groups in Serbia". Frontiers in Public Health 3, no 194 (2015): 1–4. doi: 10.3389/fpubh.2015.00194.

Bertelsmann Stiftung. BTI 2020 Country Report – Kosovo. Gütersloh: Bertelsmann Stiftung, 2020.

Bertelsmann Stiftung. BTI 2020 Country Report – Serbia. Gütersloh: Bertelsmann Stiftung, 2020.

Bjegovic-Mikanovic, Vesna, Milena Vasic, Dejana Vukovic, Janko Jankovic, Aleksandra, Jovic-Vranes, Milena Santric-Milicevic, Zorica Terzic-Supic. "Cristina Hernandez-Quevedo. Serbia: Health System Review". Health Systems in Transition 21, no. 3 (2019): 1–211.

Björnberg, Arne, Ann Yung Phang. Euro Health Consumer Index 2018. Report. Accessed November 28, 2020. https://healthpowerhouse.com/media/EHCI-2018/EHCI-2018-report.pdf.

Brodmann, Stefanie, Boryana Gotcheva, Florentin Kerschbaumer, and Erëblina Elezaj. Kosovo Social Assistance Scheme Study. Assessment and Reform Options, Report No. AUS0000628. Washington: World Bank Group, 2019.

Commission of the European Communities. Kosovo – Fulfilling its European Perspective, COM (2009) 534 final, Brussels, October 14, 2009. Accessed November 16, 2020. https://eur-lex.europa.eu/LexUriServ/LexUriServ.do?uri=COM:2009:0534:FIN:EN:PDF.

Council of Europe – European Committee for Social Cohesion. A New Strategy for Social Cohesion, 2004. Accessed January 7, 2021. https://www.coe.int/t/dg3/socialpolicies/socialcohesiondev/source/RevisedStrategy_en.pdf.

European Commission. A Credible Enlargement Perspective for and Enhanced EU Engagement with the Western Balkans, COM(2018) 65 final. Strasbourg, 2 June 2018. Accessed November 18, 2020. https://ec.europa.eu/info/sites/default/files/communication-credible-enlargement-perspective-western-balkans_en.pdf.

European Commission. EU-Western Balkans Summit Thessaloniki, 21 June 2003. Accessed November 15, 2020. https://ec.europa.eu/commission/presscorner/detail/en/PRES_03_163.

European Commission. Kosovo 2020 Report, SWD (2020) 356 final. Brussels, October 6, 2020. Accessed November 21, 2020. https://ec.europa.eu/neighbourhood-enlargement/system/files/2020-10/kosovo_report_2020.pdf.

European Commission. Serbia 2020 Report, SWD (2020) 352 final. Brussels, October 6, 2020. Accessed December 5, 2020. https://ec.europa.eu/neighbourhood-enlargement/system/files/2020-10/serbia_report_2020.pdf.

European Commission. Strategy and Reports – Previous Documents. Accessed November 15, 2020. https://tinyurl.com/mw34t6wx.

European Council and Council of the European Union. Serbia. Status of Negotiations. Accessed November 15, 2020. https://www.consilium.europa.eu/en/policies/enlargement/serbia/.

European Council. Stabilisation and Association Agreement (SAA) between the European Union and Kosovo signed. November 18, 2020. https://www.consilium.europa.eu/en/press/press-releases/2015/10/27/kosovo-eu-stabilisation-association-agreement/.

European Training Foundation. Kosovo Education, Training and Employment Developments, 2020. Accessed May 4, 2021. https://www.etf.europa.eu/sites/default/files/document/Country%20Fiche%202020%20Kosovo%20Education%20Training%20and%20Employment%20Developments.pdf.

Eurostat. At-risk-of-poverty Rate by Poverty Threshold, Age and Sex – EU-SILC and ECHP surveys. Accessed December 5, 2020. https://ec.europa.eu/eurostat/databrowser/view/ILC_LI02/default/table?lang=en.

Eurostat. People at Risk of Poverty or Social Exclusion. Accessed December 5, 2020. https://ec.europa.eu/eurostat/databrowser/view/t2020_50/default/table?lang=en.

Eurostat, Euro Area Unemployment at 7.4%. Accessed January 7, 2021. https://ec.europa.eu/eurostat/documents/portlet_file_entry/%202995521/3-30012020-AP-EN.pdf/b9a98100-6917-c3ea-a544-ce288ac09675.

Gashi, Krenar, Vjosa Musliu, Jan Orbie. "Mediation Through Recontextualization: The European Union and The Dialogue Between Kosovo and Serbia". European Foreign Affairs Review 22, no. 4 (2017): 533–550.

Government of the Republic of Serbia. Third National Report for Social Inclusion and Poverty Reduction in the Republic of Serbia: The Status of Social Exclusion and Poverty Trends in the Period 2014–2017 and Future Priorities. Belgrade 2018. Accessed November 24, 2020. https://media.srbija.gov.rs/medeng/documents/third-national-report-on-social-inclusion-and-poverty-reduction2014-17_eng.pdf.

Gubbels, John, David Snelbecker, Lena Zezulin. The Kosovo Pension Reform: Achievements and Lessons. SP Discussion Paper No. 0707 (2007). Accessed November 26, 2020. https://documents1.worldbank.org/curated/en/523821468264528122/pdf/394060XK00707o1PUBLIC1.pdf.

Hamilton, Douglas. Kosovo Declares Independence from Serbia. Accessed November 15, 2020. https://www.reuters.com/article/us-kosovo-serbia-idUSHAM53437920080217.

Haxhikadrija, Amir. Kosovo Moves towards a Strengthening of the Social Assistance Scheme. European Social Policy Network Flash Report 2020/62. September 2020.

Jasarevic, Senad. Social Security Law in Serbia, Second edition. Wolters Kluwer, 2020.

Kllokoqi, Selatin. Pensions in Kosovo – Challenges and Opportunities. Kosovo: Institute for Development Policy, Swiss Cooperation Office. Accessed November 28, 2020. https://indep.info/wp-content/uploads/2018/09/INDEP_Pension-system-reform.pdf.

Kosovo Agency of Statistics. Labor Force Survey in Kosovo, 2019. Accessed December 12, 2020. https://ask.rks-gov.net/media/5412/labour-force-survey-2019.pdf.

Law No. 04/L-096 on Amending and Supplementing the Law No. 2003/15 on Social Assistance Scheme in Kosovo.

Levizja FOL. Corruption in Public Health Care Institutions in Kosovo, Public Opinion Survey, February 2016. Accessed December 4, 2020. http://levizjafol.org/wp-content/uploads/2016/02/Health-Corrup-Scan-En.pdf.

Macrotrends. Serbia Poverty Rate 2012–2021. Accessed January 7, 2021. https://www.macrotrends.net/countries/SRB/serbia/poverty-rate.

Matković, Gordana, Katarina Stanić. "The Serbian Pension System in Transition: A Silent Break with Bismarck". Economic Annals 65, no. 225 (2020): 110–113.

Ministry of European Integration Government of the Republic of Serbia. Annual Progress Reports of the European Commission for Serbia. Accessed November 15. 2020. https://www.mei.gov.rs/eng/documents/eu-documents/annual-progress-reports-of-the-european-commision-for-serbia.

Ministry of Health Republic of Kosovo. National Health Accounts Report for 2017, Prishtina 2019. Accessed December 2, 2020. https://msh.rks-gov.net/wp-content/uploads/2019/10/Raporti-p%C3%ABr-NHA-ENG.pdf.

Mustafa, Artan. Kosovo Plans Significant Pension Policy Shift. European Social Policy Network. ESPN Flash Report 2018/77, December 2018.

Mustafa, Mybera, Merita Berisha, and Basri Lenjani. "Reforms and Challenges of Post-conflict Kosovo Health System". Mater Sociomed 26, no. 2, (2014): 125–128. doi: https://doi.org/10.5455/msm.2014.26.125-128.

Penev, Goran. "Population Ageing Trends in Serbia from the Beginning of the 21st Century and Prospects until 2061: Regional Aspect". Zbornik Matice srpske za drustvene nauke, no. 148 (2014): 687–700. doi: https://doi.org/10.2298/ ZMSDN1448687P.

Percival, Valerie, Egbert Sondorp. "A Case Study of Health Sector Reform in Kosovo". Conflict and Health 4, no. 7, (2010): 1–14. doi: https://doi.org/10.1186/1752-1505-4-7.

Security Council. Economic Agreement, Resumed Talks between Belgrade, Pristina, Mark Important Steps towards Reconciliation in Kosovo, Mission Head Tells Security Council. Press Release, SC14334 (21 October 2020). Accessed November 19, 2020. https://www.un.org/press/en/2020/sc14334.doc.htm.

Security Council. Security Council Meets in Emergency Session following Kosovo's Declaration, SC/9252, 18 February 2008. Accessed November 16, 2020. https://www.un.org/press/en/2008/sc9252.doc.htm.

Stanic, Katarina. Pension system in System in Serbia – Design, Characteristics, and Policy Recommendation. Beograd: USAID SEGA projekat, Center for Liberal-Democratic Study, 2010.

Statista. Serbia: Labor Force Participation Rate from 2009 to 2019. Accessed April 7, 2021. https://www.statista.com/statistics/993701/labor-force-participation-rate-in-serbia/.

Statista. Serbia: Unemployment Rate from 1999 to 2020. Accessed April 7, 2021. https://www.statista.com/statistics/440532/unemployment-rate-in-serbia/.

Statista. Serbia: Youth Unemployment Rate from 1999 to 2020. Accessed January 7, 2021. https://www.statista.com/statistics/812963/youth-unemployment-rate-in-serbia/.

Statistical Office of the Republic of Serbia, Assessment of Absolute Poverty in Serbia in 2018. Accessed December 5, 2020. http://socijalnoukljucivanje.gov.rs/wp-content/uploads/2019/10/Assessment_of_Absolute_Poverty_in_2018.pdf.

Statistical Office of the Republic of Serbia, Poverty and Social Inequality, 2018. Accessed December 5, 2020. https://www.stat.gov.rs/en-us/vesti/20191015-siromastvo-i-socijalna-nejednakost-2018/.

Statistical Office of The Republic of Serbia. Labor Force Survey 2013, Bulletin 578, Belgrade 2014. Accessed December 10, 2020. https://publikacije.stat.gov.rs/G2014/PdfE/G20145578.pdf.

Statistical Office of The Republic of Serbia. Labor Force Survey in the Republic of Serbia, 2019, Bulletin 658, Belgrade 2020. Accessed December 10, 2020. https://publikacije.stat.gov.rs/G2020/PdfE/G20205658.pdf.

Szpala, Marta. Serbia-Kosovo Negotiations – Playing for Time under Pressure from the West. Accessed November 18, 2020. https://www.osw.waw.pl/en/publikacje/osw-commentary/2018-08-21/serbia-kosovo-negotiations-playing-time-under-pressure-west-o.

The Government of the Republic of Serbia. Social Benefits. Accessed November 20, 2020. https://www.srbija.gov.rs/tekst/en/129940/social-benefits.php.

The World Bank Group. Kosovo Social Assistance Scheme Study. Assessment and Reform Option. Report No. AUS0000628, March 2019. Accessed December 12, 2020. https://documents1.worldbank.org/curated/en/994991557470271998/pdf/Kosovo-Social-Assistance-Scheme-Study-Assessment-and-Reform-Options.pdf.

The World Bank Group. Kosovo. Poverty & Equity Brief, April 2021. Accessed April 7, 2021. https://databank.worldbank.org/data/download/poverty/987B9C90-CB9F-4D93-AE8C-750588BF00QA/SM2021/Global_POVEQ_XKX.pdf.

The World Bank and Kosovo Agency of Statistics. Results of the Kosovo 2012 Labor Force Survey, September 2013. Accessed December 12, 2020. https://ask.rks-gov.net/media/1671/results-of-the-kosovo-2012-labour-force-survey.pdf.

The World Bank and Statistics Office of Kosovo. Consumption Poverty in the Republic of Kosovo May 2019. Accessed December 15, 2020. https://ask.rks-gov.net/media/4901/poverty-statistics-2012-2017.pdf.

The World Bank Group. An Uncertain Recovery, Western Balkans Regular Economic Report No. 18, Fall 2020. Accessed December 17, 2020. https://openknowledge.worldbank.org/bitstream/handle/10986/34644/153774.pdf?sequence%20=1&isAllowed=y.

The World Bank. Current Health Expenditure (% of GDP) – European Union. Accessed November 28, 2020. https://data.worldbank.org/indicator/SH.XPD.CHEX.GD.ZS?locations=EU.

The World Bank. Health Expenditure (% of GDP) – Serbia. Accessed November 28, 2020. https://data.worldbank.org/indicator/SH.XPD.CHEX.GD.ZS?locations=RS.

Tota, Elton. EU Enlargement and its Impact to the Western Balkans. Berlin: Logos Verlag, 2019.

Transparency International. Corruption Perceptions Index 2020. Accessed January 7, 2021. https://www.transparency.org/en/cpi/2020/index/nzl.

Turp-Balazs, Craig. The Explainer: The EU's Kosovo Awkward Squad. Accessed February 10, 2021. https://emerging-europe.com/news/the-explainer-the-eus-kosovo-refuseniks/.

UN Kosovo Team. Socio-Economic Response Plan to COVID-19. August 2020.

UNDP Kosovo – Public Pulse Project Team. Challenges and Perspectives of Youth in Kosovo. Pristina August 2018.

UNDP Serbia. COVID 19 Socio Economic Response Plan. October 2020.

United Nations Development Programme in Kosovo and Folke Bernadotte Academy. Social Cohesion in Kosovo: Context Review and Entry-Points, Kosovo 2019. Accessed January 7, 2021. https://www.ks.undp.org/content/kosovo/en/home/library/democratic_governance/social-cohesion-in-kosovo--context-review-and-entry-points.html.

UNMIK. Law No. 2003/15 on The Social Assistance Scheme in Kosovo. Accessed November 20, 2020. http://old.kuvendikosoves.org/common/docs/ligjet/2003_15_en.pdf.

UNMIK. On Pensions in Kosovo, Regulation No. 2001/35, 22 December 2001. Accessed November 22, 2020. https://www.atk-ks.org/wp-content/uploads/2017/11/Regulation_2001_35.pdf.

Veljanovska Blazhevska, Katerina. "Factors that Influence the Process of Migration of Youth: A Case Study of Kosovo". Security and Defence Quarterly 17, no. 4 (2017): 48–73. doi: https://doi.org/10.5604/01.3001.0011.7846.

Vian, Taryn. Corruption Risk Assessment in the Health Sector in Kosovo. Findings and Recommendations. Pristina: United Nations Development Programme, 2014.

Vuković, Drenka, Natalija Perisić. "Social Security in Serbia – Twenty Years Later". In Welfare States in Transition – 20 years after Yugoslav Welfare Model, edited by Marija Stambolieva and Stefan Dehnert. Bulgaria: Friedrich Ebert Foundation, 2011.

Weller, Marc. Contested Statehood. Kosovo's Struggle for Independence. Oxford: Oxford University Press, 2009.

World Population Review. Countries that Recognize Kosovo 2021. Accessed January 10, 2021. https://worldpopulationreview.com/country-rankings/countries-that-recognize-kosovo.

Zakon o doprinosima za obavezno socijalno osiguranje, "Službeni glasnik RS", br. 84/2004, 61/2005, 62/2006, 5/2009, 52/2011, 101/2011, 7/2012 – usklađeni din. izn., 8/2013 – usklađeni din. izn., 47/2013, 108/2013, 6/2014 – usklađeni din. izn., 57/2014, 68/2014 – dr. zakon, 5/2015 – usklađeni din. izn., 112/2015, 5/2016 – usklađeni din. izn., 7/2017 – usklađeni din. izn., 113/2017, 7/2018 – usklađeni din. izn., 95/2018, 4/2019 – usklađeni din. izn., 86/2019 i 5/2020 – usklađeni din. Izn; Zakon o socijalnoj zaštiti, "Sl. glasnik RS", br. 24/2011.

Zakon o finansijskoj podršci porodica sa decom, "Sl. glasnik RS", br. 113/2017 i 50/2018; Zakon o pravima boraca, vojnih invalida i članova njihovih porodica, "Službeni glasnik RS" br. 137 od 24. decembra 2004, 69 od 20. jula 2012 – us, 50 od 29.

Zakon o penzijsko invalidskom osiguranju, "Sl. glasnik RS", br. 34/2003, 64/2004 – odluka USRS, 84/2004 – dr. zakon, 85/2005, 101/2005 – dr. zakon, 63/2006 – odluka USRS, 5/2009, 107/2009, 101/2010, 93/2012, 62/2013, 108/2013, 75/2014, 142/2014, 73/2018, 46/2019 – odluka US i 86/2019.

Zakon o zapošljavanju i osiguranju u slučaju nezaposlenosti, "Sl. glasnik RS", br. 36/2009, 88/2010, 38/2015, 113/2017.

Żakowska, Marzena. "Strategic Challenges for Serbia's Integration with the European Union". Security and Defence Quarterly 11, no. 2 (2016): 3–29. doi: https://doi.org/10.5604/01.3001.0010.5631.

PART 1

Social Security in Serbia

∴

CHAPTER 1

Overview of Social Protection in Serbia: Current Perspectives and Challenges

Katarina Stanić and Gordana Matković

1 Introduction

Serbia is an upper-middle-income country with a per capita GDP of 4,904 EUR in 2016 and an estimated population of 7.05 million. Depopulation and pronounced population aging have been perceived as a major challenge for the welfare state and for society as a whole.[1] The unemployment rate is high 15.9% in 2016 while the standard of living is low and poverty is widespread.[2] The absolute consumption poverty rate is persistently high around 7% while the at-risk-of-poverty rate stands at a very high 25.5%.[3] Child poverty rates are considerably higher than the average and various surveys have documented the presence of extreme vulnerability in Roma settlements.

This poses a strain on the social protection system and places a high pressure on the pension system, healthcare, and long-term care. Widespread poverty, informal employment, and high unemployment impose "high demands on the fragile welfare state", similarly to the situation in all Western Balkan countries.[4] Vulnerable groups, such as the Roma population, need coordinated multisector measures, which is challenging for an inefficient welfare state. The aim of this chapter is to depict the overall social protection system in Serbia and to assess its coverage and adequacy. The research identifies the main challenges and areas for improvement; and was conducted using the desk research method to collect and analyze secondary data such as social policies and

---

1 Gordana Matković, "The Welfare State in Western Balkan Countries: Challenges and Options", Stanovnistvo 57, no. 1 (2019): 30.
2 Republika Srbija: Republički Zavod za statistiku, Anketa o radnoj snazi u Republici Srbiji 2016, Republički Zavod za statistiku (Belgrade: Republički Zavod za statistiku, 2017), 17, https://publikacije.stat.gov.rs/G2017/Pdf/G20175623.pdf (accessed March 16, 2020).
3 Vlada Siromaštva, RS: TIM za socijalno uključivanje i smanjenje siromaštva, Ocena apsolutnog siromaštva u Srbiji u 2018.godini (Belgrade, 2019), 3, http://socijalnoukljucivanje.gov.rs/wp-content/uploads/2019/10/Ocena_apsolutnog_siromastva_u_2018_lat.pdf (accessed March 16, 2020).
4 Gordana Matković, The Welfare State in Western Balkan Countries, 34.

legislation, research studies, and national and EU statistics. Finally, a regulatory framework that defines the social protection system in Serbia has been formulated.

The main argument of the research is that the social protection system is of Bismarckian origin, meaning it is based on a social insurance system. Although there is room for improvement in the coverage and adequacy of the social insurance component, the main area for improvement and further research is the vulnerable groups not covered by the insurance system, namely, the disabled and the elderly not covered by the pension system.

2   The Social Protection System in Serbia

The social protection system in Serbia is Bismarckian in origin, where the upper layers of protection are organized through social insurance and employment-related benefits. In addition, there are various cash and in-kind benefits within the system of social welfare, child and veteran protection. The majority of social protection cash benefit expenditures are insurance-based. Out of a total of 16.2% of GDP spent on cash benefits for social protection, 14.9% of GDP or as much as 92.5% is insurance or employment-based; around 5% of expenditures are means-tested and only 2.5% are categorically targeted, i.e., universal benefits (Figure 1.1).

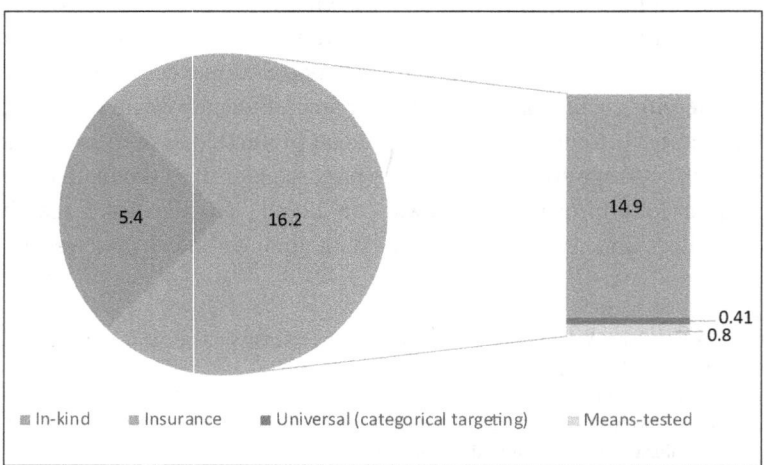

FIGURE 1.1   Social protection benefits (% of GDP) in 2015
SOURCE: OWN ELABORATION BASED ON EUROSTAT, TABLE BY BENEFITS – ALL FUNCTIONS, APPSSO.EUROSTAT.EC.EUROPA.EU/NUI/SUBMITVIEWTABLEACTION.DO (ACCESSED JANUARY 10, 2018).

The total expenditure on social protection (including administration) ranged between 21% and 23% of GDP in Serbia in the past few years, in comparison to the EU-28 weighted average of 28%–29% (Table 1.1).[5] In addition to the 16.2% of GDP spent on cash benefits, around 5%–6% is spent on in-kind benefits, mainly health services.[6] The largest proportion of social protection cash expenditure is spent on pensions, amounting to as much as 14% of GDP in the years following the financial crisis and currently standing at around 11% of GDP.[7]

TABLE 1.1 Social protection expenditure in Serbia (% of GDP), 2010–2015

	2010	2011	2012	2013	2014	2015
Total SP expenditure[a]	22.6	21.4	22.6	21.9	22.0	20.7
Social protection benefits	22.1	21.0	22.1	21.4	21.6	20.2
Sickness/Health care	5.7	5.5	5.7	5.5	5.6	5.1
Disability	2.1	1.9	1.8	1.6	1.7	1.3
Old age	9.5	9.3	10.1	9.9	9.9	9.3
Survivors	2.1	2.0	2.2	2.1	2.1	2.0
Family/Children	1.2	1.1	1.2	1.2	1.3	1.3
Unemployment	0.9	0.8	0.7	0.6	0.6	0.6
Housing	0.0	0.0	0.0	0.0	0.0	0.1
Social exclusion n.e.c.	0.6	0.3	0.4	0.4	0.5	0.5
EU-28 average[a]	28.6	28.3	28.7	28.9	28.6	28.3

a including administrative costs
SOURCE: EUROSTAT, EXPENDITURE: MAIN RESULTS, HTTPS://EC.EUROPA.EU/EUROSTAT/DATABROWSER/BOOKMARK/3C8B0F0C-023B-47F5-B8D8-211B7CC33088?LANG=EN (ACCESSED ON MARCH 10, 2020).

The social protection system in Serbia is organized via the social insurance system, social welfare, and child and veteran protection (Figure 1.2). The social insurance system protects against various risks, specifically sickness,

---

5 Eurostat, Expenditure: Main Results, https://ec.europa.eu/eurostat/databrowser/bookmark/3c8b0f0c-023b-47f5-b8d8-211b7cc33088?lang=en (accessed January 10, 2018).
6 Eurostat, Table by Benefits – All Functions, appsso.eurostat.ec.europa.eu/nui/submitViewTableAction.do (accessed January 10, 2018).
7 Government of the Republic of Serbia, Third National Report for Social Inclusion and Poverty Reduction in the Republic of Serbia: The Status of Social Exclusion and Poverty Trends in the Period 2014–2017 and Future Priorities (Government of Serbia, 2018).

FIGURE 1.2   System of social protection in Serbia
SOURCE: OWN ELABORATION BASED ON THE PENSION AND DISABILITY
INSURANCE LAW, UNEMPLOYMENT INSURANCE LAW; HEALTH CARE
INSURANCE LAW, SOCIAL WELFARE LAW AND LAW ON FINANCIAL SUPPORT
FOR FAMILIES WITH CHILDREN.

unemployment, employment injury, old age (longevity), disability, long-term care, and death.[8] It is organized by three different insurance institutions the Pension and Disability Insurance Fund (PDI Fund), which is responsible for pension and disability insurance, the Health Insurance Fund (HI Fund), which is responsible for health insurance, and the National Employment Service (NES), which is responsible for unemployment insurance (Figure 1.2).[9] The corresponding cash benefits are sick leave (including pregnancy-related leave) compensation, pensions (old-age, disability, and survivors), long-term care benefit, compensation for physical injury at work, etc. Maternity and parental/childcare leave are not covered under social insurance but are under the social welfare and child protection system. However, these leave benefits follow the social

---

8 Zakon o penzijskom i invalidskom osiguranju, "Sl. glasnik RS", br. 34/2003, 64/2004 – odluka USRS, 84/2004 – dr. zakon, 85/2005, 101/2005 – dr. zakon, 63/2006 – odluka USRS, 5/2009, 107/2009, 101/2010, 93/2012, 62/2013, 108/2013, 75/2014, 142/2014, 73/2018, 46/2019 – odluka US i 86/2019, https://www.paragraf.rs/propisi/zakon_o_penzijskom_i_invalidskom_osiguranju.html (accessed March 4, 2020); Katarina Stanić, Pension System in Serbia – Design, Characteristics and Policy Recommendations (Belgrade: USAID SEGA project, 2010); Zakon o zapošljavanju i osiguranju za slučaj nezaposlenosti, "Sl. glasnik RS", br. 36/2009, 88/2010, 38/2015, 113/2017 i 113/2017 – dr. zakon, https://www.paragraf.rs/propisi/zakon_o_zaposljavanju_i_osiguranju_za_slucaj_nezaposlenosti.html (accessed March 4 2020).

9 For more information see The Pension and Disability Insurance Fund of the Republic of Serbia, https://www.pio.rs/en (accessed May 25, 2020); Republic Found of Health Insurance, http://www.eng.rfzo.rs (accessed May 25, 2020); National Employment Service, https://www.nsz.gov.rs (accessed May 25, 2020).

insurance logic and are based on employment; therefore, they are very similar to social insurance. The social welfare and child protection system also provides near-universal benefits – maternity birth grant for all parents[10] and universal care allowance for everyone in need, regardless of his/her financial situation.[11] Finally, this system provides two cash benefits aimed at poverty reduction: the child allowance (CA) and the financial social assistance (FSA), being a means-tested benefit of last resort.[12] According to the latest changes to the legislation, a universal child allowance is also granted to children with severe disability.[13]

The veteran protection system aims to protect war invalids and civilian victims of war. This system encompasses various cash benefits, such as personal disability allowance, long-term care allowance, and an allowance for orthopedic aids, etc.[14]

The social insurance system is financed by social contributions and budget transfers when needed, which is particularly the case with a pension and disability insurance deficit. Contributions, calculated on the basis of gross wages, amount to a total of 26% for the PDI Fund (12% for employers, 14% for employees), 10.3% for the HI Fund, and 1.5% for unemployment insurance. Contributions to the PDI Fund are also paid through other types of contracts, such as service contracts, temporary contracts, etc., while health insurance contribution is only paid if the person is not insured on any other basis.[15] Other benefits are financed by general taxation. Income tax in Serbia is a partial (not synthetic) flat rate that differs for various incomes; for example, a 10% tax on

---

10   There have been an asset ceiling for the birth grant, but it is very high.
11   Gordana Matković, Boško Mijatović, and Katarina Stanić, Novčana davanja za decu i porodice sa decom, CLDS; CSP; UNICEF (Belgrade, CLDS/CSP/UNICEF, 2013), 64; Gordana Matković, Boško Mijatović and Katarina Stanić, "Novčana davanja za decu i porodice sa decom u Srbiji. Karakteristike programa i opcije za unapređenje", Stanovništvo 52, no. 2 (2014), 9.
12   Biljana Bogićević, Gorana Krstić, Boško Mijatović, and Branko Milanović, Siromaštvo i reforma finansijske podrške siromašnima (Belgrade: Centar za liberalno-demokratske studije2003), 75; Gordana Matković and Boško Mijatović, "Analiza uticaja državne finansijske podrške siromašnima", in Tim potpredsednika Vlade za implementaciju Strategije za smanjenje siromaštva, Vlada Republike Srbije, Belgrade (2009), 8.
13   Zakon o finansijskoj podršci porodici sa decom, "Sl. glasnik RS", br. 113/2017, 50/2018.
14   Zakon o pravima boraca, vojnih invalida i članova njihovih porodica, "Službeni glasnik RS", br. 137 od 24. decembra 2004, 69 od 20. jula 2012 – us, 50 od 29, Article 5.
15   Zakon o doprinosima za obavezno socijalno osiguranje, "Službeni glasnik RS", br. 84/2004, 61/2005, 62/2006, 5/2009, 52/2011, 101/2011, 7/2012 – usklađeni din. izn., 8/2013 – usklađeni din. izn., 47/2013, 108/2013, 6/2014 – usklađeni din. izn., 57/2014, 68/2014 – dr. zakon, 5/2015 – usklađeni din. izn., 112/2015, 5/2016 – usklađeni din. izn., 7/2017 – usklađeni din. izn., 113/2017, 7/2018 – usklađeni din. izn., 95/2018, 4/2019 – usklađeni din. izn., 86/2019 i 5/2020 – usklađeni din. izn.

gross wages (with a standard deduction that entails progressivity), 20% for other types of work contracts, 10% for self-employed people, etc. In addition, there is an annual income tax of 10% for those earning more than three times the average salary, and for individuals earning six times the average salary, an additional 15% is applied to the difference.[16]

3 Social Insurance

Pension insurance is earnings-related and financed on a pay-as-you-go basis. It covers old age, disability, and death risk.[17] The coverage of the population aged 65 years and older with any of these three types of pension is quite high, amounting to 88% (95% for men and 82% for women).[18] The old-age pension benefit is calculated using a points system, which closely links work history and benefits.[19] Workers with 40 years of service can receive approximately 62% of their work-life average earnings in 2017.[20] The average old-age pension[21] amounted to 29,000 Serbian (RSD) per month in 2017, and the benefit ratio was 61% of the average wage.[22] Retirees are allowed to work while in retirement on any type of contract.

Disability pension, in cases of employment injury, is calculated on a full-service basis, while in other cases a portion of years of service is added.[23] To

---

16 Zakon o porezu na dohodak građana, "Sl. glasnik RS", br. 24/2001, 80/2002, 80/2002 – dr. zakon, 135/2004, 62/2006, 65/2006 – ispr., 31/2009, 44/2009, 18/2010, 50/2011, 91/2011 – odluka US, 7/2012 – usklađeni din. izn., 93/2012, 114/2012 – odluka US, 8/2013 – usklađeni din. izn., 47/2013, 48/2013 – ispr., 108/2013, 6/2014 – usklađeni din. izn., 57/2014, 68/2014 – dr. zakon, 5/2015 – usklađeni din. izn., 112/2015, 5/2016 – usklađeni din. izn., 7/2017 – usklađeni din. izn., 113/2017, 7/2018 – usklađeni din. izn., 95/2018, 4/2019 – usklađeni din. izn., 86/2019 i 5/2020 – usklađeni din. izn.
17 Katarina Stanić, Pension System in Serbia – Design, Characteristics and Policy Recommendations (Belgrade: USAID and CLDS, 2010), 35.
18 Government of the Republic of Serbia, Third National Report for Social Inclusion and Poverty Reduction, 218.
19 System was slightly disrupted with the Law on temporary pension reductions during 2014–2019.
20 Gordana Matković and Katarina Stanić, "Serbian Pension System in Transition: Silent Break with Bismarck", Economic Annals 2020, 65, Issue 225: 105–133; Government of the Republic of Serbia, Third National Report for Social Inclusion and Poverty Reduction.
21 This is without old-age farmers pension.
22 Government of the Republic of Serbia, Third National Report for Social Inclusion and Poverty Reduction, 221–224.
23 For those under the age of 53, two thirds of the years of pension able service are added for the years missing up to 53 years of age and half of the pensionable service which is

receive a disability pension, one must have been insured for at least five years. There are exemptions for those younger than 30 years of age, who need to have been insured for at least three years, those younger than 25 years of age (at least two years of insurance), and those under 20 years of age (at least one year of insurance).[24] The disability pension is naturally lower than the old-age pension, amounting to 24,600 RSD monthly in 2017 (SIPRU, 2018).[25] Disability beneficiaries are allowed to work on certain types of contract, such as a service contract, but not on a labor contract. The survivor's pension is determined as a percentage of an old-age or disability pension that the beneficiary would be entitled to at the time of their death. The percentage is calculated according to the number of family members entitled to the pension: 70% for one family member, 80% for two, 90% for three, and 100% for four or more family members. A minimum of five years of service is necessary to receive a survivor's pension, while for those with fewer than 20 years of service, the pension calculation formula counts 20 years.[26] The average survivor's pension was less than 21,000 RSD in 2017.[27]

Farmers are also covered by pension insurance, and the calculation formula is the same as for employees and the self-employed. However, their pensions are lower due to the very low contributions they make and the small number of years that contributions are paid due to poor collection.[28] As such, the farmer's pension is in reality a flat-rate pension, as the majority of farmers receive the minimum, which amounted to 11,272 RSD in December 2017.[29]

---

missing up to 63 years of life for men, i.e. up to 58 years of life for the insured women. For the insured older than 53, half the missing service is added to 58 for women, 63 for men.

24 Zakon o penzijsko invalidskom osiguranju, "Sl. glasnik RS", br. 34/2003, 64/2004 – odluka USRS, 84/2004 – dr. zakon, 85/2005, 101/2005 – dr. zakon, 63/2006 – odluka USRS, 5/2009, 107/2009, 101/2010, 93/2012, 62/2013, 108/2013, 75/2014, 142/2014, 73/2018, 46/2019 – odluka US i 86/2019, Articles 21–26, https://www.paragraf.rs/propisi/zakon_o_penzijskom_i_inv alidskom_osiguranju.html (accessed March 4, 2020).

25 Government of the Republic of Serbia, National Report for Social Inclusion and Poverty, 221.

26 Katarina Stanić, Pension System in Serbia – Design, 57.

27 Government of the Republic of Serbia, Third National Report for Social Inclusion and Poverty, 221.

28 Boško Mijatović, Penzijsko osiguranje poljoprivrednika (Belgrade: Centar za liberalno-demokratske studije, 2010), 17.

29 Republički Fond za Penzijsko i Invalidsko Osiguranje, Statistički mesečni bilten 12, 2017, 8, https://www.pio.rs/sites/default/files/old/images/dokumenta/statistike/2017/decembar%202017.%20godine.pdf (accessed March 10, 2020).

The minimum pension is a redistributive component of the pension system which is also organized within the insurance system[30] and it amounted to around 14,338 RSD in December 2017 for old-age/disability beneficiaries,[31] which is about 22% of the average gross wage and 30% of the average net wage. The amount of the survivor's pension can be even lower, i.e.,70% of the minimum old-age pension.[32] The minimum old-age/disability pension has always been higher than the absolute poverty line for a one-member household. The (minimum) farmer's pension is generally below the absolute poverty line, but one should take into account the in-kind income of the agricultural population. The minimum amount of the survivor's pension is also below the poverty line (Figure 1.3).

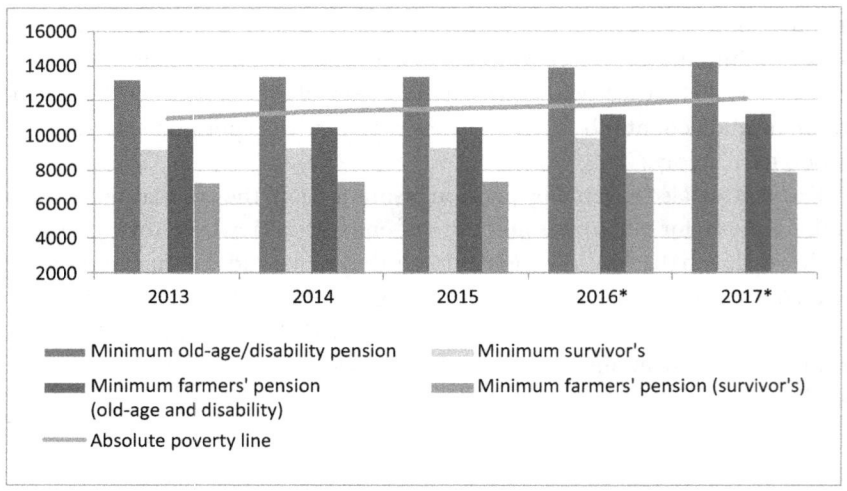

FIGURE 1.3   Absolute poverty line and minimum pension
SOURCE: THIRD NATIONAL REPORT FOR SOCIAL INCLUSION AND POVERTY REDUCTION IN THE REPUBLIC OF SERBIA: THE STATUS OF SOCIAL EXCLUSION AND POVERTY,TRENDS IN THE PERIOD 2014–2017 AND FUTURE PRIORITIES, 227, KATARINA STANIĆ, PENSION SYSTEM IN SERBIA – DESIGN, CHARACTERISTICS AND POLICY RECOMMENDATIONS. BELGRADE: USAID SEGA PROJEKAT, 2010.

Pension expenditures in Serbia are traditionally quite high, consuming up to 14% of GDP in 2009. In recent years, expenditures have been decreasing, to 11.6% of GDP in 2016 and with projections of 11.2% in 2017.[33] In addition

---

30   Katarina Stanić, Pension System in Serbia – Design, 55.
31   Republički Fond za Penzijsko i Invalidsko Osiguranje, Statistički mesečni bilten 12, 2017, 7.
32   Authors' calculation.
33   Government of the Republic of Serbia, Third National Report for Social Inclusion and Poverty Reduction, 232.

to pensions, PDI insurance also includes long-term care benefit and employment injury (physical injury) benefit.[34] The long-term care benefit is a flat-rate benefit amounting to approx. 17,000 RSD as of the end of 2017. Around 77,000 beneficiaries receive this benefit, two-thirds of whom are older than 65 years old.[35] Those with 100% disability are eligible for an augmented allowance and receive a top-up from the social welfare system.[36] The number of beneficiaries of the employment injury benefit was around 63,000 at the end of 2017, out of which only 7,000 had a work-related physical injury; the remaining 56,000 were existing beneficiaries from the old regulations, when this benefit was paid for injuries outside of work. This benefit is approximately 3,000 RSD for those injured at work.[37]

The unemployment benefit (a passive labor market measure) is an insurance benefit that can be acquired if the unemployed person had been working/insured for at least 12 continuous months prior to the loss of their job, or 18 months with breaks, with the condition that they report job searching activity once a month. The benefit amounts to 50% of the last 6-month average wage but cannot be higher than 160% (or lower than 80%) of the minimum wage. This means that the benefit range is rather small, while its duration depends on the recipient's work history spanning from three months for less than five years of service to twelve months for more than 25 years of service. The unemployment benefit also covers social insurance, healthcare insurance, healthcare, and pensions.[38] Around 5% of the total number of registered unemployed people are covered by the unemployment benefit as a huge percentage of the unemployed are searching for their first job, thus, they do not qualify for the unemployment benefit. A large percentage of unemployment is

---

34 Zakon o penzijsko invalidskom osiguranju, "Sl. glasnik RS", br. 34/2003, 64/2004 – odluka USRS, 84/2004 – dr. zakon, 85/2005, 101/2005 – dr. zakon, 63/2006 – odluka USRS, 5/2009, 107/2009, 101/2010, 93/2012, 62/2013, 108/2013, 75/2014, 142/2014, 73/2018, 46/2019 – odluka US i 86/2019, https://www.paragraf.rs/propisi/zakon_o_penzijskom_i_invalidskom_osig uranju.html (accessed March 04, 2020).

35 Republički Fond za Penzijsko i Invalidsko Osiguranje, Statistički mesečni bilten, 12, 2017, 27–28, https://www.pio.rs/sites/default/files/old/images/dokumenta/statistike/2017/decembar%202017.%20godine.pdf (accessed March 10, 2020).

36 Gordana Matković and Katarina Stanić, Socijalna zaštita u starosti: dugotrajna nega i socijalne penzije (Belgrade: Centar za socijalnu politiku/FEFA/SIPRU, 2014), 52.

37 Republički Fond za Penzijsko i Invalidsko Osiguranje, Statistički mesečni bilten 12, 2017, 29, https://www.pio.rs/sites/default/files/old/images/dokumenta/statistike/2017/decembar%202017.%20godine.pdf (accessed March 10, 2020).

38 Zakon o zapošljavanju i osiguranju za slučaj nezaposlenosti, "Sl. glasnik RS", br. 36/ 2009, 88/ 2010, 38/ 2015, 113/ 2017 i 113/ 2017 – dr. zakon, https://www.paragraf.rs/propisi/zakon_o _zaposljavanju_i_osiguranju_za_slucaj_nezaposlenosti.html (accessed March 10, 2020).

long-term, though the benefit duration may be very short.[39] The proportion of these expenditures as a share of GDP spending has been relatively stable over the years, totaling some 0.5%,[40] while the total expenditure on unemployment function is around 0.7% (Table 1.1).

The HI Fund covered 97.2% of the population's health insurance in 2016.[41] According to the Law on Health Insurance, apart from employees, retirees, and those receiving an unemployment benefit for whom contributions are paid by employers, the PDI Fund, or National Employment Service (NES) contributions must be paid for those defined as vulnerable groups by the general budget, and 20% of the total number of insured people are covered on this basis. The most important cash benefit within the health insurance system is the sick leave benefit. Spending on this benefit accounted for 4.2% on average, while administrative costs accounted for 2.1% on average of gross expenditure by the HIF.[42]

4 Social Welfare and Child Protection

The responsibility for social welfare and child protection in Serbia is divided between the national and local governments. The national government finances and regulates non-contributory cash benefits, such as means-tested FSA benefits and CA, categorically targeted maternity benefit grant and long-term care allowance and employment-related maternity/parental leave benefits. Centers for Social Work (CSW) and the respective local government departments administer cash benefits.[43]

Childbirth-related leave benefits are paid through the social welfare and child protection system and financed by the budget (general taxation), though these benefits follow the social insurance logic and are based on employment.[44]

---

39   Republic of Serbia: National Employment Service, Monthly Statistic Bulletin, no. 184, Republic of Serbia: National Employment Service (Belgrade, 2017), 10.
40   Government of the Republic of Serbia. Second National Report for Social Inclusion and Poverty Reduction in the Republic of Serbia: The Status of Social Exclusion and Poverty Trends in the Period 2011–2014 and Future Priorities (Belgrade: Government of Serbia), 2014.
41   Government of the Rapablic of Serbia, Third National Report for Social Inclusion and Poverty Reduction, 243.
42   Zakon o zdravstvenom osiguranju, "Sl. glasnik RS", br. 25/2019; Ljiljana Pejin Stokić, Jurij Bajec, ESPN Thematic Report on Financing Social Protection. Serbia 2019, (European Commission – European Social Policy Network, 2019), 10.
43   Zakon o finansijskoj podršci porodica sa decom, "Sl. glasnik RS", br. 113/ 2017, 50/ 2018, https://www.paragraf.rs/propisi/zakon-o-finansijskoj-podrsci-porodici-sa-decom.html (accessed January 25, 2020). Zakon o socijalnoj zaštiti, "Sl. glasnik RS", br. 24/2011, https://www.paragraf.rs/propisi/zakon_o_socijalnoj_zastiti.html (accessed January 25, 2020).
44   Gordana Matković, Boško Mijatović, and Katarina Stanić, Novčana davanja za decu i porodice sa decom, CLDS; CSP; UNICEF (Belgrade, CLDS/CSP/UNICEF, 2013); Gordana

The maternity/parental leave benefit is paid at the rate of 100% wage replacement for one year, or two years for the third and subsequent children. There were around 40,000 beneficiaries in 2016, i.e., above 50% of newborn children's parents were covered by maternity/parental leave. Over the past few years, public expenditures for childbirth-related leave benefits have more than doubled, in 2015 they were 0.7% of GDP, compared to 0.3% of GDP in 2002, mainly due to the increase in the number of beneficiaries.[45] This program is adequate in terms of a work–family life balance, and it is quite generous among the programs in EU countries. The main flaw is a lack of flexibility, since the system does not allow leave to be combined with part-time work or a longer leave to be combined with a reduced benefit.[46] Until recently, the system did not recognize non-standard forms of employment such as service contracts, temporary contracts, farming, etc., despite taxes and contributions being paid. This problem has been resolved with the new Law on Financial Support of Children and Families with Children, which was adopted in December 2017.

Maternity grants are near-universal benefits (the property test is quite high), with the main goal of supporting and encouraging childbirth. This is the main population policy program in Serbia. The amount ranges from 38,000 RSD for the first child to 360,000 RSD for the fourth. Around 60,000 families receive maternity grants, which covers more than 90% of newborn children, and the coverage is higher for higher-order births.[47] Expenditure for maternity grants in 2016 was 0.17% of GDP, which is relatively high considering that the maternity grant in Serbia is generous.[48]

The long-term care (LTC) allowance is a universal benefit for children and adults with disabilities who are not insured under the pension and disability insurance. It is granted to people with disabilities in need of long-term care, regardless of income; it is unconditional there is no restriction on how the cash may be spent. In general, long-term support in Serbia relies primarily on

---

Matković, Boško Mijatović and Katarina Stanić, "Novčana davanja za decu i porodice sa decom u Srbiji. Karakteristike programa i opcije za unapređenje", Stanovništvo 52, no. 2 (2014).

45 Katarina Stanić and Gordana Matković, "Understanding the Increase in the Number of Childbirth- Related Leave Beneficiaries in Serbia", Stanovništvo 55, no. 1 (2017): 41.

46 Gordana Matković, Boško Mijatović and Katarina Stanić, "Politike usmerene na smanjenje ekonomske cene roditeljstva u Srbiji", in Ka boljoj demografskoj budućnosti Srbije, ed. Vladmir S. Kostić, Slavica Đukić Dejanović, and Mirjana Rašević (Belgrade: SANU i IDN, 2018), 83–84.

47 Gordana Matković, Boško Mijatović, and Katarina Stanić, Novčana davanja za decu i porodice sa decom, 81–85.

48 Gordana Matković, Boško Mijatović, and Katarina Stanić, "Politike usmerene na smanjenje ekonomske cene roditeljstva u Srbiji", 76.

cash benefits and less on support services, which is a feature of a number of European countries (Germany and Austria, for example).[49] There are only two levels of long-term care allowance: a basic allowance that amounted to about 10,000 RSD per month in 2017, and an augmented allowance for those with severe disability,[50] which was 27,568 RSD.[51] For severely disabled people who are insured by the PDI Fund, the social welfare system pays an additional top-up from the budget up to the amount of augmented allowance.[52] There were 16,197 beneficiaries of the basic attendance allowance in 2017, and approximately 36,000 for the augmented allowance, including around 20,000 top-ups (those entitled to LTC benefits from the PDI system).[53] Coverage of disabled individuals with care allowance appears to be very high.[54] Expenditures for the LTC allowance reached 0.24% of GDP in 2017.[55] The augmented care allowance is set at an adequate level 27.5% higher than the net minimum wage given that the purpose of this allowance is to compensate for the lost earnings of family members who decide to stay outside of the workforce and instead take care of the child/person with disabilities.[56]

FSA and CA are the most important cash benefits aimed at poverty prevention/reduction in Serbia. The CA is a means-tested benefit which is conditional upon regular child education.[57] The monthly income threshold for CA eligibility was 8,264 RSD per household member in 2016, and the threshold is raised by 20% for single-parent families and children with disabilities. The CA

---

49 Gordana Matković and Katarina Stanić, Socijalna zaštita u starosti: dugotrajna nega i socijalne penzije (Belgrade: Centar za socijalnu politiku/FEFA/SIPRU, 2014).
50 Severe disability refers to a 100% disability for a single impairment or at least a 70% disability for each of two or more impairments.
51 Government of the Republic of Serbia, Third National Report for Social Inclusion and Poverty Reduction, 197.
52 Zakon o socijalnoj zaštiti, "Sl. glasnik RS", br. 24/2011, Article 94, https://www.paragraf.rs/propisi/zakon_o_socijalnoj_zastiti.html (accessed January 25, 2018).
53 Government of the Republic of Serbia, Third National Report for Social Inclusion and Poverty Reduction, 197.
54 Gordana Matković and Katarina Stanić, Socijalna zaštita u starosti: dugotrajna nega i socijalne penzije, 55–56.
55 Government of the Republic of Serbia, Third National Report for Social Inclusion and Poverty Reduction, 197.
56 Authors' calculation based on the amount of augmented attendance allowance and minimum wage, data for minimum wage: Paragraf, Minimalna zarada, http://demo.paragraf.rs/demo/documents/editorial/statistika/02_stat_arh.htm (accessed January 26, 2018).
57 Gordana Matković and Boško Mijatović, Program dečijih dodataka u Srbiji: Analiza i predlozi za unapređenje (Belgrade: Centar za liberalno-demokratske studije, 2012), 102; Gordana Matković, Boško Mijatović, and Katarina Stanić, Novčana davanja za decu i porodice sa decom, CLDS; CSP; UNICEF, 64.

benefit is 2,660 RSD, and the augmented CA is 3,450 RSD. The CA is granted for a maximum of four children in a family.[58] The newly adopted Law on Financial Support to Families with Children improves the coverage and adequacy of child allowance for children with disabilities. Instead of a means test, the CA for children with severe disability will be universal and 50% higher than the regular CA.[59] Approximately 342,000 children, or about 21% of those under the age of 19, are covered by the CA.[60] The coverage is significantly below average for the children of secondary-school age, and this is particularly pronounced in Roma settlements. Of the total number of children in Roma settlements of elementary-school age, over 70% receive a child allowance, while for secondary-school children the rate is less than 30%.[61] The findings of the MICS survey show that complicated administrative procedures continue to be a significant obstacle for the poorest and least-educated parents, especially in Roma settlements.[62]

The targeting accuracy of the CA is adequate. SILC data (2016) show that over 70% of the total funding for this program goes to the population in the first (the poorest) and second quintile.[63] Expenditures for the CA in 2017 amounted to 0.28% of GDP.[64] According to the World Bank, "implications for poverty are not insignificant without the child allowance program, the risk of poverty would increase by 0.8 percentage points".[65] The adequacy of the CA could be assessed against the poverty line. The regular CA makes up about half of the expenditure for children under the age of 14 years, and only one-third for older children. This applies to both the absolute and the relative poverty line.[66]

---

58   Nominalni iznosi roditeljskog dodatka, paušala za nabavku opreme za dete i dečijeg dodatka i cenzusa za ostvarivanje prava na dečiji dodatak, Cekos, 2017, http://www.cekos.rs/nominalni-iznosi-roditeljskog-dodatka-pau%C5%A1ala-za-nabavku-opreme-za-dete-i-de%C4%8Dijeg-dodatka-i-cenzus-1 (accessed 25 December, 2017).

59   Zakon o finansijskoj podršci porodica sa decom, https://www.paragraf.rs/propisi/zakon-o-finansijskoj-podrsci-porodici-sa-decom.html (accessed 25 December, 2017).

60   Government of the Republic of Serbia, Third National Report for Social Inclusion and Poverty Reduction, 197.

61   Republički zavod za statistiku i UNICEF, Istraživanje višestrukih pokazatelja položaja žena i dece u Srbiji i Istraživanje višestrukih pokazatelja položaja žena i dece u romskim naseljima u Srbiji 2014, Konačni Izveštaj. (Belgrade, 2014), 244.

62   Ibid.

63   Government of the Republic of Serbia, Third National Report for Social Inclusion and Poverty Reduction, 343.

64   Ibid., 193.

65   World Bank, Republic of Serbia: Restructuring and Right Sizing Project Vertical Review of Ministry of Labor – Review of Social Assistance Programs in Serbia (Washington DC: World Bank, 2017), 27.

66   Gordana Matković, Boško Mijatović and Katarina Stanić, "Politike usmerene na smanjenje ekonomske cene roditeljstva u Srbiji", 80.

The FSA is a minimum income guarantee scheme, a last resort type of benefit that fills a gap up to a defined income threshold. The maximum amount of assistance for the beneficiary is equal to the amount of the threshold, while it is weighted for each additional adult family member by 50% and by 30% for children under 14 years of age. Households in which all members are incapable of work and single-parent families can exercise their right to an increased FSA and a 20% higher threshold.[67] In the second half of 2017, the FSA threshold/assistance level amounted to 8,201 RSD (around 130 PPS) for equivalent adults, and the increased FSA was close to 9,841RSD (around 160 PPS).[68] The right to an FSA benefit in 2017 was exercised by more than 106,000 households, with approximately 260,000 adults and children, i.e., 3.7% of the total population.[69] According to the Republican Statistical Office data, the coverage of vulnerable groups is low; only 11% of the poorest quintile receives FSA benefits.[70] According to the MICS–UNICEF survey, coverage of the population in Roma settlements is quite high; almost every other household is a beneficiary.[71] On the other hand, targeting in terms of vertical efficiency is very good, even commensurate with the most developed countries, according to the World Bank's estimates.[72] According to the SILC (2016), approximately 60% of the total FSA program expenditure goes to the lowest-income quintile.[73] Expenditures for the FSA in 2016 amounted to 0.33% of GDP. According to the latest World Bank report, the FSA is the most successful of all social programs financed from the budget, as measured by cost-effectiveness.[74] The adequacy of the FSA is unsatisfactory when assessing the amount of assistance from the point of view of meeting basic needs, despite the fact that there are various other benefits for which the FSA often presents some

---

67   Zakon o socijalnoj zaštiti, "Sl. glasnik RS", br. 24/2011, https://www.paragraf.rs/propisi/zakon_o_socijalnoj_zastiti.html (accessed January 25, 2018).
68   Rešenje o nominalnim iznosima novčane socijalne pomoći, "Sl. glasnik RS", br. 94/2017, https://www.pravno-informacioni-sistem.rs/SlGlasnikPortal/eli/rep/sgrs/ministarstva/resenje/2019/%2036/1/reg (accessed January 25, 2018).
69   Government of the Republic of Serbia, Third National Report for Social Inclusion and Poverty Reduction, 193.
70   Ibid., 343.
71   Republički zavod za statistiku i UNICEF, Istraživanje višestrukih pokazatelja položaja žena i dece u Srbiji i Istraživanje višestrukih pokazatelja položaja žena i dece u romskim naseljima u Srbiji 2014, 240.
72   World Bank, Republic of Serbia: Restructuring and Right Sizing Project Vertical Review of Ministry of Labor – Review of Social Assistance Programs in Serbia (Washington DC: World Bank, 2017), 5.
73   Government of the Republic of Serbia, Third National Report for Social Inclusion and Poverty Reduction, 343.
74   Ibid.

sort of 'passport' (for example, reducing monthly bills for electricity or gas).[75] If we evaluate the adequacy from the aspect of (de)motivation for work, the percentage of the assistance given to an individual who is able to work at the net minimum wage is 37%. Only families with four children receive an FSA benefit that reaches the minimum wage. When CA is taken into account, the program is still not adequate in terms of meeting basic needs, though the total amount of assistance significantly exceeds minimum wage (Figure 1.4).

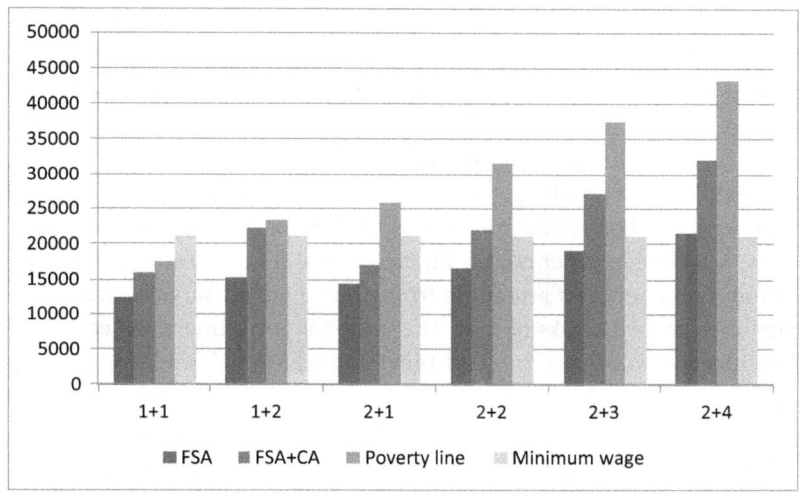

FIGURE 1.4 Amounts of FSA and CA for different family types vs. the poverty line and minimum wage, 2016
SOURCE: GORDANA MATKOVIĆ, BOŠKO MIJATOVIĆ, AND KATARINA STANIĆ, "POLITIKE USMERENE NA SMANJENJE EKONOMSKE CENE RODITELJSTVA U SRBIJI", 79.

In the area of social care services, the mandate of the national level includes residential and foster care services, shelters for victims of trafficking, and supported housing for people with disabilities in less-developed municipalities. CSW activities related to assessment and planning services are also funded from the national budget. Public expenditure for these purposes amounts to 0.2% of GDP.[76] Additionally, the national government regulates the services and establishes the control mechanism.

---

75 Decree on Energy Protected Customer, Official Gazette of the Republic of Serbia, no. 90/2013, 44/2014 and 124/14, last amended on December 30, 2015.
76 Gordana Matković, Social and Child Protection in Serbia, 2017, Unpublished Report, Center for Social Policy Belgrade, http://futureofthewelfarestate.org/wp-content/uploads/2018/04/Serbia-CountryBrief.pdf (accessed January 25, 2018).

Local governments (LGs) are mainly responsible for one-off cash benefits and community-based services. Cash benefits regulated and financed by LGs include additional maternity grants and means-tested cash benefits awarded to the poor in their communities. Many LGs distribute cash assistance to FSA households during the three-month interruption of benefits from the national level. Larger and better-off communities usually award additional cash assistance to FSA households reflecting the higher costs of living in the big cities. Some local governments distribute in-kind assistance in commodities (food or clothing), subsidize utility bills, cover transportation costs for school children, and/or provide free meals in soup kitchen/children's kitchens. Children in receipt of financial social assistance are occasionally awarded one-off aid for school trips, summer holidays, textbooks, and school supplies. Services within the mandate of LGs include community-based day-care services, services for independent living, counselling, therapy, and social education services, as well as shelter services. The beneficiaries are referred to social care services by their local CSW. Local governments also finance CSWs' facilities and the salaries of additional professionals attending to the benefits and services funded by municipalities and cities. As of 2016, the national government allocates earmarked transfers with the purpose of providing additional funds for care services in the local mandate. According to the data gathered by mapping social care, the services within the mandate of the LGs are still insufficiently available, unevenly developed, and often unsustainable. In 2015, different social care services in the LG's mandate were provided in 133 out of the 145 local governments. The total expenditures for these services in 2015 amounted to 2.6 billion RSD (0.06% of GDP).[77] Among the services in the LG's mandate, home care for the elderly and day care centers for children with disabilities dominate. These two services cover the vast majority of the total number of beneficiaries and represent almost two-thirds of the total expenditures for services in the LG's mandate. Other services are mainly available only in the larger cities.[78]

The effectiveness of social transfers in Serbia is satisfactory, although there is room for improvement. This assessment is based on a comparison of the poverty risk rate before and after the allocation of all social transfers, which include all social and child protection cash benefits, unemployment benefits, sickness benefits, veterans' protection benefits and disability pensions.

---

77 Gordana Matković and Milica Stranjaković, Mapping Social Care Services within the Mandate of Local Governments in the Republic of Serbia (Belgrade: Social Inclusion and Poverty Reduction Unit Government of the Republic of Serbia, 2016), 17, 37.
78 Ibid.

According to the SILC (2016), all social transfers (excluding survivor and old-age pensions) reduce the poverty risk by as much as 10.4 percentage points in the Republic of Serbia; hence, the effectiveness rate is 29.0%, which is still lower than in the EU-28, where the rate was 33.7%, based on SILC data from 2015. The effectiveness is significantly higher when pensions are also treated as social transfers.[79]

5   Major Challenges of the Social Protection Sector in Serbia

The majority of cash benefits in Serbia are traditionally insurance-based, including maternity/parental leave, which is employment-related though not financed by contributions. Coverage of the elderly with pensions is quite high. Still, there are more than 150,000 elderly people mainly women without a pension. The minimum pension income is organized within the social insurance system. There is no specific social assistance for the elderly, but they may apply for regular FSA (which is augmented for one's inability to work, which includes the elderly) if eligible. However, the means-test conditions are quite strict, particularly those pertaining to property, while the income test threshold is quite low.

Several options for improving the coverage and adequacy of the minimum income in old age have been analyzed.[80] The first option is universal pensions for everyone older than 65 years, but this option has two main disadvantages: the majority of elderly people are already covered by an insurance-based pension, and a universal pension is a very expensive option, while the tax system is not synthetic and pension income is currently not taxed. The second option analyzed is a guaranteed pension, something like the Swedish *garanti pension*, which is an aid or a top-up to a certain guaranteed pension for all citizens, regardless of work history. The main advantage of this option is the achievement of full coverage. However, this option is quite expensive, and the issue of cost-effectiveness may be raised because of an inclusion error in the context of the tax system in Serbia. In addition, this pension may cause a disincentive effect on workers in the grey economy in terms of motivation for formally registering and paying contributions. The third option which was

---

[79] Eurostat, At-risk-of-poverty Rate before Social Transfers by Sex – EU-SILC survey, https://ec.europa.eu/eurostat/databrowser/view/tesov250/default/table?lang=en (accessed December 20, 2017).

[80] Gordana Matković and Katarina Stanić, Socijalna zaštita u starosti: dugotrajna nega i socijalne penzije (Belgrade: Centar za socijalnu politiku/FEFA/SIPRU, 2014), 155.

assessed is a special 'module' for the elderly within the FSA. This "module" could include a higher threshold/assistance level for old-age households and/ or a higher coefficient for every elderly person 0.7 instead of the current 0.5 and/or the abolition of the property criteria. Estimated expenditures for "FSA for the elderly" range from 0.033% of GDP to 0.3% of GDP. In addition to cost efficiency, the advantage of this targeted pension is that it is less demotivating for working and paying contributions than would be the case with the guaranteed or current minimum pension.[81]

Disability risk in Serbia is covered through insurance/employment. The only universal benefit is the long-term care benefit, while some sort of basic income for people with disabilities in Serbia is missing. It is true that due to the disability pension's adjusted requirement of minimum years of service for individuals under 30 years of age, it is possible to find a way to acquire a disability pension, even for those who are born with a disability or who became disabled prior to employment.[82] However, this solution is harmful both to the disability insurance system, as it distorts the insurance system with a very redistributive element, and to people with disabilities, since it limits their work options. In particular, people with disabilities who receive a disability pension are allowed to work only under a service contract, while the Law on Professional Rehabilitation and Employment of Persons with Disabilities requires employers to hire people with disabilities on a labor contract.

Similarly, survivors, particularly children whose breadwinner was not insured or was insured for fewer than five years, are not covered. A marginal improvement for these children was made with the recently adopted Law on Financial Support of Children and Families with Children, which increased the income threshold by 30% for single-parent families where one parent is dead and the child does not receive a survivor's pension.[83] The amount of CA was also increased by 30%.[84] Additionally, the state provides services for children without any parents (mainly foster care). Once they reach the legal age of adulthood, or after acquiring a university education, they are no longer covered by any kind of assistance.

---

81 Ibid.
82 There are no data to support this hypothesis, but is anecdotic evidence indicates this practice.
83 Previous regulations increased census for 20%, see Zakon o finansijskoj podršci porodica decom, https://www.paragraf.rs/propisi_download/zakon_o_finansijskoj_podrsci _porodici_sa_decom.pdf, Article 20 (accessed January 25, 2018).
84 Zakon o finansijskoj podršci porodica decom, Article 33, https://www.paragraf.rs/propisi/ zakon-o-finansijskoj-podrsci-porodici-sa-decom.html (accessed January 25, 2018).

When it comes to unemployment, there is an insurance-based benefit for those who lose their job, though first-time jobseekers and long-term unemployed people are not covered by any kind of cash assistance apart from FSA. However, the extremely high level of unemployment and inactivity coupled with a large grey economy limits the options. The risk of childbearing is also covered throughout employment, however while there is a maternity grant as a universal and quite generous benefit this in no way compensates for the maternity allowance.

The coverage and adequacy of the cash benefits awarded to the poor are still modest; the minimum income benefit is below the absolute poverty line. At the same time, there is little room for increasing the amount of the benefit, due to the extremely low minimum wage in Serbia.

When it comes to social welfare services, the main challenges are the fact that community-based services are insufficiently available, especially in less-developed municipalities and in rural areas; cash benefits are not linked to services; and deinstitutionalization is still an issue, primarily for adults with intellectual disabilities.

6   Conclusions

The social protection system in Serbia is Bismarckian in origin, where the upper layers of protection are organized through social insurance and employment-related benefits. In addition, there are various cash and in-kind benefits within the system of social welfare and child and veteran protection, the most important being means-tested financial social assistance (FSA) and a child allowance, both aimed at reducing poverty. There are only two categorical benefits: an attendance allowance and a maternity grant.

Consequently, there are certain vulnerable groups which are not covered by the insurance system, yet simultaneously not poor enough according to the administrative criteria to be eligible for the last-resort benefits aimed at poverty reduction. This is the main area for improvement and further development of the social protection system in Serbia: coverage of the group which is in some way excluded from social protection. In particular, this refers to elderly people who are not covered by insurance (around 10% of this population), people with disabilities, surviving children whose parent(s) were not insured or were insured for a very short period. In addition, some groups are particularly vulnerable, such as children and the Roma population. When it comes to old age, one of the options to protect the uninsured elderly population is a means-tested social pension (or a 'module' within the FSA program). This is a cost-effective option which does not introduce a strong demotivating factor for paying contributions in a country like Serbia with a significant grey economy. Revision of the guaranteed minimum income system for old age in Serbia has become a priority, not only because of the current generation, but also bearing in mind the now almost 30 years of grey economy activity in Serbia with underreported or unregistered employment which will inevitably lead to very low pension benefits or no benefits at all.

Another important vulnerable group is people with disabilities, who are eligible for an attendance allowance if uninsured, but not for any kind of living allowance. Consequently, the social protection of people with disabilities is an area where research, experimentation, and reforms are needed. Policy research related to survivors, particularly children and teenagers who live in institutions of social protection until the age of 18, is also needed, together with a rethinking of the survivor's pension scheme. Improvement of child protection entails improving the adequacy of the child allowance scheme, in particular raising the benefit to a level that would cover at least half of the costs attributed to children in families whose consumption is equal to the poverty line. Additionally, a universal child allowance for children living in substandard Roma settlements should be considered.

Finally, there is always a way to increase the adequacy level of the FSA while taking into account the danger of demotivation towards work. One of the measures is to increase the weight from 0.3 to 0.5 for children over the age of 14, in line with the OECD equivalence scale, as well as an additional increase of the weight for children with disabilities. Relaxing the property-related requirements, raising the land ownership ceiling in particular, would allow the coverage to be increased without increasing the benefit amount. In the medium-term, the FSA benefit/income ceilings could be increased to the level of the absolute poverty line or some other minimum living standard threshold. When it comes to welfare services, community-based services are insufficiently available, especially in less-developed municipalities and in rural areas, while cash benefits are not linked to services, which is primarily an issue in the area of long-term care and activation policies. Developing and expanding the community-based services of LGs, which need to be supported from the national level including the evaluation of the earmarked transfer scheme is crucial.

Bibliography

Bogićević, Biljana, Gorana Krstić, Boško Mijatović, and Branko Milanović. Siromaštvo i reforma finansijske podrške siromašnima. Belgrade: Centar za liberalno-demokratske studije, 2003.

Decree on Energy Protected Customer, Official Gazette of the Republic of Serbia, no. 90/2013, 44/2014 and 124/14, last amended on December 30, 2015.

Eurostat. At-Risk-of-Poverty Rate before Social Transfers by Sex – EU-SILC Survey. Accessed December 20, 2017. https://ec.europa.eu/eurostat/databrowser/view/tesov250/default/table?Lang=en.

Eurostat. Expenditure: Main Results. Accessed January 10, 2020. https://ec.europa.eu/eurostat/databrowser/bookmark/3c8b0f0c-023b-47f5-b8d8-211b7cc33088?lang=en.

Eurostat. Tables by Benefits – All Functions. Accessed January 10, 2018. appsso.eurostat.ec.europa.eu/nui/submitViewTableAction.do.

Government of the Republic of Serbia. Second National Report for Social Inclusion and Poverty Reduction in the Republic of Serbia: The Status of Social Exclusion and Poverty Trends in the Period 2011–2014 and Future Priorities. Belgrade: Government of Serbia, 2014.

Government of the Republic of Serbia. Third National Report for Social Inclusion and Poverty Reduction in the Republic of Serbia: The Status of Social Exclusion and Poverty Trends in the Period 2014–2017 and Future Priorities. Belgrade: Government of Serbia, 2018.

Matković, Gordana. "The Welfare State in Western Balkan Countries: Challenges and Options". Stanovnistvo 57, no. 1 (2019): 27–52.

Matković, Gordana. Social and Child Protection in Serbia. Unpublished Report. Belgrade: Center for Social Policy, 2017.

Matković, Gordana, and Boško Mijatović. Analiza uticaja državne finansijske podrške siromašnima. Belgrade: Tim potpredsednika Vlade za implementaciju Strategije za smanjenje siromaštva, Vlada Republike Srbije, 2009.

Matković, Gordana, and Boško Mijatović. Program dečijih dodataka u Srbiji: Analiza i predlozi za unapređenje. Belgrade: Centar za liberalno-demokratske studije, 2012.

Matković, Gordana, and Katarina Stanić. "Serbian Pension System in Transition: Silent Break with Bismarck". Economic Annals 2020, 65, Issue 225: 105–133.

Matković, Gordana, and Katarina Stanić. Socijalna zaštita u starosti: dugotrajna nega i socijalne penzije. Belgrade: Centar Za Socijalnu Politiku/Fefa/Sipru, 2014.

Matković, Gordana, and Milica Stranjaković. Mapping Social Care Services within the Mandate of Local Governments in the Republic of Serbia. Belgrade: Social Inclusion and Poverty Reduction Unit Government of the Republic of Serbia, 2016.

Matković, Gordana, Boško Mijatović, and Katarina Stanić. "Novčana davanja za decu i porodice sa decom u Srbiji. Karakteristike Programa i Opcije za Unapređenje". Stanovnistvo 52, no. 2 (2014): 1–20.

Matković, Gordana, Boško Mijatović, and Katarina Stanić. "Politike usmerene na smanjenje ekonomske cene roditeljstva u Srbiji". In Ka boljoj demografskoj budućnosti Srbije, edited by Vladmir S. Kostić, Slavica Đukić Dejanović and Mirjana Rašević, 67–91. Belgrade: SANU i IDN, 2018.

Matković, Gordana, Boško Mijatović, and Katarina Stanić. Novčana davanja za decu i porodice sa decom. Belgrade: CLDS; CSP; UNICEF, 2013.

Mijatović, Boško. Penzijsko Osiguranje Poljoprivrednika. Belgrade: Centar za liberalno-demokratske studije, 2010.

Minimalna zarada. Accessed January 26, 2018. http://demo.paragraf.rs/demo/documents/editorial/statistika/02_stat_arh.htm.

Nominalni iznosi roditeljskog dodatka, paušala za nabavku opreme za dete i dečijeg dodatka i cenzusa za ostvarivanje prava na dečiji dodatak. Cekos, 2017. Accessed December 25, 2017. http://www.cekos.rs/nominalni-iznosi-roditeljskog-dodatka-pau%C5%A1ala-za-nabavku-opreme-za-dete-i-de%C4%8Dijeg-dodatka-i-cenzus-1.

Pejin Stokić, Ljiljana and Jurij Bajec. ESPN Thematic Report on Financing Social Protection. Serbia 2019. European Commission – European Social Policy Network, 2019.

Republic of Serbia. National Employment Service. Monthly Statistic Bulletin no. 184. Belgrade: Republic of Serbia: National Employment Service, 2017.

Republički Fond za Penzijsko i Invalidsko Osiguranje. Statistički mesečni bilten, 12, 2017. Accessed March 10, 2020. https://www.pio.rs/sites/default/files/old/images/dokumenta/statistike/2017/decembar%202017.%20godine.pdf.

Republički zavod za statistiku i UNICEF. Istraživanje višestrukih pokazatelja položaja žena i dece u Srbiji i Istraživanje višestrukih pokazatelja položaja žena i dece u romskim naseljima u Srbiji 2014, Konačni Izveštaj. Belgrade, 2014.

Republika Srbija: Republički Zavod za statistiku. Anketa o radnoj snazi u Republici Srbiji 2016. Belgrade: Republički Zavod za statistiku, 2017. Accessed March 16, 2020. https://publikacije.stat.gov.rs/G2017/Pdf/G20175623.pdf.

"Rešenje o Nominalnim Iznosima Novčane Socijalne Pomoći". "Sl. glasnik RS", br. 94/2017. Accessed January 25, 2018. https://www.pravno-informacioni-sistem.rs/SlGlasnikPortal/eli/rep/sgrs/ministarstva/resenje/2019/%2036/1/reg.

Siromaštva, Vlada. RS: TIM za socijalno uključivanje i smanjenje. Ocena Apsolutnog Siromaštva u Srbiji u 2018. Godini. Belgrade: 2019. Accessed January 25, 2018. http://socijalnoukljucivanje.gov.rs/wp-content/uploads/2019/10/Ocena_apsolutnog_siromastva_u_2018_lat.pdf.

Skupština RS. Zakon o Pravima Boraca, Vojnih Invalida i Članova Njihovih Porodica. "Službeni glasnik RS", br. 137 od 24. decembra 2004, 69 od 20. jula 2012 – us, 50 od 29. juna 2018.

Stanić, Katarina. Pension System in Serbia – Design, Characteristics and Policy Recommendations. Belgrade: USAID SEGA projekat, 2010.

Stanić, Katarina. Penzijski Sistem u Srbiji: Dizajn, Karakteristike i Preporuke. Belgrade: USAID SEGA projekat, 2010.

Stanić, Katarina, and Gordana Matković. "Understanding the Increase in the Number of Childbirth-Related Leave Beneficiaries in Serbia". Stanovnistvo 55, no. 1 (2017): 41–62.

World Bank. Republic of Serbia. Restructuring and Right Sizing Project Vertical Review of Ministry of Labor – Review of Social Assistance Programs in Serbia. Washington DC: World Bank, 2017.

Zakon o doprinosima za obavezno socijalno osiguranje. "Službeni glasnik RS", br. 84/2004, 61/2005, 62/2006, 5/2009, 52/2011, 101/2011, 7/2012 – usklađeni din. izn., 8/2013 – usklađeni din. izn., 47/2013, 108/2013, 6/2014 – usklađeni din. izn., 57/2014, 68/2014 – dr. zakon, 5/2015 – usklađeni din. izn., 112/2015, 5/2016 – usklađeni din. izn., 7/2017 – usklađeni din. izn., 113/2017, 7/2018 – usklađeni din. izn., 95/2018, 4/2019 – usklađeni din. izn., 86/2019 i 5/2020 – usklađeni din. izn.

Zakon o finansijskoj podršci porodica sa decom. "Sl. glasnik RS", br. 113/2017 i 50/2018. Accessed January 25, 2020. https://www.paragraf.rs/propisi/zakon-o-finansijskoj-podrsci-porodici-sa-decom.html.

Zakon o penzijskom i invalidskom osiguranju. "Sl. glasnik RS", br. 34/2003, 64/2004 – odluka USRS, 84/2004 – dr. zakon, 85/2005, 101/2005 – dr. zakon, 63/2006 – odluka USRS, 5/2009, 107/2009, 101/2010, 93/2012, 62/2013, 108/2013, 75/2014, 142/2014, 73/2018, 46/2019 – odluka US i 86/2019. Accessed March 4, 2020. https://www.paragraf.rs/propisi/zakon_o_penzijskom_i_invalidskom_osiguranju.html.

Zakon o porezu na dohodak građana. "Sl. glasnik RS", br. 24/2001, 80/2002, 80/2002 – dr. zakon, 135/2004, 62/2006, 65/2006 – ispr., 31/2009, 44/2009, 18/2010, 50/2011, 91/2011 – odluka US, 7/2012 – usklađeni din. izn., 93/2012, 114/2012 – odluka US, 8/2013 – usklađeni din. izn., 47/2013, 48/2013 – ispr., 108/2013, 6/2014 – usklađeni din. izn., 57/2014, 68/2014 – dr. zakon, 5/2015 – usklađeni din. izn., 112/2015, 5/2016 – usklađeni din. izn., 7/2017 – usklađeni din. izn., 113/2017, 7/2018 – usklađeni din. izn., 95/2018, 4/2019 – usklađeni din. izn., 86/2019 i 5/2020 – usklađeni din. izn.

Zakon o pravima boraca, vojnih invalida i članova njihovih porodica, "Službeni glasnik RS" br. 137 od 24. decembra 2004, 69 od 20. jula 2012 – us, 50 od 29.

Zakon o socijalnoj zaštiti. "Sl. glasnik RS", br. 24/2011. Accessed January 25, 2018. https://www.paragraf.rs/propisi/zakon_o_socijalnoj_zastiti.html.

Zakon o zapošljavanju i osiguranju za slučaj nezaposlenosti. "Sl. glasnik RS", br. 36/2009, 88/2010, 38/2015, 113/2017 i 113/2017 – dr. zakon. Accessed March 4, 2020. https://www.paragraf.rs/propisi/zakon_o_zaposljavanju_i_osiguranju_za_slucaj_nezaposlenosti.html.

Zakon o zdravstvenom osiguranju. "Sl. glasnik RS", br. 25/2019.

CHAPTER 2

The Pension System in Serbia: Developments, Current State and Challenges

Katarina Stanić

1   Introduction

The Serbian pension system dating back to the 19th century and developed under Bismarckian influence in the 1920s, was finally set up after the Second World War.[1] The system was organized as a traditionally defined benefit system with quite generous payments: the reference period was 10 consecutive years of insurance which is the most favorable period for the insured while the valorization was calculated on the basis of net wage growth. The maximum pension benefit was 85% of the pension base.[2]

Difficulties in financing pensions in Serbia had arisen by the mid-80s but culminated at the time of the deep political and economic crises during the '90s. A reduction in the number of employees, evasion of contribution payments, and widespread grey-economy activity led to a reduction in the number of people insured, while the number of pensioners rose continually due to the very liberal retirement policy. During these years, pension financing became increasingly 'creative'.[3] For example, in the period 1995-2000, only in 1996 were all 12 monthly pension payments made, with 10.5 to 11.5 monthly payments being paid during the rest of the period. This created the so-called 'big debt', amounting to 2.4 monthly pensions payments. In addition, there was a delay in the payment of pension benefits, which saved a lot of money under the high inflation of the time.[4]

At the outset of the 2000s democratic changes and a reform of the pension system was initiated in December 2001 and rounded out in 2003 with the

---

[1] Filip P. Bojić, Pravo na socijalnu penziju u sistemu prava socijalne sigurnosti (Belgrade: Univerzitet u Beogradu – Pravni fakultet, 2018), 188–91.
[2] Katarina Stanić, Pension System in Serbia – Design, Characteristics and Policy Recommendations (Belgrade: USAID and CLDS, 2010), 36.
[3] Gordana Matković, "Reform of Pension and Disability System", in Four Years of Transition in Serbia, eds. Boris Begović and Boško Mijatović (Belgrade: CLDS, 2005), 337.
[4] Katarina Stanić and Jurij Bajec, "What is Actually the Size of the Pension System Deficit in Serbia?", Quarterly Monitor of Economic Trends and Policies in Serbia 1 (2005): 58.

adoption of the new Act on Pension and Disability Insurance. The basic goal of the reform was to establish a fiscally viable pension system with regular payment of pension benefits, including the repayment of inherited debts. With regard to the financial consolidation of the system, in 2001 the two key changes were the one-off rise in the retirement age by three years (from 60 to 63 for men and from 55 to 58 for women), which had not been changed for 30 years, and the shift from wage indexation to mixed wage and cost-of-living indexation, the "Swiss formula", that gives equal weight to rises in wages and cost of living.[5] Parallel with the work on reforms, other activities were instituted for the purpose of contributing to savings, such as fighting against corruption in the disability pension system.[6] During this phase, the nominal contribution rates were substantially and effectively reduced (from 32% to 19.6%), despite the broadening tax base.[7]

In April 2003, with the new Act, the traditional defined-benefit system was changed to the "German points system", with the aim of tightening the link between contributions and benefits. This included extension of the reference period from the ten best years to lifelong earnings, extension of mandatory coverage to employees in non-standard employment, and tightening of the eligibility criteria regarding disability pensions and accelerated pension benefits. The concept of total disability was introduced instead of the inability to perform a particular job, and the regular evaluation of disability benefits was enforced.[8]

At that time, pension reforms in most Central and Eastern European countries were strongly influenced by the World Bank and the 'three-pillar' system. Serbia is one of the rare eastern European countries that decisively refused to implement the second pension pillar, despite having active arrangements with the World Bank. Instead, "Serbia opted for the more traditional path-dependent approach" by combining first-pillar parametric reforms with the introduction of a voluntary third pillar.[9] Despite differing views on the multi-pillar

---

5   Gordana Matković, "Reform of Pension and Disability System", 341; Nikola Altiparmakov and Gordana Matković, "The Development of Private Pensions in Serbia: Caught between a Generic Blueprint and an Unconducive Local Environment", Transfer: European Review of Labour and Research 24, no. 1 (2018), 60.
6   Gordana Matković, "Reform of Pension and Disability System", 340.
7   Katarina Stanić and Jurij Bajec, What is Actually the Size of the Pension System Deficit in Serbia?, 60.
8   Gordana Matković and Katarina Stanić, "Serbian Pension System in Transition: Silent Break with Bismarck", Economic Annals 2020 65, Issue 225: 105–133.
9   Nikola Altiparmakov and Gordana Matković, "The Development of Private Pensions in Serbia: Caught between a Generic Blueprint and an Unconducive Local Environment", 59.

system, the World Bank stated, "bold changes in the pension system of Serbia, implemented on two occasions, during 2001 and 2003, are among the most important achievements in the overall reform program".[10]

Notwithstanding the bold reforms, pension expenditure and pension fund deficit actually started to increase, which became the main topic of concern in 2005. This resulted in changes to the Act on Pension and Disability Insurance further increasing the retirement age by two years and changing the indexation method to only the Consumer Price Index (CPI) with a transition period, while at the same time there were some changes that were not coherent with these quite strict saving measures (such as a one-off increase in the minimum pension, relaxation of accelerated service pension criteria, etc.).[11]

What followed has been a long period of frequent changes in pension policy, particularly ad hoc indexation, and the absence of a clear strategic vision, that resulted in "patchwork reforms" constant changes with arguments that are sometimes contradictory, for example, introducing pension penalties for anticipated pensions justified by actuarial fairness, while at the same time increasing redistribution with the increase in minimum pensions.[12]

The aim of this chapter is to depict the developments and the state of the pension system in Serbia and to identify the key challenges and areas for improvement. The study adopted the desk research method to collect and analyze the main design and performance indicators, and where possible to compare them to EU statistics.

The main argument of the chapter is that though still fragile, the financial position of the pension system in Serbia has improved significantly at the expense of relative pension adequacy. Consequently, it is the right time to prevent any further decline in the replacement rate. When it comes to absolute pension adequacy, i.e., preventing old-age poverty, the pension system is

---

10   Ibid., 62; World Bank, "Serbia and Montenegro Recent Progress on Structural Reforms", (Washington, D.C.: World Bank Group, 2003), 21, http://documents.worldbank.org/curated/en/956521468781161590/Serbia-and-Montenegro-recent-progress-on-structural-reforms (accessed 10 June 2020).

11   Boško Mijatović, "Penzijski sistem", in Reforme u Srbiji: dostignuća i izazovi, ed. Boško Mijatović (Beograd: Centar za Liberalno-Demokratske Studije, 2008), 87; Gordana Matković, "Penzijski sistem u Srbiji – karakteristike, dosadašnje reforme, dileme i opcije", in Penzijski sistem u Srbiji, ed. Katarina Stanić (Belgrade: USAID/Bearing Point, 2009), 21; Katarina Stanić, Pension System in Serbia – Design, Characteristics and Policy Recommendations, 50.

12   Gordana Matković, "Mirovinski sustav Srbije u svjetlu krize", Revija za socijalnu politiku 23, no. 1 (2016): 115.

adequately achieving its goal. Still, some 150,000–160,000 elderly people are not covered by a pension, which is a gap that needs to be improved.

2   Main Characteristics of the Pension System in Serbia

The pension system in Serbia is predominantly public, insurance-based, and financed on a pay-as-you-go basis. It provides three types of benefits: old-age, disability, and survivors' pensions. In addition, there is a group of privileged pensions based on accelerated service for a special group of jobs which are arduous or hazardous, and those that are detrimental to health as well as those which cannot be successfully performed after a certain age.[13] The system covers employees, the self-employed, and farmers. This used to be handled through three separate 'funds' which were consolidated into one in 2011.[14]

The public pension system is mainly financed by contributions, the rate of which since May 2014 has been 26% of gross wages (the employee contribution rate is 14% and the employer contributes 12%). This contribution rate is meant to finance all three types of pensions (old-age, disability, and survivors'), pensioners' health insurance, and other benefits related to insurance for old age and disability, such as a long-term care allowance, an employment injury benefit, etc. As contribution revenues are insufficient, subsidies from the national budget are an important part of financing.[15]

Pension benefits are calculated using a pension point formula which tightly links employment history to benefits. People collect points throughout their career to obtain their personal point up to 45 years using a personal coefficient as a lifetime earnings average, multiplied by years of service. It is possible to receive an old-age pension before the standard retirement age with a 0.34% monthly penalty.[16] Privileged pensions are based on accelerated service and

---

13   CLDS, General Point and Extra Credited (Accelerated) Services Analyses (Belgrade: CLDS, 2011).

14   Government of Republic of Serbia, "Second National Report for Social Inclusion and Poverty Reduction in the Republic of Serbia: The Status of Social Exclusion and Poverty Trends in the Period 2011–2014 and Future Priorities", (2014), http://socijalnoukljucivanje .gov.rs/wp-content/uploads/2014/11/Second-National-Report-on-Social-Inclusion-and -Poverty-Reduction-final.pdf (accessed June 7, 2020), 180.

15   Government of the Republic of Serbia, Third National Report for Social Inclusion and Poverty Reduction in the Republic of Serbia: The Status of Social Exclusion and Poverty Trends in the Period 2014–2017 and Future Priorities, (Belgrade 2018), 214, https://media .srbija.gov.rs/medeng/documents/third-national-report-on-social-inclusion-and-pove rty-reduction2014-17_eng.pdf, (accessed August 15, 2020).

16   Zakon o penzijsko invalidskom osiguranju, "Sl. glasnik RS", br. 46/2019.

lower retirement age. They are also calculated using a point formula, according to which years of service are accelerated from 12 months to 14–18 months depending on how hazardous the jobs are. Employers compensate for this acceleration with higher contribution rates, though this is insufficient when a longer pension duration is taken into account.[17]

Disability pensions are calculated in a similar manner, summing up the missing years of service according to certain rules. In particular, for those under the age of 53 years, 2/3 of service length is added to the age of 53, and 1/2 of the pension service that is missing for insured women for an additional 5 years and 10 years for men.[18] In case of occupational injury, 40 years of pensionable service is counted regardless of the individual's age.[19]

The survivors' pension is calculated as a percentage of the old-age or disability pension that an insured person/pensioner would be entitled to at the moment of death, depending on the number of family members entitled to the pension: 70% for one family member, 80% for two, 90% for three, and 100% for four or more family members.[20]

Minimum income in old age is also provided for within the insurance system as a minimum pension benefit, for those insured at least 15 years. Survivors' pensions are not raised to the minimum pension level, only the old age/disability pension, which serves as the basis for calculating the survivors' pension. There is no social pension in Serbia or specific old-age assistance scheme for an elderly person who never worked or did not work for the minimum number of years required in order to qualify for a pension.[21]

Farmers' pensions are a part of the general pension insurance system; the pension calculation formula is the same for employees and the self-employed. However, farmers' pensions are very low, since they pay contributions against the minimum base and for a limited number of years, so the calculated old age pension is usually lower than the minimum pension. In addition, the minimum pension for farmers is lower than the minimum pension for employees and self-employed persons. This difference was established in 2005, when the

---

17   Katarina Stanić, Pension System in Serbia – Design, Characteristics and Policy Recommendations, 49.
18   This used to be a difference up to standard retirement age which was 58 for women and 63 for men. When SPA increased this rule was not changed.
19   Zakon o penzijsko invalidskom osiguranju, Article 69.
20   Ibid., Article 71.
21   Government of Serbia, Third National Report for Social Inclusion and Poverty Reduction in the Republic of Serbia: The Status of Social Exclusion and Poverty Trends, 214.

minimum pension of these two categories was increased from 20% to 25% of the average wage from the previous year, while the old one was left for farmers.[22]

The retirement age for the standard old-age pension is 65 for men and 63 for women, equalizing with men at 65 years old in 2032. In addition to the age condition, in order to obtain the standard old-age pension, a minimum of 15 years of contributions are required. Those with 40 years of service are eligible for anticipated pension, currently at the minimum age of 58 years for men and slightly looser conditions for women, reaching 40 years of service and a minimum of 60 years of age for both men and women in 2024.[23] Pension in payment and general point are indexed/uprated in the same manner. Initially, the indexation method was the Swiss formula, which takes into account half of the wage growth and half of the CPI growth. Afterwards, the indexation method was changed frequently, often on an ad hoc basis. Since 2010, pensions have been either 'frozen' without indexation or they were indexed at a rate below the CPI growth.[24] In addition, from November 2014 until September 2018 higher pensions were progressively reduced.[25] The most recent change was the return to the Swiss formula in January 2020.[26]

Since 2005, the pension system in Serbia has included a voluntary, private component which is still very meagre, amounting only to 0.8% of GDP in 2017–18.[27] A mandatory private component, a 'second pillar' according to World Bank taxonomy, was rejected at the beginning of the 2000s' transition process, with the argument of high transitional cost, underdeveloped financial markets, no administrative capacity for supervision and control of pension funds, and emerging doubts about the effects of the second pillar.[28]

---

22   Boško Mijatović, Farmers' Pension Insurance (Belgrade: USAID and Centre for Liberal Democratic Studies, 2010), 17.
23   Zakon o penzijsko invalidskom osiguranju.
24   Government of the Republic of Serbia, Third National Report for Social Inclusion and Poverty Reduction in the Republic of Serbia: The Status of Social Exclusion and Poverty Trends, 216.
25   Gordana Matković and Katarina Stanić, "Serbian Pension System in Transition: Silent Break with Bismarck", 15–16.
26   Zakon o penzijsko invalidskom osiguranju, Article 80.
27   Pension Market in Focus (OECD: 2019), 73, https://www.oecd.org/pensions/private-pensions/Pension-Markets-in-Focus-2019.pdf (accessed June 12, 2020).
28   Gordana Matković et al., Challenges of Introduction of the Mandatory Private Pension System in Serbia (Belgrade: Center for Liberal-Democratic studies, 2009), 8.

3   Developments and Current State

Coverage of the elderly with the pension insurance is relatively high and has been increasing over the last few decades. In 2016, it amounted to almost 90% (Table 2.1). However, around 160,000 people, predominantly women, are still without a pension.[29]

TABLE 2.1   Pension coverage of elderly people (65+ years of age)

Gender	2009	2011	2016
Male	87.2%	89.5%	95%
Female	69.5	73.5%	82.5%
Total	77%	80.8%	88%

SOURCES: GOVERNMENT OF THE REPUBLIC OF SERBIA, THIRD NATIONAL REPORT FOR SOCIAL INCLUSION AND POVERTY REDUCTION IN THE REPUBLIC OF SERBIA: THE STATUS OF SOCIAL EXCLUSION AND POVERTY TRENDS IN THE PERIOD 2014–2017 AND FUTURE PRIORITIES (BELGRADE, 2018), HTTPS://MEDIA.SRBIJA.GOV.RS/MEDENG/DOCUMENTS/THIRD-NATIONAL-REPORT-ON-SOCIAL-INCLUSION-AND-POVERTY-REDUCTION2014-17_ENG.PDF (ACCESSED AUGUST 15, 2020), 218; GORDANA MATKOVIĆ AND KATARINA STANIĆ, SOCIJALNA ZAŠTITA U STAROSTI: DUGOTRAJNA NEGA I SOCIJALNE PENZIJE (BELGRADE: CENTAR ZA SOCIJALNU POLITIKU I FEFA, 2014), 128.

The number of pensioners has been increasing over the years, with a clear shift in the breakdown of pensioners towards old-age pensioners and a decline in disability pensions. This long-term trend is a result of the 2001–2003 reform period, when reformers sought to fight against corruption in the disability pension system, the concept of disability changed, and a regular revision of disability pensions was envisaged.[30] The number and proportion of people receiving a survivor's pension has been quite stable over time (Figure 2.1).

Pension adequacy, measured by the replacement rate (RR) for a hypothetical worker with an average of 40 years of service, has become quite low in recent years. During the last two decades, Serbia has seen a constant decline in net RR (Figure 2.2) with the exception of 2009, when an extraordinary indexation was due to political reasons as well as a change in wage statistics methodology.[31]

---

29 Calculation based on demographic data from the Republic Statistical Office.
30 Gordana Matković, "Reform of the Pension and Disability System", 340–343.
31 Gordana Matković and Katarina Stanić, "Serbian Pension System in Transition: Silent Break with Bismarck".

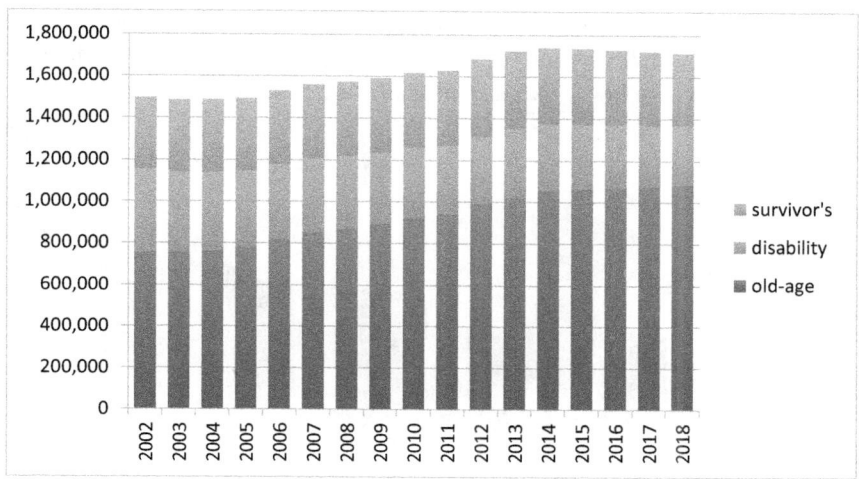

FIGURE 2.1 Number of pensioners by type of pension, 2002–2018 (end of year)
Note: Flat, 40-year career, average earner
SOURCE: PIO FUND, HTTPS://WWW.PIO.RS/SR/GODISHNI-BILTEN (ACCESSED MAY 24, 2020).

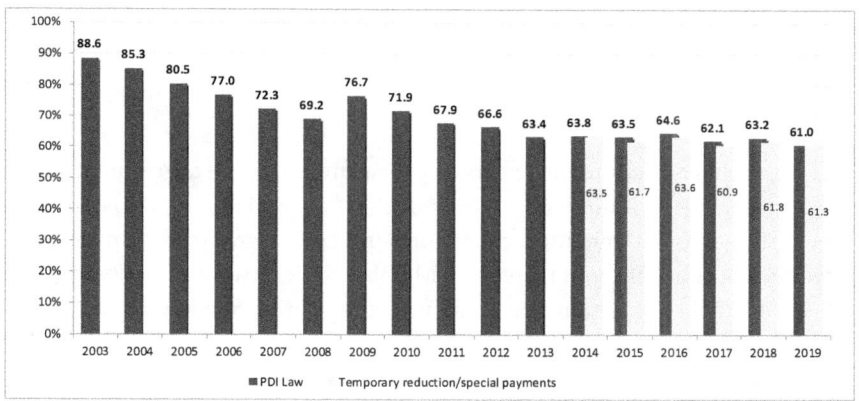

FIGURE 2.2 Net replacement rate in Serbia, 2003–2019 (in%)
SOURCE: GORDANA MATKOVIĆ AND KATARINA STANIĆ, "SERBIAN PENSION SYSTEM IN TRANSITION: SILENT BREAK WITH BISMARCK", ECONOMIC ANNALS 2020, 65, ISSUE 225: 105–133.

Compared to EU countries, net RR in 2016 was lower than the net RRs in all old EU countries apart from Germany and Sweden (Figure 2.3). New Member States typically have lower RRs, except Malta and Poland.

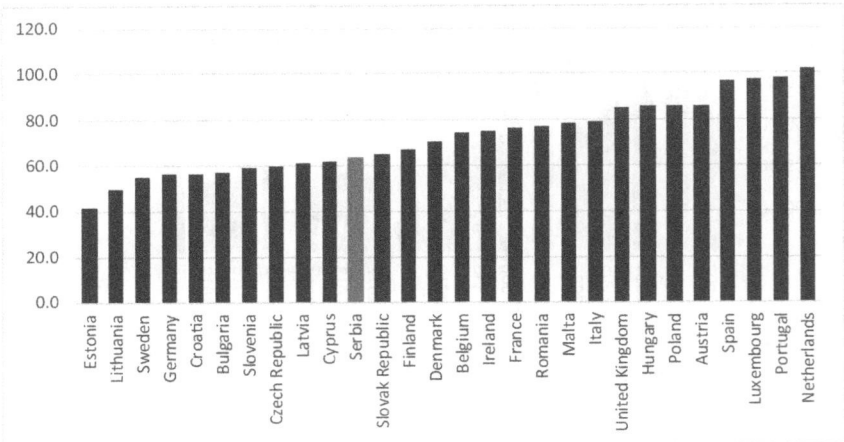

FIGURE 2.3   Net replacement rate in EU and Serbia, 2016
SOURCE: EUROPEAN COMMISSION. THE 2018 PENSION ADEQUACY REPORT: CURRENT AND FUTURE INCOME ADEQUACY IN OLD AGE IN THE EU (BRUSSELS: PUBLICATIONS OFFICE OF THE EUROPEAN UNION, 2018). OWN ELABORATION FOR SERBIA.

The actual pension income adequacy measured with the aggregate replacement ratio (ARR)[32] is quite low: 46% in 2018. The comparison to EU countries is very similar as with net RR comparison Serbia is in a group of countries with lower ratios, most of them being new Member States. However, when income adequacy in old age is analyzed along with the relative median income of the elderly (RMI) which compares the median equalized disposable income of the population aged 65+ and the median equalized disposable income of the remainder of the population (below 65) the ratio is very high: over 102% in the same year (Figure 2.4). Serbia is one of the countries with the greatest difference between the two ratios, which may be explained by factors such as the availability of other sources of income, the fact that pension income in Serbia

---

32   This macro-measure focuses on gross pension income of 65–74 year-olds that pertains to old-age and survivors' pensions and to individual pension plans (while disability pensions are considered other social benefits) and compares it to the gross labor income of the population aged 50–59.

is not taxed, and the differences in household structure, since RMI takes into account equalization of income between household members.[33]

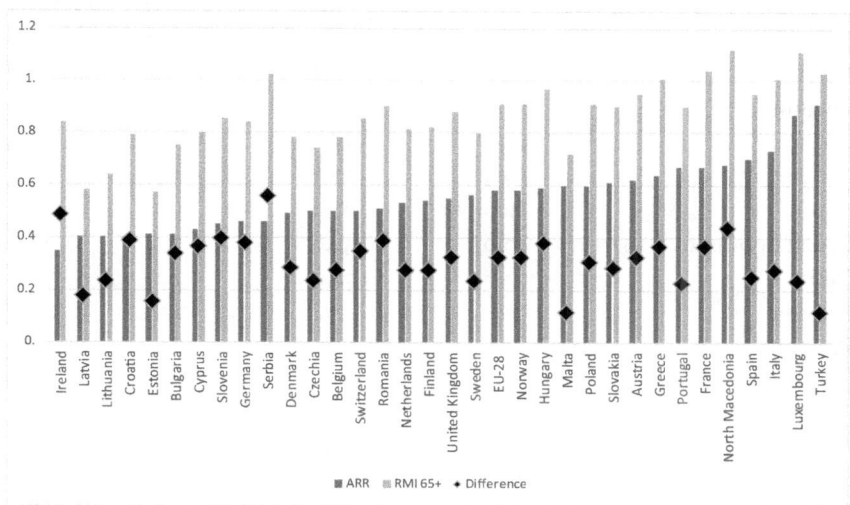

FIGURE 2.4 Aggregate replacement ratio (ARR) and relative median income of the elderly (RMI 65 and above) in EU and Serbia, 2018
SOURCE: EUROSTAT, HTTPS://EC.EUROPA.EU/EUROSTAT/DATABROWSER/VIEW/TESPM100/DEFAULT/TABLE?LANG=EN (ACCESSED MAY 25, 2020).

When it comes to future adequacy of the pension system, the perspective net RR – the one that takes into account the current legislation, shows a decline in relative income adequacy. This holds despite the fact that Serbia recently changed the indexation calculation, readopting the Swiss formula, which takes into account 50% of real wage growth. Consequently, the perspective RR is not falling as dramatically as previous projections predicted.[34] Nevertheless, apart from Poland and Romania, Serbia is the country with the largest negative percentage point change between the current and perspective net RRs, and the country with the lowest perspective net RR (Table 2.2).[35]

---

33   Katarina Stanić, Monitoring Social Inclusion in the Republic of Serbia – Indicators in the Field of Pensions (Belgrade: Social Inclusion and Poverty Reduction Unit Government of the Republic of Serbia, 2017), 19.
34   Gordana Matković and Katarina Stanić, "Serbian Pension System in Transition: Silent Break with Bismarck", 20.
35   One should bear in mind, though, that macroeconomic assumptions are specific to each country, making cross-country comparisons difficult on the basis of EU perspective RR data.

TABLE 2.2 Perspective net replacement rate (1st & 2nd pillars), EU and Serbia

Country	2016	2056	Change (in p.p.)
Austria	86.1	84.8	-1.3
Belgium	74.6	75.0	0.4
Bulgaria	57.3	73.8	16.5
Croatia	56.6	40.2	-16.4
Cyprus	62.0	67.0	5.0
Czech Republic	60.0	54.6	-5.4
Denmark	70.7	72.9	2.2
Estonia	41.8	47.8	6.0
Finland	67.1	59.1	-8.0
France	76.3	68.6	-7.7
Germany	56.2	61.6	5.4
Hungary	85.6	81.7	-3.9
Ireland	75.4	69.5	-5.9
Italy	78.9	75.7	-3.2
Latvia	61.0	51.1	-9.9
Lithuania	49.6	49.1	-0.5
Luxembourg	97.5	90.1	-7.4
Malta	78.3	70.0	-8.3
Netherlands	101.8	96.1	-5.7
Poland	85.9	44.7	-41.2
Portugal	97.8	89.3	-8.5
Romania	77.2	32.2	-45.0
Slovak Republic	65.0	66.2	1.2
Slovenia	58.8	58.8	0.0
Spain	96.8	86.5	-10.3
Sweden	54.9	45.9	-9.0
United Kingdom	85.0	62.7	-22.3
Serbia (2% real wage growth)	63.4	42.8	-20.6
Serbia (3% real wage growth)	63.4	36.0	-27.4

SOURCE: EUROPEAN COMMISSION, THE 2018 PENSION ADEQUACY REPORT: CURRENT AND FUTURE INCOME ADEQUACY IN OLD EGE IN THE EU, VOLUME I, 2018, 49, HTTPS://OP.EUROPA.EU/EN/PUBLICATION-DETAIL/-/PUBLICATION/F0E89C3F-7821-11E8-AC6A-01AA75ED71A1/LANGUAGE-EN (ACCESSED MAY 25, 2020). OWN ELABORATION FOR SERBIA.

The minimum pension (old-age and disability) stands above absolute poverty line and serves as the main instrument to safeguard a basic standard of living through pension insurance. The farmers' minimum pension is usually below the poverty line, except for the period 2008–2011, when it was around the poverty line. The survivors' pension, for both those insured as employees and self-employed persons, and particularly under farmers' insurance, is significantly lower than the absolute poverty line (Figure 2.5).

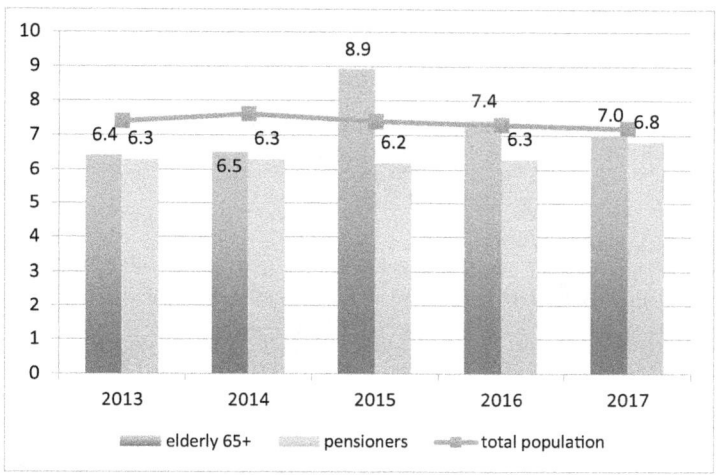

FIGURE 2.5   Minimum pension and the absolute poverty line (in %)
SOURCE: SIPRU FOR POVERTY LINE; PIO FUND, HTTPS://WWW.PIO.RS/SR/
MESECHNI-BILTEN (ACCESSED MAY 25, 2020).

The majority of farmers receive the minimum old-age pension. In December 2016, the minimum farmers' old-age pension was received by 76.5% of retired farmers; about 15% of farmers' pension recipients received pensions below the minimum level of that for survivors and only about 5% of pensioners received pensions above the minimum level.[36] The proportion of pensioners living in absolute poverty is below that of the overall population. Broken down by age groups, the poverty of people aged 65+ is lower than or equal to that of the overall population, except in 2015 (Figure 2.6). The rate of pensioners and those 65+ years old who are at risk of poverty is lower than that of the overall

---

36   Government of the Republic of Serbia, Third National Report for Social Inclusion and Poverty Reduction in the Republic of Serbia: The Status of Social Exclusion and Poverty Trends, 224.

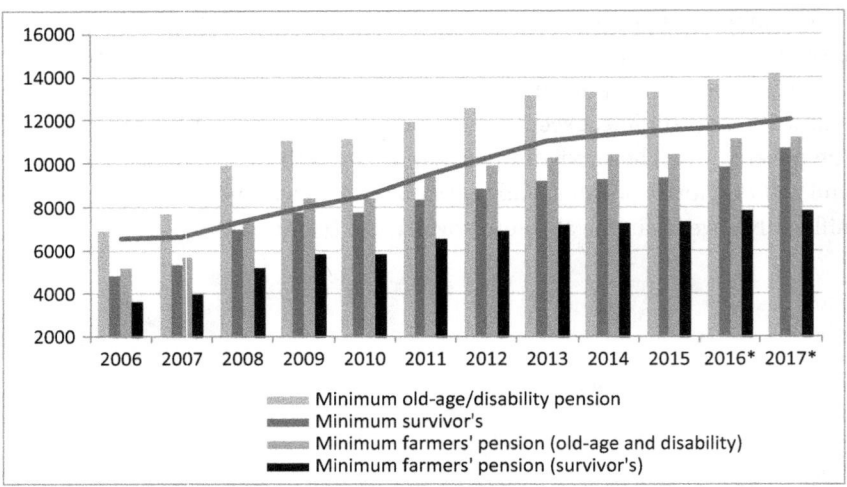

FIGURE 2.6 Absolute poverty rate, 2006–2017
* In 2016 and 2017 there was a one-off payment for all pensioners at the end of the year, which was allocated into the amount of minimum pension
SOURCE: GOVERNMENT OF SERBIA – SIPRU ASSESSMENT OF ABSOLUTE POVERTY IN SERBIA IN 2018, HTTP://SOCIJALNOUKLJUCIVANJE.GOV.RS/EN/ASSESSMENT-OF-ABSOLUTE-POVERTY-IN-SERBIA-IN-2018/ (ACCESSED MAY 25, 2020).

population, while women 65+ are at a significantly higher risk of poverty than men (Figure 2.7). This can be explained by the higher life expectancy of women, meaning that they more frequently live in single-person households, which are typically at a higher risk of poverty, and receive less pension coverage.

FIGURE 2.7 At-risk-of-poverty rate, total and by gender (in %, income in 2018)
SOURCE: STATISTICAL OFFICE OF THE REPUBLIC OF SERBIA, POVERTY AND SOCIAL INEQUALITY, 2018, HTTPS://PUBLIKACIJE.STAT.GOV.RS/G2019/PDFE/G20191281.PDF (ACCESSED MAY 25, 2020).

Pension expenditures have been quite high, leveling off at around 12% and even hitting 13% of GDP in 2009 (Figure 2.8).[37] Since then, expenditures have been decreasing due to pensions being frozen in 2010 and subsequently only being uprated at a lower rate than CPI. This decrease has been particularly pronounced since 2014 when pensions were progressively reduced for those with average and higher pensions.

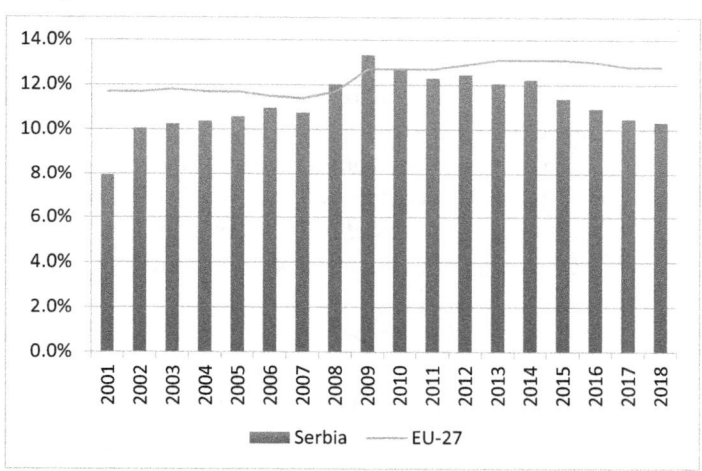

FIGURE 2.8 Pension expenditures in the EU and Serbia (% of GDP)
SOURCE: PENSION AND DISABILITY INSURANCE FUND OF THE REPUBLIC OF SERBIA, VARIOUS FINANCIAL REPORTS FOR PENSION EXPENDITURES HTTPS://WWW.PIO.RS/SR/FINANSIJE (ACCESSED MAY 27, 2020); MINISTRY OF FINANCE OF THE REPUBLIC OF SERBIA FOR GDP, HTTPS://MFIN.GOV.RS/DOKUMENTI2/MAKROEKONOMSKI-I-FISKALNI-PODACI (ACCESSED MAY 27, 2020); EUROSTAT FOR EU-27AVERAGE, HTTPS://EC.EUROPA.EU/EUROSTAT/DATABROWSER/VIEW/TPS00103/DEFAULT/TABLE?LANG=EN (ACCESSED MAY 27, 2020).

Financing pension expenditures had been an issue for a long time. At the beginning of the 2000s, just after the reforms, the PDI fund deficit rose and reached 5% of GDP in 2002, staying at that level in subsequent years; it turned out that there were several reasons for this. Firstly, a tax reform conducted in June brought down both the nominal and effective contribution rates for PDI, thereby affecting the revenue side. Secondly, the regular

---

37   It used to be considered even higher until recently, when changes to the GDP methodology increased the GDP, hence proportions were lowered.

payment of entitlements to pensioners without arrears increased expenditures by as much as 1.5 percentage points of GDP. In addition, some other expenditures such as health care transfers and repayment of debts and loans also increased the expenditure side of the PDI fund. Finally, the deficit was somewhat influenced by the exceptionally high growth of wages apparent in the official statistics, which notwithstanding indexation, which according to the Swiss formula takes into account only 50% of wage growth, still led to such a growth of pensions that was not accompanied by increased contribution revenues, since it turned out that the wage growth was overstated by the statistics.[38]

Budgetary transfers to the PDI fund remained at the level of 5% of GDP in the following years and rose to 7% of GDP in 2009 as a result of a surge in pension expenditure, which in turn was a consequence of the extraordinary pension indexation due to political pressures in October 2008.[39] Since 2012, transfers from the budget began to fall, reaching 3.4% of GDP in 2018. This resulted from both decreased expenditures and the increased contribution rate since 2014.

It is also important to make a distinction between the PIO fund deficit and the deficit of the pension system. On the revenue side, in addition to contributions there are budgetary transfers for special entitlements according to the PDI law, transfers for topping up the minimum pension, etc., which should be considered as pension system revenue. On the expenditure side, apart from expenditures on net pensions the PDI fund also covers some other social insurance benefits, such as compensation for physical injury, a long-term care benefit, purchase of aids for the blind, compensation for funeral expenses of pensioners, the health insurance of pensioners, administrative costs, etc.[40] The aforementioned pension system deficit is significantly lower than budgetary transfers to the PDI fund and has fallen to almost 1% of GDP in recent years (Figure 2.9).

---

[38] Katarina Stanić and Jurij Bajec, What is Actually the Size of the Pension System Deficit in Serbia?, 60; Katarina Stanić, "Registered Employment and Wages – Statistical Data and Trends 2000–2005", Quarterly Monitor of Economic Trends and Policies in Serbia 3 (2005): 61.

[39] Katarina Stanić, "Efekti dosadašnjih i nove promene u penzijskom sistemu", in Institucionalne promene u 2010 (Belgrade: CLDS, 2011), 119.

[40] Ibid., 118.

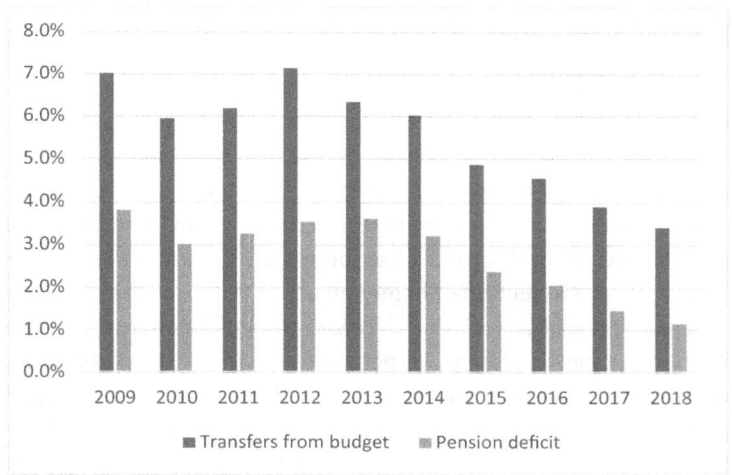

FIGURE 2.9 Budgetary transfers to PDI fund and pension deficit (% of GDP), 2009–2018
SOURCE: OWN ELABORATION BASED ON PIO FUND FINANCIAL STATEMENTS, HTTPS://WWW.PIO.RS/SR/FINANSIJE (ACCESSED JUNE 10, 2020).

4   Challenges for the Pension System

As with most pension systems around the world, the Serbian pension system is facing the challenge of delivering adequate and sustainable pensions. At the beginning of the 2000s, the replacement rate was nominally very high, above 90%, while in fact real pensions were significantly lower due to arrears and high inflation. Consequently, regular payment and macroeconomic stabilization led to a surge in pension expenditure and the need for a change in the pension adjustment. In 2001, wage indexation was replaced with the Swiss formula combination of wage increases and the cost of living. In this way, the rapid growth of pensions, which was unsustainable due to the deficit in the pension fund, was slowed down.[41] Another important decision was to index the general point and pension in payment in the same manner, since different formulas of valorization (general point indexation) and indexation of pensions in payment can create large differences between new and old pensioners of the same professional profile.[42] At that time, a substantial increase in wages

---

41   Gordana Matković, "Reform of Pension and Disability System", 341.
42   Katarina Stanić, Pension System in Serbia – Design, Characteristics and Policy Recommendations, 33.

was rightfully expected, hence a different indexation of general point and pensions in payment would have left existing pensioners behind and excluded them from the benefits of the transition.

Meanwhile, the pension policy in Serbia has been wandering between two different approaches the Beveridge system, where the main aim is to prevent poverty in old age, and the Bismarck system, where the main goal is to ensure a relative standard of living for pensioners. "Freezing" the pensions ad hoc indexation without indexation often below the growth in consumer prices and the progressive reduction of higher pensions that occurred between November 2014 and September 2018, coupled with one-off payments either to pensioners with lower pensions or to all pensioners is in fact a "silent break with Bismarck", where this policy has not been really defined or understood as a new strategic course of action, nor has it been debated or analyzed. These silent reforms seem to be a "quick and easy" solution for tackling high public expenditures and deficit without understanding the implications and the fact that this shift implies a significant transition cost.[43]

Currently, the net replacement rate is at around 60% of lifelong earnings, and it will fall further: the perspective net RR is very low despite the recent switch to the Swiss formula. The aggregate RR is quite low, at 46% in 2018, and although RMI for the elderly is above 100%, it rather indicates a lack of income of inactive under 65-year-olds than the relative adequacy of the pension system. Taking all of these indicators together, coupled with the very low level of wages in Serbia, implies that the goal of the pension system to assure a relatively good standard of living for pensioners is in jeopardy.

This in turn implies a need to shift the general point indexation to wages as the only way to keep the RR at the current level. On the other hand, given the system's financial sustainability, pensions in payment certainly cannot be indexed with real wage growth, so the separation of the indexation of the general point and pensions in payment is unavoidable. This is very sensible, as it raises the issue of horizontal equity between existing and new pensioners, particularly in an economy with growth in real wages. Basically, it reflects the dilemma between lower initial pensions with real growth over retirement years (same indexation) or higher initial pensions, which would ensure more adequate pensions for new pensioners, with slower or no real growth during retirement years (separate indexation).[44]

---

43   Gordana Matković and Katarina Stanić, "Serbian Pension System in Transition: Silent Break with Bismarck", 1.
44   CLDS, General Point and Extra Credited (Accelerated) Service Analyses, 29–31.

When it comes to safeguarding an absolute standard of living, i.e., preventing poverty in old age, the role of the pension system is essential; it can be said that the system is successfully achieving this goal, since the poverty rate among pensioners (under both absolute and relative concepts) is below that of the overall population. Nevertheless, there are still around 150,000–160,000 people, or over 10% of the population aged 65+, who are not covered by pension insurance. There is no specific social assistance program for the elderly in Serbia, though they may apply for regular financial social assistance (FSA), which is augmented by 20% when one is unable to work, as with the elderly. However, the eligibility criteria are quite strict, particularly those pertaining to property, while the income test threshold is lower than the absolute poverty line. Therefore, this program is not appropriate for the elderly, particularly for those in rural areas who usually own land and in fact only a small number of elderly people around 10,000 are FSA beneficiaries.[45]

Farmers' pensions are quite unique. Although they nominally fit into the comprehensive pension insurance system, in reality farmers' pensions are flat and set at a very low level, below the absolute poverty line. This is due to the problems with tax and contribution collection in agriculture contributions are paid at a minimum level for a limited number of years, if at all. This has effectively turned farmers' pension insurance into voluntary insurance instead of a mandatory system, as it was designed.[46] This introduces a challenge into the pension system, again raising the issue of adequacy and financial stability for this specific category.

Similarly, survivors' pensions are very low often below the absolute poverty line and the research on pensioners' poverty combined with the distribution of the survivors' pensions indicates a potential risk of poverty,[47] while at the same time it represents a significant portion of pension expenditure: around 16% of total pension expenditure compared to the EU average of 13%.[48]

Privileged pensions represent around 15%–20% of the total number of pension beneficiaries. Although service acceleration is coupled with higher contributions, the horizontal equity principle does not hold true, since privileged

---

45 Gordana Matković and Katarina Stanić, Socijalna zaštita u starosti: dugotrajna nega i socijalne penzije, (Belgrade: Centar za socijalnu politiku i FEFA, 2014), 147.
46 Boško Mijatović, Farmers' Pension Insurance, 49.
47 Katarina Stanić, Pension System in Serbia – Design, Characteristics and Policy Recommendations, 104.
48 Eurostat, Database by Themes: Social Protection Expenditure, https://ec.europa.eu/eurostat/databrowser/view/spr_exp_sum/default/table?lang=en (accessed June 14, 2020).

pensioners are not in an equal position among themselves and they are in a significantly more favorable position than standard old-age pensioners.[49]

5 Conclusion

The pension system in Serbia is successfully preventing poverty in old age; however, the declining net RR (currently at around 60%) threatens to jeopardize the relative standard of living of pensioners. The financial stability of the pension system, which has been an issue for a long time, now appears to be being brought under control: pension expenditures as a share of GDP have declined by 3 percentage points and the fall in the pension fund and pension system deficits was even more pronounced.

Consequently, it seems to be the right time to separate general point and pension in payment indexation. In order to prevent the RR from declining further, the general point value should be uprated by the real wage growth rate. For the sake of the system's financial stability, pensions in payment should be indexed with either a combination of real wages and CPI growth, such as the Swiss formula, or CPI indexation only.

When it comes to improving the coverage of the elderly, introducing some form of social pension in Serbia is desirable. Several options have been analyzed, such as universal pensions for everyone older than 65 years, a guaranteed pension like the Swedish guarantee pension, which is a top-up to a certain guaranteed pension for all citizens, regardless of work history, or a special 'module' for the elderly within the FSA. This module could include a higher threshold/assistance level for old-age households and/or a higher coefficient for every elderly person 0.7 instead of the current 0.5 and/or the abolition of the property criteria. Estimated expenditures of "FSA for the elderly" range from 0.033% of GDP to 0.3% of GDP. In addition to cost efficiency, the advantage of this targeted pension is that it is less motivating for working and paying contributions than the current minimum pension or a guaranteed minimum would be.[50]

Farmers' pensions as a component of the pension insurance system need to be redesigned due to the unique position of agriculture within the tax system of Serbia. Some options have been analyzed, such as radically rehabilitating the farmers' pension insurance to upgrade the existing model, extending the

---

49 CLDS, General Point and Extra Credited (Accelerated) Services Analyses, 81.
50 Katarina Matković and Katarina Stanić, Socijalna zaštita u starosti: dugotrajna nega i socijalne penzije, 160.

existing situation, and dissolving mandatory insurance for farmers, formally turning it into a voluntary system.[51] Further research and analysis is needed in the field of farmers` pensions. Survivors' pension is another field that requires policy research and analysis in a wider context, particularly of surviving children.

There is room for further improvement and streamlining of the pension system, in particular by fine-tuning the existing system. For example, privileged pensions with accelerated service (including pensions under special regulations) could also be subject to the same system of penalties as for anticipated old-age pensions, with the exception of occupations in which life expectancy is lower.[52]

When it comes to retirement age, there is currently no need for further increases, since the life expectancy in Serbia is lower than in more developed EU countries, so the duration of pensions is lower. Therefore, any future increases should be linked with life expectancy.

Bibliography

Altiparmakov, Nikola, and Gordana Matković. "The Development of Private Pensions in Serbia: Caught between a Generic Blueprint and an Unconducive Local Environment ". Transfer: European Review of Labor and Research 24, no. 1 (2018): 57–71.

Bojić, Filip P., Pravo na socijalnu penziju u sistemu prava socijalne sigurnosti. Belgrade: Univerzitet u Beogradu-Pravni fakultet, 2018.

CLDS. General Point and Extra Credited (Accelerated) Services Analyses. Belgrade: Publisher, 2011.

European Commission. The 2018 Pension Adequacy Report: Current and Future Income Adequacy in Old Ege in the EU, Volume I, 2018. Accessed May 25, 2020. https://op.europa.eu/en/publication-detail/-/publication/f0e89c3f-7821-11e8-ac6a-01aa75ed71a1/language-en.

Eurostat. Database by Themes: Social Protection Expenditure. Accessed June 14, 2020. https://ec.europa.eu/eurostat/databrowser/view/spr_exp_sum/default/table?lang=en.

Government of the Republic of Serbia. Second National Report for Social Inclusion and Poverty Reduction in the Republic of Serbia: The Status of Social Exclusion and Poverty Trends in the Period 2011–2014 and Future Priorities. 2014. Accessed June

---

51   Boško Mijatović, "Farmers' Pension Insurance", 51–67.
52   Third National Report for Social Inclusion and Poverty Reduction in the Republic of Serbia: The Status of Social Exclusion and Poverty Trends, 235.

7, 2020. http://socijalnoukljucivanje.gov.rs/wp-content/uploads/2014/11/Second-National-Report-on-Social-Inclusion-and-Poverty-Reduction-final.pdf.

Government of the Republic of Serbia. Third National Report for Social Inclusion and Poverty Reduction in the Republic of Serbia: The Status of Social Exclusion and Poverty Trends in the Period 2014–2017 and Future Priorities. 2018. Accessed August 15, 2020. https://media.srbija.gov.rs/medeng/documents/third-national-report-on-social-inclusion-and-poverty-reduction2014-17_eng.pdf.

Government of the Republic of Serbia – SIPRU. Assessment of Absolute Poverty in Serbia in 2018. 2019. Accessed May 25, 2020. http://socijalnoukljucivanje.gov.rs/en/assessment-of-absolute-poverty-in-serbia-in-2018/.

Matković, Gordana. "Mirovinski Sustav Srbije u Svjetlu Krize". Revija za socijalnu politiku 23, no. 1 (2016): 99–119.

Matković, Gordana. "Penzijski Sistem u Srbiji – Karakteristike, Dosadašnje Reforme, Dileme i Opcije". In Penzijski Sistem u Srbiji, edited by Katarina Stanić. Belgrade: USAID/BearingPoint, 2009.

Matković, Gordana. "Reform of Pension and Disability System". In Four Years of Transition in Serbia, edited by Boris Begović and Boško Mijatović, 337–345. Belgrade: CLDS, 2005.

Matković, Gordana, Jurij Bajec, Boško Mijatović, Boško Živković, and Katarina Stanić. Challenges of Introduction of the Mandatory Private Pension System in Serbia. Belgrade: Center for Liberal-Democratic studies – CLDS, 2009.

Matković, Gordana, and Katarina Stanić. "Serbian Pension System in Transition: Silent Break with Bismarck". Economic Annals 2020, 65, Issue 225: 105–133.

Matković, Gordana, and Katarina Stanić. Socijalna Zaštita u Starosti: Dugotrajna Nega i Socijalne Penzije. Belgrade: Centar za Socijalnu Politiku i Fefa, 2014.

Mijatović, Boško. Farmers' Pension Insurance. Belgrade: USAID and Centre for Liberal Democratic Studies, 2010.

Mijatović, Boško. "Penzijski Sistem". In Reforme u Srbiji: Dostignuća i Izazovi, edited by Boško Mijatović. Beograd: Centar za Liberalno-Demokratske Studije, 2008.

OECD. "Pension Market in Focus". 2019. Accessed June 14, 2020. https://www.oecd.org/pensions/private-pensions/Pension-Markets-in-Focus-2019.pdf.

Statistical Office of the Republic of Serbia. Poverty and Social Inequality, 2018. Accessed May 25, 2020. https://publikacije.stat.gov.rs/G2019/PdfE/G20191281.pdf.

Stanić, Katarina. "Efekti Dosadašnjih i Nove Promene u Penzijskom Sistemu". In Institucionalne Promene u 2010. Belgrade: CLDS, 2011.

Stanić, Katarina. Monitoring Social Inclusion in the Republic of Serbia – Indicators in the Field of Pensions. Belgrade: Social Inclusion and Poverty Reduction Unit Government of the Republic of Serbia, 2017.

Stanić, Katarina. Pension System in Serbia – Design, Characteristics and Policy Recommendations. Belgrade: USAID and CLDS, 2010.

Stanić, Katarina. "Registered Employment and Wages – Statistical Data and Trends 2000–2005". Quarterly Monitor of Economic Trends and Policies in Serbia 3 (2005): 61–70.

Stanić, Katarina, and Jurij Bajec. "What is Actually the Size of the Pension System Deficit in Serbia?". Quarterly Monitor of Economic Trends and Policies in Serbia 1 (2005): 58–64.

World Bank. Serbia and Montenegro Recent Progress on Structural Reforms. Washington, D.C.: World Bank Group, 2003. Accessed 10 June 2020. http://documents.worldbank.org/curated/en/956521468781161590/Serbia-and-Montenegro-recent-progress-on-structural-reforms.

Zakon o penzijsko invalidskom osiguranju. "Sl. glasnik RS", br. 46/2019, 86/2019.

CHAPTER 3

Decentralization of Social Care Services in Serbia

Gordana Matković

1 Introduction

Over the past twenty years, the decentralization of social welfare in Serbia has mainly taken place through the expansion of social care community-based services within the jurisdiction of local governments. Strategic decisions have been made to keep cash benefits and the majority of accommodation services (residential and foster care) as the responsibility of the national government.[1] While it has been considered that responsibility for care homes for older people should be transferred to cities in the form of asymmetric decentralization, this has not been implemented.[2]

Social care services are within the jurisdiction of the national and local governments. Through laws and bylaws, the national government regulates social care services, establishes minimum standards and control mechanisms. Development of community-based services (CBS), together with decentralization and deinstitutionalization, remain a formal priority of the reform agenda. Two documents, Poverty Reduction Strategy[3] and Social Welfare Development Strategy[4] provided an outline of the agenda for reform and made clear the institutional relationships between mandates at the central and local levels, the essential function of community-based services and introduced civil society organizations as service providers and case management concepts. More recent strategic documents have not yet been adopted.

Local governments (LGs) in Serbia consist of municipalities and cities. There are 145 local governments, some of which are small, sparsely populated, and under-capacitated (underprovisioned or under-resourced) municipalities, and some are large cities. Based on their level of development and according

---

1 Social Welfare Development Strategy, 2005, https://npm.rs/attachments/strateg.razvoja.soc.zastite.pdf (accessed May 16, 2020).
2 Gordana Matković, Decentralization of Social Welfare in Serbia (Belgrade: CLDS, 2006), 72.
3 Poverty Reduction Strategy, 2003, http://socijalnoukljucivanje.gov.rs/wp-content/uploads/2014/06/1.-Strategija-za-smanjenje-siromastva-u-Srbiji-Rezime-i-matrice.pdf (accessed May 16, 2020).
4 Social Welfare Development Strategy, 2005.

to national regulations, the LGs have been classified into four groups, ranging from the first, consisting of the most developed municipalities and cities, with the level of development above the Republic average, to the fourth group, consisting of the least developed LGs.[5] LGs derive their revenues from shared taxes, block transfers, local taxes, as well as fees and charges. The primary responsibilities of LGs are confined to infrastructure services, preschool education, and a limited set of social care services.[6] In the area of social welfare, local governments are also responsible for one-off benefits, both cash and in-kind.

To assess the decentralization process, several cycles of mapping social care services were implemented. The first mapping process was carried out in 2013, the second one in 2016 and the third in 2019.[7] The mapping process entailed efforts to scan all existing social care services within the mandate of LGs, to collect data on the overall expenditures and the number of beneficiaries of local services, as well as to highlight sustainability issues. The database produced through the mapping process enables LGs to compare their performance across a number of indicators, and also provides the national government with inputs for the conceptualization of earmarked transfers and policies that are important for advancing the development of non-institutional social care services. Mapping of social care services consisted of three phases: a preparatory phase (questionnaire development and testing) the data collection phase (including entering the data and verification) and the report writing phase. In the 2019 mapping cycle, the data collection phase lasted from June to September. A total of 439 professionals from 145 LGUs participated in the mapping process. All data refer to 2018.

---

5 The main indicator for measuring the level of development is the total sum of wage bill and pensions and the budget revenue of the local government units, while corrective indicators include demographic decline or growth, unemployment rate and the level of education. National Agency for Regional Development, Developments of the Regions and Local Self-Government Units, http://www.regionalnirazvoj.gov.rs/Lat/ShowNARRFolder.aspx?mi=4 (accessed June 4, 2020).
6 World Bank: Serbia – Municipal Finance and Expenditure Review (Washington DC: World Bank, 2013), 14, http://documents.worldbank.org/curated/en/400441468103148742/Serbia-Municipal-finance-and-expendit ure-review (accessed June 4, 2020).
7 Gordana Matković and Milica Stranjaković, Mapping Social Care Services within the Mandate of Local Governments in the Republic of Serbia (Belgrade: Social Inclusion and Poverty Reduction Unit Government of the Republic of Serbia, 2016); Center for Liberal Democratic Studies: Mapping Social Care Services within the Mandate of Local Governments in the Republic of Serbia (Belgrade: Social Inclusion and Poverty Reduction Unit, Office of the Minister without Portfolio in charge of European Integration Government of the Republic of Serbia, 2013).

The aim of this chapter is to analyze the availability of community-based services in Serbia and the adequacy of earmarked transfers from the national level that have been introduced to boost the development of these services. This research relies on mapping of social care services within the jurisdiction of local governments and analysis of legal and public documents.

2   Mandates for Social Care Services

The responsibility for social care services in Serbia is divided between the local and the national levels. According to the Social Welfare Law,[8] there are five types of social care services:
- assessment and planning services (national responsibility);
- day-care community-based services (local);
- services for independent living (mixed);
- counseling, therapy, and social education services (local);
- accommodation and shelter services (mixed).

The national level mandate includes the majority of accommodation and shelter services (for services in foster and residential care, providing shelters for people who have been victims of human trafficking) as well as supported housing for persons with disabilities (PWD) in LGs belonging to groups II, III and IV based on their level of development.[9] The national budget also provides funding for assessment and planning of services in centers for social work (CSW). Of two thousand professionals employed in 140 local centers for social work, four fifths are funded from the national budget.[10] Public expenditure for social care services within the national jurisdiction amounts to approximately 0.2% of GDP (0.14% of GDP for 20,000 beneficiaries of residential and foster care services and 0.06% of GDP for CSW staff and the part of operating costs).[11] The local government's mandate covers the remainder of the services, mostly community-based non-institutional services (Figure 3.1). LGs are also responsible for the

---

8   Social Welfare Law, 2011.
9   National Agency for Regional Development, Developments of the Regions and Local Self-Government Units, http://www.regionalnirazvoj.gov.rs/Lat/ShowNARRFolder.aspx?mi=4 (accessed June 4, 2020).
10   Government of the Republic of Serbia: Second National Report for Social Inclusion and Poverty Reduction in the Republic of Serbia: The Status of Social Exclusion and Poverty Trends in the Period 2011–2014 and Future Priorities (Belgrade, 2014), 169.
11   Government of the Republic of Serbia: Third National Report for Social Inclusion and Poverty Reduction in the Republic of Serbia: The Status of Social Exclusion and Poverty Trends in the Period 2014–2017 and Future Priorities (Belgrade, 2018), 199.

maintenance of CSW facilities and for funding the salaries of additional social workers attending to the entitlements and services within the mandate of LG s.

Pre-2011 legislation did not allow additional direct transfers from the national government to local governments for the purpose of financing services that were part of the LG's mandate. However, during the last fifteen years these services have been partly financed through the extra budgetary Social Innovation Fund, public works, and the Budget Fund for PWD. Part of the funding has come from donations as well. The 2011 Social Welfare Law introduced earmarked transfers to provide supplemental funds for care services which are mandated to local authorities. However, the decree regulating the transfers was only adopted much later (March 2016).

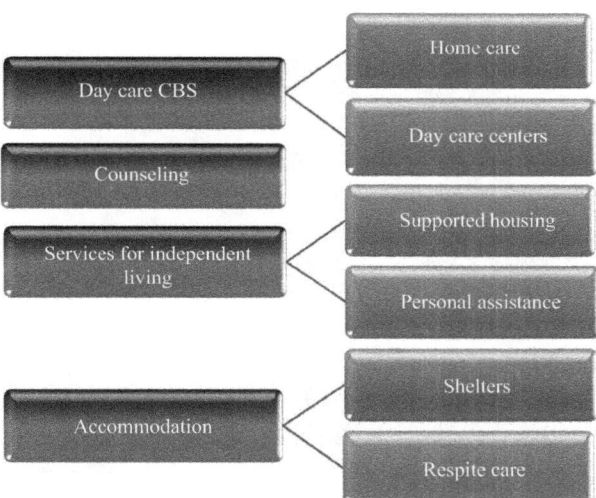

FIGURE 3.1 Social care services within the mandate of LG s
SOURCE: AUTHOR'S ELABORATION BASED ON THE SOCIAL WELFARE LAW, 2011.

3 Social Care Services within the Jurisdiction of Local Governments

According to the mapping data, 137 of 145 local governments provided different CBS in 2018.[12] Home care for older people, day care centers for children with disabilities (CWD) and children's personal attendants, which belong to the group of day-care community-based services, dominated the services

---

12 Gordana Matković and Milica Stranjaković, Mapping Social Care Services and Material Support within the Mandate of Local Governments in the Republic of Serbia, 12.

under LG mandate (Table 3.1). These three services, which account for nearly 75% of total expenditures for services that are the responsibility of LGs, cover the greatest part of all beneficiaries. In many LGs only limited services are provided, and many services are not available countrywide (Table 3.1). Even the coverage rate for older people receiving the most widespread home care services is low (1.2% of the population over 65 years of age) compared to more developed European countries.[13]

TABLE 3.1 LG social care services, Serbia, 2018

Type of services	Number of LG	Number of beneficiaries	Total expenditure (RSD)
Home care for PWD and elderly	123	16,678	1,255,910,687
Children's personal attendants	76	1,762	576,453,922
Day care centers for CWD	64	1,999	894,664,947
Counseling	37	1,239	93,440,022
Day care centers for PWD	20	449	90,644,407
Shelters for victims of violence	15	358	115,136,827
Personal assistance for PWD	17	223	97,730,672
Home care for CWD	14	227	38,442,265
Supported housing for youth	14	50	12,766,264

Note: only services provided in more than 10% LG are presented

SOURCE: GORDANA MATKOVIĆ AND MILICA STRANJAKOVIĆ, MAPPING SOCIAL CARE SERVICES AND MATERIAL SUPPORT WITHIN THE MANDATE OF LOCAL GOVERNMENTS IN THE REPUBLIC OF SERBIA (BELGRADE: SOCIAL INCLUSION AND POVERTY REDUCTION UNIT, GOVERNMENT OF THE REPUBLIC OF SERBIA, 2020), 13–37.

Total expenditures were RSD 3.65 billion (0,07% of GDP), according to the mapping data gathered. Expenditures for local community-based services are twice as low as for accommodation, mostly residential, services (0,14% of GDP).[14]

---

[13] Gordana Matković and Katarina Stanić, Socijalna zaštita u starosti: dugotrajna nega i socijalne penzije (Belgrade: Center za socijalnu politiku/FEFA/SIPRU, 2014), 70.

[14] Government of the Republic of Serbia: Third National Report for Social Inclusion and Poverty Reduction in the Republic of Serbia: The Status of Social Exclusion and Poverty Trends, 199.

The highest expenditures for CBS in absolute terms were recorded in the capital city Belgrade[15] (1.26 billion), more than a third of the total expenditures for these purposes in all of Serbia. On the other hand, eight municipalities had no services at all and thus no expenditures. An additional dozen municipalities also in effect belong to this group, given the very small number of beneficiaries and low expenditures for services. Approximately one-fifth of LGs provides only one service, predominantly home care for the elderly. Most LGs provide two to three services. More diverse and complex services are present only in some larger cities.

Local government budgets excluding earmarked transfers (EET) funded the largest share of total CBS expenditures in 2018 (76.5%), according to the mapping data (Figure 3.2). The largest allocations from local budgets EET, of over 2.5%, were recorded in five small municipalities, four of which belong to the group of the least developed municipalities in Serbia, mostly in the south of the country (Table 3.2). Belgrade and Novi Sad, the two largest cities, have respectively allocated 1.2% and 1.7% of their budgets EET for CBS. On the other hand, a large number of municipalities and cities did not allocate any funds for services or allocated less than 0.01% (30 LGs). The median share of expenditures from local budgets EET for these purposes was only 0.35%, which means that half of the municipalities and cities have assigned a very low priority to the protection of vulnerable groups through social care services (Table 3.2). Among them are some of the most developed LGs.

TABLE 3.2   Distribution of LGs by share of expenditures on social care services in local budgets, 2018

Number of LGs	Share of local expenditures on social care services
72	below median (< 0.35%)
24	between median and twice the median (0.35–0.69%)
43	0.7%–2.5%
5	>2.5%

SOURCE: GORDANA MATKOVIĆ AND MILICA STRANJAKOVIĆ, MAPPING SOCIAL CARE SERVICES AND MATERIAL SUPPORT WITHIN THE MANDATE OF LOCAL GOVERNMENTS IN THE REPUBLIC OF SERBIA (BELGRADE: SOCIAL INCLUSION AND POVERTY REDUCTION UNIT, GOVERNMENT OF THE REPUBLIC OF SERBIA, 2020), 30.

---

15   The City of Belgrade is the largest territorial unit, with the largest population and the highest local budget, as well as a long-standing tradition in the provision of social care services.

Differences between LGs in local budget expenditures for CBS cannot be explained by differences in the number of residents, and a weak correlation is observed with respect to the degree of self-financing, which approximates the level of development.[16] The differences cannot be attributed to ideology either, considering that the same party is in power in almost all municipalities and cities. Further research is needed to better understand the reasons for such significant differences.

Apart from local budgets EET, the remainder of the funds came from earmarked transfers (17%), international donors (2.8%) and copayments from beneficiaries (2.2%) (Figure 3.2). According to the mapping data, the highest share of earmarked transfers from the national level is noted among home care services, children's personal attendant and counseling services.

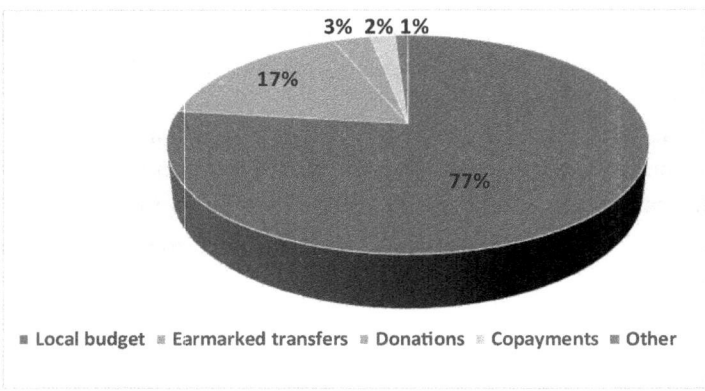

FIGURE 3.2   Sources of CBS financing 2018
SOURCE: GORDANA MATKOVIĆ AND MILICA STRANJAKOVIĆ, MAPPING SOCIAL CARE SERVICES AND MATERIAL SUPPORT WITHIN THE MANDATE OF LOCAL GOVERNMENTS IN THE REPUBLIC OF SERBIA (BELGRADE: SOCIAL INCLUSION AND POVERTY REDUCTION UNIT, GOVERNMENT OF THE REPUBLIC OF SERBIA, 2020), 43.

Among the LGs that received an earmarked transfer in 2018 (105 LGs), one in five (23 LGs) relied almost exclusively on this source of funding, with share

---

16   This indicator points to "the ability of local self-government units to be financed from own-source revenues and assigned taxes. The high value of the indicator indicates high financial independence and sustainability of local self-government", Public Policy Secretariat of the Republic of Serbia, Analytical Tool for LGs, Methodological Notes, https://jls1.rsjp.gov.rs/vox/Napomene (accessed May 18, 2020).

of transfers 90% and more (Table 3.3). In this group, there are nine local self-governments that are not underdeveloped, and which, according to the decree, had to provide between 10 and 30% of their own funds in order to receive earmarked transfers. The share of earmarked transfer was high in 42 LGs (between 50 and 89%).

TABLE 3.3 Distribution of LGs by share of earmarked transfers, 2018

Number of LGs	Share of earmarked transfers (%)
40	without transfers
40	<49
42	50–89
23	>90

SOURCE: GORDANA MATKOVIĆ AND MILICA STRANJAKOVIĆ, MAPPING SOCIAL CARE SERVICES AND MATERIAL SUPPORT WITHIN THE MANDATE OF LOCAL GOVERNMENTS IN THE REPUBLIC OF SERBIA (BELGRADE: SOCIAL INCLUSION AND POVERTY REDUCTION UNIT, GOVERNMENT OF THE REPUBLIC OF SERBIA, 2020), 32.

Services within the mandate of local governments are provided by both public institutions and civil society organizations (CSOs). According to the Social Welfare Law, services are to be subject to the public procurement process if previously established, existing public social welfare institutions are unable to provide them. The significance of civil society organizations in the provision of care services has increased substantially in the past ten years. CSOs deliver services to 46% of elderly and PWD home care beneficiaries and to 60% of child beneficiaries of personal attendant services.[17] CSOs are also dominant providers of personal assistance, home care for CWD and daycare centers for adult persons with disabilities. For other types of services, state providers are dominant. The issue of sustainability is notable among the services provided by CSOs and when donations are the dominant source of funding.

Changes from previous years in which the mapping was carried out are small, especially in relative terms. According to the revised GDP figures,[18] the

---

17 Gordana Matković and Milica Stranjaković, Mapping Social Care Services and Material Support within the Mandate of Local Governments in the Republic of Serbia, 24.
18 Republički zavod za statistiku, "Bruto domaći proizvod 2015–2017 – revidirani podaci", Saopštenje 271 (Belgrade: RZS, 2018), https://publikacije.stat.gov.rs/G2018/Pdf/G20181271.pdf (accessed June 24, 2020).

share of expenditures for social care services was 0.06% in 2012 and 2015, which is 0.01 percentage point less than in 2018 (Table 3.4). Unlike, the slight increase in the period between the first two mapping cycles, in 2018 real expenditures increased by almost 30% compared to 2015. This increase is primarily due to earmarked transfers, which were not yet introduced in 2015, since the government was late in passing the decree.

TABLE 3.4   Expenditures for CBS, Serbia, 2012–2018

	Expenditures (RSD)	Expenditures (2018 RSD)	Increase	Increase (%)	% GDP
2012	2,435,730,000	2,743,889,948			0.06
2015	2,615,640,281	2,790,207,083	46,317,135	1.7	0.06
2018	3,647,501,623	3,647,501,623	857,294,539	30.7	0.07

SOURCE: GORDANA MATKOVIĆ AND MILICA STRANJAKOVIĆ, MAPPING SOCIAL CARE SERVICES AND MATERIAL SUPPORT WITHIN THE MANDATE OF LOCAL GOVERNMENTS IN THE REPUBLIC OF SERBIA (BELGRADE: SOCIAL INCLUSION AND POVERTY REDUCTION UNIT, GOVERNMENT OF THE REPUBLIC OF SERBIA, 2020), 34.

In the observed period, children's personal attendant services expanded the most. This service did not exist in 2013. Compared to 2015, the number of LGs in which this service was provided has more than doubled (from 30 to 76), and the number of beneficiaries has increased 2.5 times.[19] The service was introduced to support inclusive education for children with disabilities. The indicators did not change significantly for other services.

Nonetheless, the situation is more favorable compared to the early phase of reforms. The 2004 survey disclosed that the most widespread services, home care for older people and day care services for children with disabilities, were present in only one in five municipalities. At the same time, local governments allocated on average from local budgets only 2% for both social care services and cash welfare benefits.[20]

---

19 Gordana Matković and Milica Stranjaković, Mapping Social Care Services and Material Support within the Mandate of Local Governments in the Republic of Serbia, 19.
20 Gordana Matković, Decentralization of Social Welfare in Serbia, 44.

4 Earmarked Transfers for Local Social Care Services

With the purpose of boosting the growth of social care services that fall under the mandate of LGs, the Social Welfare Law introduced earmarked transfers for these services in 2011.[21] Earmarked transfers are designed based on the experiences of the Social Innovation Fund (SIF).[22] Established in 2003, SIF was designed as a mechanism for reform and for the development of local-level, non-institutional community-based services and to involve non-state actors in the provision of services.[23] It promoted the transfer of good practice as well as partnering between non-governmental actors and the governmental sector. The Fund also successfully sought support and input for reforms at the central level by shifting its focus each year to different types of projects. Good examples of projects that the Fund financed include home care services, day care centers for children with disabilities, shelters for victims of violence. During the six years in which the Fund was in operation, nearly 300 local projects in 100 LGs were supported with over €7 million in financing.[24]

The Social Welfare Law of 2011 introduced three types of earmarked transfers which can be used by LGs as funding for CBS within their mandate:
– the first type was meant for cities and municipalities with a below average level of development i.e., LGs belonging to groups II, III and IV;
– the second type was meant for local governments that had residential care facilities which were in the process of transformation;
– the third type of earmarked transfer was intended to foster the growth of services that are innovative and those of national importance.

In March 2016, the government adopted a decree on earmarked transfers that specifies the criteria and rules for the allocation of additional funds to local governments for social care services that are in their mandate.[25] The decree sets the total amount of expenditures for earmarked transfers at the level of 1.5% of the respective ministry's budgetary resources allocated for the program related to social assistance and care in the previous year (Partition 28, Program 0902, Function 70 in 2017).[26] As an exception, this ratio was set at 0.86% in

---

21   Social Welfare Law, 2011, Article 207.
22   Gordana Matković, Decentralization of Social Welfare in Serbia, 71.
23   Pavle Golicin and Galjina Ognjanov, Assessment of Results of the Social Innovation Fund (Belgrade: FREN and UNDP, 2010), 9.
24   Jelena Tadzić, Doprinos fonda za socijalne inovacije reformi i modernizaciji sistema socijalne zaštite na lokalnom nivou (Belgrade: University of Singidunum, FEFA, 2015), 58.
25   Decree on Earmarked Transfers in Social Protection, 2016.
26   Budget System Law, 2017, 145.

2016 (400 million RSD), according to the decree. The decree lays out the structure of the fund by type of earmarked transfers (Table 3.5). For the second and third types of earmarked transfers, no more than 20% of total funds may be spent. So at least 80%, or potentially even more resources are to be allocated to LGs in groups II, III and IV according to their level of development. Funds for the second type of earmarked transfers are to be allocated on the basis of the data on persons in residential institutions in transformation that have been relocated or on the basis of planned relocations. It is envisaged that for these purposes per capita allocated funds cannot exceed the level of the average per capita annual expenditures per residential institution beneficiary. The third type of earmarked funds is to be allocated to local governments on the basis of programs and projects approved by the respective ministry. The decree defines that services of national importance are those that relate to family support services and services aimed at the prevention of the separation of children from their families, as well as support for older people in rural and sparsely populated areas.

TABLE 3.5 Eligible LGs, type of services, structure of funds and criteria, according to type of transfers

Type of transfer	I	II	III
Eligible LGs	Less developed LGs (groups II, III and IV)	LGs with institutions in transformation	All LGs
Type of services	All local social care services	All local social care services	Innovative and services of national importance
Structure of total funds	At least 80%	Not more than 20%	
Criteria	Set of six criteria	Data on persons reallocated	Approved programs and projects

SOURCE: OWN ELABORATION BASED ON THE DECREE ON EARMARKED TRANSFERS IN SOCIAL PROTECTION, 2016.

Allocation of the funds for the first type of earmarked transfers is based on the six initial criteria, presented in the Decree. These criteria are weighted differently, and thus on the basis of the second and third criteria, 50% of total funds for the first type of earmarked transfers are allocated. On the basis of the first and fourth criteria, 30% of funds are allocated, and based on the last two criteria, 20%. The criteria and weights are presented in Table 3.6. It seems that the idea behind the above criteria is to approximate the social situation in the municipalities and cities and respect the differences in the size of the potentially vulnerable population.

TABLE 3.6 Criteria and weights for the allocation of earmarked transfers

Initial criteria	Weight (in %)
Total population of LG	15
Number of children and young people up to 19 years of age and the number of people older than 65 years of age	25
Number of national cash and in-kind benefit program recipients that reside in a given LG	25
Number of cash and in-kind benefit program recipients in a given LG	15
Number of persons in residential institutions residing in a given LG	10
Territory of the municipality or city	10

SOURCE: OWN ELABORATION BASED ON THE DECREE ON EARMARKED TRANSFERS IN SOCIAL PROTECTION, 2016.

Funds distributed to local governments are further adjusted depending on their fiscal capacity. The measure of fiscal capacity is the amount of shared revenue per capita.[27] According to the Decree on earmarked transfers, the funds are increased by 20% for LGs from groups II, II and IV whose shared revenues (per capita) are less than half the average. For LGs with a financial capacity between 50% and 80% of the average, funds are increased by 10%. LGs whose fiscal capacity is above average will receive 20% less than anticipated by the formula. The decree imposes that LGs from groups II and III according to their level of development must allocate from their own budgets 30% and 10% of the funds, respectively. LGs belonging to group IV do not have to contribute

---

27 Shared revenues are centrally administered, imposed at centrally determined rates and shared with the LG in which they are collected. Shared revenues come from shared taxes (including payroll taxes) and fees.

anything from their own budget. An important condition is that services must meet the minimum standards prescribed by the Social Welfare Law.

5 Lessons Learned

There are a number of dilemmas and shortcomings regarding the decree. The most important shortcoming is that the decree has not sought to prevent the substitution effect. It is possible for local governments to seize funds from the national level to finance previously established, existing services and to redirect resources from the local budget for other purposes. This could be prevented by adding the requirement that LGs must increase the overall level of social care expenditures by the amount of earmarked transfers.

Additionally, one of the criteria for the allocation of earmarked transfers is the number of recipients of the LG's cash and in-kind benefits program (fourth criterion). Based on this criterion, 10% of the funds that are available for the first type of earmarked funds are distributed. This criterion is inadequate since LGs are in charge of allocating only one-off assistance and supplementary cash assistance to the poor. To date, the data on these benefits have not been collected regularly. The Ministry requested that LGs fill out a questionnaire and submit the required data. According to the mapping project, LGs have very different criteria for awarding these benefits. Some LGs award very small amounts of cash assistance to a large number of recipients, and some have adopted the opposite model. Consequently, the comparison of LGs and/or ranking according to this criterion is pointless. In addition, the number of the recipients of an LG's cash benefit program are not a proxy for the social situation in the municipality/city.

The considerations are quite similar with respect to social care services. The number of beneficiaries who receive social care services that are the responsibility of local governments, is of no real value when viewed in isolation and outside the context of the service model. Some local governments opt for a model involving a large number of beneficiaries and a low intensity of services (once a week or part time). Other municipalities and cities prefer yet another model, providing high intensity services, targeting only a relatively small number of beneficiaries. Simply adding up the total number of beneficiaries of diverse services such as, for example, day care community-based services and counseling, is also inadequate.

In addition, the results of the mapping project indicate that some LGs regard social care services as high priority programs and some simply have not established any services at all. The social situation is not reflected simply by the number of beneficiaries of social care services within the mandate of LGs in the municipalities and cities, nor is the need for services. As mentioned, sometimes it is an issue of policy choice (in LGs that do not perceive services as a priority), but sometimes the low number of beneficiaries is the result of a very modest local budget. In the latter case, the stated criterion 'punishes' precisely those local governments that need the transfers the most. Finally, the criterion obviously imposes an obligation to collect data systematically on local level social care services. Although it may be unintended, this will be a positive consequence of the implementation of this criterion.

Apart from the fourth criterion, the remaining criteria are all essentially related to the size of the municipality/city. As a result, larger cities and municipalities are awarded with funds, which in some cases substantially exceed their expenditures for social care services in previous years. It is obvious that both time and substantial professional capacities are required to establish social care services, not to mention that potential service providers must be available. The question that arises then in this context is whether or not the cities are able to use the transfers they are allocated effectively. In small municipalities, this problem may be more pronounced.

Finally, some small, underdeveloped municipalities, which gave high priority to services, received in relative terms less funding than more developed municipalities for which social care services were hardly a high priority. This demonstrates that expenditures by local governments on social care services need to be considered, at the very least as a criterion serving as a corrective, in order to ensure that resources will be used efficiently. In 2018, one in five LGs received more than twice the amount they spent on services in previous years through earmarked transfers. It is positive that the decree imposes co-financing by local governments, and that the services must meet the minimum standards prescribed by the Social Welfare Law. However, the latest mapping of services showed that a number of LGs did not meet this requirement. What also remains unclear is if innovative services must meet this requirement as well. If this is the case, it is not appropriate, since innovative services are not yet part of the system, and the minimum standards for these services are yet to be designed. Monitoring and evaluation of the implementation of the decree, publication of data on the distribution of transfers, and organization of the exchange of LG experiences are also essential if earmarked transfers are to avoid being regarded as a failure and then rejected because of their inadequate design. However, the general issue is whether the transfers should be distributed to LGs in group II (80% to 100% the Republic average) or whether the funds should be allocated only to the least developed and small municipalities. Additionally, the funds should be approved for a period of several years. These are conceptual issues and require additional research and deliberation. On the topic of earmarked transfers, the report of the European Commission also highlights the lack of transparency and the lack of a multi-year commitment.[28]

6 Conclusion

Decentralization in the form of expansion of social care services that are under the mandate of local governments in Serbia has not progressed substantially. In general, these services remain not available at an adequate level especially in some parts of the country and are often not sustainable. Over the years, reforms have been implemented that were a prerequisite for decentralization including the setting up of structural and operational standards for social care services, as well as control mechanisms and the establishment of a licensing process. Earmarked transfers have been allocated by the national government since 2016 intended to provide supplemental funds for care services that are part of the local mandate.

In 2018, 137 of 145 local governments provided a range of social care services within their mandate. Total expenditures on these services were RSD 3.6 billion (0.07% GDP) in 2018, according to the data collected. Dominant among the services offered within the LG mandate are home care for the elderly, day care centers for children with disabilities (CWD) and children's personal attendants. The expansion of the latter services in just a few years is proof that it is indeed feasible to develop services in the community quickly and successfully if there is a clearly articulated demand and pressure to introduce them. Services for independent living, targeted at persons with disabilities, are the least developed.

The research demonstrates that earmarked transfers from the central level are critical to continue the development of services that are the responsibility of local authorities, but there is a need to redefine certain legal provisions governing this matter. Therefore, the main constraints on further decentralization in Serbia include the absence of regional level administration, huge differences in the size, professional capacities, and level of development of LGs, a lack of political interest in allocating funds for social welfare both on the local and national levels and insufficiently developed control and monitoring and evaluation mechanisms that could adequately support a highly decentralized

---

28 European Union, Commission Staff Working Document: Serbia 2019 Report. Brussels: European Commission, 2019. https://ec.europa.eu/neighbourhood-enlargement/sites/near/files/20190529-serbia-report.pdf (accessed May 10, 2020).

system. Additionally, social welfare beneficiaries and vulnerable groups are insufficiently informed and lack political power.

Among the policy recommendations this study leads to is first, that additional effort is needed to increase the availability of community-based services that are crucial not only for the continuation of the decentralization process but also for deinstitutionalization. In this context, greater significance should be attributed to services for independent living of persons with disabilities, especially personal assistance. Second, the Decree on Earmarked Transfers in Social Protection should be revised. It is necessary to include the expenditures of local governments on social care services among the criteria for the allocation of earmarked transfers and to abolish the criteria such as the number of social care services beneficiaries and the number of recipients of the LG's cash and in kind benefits program. It is also necessary to monitor and evaluate the implementation of the Decree. Finally, a prerequisite to understanding the problems, obstacles to development, and shortcomings of the existing situation is the monitoring and evaluation of local social care services. In the absence of information systems at the local level, mapping of services should continue on a regular basis.

Hence, topics for further research include a better understanding of the differences between individual local governments, an assessment of the optimal level of distribution and availability of social care services within the LGs mandate, and options for further decentralization.

Bibliography

Budget System Law, 2017.

Center for Liberal Democratic Studies. Mapping Social Care Services within the Mandate of Local Governments in the Republic of Serbia. Belgrade: Social Inclusion and Poverty Reduction Unit, Office of the Minister without Portfolio in charge of European Integration Government of the Republic of Serbia, 2013.

Decree on Earmarked Transfers in Social Protection, 2016.

European Union. Commission Staff Working Document: Serbia 2019 Report. Brussels: European Commission, 2019. Accessed May 10, 2020. https://ec.europa.eu/neighbourhood-enlargement/sites/near/files/20190529-serbia-report.pdf.

Golicin, Pavle, and Galjina Ognjanov. Assessment of Results of the Social Innovation Fund. Belgrade: FREN and UNDP, 2010.

Government of Serbia: Second National Report for Social Inclusion and Poverty Reduction in the Republic of Serbia: The Status of Social Exclusion and Poverty Trends in the Period 2011 –2014 and Future Priorities. Belgrade, 2014.

Government of Serbia. Third National Report for Social Inclusion and Poverty Reduction in the Republic of Serbia: The Status of Social Exclusion and Poverty Trends in the Period 2014–2017 and Future Priorities. Belgrade, 2018.

Matković, Gordana. Decentralization of Social Welfare in Serbia. Belgrade: CLDS, 2006.

Matković, Gordana, and Katarina Stanić. Socijalna zaštita u starosti: dugotrajna nega i socijalne penzije. Belgrade: Centar za socijalnu politiku/FEFA/SIPRU, 2014.

Matković, Gordana, and Milica Stranjaković. Mapping Social Care Services and Material Support within the Mandate of Local Governments in the Republic of Serbia. Belgrade: Social Inclusion and Poverty Reduction Unit, Government of the Republic of Serbia, 2020.

Matković, Gordana, and Milica Stranjaković. Mapping Social Care Services within the Mandate of Local Governments in the Republic of Serbia. Belgrade: Social Inclusion and Poverty Reduction Unit, Government of the Republic of Serbia, 2016.

National Agency for Regional Development. Developments of the Regions and Local Self-Government Units. Accessed June 4, 2020. http://www.regionalnirazvoj.gov.rs/Lat/ShowNARRFolder.aspx?mi=4.

Poverty Reduction Strategy, 2003. Accessed May 16, 2020. http://socijalnoukljucivanje.gov.rs/wp-content/uploads/2014/06/1.-Strategija-za-smanjenje-siromastva-u-Srbiji-Rezime-i-matrice.pdf.

Public Policy Secretariat of the Republic of Serbia. Analytical Tool for LGs, Methodological Notes. Accessed May 18, 2020. https://jls1.rsjp.gov.rs/vox/Napomene.

Republički zavod za statistiku. "Bruto domaći proizvod 2015–2017 – revidirani podaci", Saopštenje 271. Belgrade: RZS, 2018. Accessed June 24, 2020. https://publikacije.stat.gov.rs/G2018/Pdf/G20181271.pdf.

Social Welfare Development Strategy, 2005. Accessed May 16, 2020. https://npm.rs/attachments/strateg.razvoja.soc.zastite.pdf.

Social Welfare Law, 2011.

Tadzić, Jelena. "Doprinos fonda za socijalne inovacije reformi i modernizaciji sistema socijalne zaštite na lokalnom nivou". Master's thesis. Belgrade: University of Singidunum, FEFA, 2015.

World Bank: Serbia – Municipal Finance and Expenditure Review. Washington DC: World Bank, 2013. Accessed June 4, 2020. https://documents.worldbank.org/en/publication/documents-reports/documentdetail/400441468103148742/serbia-municipal-finance-and-expenditure-review.

CHAPTER 4

Unemployment in Serbia: Characteristics and Challenges

Maja Jandrić and Marzena Żakowska

1 Introduction

Over the last two decades, the labor market in Serbia was subject to various macroeconomic shocks, such as economic crisis, the transition process, and significant changes in key labor market institutions. Alongside the effects of the restructuring, which was a part of the transition process, one of the main factors affecting the unemployment rate in Serbia was the global financial crisis of 2008/2009. The slowdown in economic growth related to a fall in demand in the EU directly affecting exports from Serbia. The crisis also had a negative influence on the banking sector. Specifically, foreign banks withdrew capital from their accounts in Serbia and put it into the accounts of parent banks in other countries where higher profits could be expected. The economy of Serbia is sensitive to any change in the EU economy. Among other reasons, this is connected to the fact that around 80% of Serbian exports go to the EU and regional non-EU countries, with the latter strongly reliant on the former. Because of insufficient national and private sector funds, investing in Serbia requires foreign financing – the most significant part of which comes from the EU. Moreover, adjusting to the legislative requirements of the EU free market has been a serious challenge, and at the same time, a great opportunity for the Serbian economy, especially since the European Union granted Serbia its candidate member status in March 2012.[1]

The main aim of this study is to examine the changes in unemployment in Serbia in the period 2001–2019, pointing out the position of some of the vulnerable groups. The major factors influencing the labor market will be discussed. The relationship between economic growth and (un)employment, as well as the role of labor market institutions will also be evaluated. The research is based on the data from the Statistical Office of the Republic of Serbia (SORS),

---

1 Nador Zemniczky, Gábor Csüllög and Zsuzsanna Császár, "Serbia's Economy in the Context of EU Integration", Dvacáté Století, no. 2 (2015): 39–41.

Eurostat, the National Employment Service (NES) and the OECD database. In the analysis of potential effects of the reforms of labor market institutions, both neoclassical and Keynesian theoretical models were taken into account. The results of the research will give deeper insight into the following issues: What are the factors determining unemployment in Serbia? What kind of approach should be applied in developing employment protection legislation and the unemployment benefit system to improve labor market performance in Serbia?

2 (Un)employment in Serbia

In the last few decades Serbia has faced many institutional and economic shocks, which have strongly affected labor market performance. Firstly, the transition process which began later than in most other former socialist countries, and the worldwide economic crisis, caused many difficulties in the labor market. However, in recent years a significant improvement of key labor market indicators is observable. There is still room for further advancement, bearing in mind the large share of long-term unemployment, potential skills mismatch, as well as the relatively lower quality of employment in comparison to most EU countries. All these phenomena will be analyzed in more detail within this chapter.

Scientific research of the unemployment phenomenon in Serbia is faced with a lot of challenges. Besides difficulties in distinguishing between the effects of factors related to transition processes and the restructuring of companies that began after 2000 and the effects of the economic crisis, an additional problem for researchers are the relatively frequent methodological changes to the Labor Force Survey (LFS) that prevent the formation of a time series with comparable data throughout the observed period. However, these changes were necessary and aimed at providing higher quality data in line with Eurostat recommendations. LFS, as the most reliable source of labor market information in Serbia, was introduced in 1994 but became internationally comparable in 2004. New methodological changes were also introduced in 2008 to better align the concept of employment with the recommendations of the International Labor Organization (ILO), which led to a significant increase in borderline forms of employment, primarily of contributing family workers and persons starting their own businesses. Better coverage of these groups contributed to methodologically induced improvement of basic labor market indicators in Serbia. Moreover, new methodological changes in the LFS were introduced in 2014. The data are fully comparable for the period from 2008 to 2013, when the survey was conducted on a semi-annual basis. In 2014, the survey was conducted quarterly, which disrupted its comparability with previous years. Since 2015, the survey has been conducted continuously. Considering that starting from 2016 the estimation system has been changed, in accordance with the regulations of Eurostat, a revision was performed to overcome the effect of this change and to ensure the comparability of data from the following years with data from 2014 and 2015.[2] The data in Table 4.1 illustrates this situation in the period from 2004 to 2013, bearing in mind that there was a significant break in the methodology in 2008.

TABLE 4.1 Employment, unemployment, and activity rate in the period 2004–2013

Year	Employment rate % (15–64)	Unemployment rate % (15–64)	Activity rate % (15–64)
2004	53.4	19.5	66.6
2005	51	21.8	65.2
2006	49.8	21.6	63.6
2007	51.5	18.8	63.4
2008 April	54.0	14.0	62.8
2008 October	53.3	14.7	62.6
2009 April	50.8	16.4	60.8
2009 October	50.0	17.4	60.5
2010 April	47.2	20.1	59.1
2010 October	47.1	20.0	58.8
2011 April	45.5	22.9	58.9
2011 November	45.3	24.4	59.9
2012 April	44.2	26.1	59.7
2012 October	46.4	23.1	60.4
2013 April	45.8	25.0	61.0
2013 October	49.2	21.0	62.2

SOURCES: OWN ELABORATION BASED ON DATA FROM SORS, RATES OF ACTIVITY, EMPLOYMENT, INACTIVITY AND UNEMPLOYMENT, HTTPS://DATA.STAT.GOV.RS/HOME/ RESULT/24000100?LANGUAGECODE=EN-US&DISPLAYMODE=TABLE&GUID=DE2DF46F -BE1C-4AE7-97CA-36D7C82E1182 (ACCESSED APRIL 20, 2020); "ZAPOSLENOST I ZARADE" IN QUARTERLY MONITOR OF ECONOMIC TRENDS AND POLICIES IN SERBIA, FREN, NO. 15 (2008): 17, HTTPS://FREN.ORG.RS/WP-CONTENT/UPLOADS/2020/06/QM15.PDF (ACCESSED APRIL 20, 2020).

---

2   For more methodological details see Labour Force Survey – Abriged Methodology, Statistical Office of the Republic of Serbia (2017), https://publikacije.stat.gov.rs/G2017/PdfE/G201720 107.pdf (accessed April 20, 2020).

Only in the short period before the economic crisis did basic labor market indicators show signs of recovery - the employment rate increased slightly in this period, while the unemployment rate decreased (Table 4.1). After the onset of the economic crisis, these two indicators continued to follow the previous deteriorating trend. However, data on employment and unemployment, which were modified to neutralize the impact of the previously described changes in the LFS methodology in 2008[3] reveal that the declining trend in the number of employed persons was constant (Figure 4.1).[4] In contrast, both adjusted and unadjusted data on unemployment indicate that there was a trend breakpoint in 2008, indicating a negative impact of the economic crisis.[5] Data in Figure 4.1

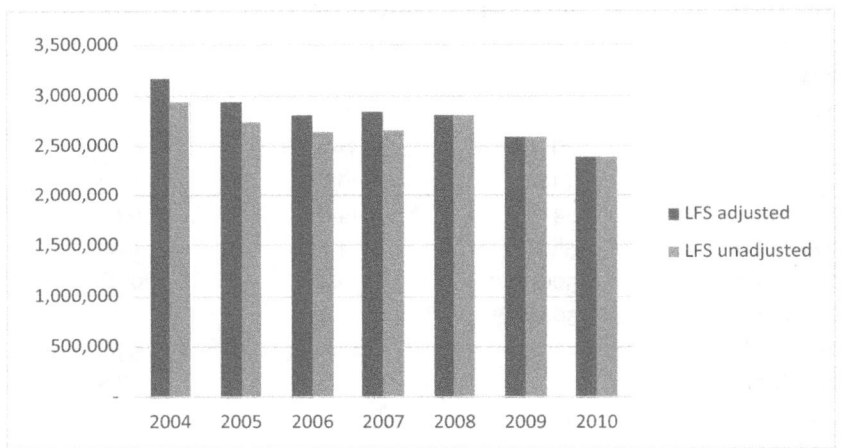

FIGURE 4.1 Employment in Serbia (15+), 2004–2010
SOURCE: MIHAIL ARANDARENKO, TRŽIŠTE RADA U SRBIJI: TRENDOVI, INSTITUCIJE, POLITIKE (BELGRADE: CENTAR ZA IZDAVAČKU DELATNOST EKONOMSKOG FAKULTETA U BEOGRADU, 2011). MIHAIL ARANDARENKO, SUPPORTING STRATEGIES TO RECOVER FROM THE CRISIS IN SOUTH EASTERN EUROPE. COUNTRY ASSESSMENT REPORT: SERBIA, INTERNATIONAL LABOUR ORGANIZATION, 2011, 22.

---

3 Ibid.
4 Farhad Mehran, Preparing Consistent Time Series on Employment and Unemployment Following Change of Definitions in Serbia's LFS, Final Report to the ILO, July 2011, 20; Mihail Arandarenko, Supporting Strategies to Recover from the Crisis in South Eastern Europe. Country Assessment Report – Serbia, International Labour Organization, 2011, https://www.ilo.org/budapest/what-we-do/publications/WCMS_167008/lang--en/index.htm.
5 Mihail Arandarenko, "The Labour Market Crisis and the Road to Job Recovery in Serbia", SEER: Journal for Labour and Social Affairs in Eastern Europe 15, no. 2 (2012): 230, https://doi.org/10.5771/1435-2869-2012-2-225.

clearly show a possible influence of methodological changes on conclusions made about employment trends. While the unadjusted series with original data shows that there was a rise in the number of the employed persons shortly before 2008, the time series that was adjusted in order to eliminate the influence of methodological changes shows that the decreasing trend in the number of employed persons was in fact constant.

In the period 2014–2019, we can observe improvement of three key labor market indicators – activity rate and employment rate have risen, while unemployment rate has significantly decreased (Figure 4.2). These trends are the consequence of the parallel influence of factors on the demand and supply side of the labor market. A primary source of rising demand for labor is economic growth, which was mostly positive in the observed period (the only exception being 2014). However, the connection between economic growth and the growth of total employment is far from straightforward. The fact that labor market improvement in this period was stronger than expected with the GDP growth rates in the same period, could be at least partly explained by factors connected to labor supply. Due to real erosion of some of the important sources of non-working incomes (e.g., decrease in the average amount of unemployment benefits after 2009), the reservation wage decreased, and this had a major influence on the labor supply. This can be corroborated by the fact that after 2012, LFS data show an increase of the share of the unemployed and

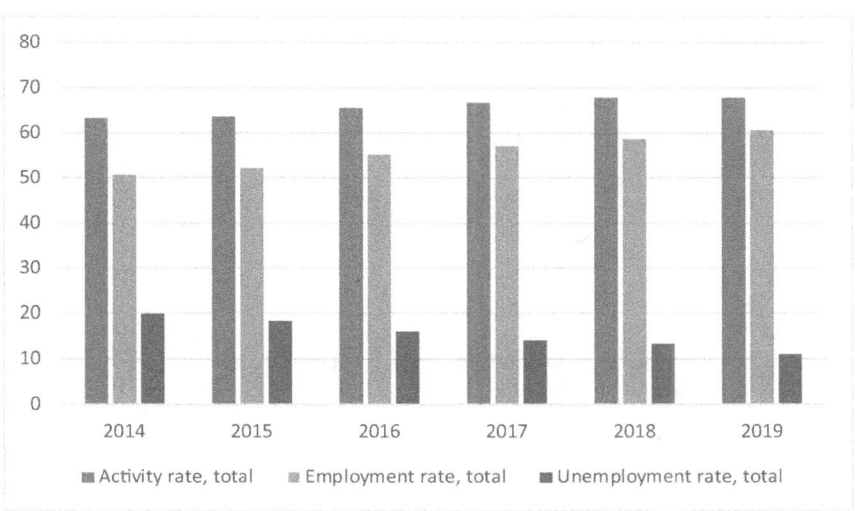

FIGURE 4.2   Employment rate, unemployment rate and activity in Serbia in 2014–2019
SOURCE: SORS, RATES OF ACTIVITY, EMPLOYMENT, INACTIVITY AND UNEMPLOYMENT BY AREA, HTTPS://DATA.STAT.GOV.RS/HOME/RESULT/2400 020102?LANGUAGECODE=EN-US&DISPLAYMODE=TABLE&GUID=E72F6780 -EEC7-4740-AEFF-F46132AE02C8 (ACCESSED JUNE 6, 2020).

discouraged inactive people who are willing to work for a salary of less than 20,000 dinars.[6]

The reduction in the unemployment rate was observed both in the working-age population (15–64) and among youth (15–24) (Figure 4.3). The structure of employment in the observed period changed slightly. In the period 2014–2019, there was an increase in the number of employees with a permanent job. However, the share of employees with a permanent contract decreased in the same period from 81.2% in 2014 to 77.2% in 2019. The share of temporary employees (as a percentage of the total number of employees) in Serbia in 2019 was still among the highest in Europe. Nevertheless, in the group aged 15–64, the share of part-time workers in total employment decreased slightly (from 10.6% in 2014 to 9.7% in 2019). The growth of LFS employment was most prominent in sectors B-D (Total industry) and F (Construction). There was a decrease in employment in agriculture, forestry, and fishing, which led to a decrease in the share of agricultural employment in total employment. In the same period, the share of services in total LFS employment rose slightly (from 55.5% in 2014 to 57% in 2019).

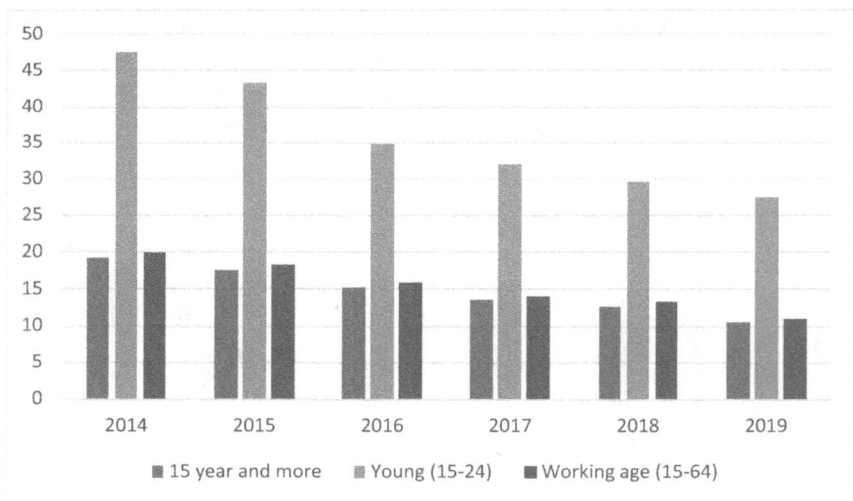

FIGURE 4.3   Unemployment rate in age groups 15+, 15–24 and 15–64
SOURCE: SORS, RATES OF ACTIVITY, EMPLOYMENT, INACTIVITY AND UNEMPLOYMENT BY AREA, HTTPS://DATA.STAT.GOV.RS/HOME/RESULT/2400 020102?LANGUAGECODE=EN-US&DISPLAYMODE=TABLE&GUID=E72F6780 -EEC7-4740-AEFF-F46132AE02C8 (ACCESSED JUNE 6, 2020).

---

6   Mihail Arandarenko, Miladin Kovačević, and Dragan Aleksić, "Zaposlenost u Srbiji između tražnje za radom i ponude rada", in Ekonomska politika Srbije u 2016. godini, ed. Dejan Šoškić and Milojko Arsić (Beograd: Centar za izdavačku delatnost, 2016), 151–176.

Young people in Serbia were strongly affected by the global economic crisis in 2008.[7] In the following years, key labor market indicators showed positive developments. However, despite the positive trends, Serbia is still in the relatively small group of European countries (e.g., Greece, Italy, Spain, Montenegro, and North Macedonia) where the youth unemployment rate is higher than 25% (Figure 4.4). Recent research found that the indicators affecting whether a young person in Serbia will be employed or not are the financial background of the participant's household, earnings, age, gender, and years of work experience.[8] Although youth unemployment decreased, the unemployment rate for the age group 15–24 is significantly higher than the unemployment rate for the working-age population. In both age groups, unemployment rates are higher for women (Figure 4.5).

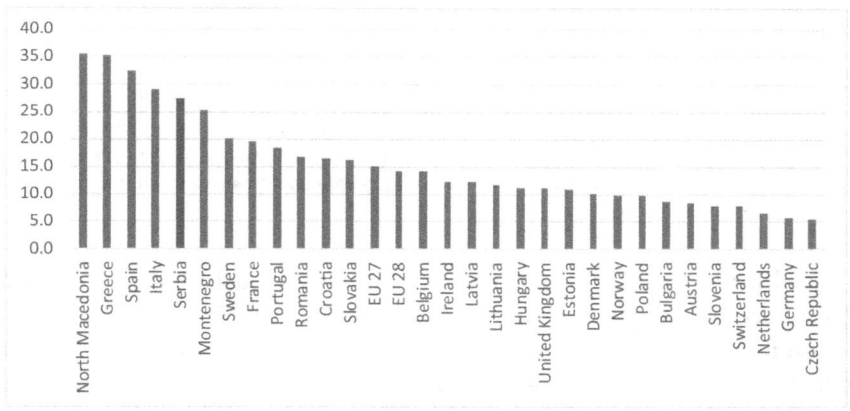

FIGURE 4.4 Youth unemployment rate (15–24) in European countries in 2019
SOURCE: EUROSTAT, UNEMPLOYMENT RATE BY AGE, SEX AND CITIZENSHIP (2019, IN%), HTTPS://EC.EUROPA.EU/EUROSTAT/DATABROWSER/VIEW/LFSA_URGAN__CUSTOM_2039879/BOOKMARK/TABLE?LANG=EN&BOOKMARK ID=41886C55-12C6-4949-B039-D884C68BDF48 (ACCESSED JUNE 20, 2020).

---

7 Government of the Republic of Serbia, Third National Report on Social Inclusion and Poverty Reduction in the Republic of Serbia, The Status of Social Exclusion and Poverty Trends in the Period 2014–2017 and Future Priorities, Belgrade, December 2018, https://media.srbija.gov.rs/medeng/documents/third-national-report-on-social-inclusion-and-poverty-reduction2014-17_eng.pdf (accessed May 20, 2020).
8 Dejana Pavlović, Dragan Bjelica and Ivana Domazet, "What Characteristics in the Youth Labour Market of Serbia are Likely to Result in Employment?", Stanovništvo 57, no. 2 (2019): 35–47, https://doi.org/10.2298/STNV190823006P.

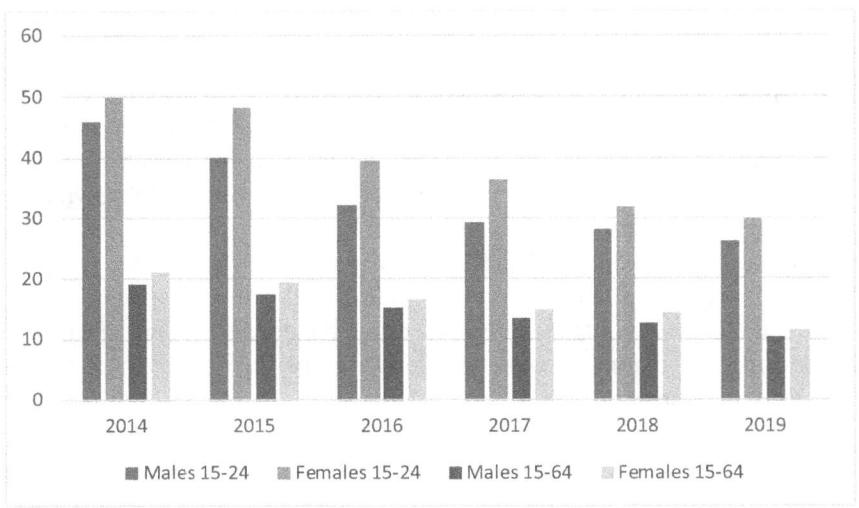

FIGURE 4.5 Unemployment rates from age and gender perspective
SOURCE: OWN ELABORATION BASED ONE SORS, RATES OF ACTIVITY, EMPLOYMENT, INACTIVITY AND UNEMPLOYMENT BY AREA, HTTPS://DATA.STAT.GOV.RS/HOME/RESULT/2400020102?LANGUAGECODE=EN-US&DISPLAYMODE=TABLE&GUID=E72F6780-EEC7-4740-AEFF-F46132AE02C8 (ACCESSED JUNE 20, 2020).

Jandrić and Molnar's research has shown that although all three observed indicators (activity rate, employment rate and unemployment rate) were worse for women than for men, these differences decrease with the level of education; the relative position of women regarding activity and employment rates was worst in the group with lower levels of education, which indicates that education is a key factor that can improve the position of women on the labor market in Serbia.[9] On the other hand, the unfavorable position of youth (15–24), which is determined not only by the unemployment rate but also by the quality of employment, has numerous personal, economic and wider social consequences related to a variety of areas, such as sustainable growth, migration, family issues, and many others. Pavlović et al. emphasize that structural changes in the labor market have forced young people to accept jobs requiring lower qualifications or part-time jobs within the grey economy.[10] Other studies

---

9   Maja Jandrić and Dejan Molnar, Kvalitet zaposlenosti i tržište rada u Srbiji (Quality of employment and labour market in Serbia), (Beograd: Friedrich Ebert Stiftung, 2017), https://library.fes.de/pdf-files/bueros/belgrad/13589.pdf (accessed May 24, 2020).

10 Dejana Pavlović, Dragan Bjelica and Ivana Domazet, "What Characteristics in the Youth Labour Market of Serbia are Likely to Result in Employment?": 35–47.

also point to problems connected to the socio-economic position of youth in Serbia. According to the study – Youth in Serbia 2018/2019[11] – three quarters of young people in Serbia express a desire or intention to emigrate. The main factors that force young people to leave the country are an unfavorable situation and pessimism about the prospect of any improvement in social conditions. In spite of the significant recovery in recent years, the overall unemployment rate is still above the levels that are observed in most EU countries (Figure 4.6).

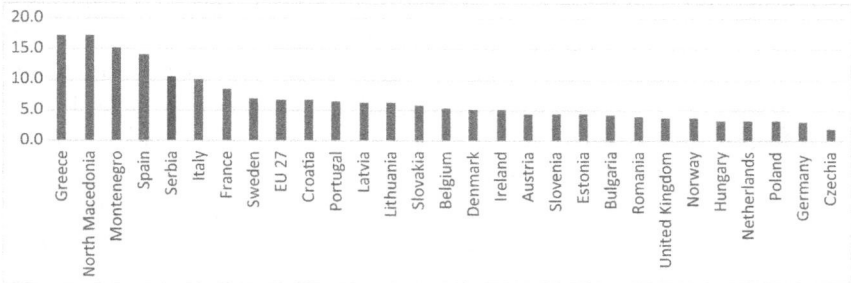

FIGURE 4.6   Unemployment rates (15–74, total in %) in European countries in 2019
SOURCE: EUROSTAT, UNEMPLOYMENT RATES BY SEX, AGE AND CITIZENSHIP HTTPS://EC.EUROPA.EU/EUROSTAT/DATABROWSER/VIEW/LFSA_URGAN __CUSTOM_2039879/BOOKMARK/TABLE?LANG=EN&BOOKMARKID=418 86C55-12C6-4949-B039-D884C68BDF48 (ACCESSED JUNE 20, 2020).

Other key labor market indicators, such as the employment and activity rates also show that there is still room for improvement to catch up with EU 27 levels (Figure 4.7). Future trends and possibilities for reaching the level of labor market performance of the more developed EU economies, besides other factors, largely depend on the effects of the current COVID-19 crisis on different economies. Arandarenko and Aleksić have stressed that "the situation in the labor market will not depend exclusively on the degree of recovery of the Serbian economy, but also on the slowing pace of the epidemic, and economic growth in the countries with which we have the strongest economic ties".[12] Currently,

---

11 Dragan Popadić, Zoran Pavlović and Srećko Mihailović, Mladi u Srbiji 2018/2019 (Youth in Serbia 2018/2019), (Belgrade: Friedrich Ebert Stiftung, 2019), 3, http://socijalnoukljuciva nje.gov.rs/wp-content/uploads/2019/05/mladi_u_srbiji_2018-2019_fes.pdf (accessed June 24, 2020).
12 Mihail Arandarenko and Dragan Aleksić, Influence of the Pandemic-caused Crisis on the Serbian Labour Market, http://mons.rs/influence-of-the-pandemic-caused-crisis-on-the -serbian-labour-market (accessed May 12, 2020).

it is not easy to forecast estimates of the macroeconomic consequences of this crisis, given that the pandemic is still ongoing. Furthermore, the effects of the pandemic on the labor market will manifest themselves gradually, most probably at first in the informal part of the labor market and then in parts of the formal labor market that are characterized by more flexibility (i.e., different forms of temporary employment).

According to research done by Sergio Torrejón et al. based on EU countries, the impact of confinement measures is likely to concentrate on the most vulnerable segments of the working population: workers with lower wages and worse employment conditions,[13] while the ILO also points to the negative impact of the crisis on informal workers.[14] Generally, changes in employment and unemployment follow changes in economic growth with a certain delay. Aside from the negative influence of the COVID-19 crisis on GDP, the labor market in Serbia will also be affected by the inflow of workers who returned to Serbia at the beginning of the pandemic. The negative effects will be at least partly mitigated by the economic policy measures that were undertaken with an aim to reduce the expected negative effects of the pandemic on the economy.

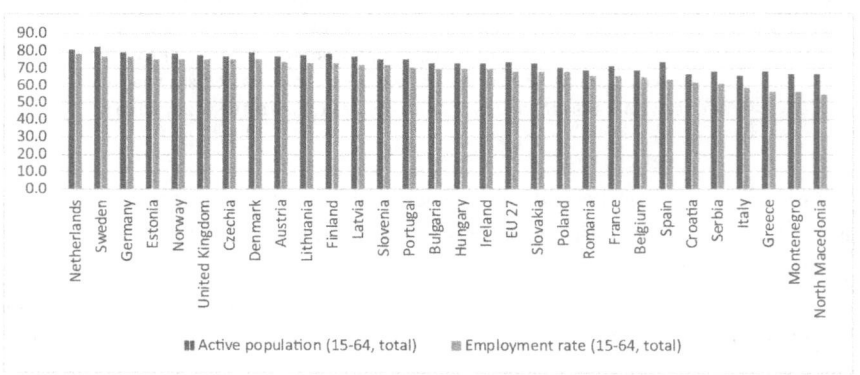

FIGURE 4.7 Employment and activity rates in European countries in 2019
SOURCE: EUROSTAT, EMPLOYMENT AND ACTIVITY RATES BY SEX, AGE AND CITIZENSHIP (%), HTTPS://EC.EUROPA.EU/EUROSTAT/DATABROWSER/BOOKMARK/DD897CE1-11CC-4CB3-803E-C8F643825D8E?LANG=EN (ACCESSED JUNE 6, 2020).

---

13 Sergio Torrejón, Ignacio González-Vázquez, Marta Fana and Enrique Fernández-Macías, The Impact of COVID Confinement Measures on EU Labour Market, European Commission, Science for Policy Briefs, 2020, https://ec.europa.eu/jrc/sites/jrcsh/files/jrc120585_policy.brief_impact.of_.covid-19.on_.eu-labour.market.pdf (accessed May 31, 2020).

14 International Labour Organization, ILO Monitor: COVID-19 and the World of Work, Third edition – Updated Estimates and Analysis, 29 April 2020. https://www.ilo.org/wcmsp5/groups/public/@dgreports/@dcomm/documents/briefingnote/wcms_743146.pdf (accessed May 17, 2020).

3 The Labor Market in Serbia

The labor market in Serbia is characterized by numerous factors, and the main ones are listed below:
- labor market duality[15] in various dimensions (e.g., public/private sector, formal/informal employment, standard/vulnerable employment);
- a comparatively low quality of employment – the lack of workforce adaptability, transitions to lower levels of security, the temporary nature of employment and the incidence of informal employment;[16]
- an unfavourable educational structure of unemployed persons – according to the records of the National Employment Service (NES), in 2018 one third of the unemployed had no qualifications or were low-skilled (33%);[17]
- an unfavourable age structure of unemployed persons – the share of the unemployed who are over 50 years old was 32% in 2018, while in young people under 30 it was 21.6%.[18]

Moreover, the share of long-term unemployment is high (Figure 4.8). Long periods of job search can lead to discouragement and loss of skills. At the same time, employers often perceive the long-term unemployed as workers with lower levels of productivity and therefore are reluctant to employ these workers. All these factors reduce the chances of employment, and without strong policy actions, have negative effects at the individual level. High shares of long-term unemployed can lead to further problems in general labor market performance.

Additionally, Serbia is generally characterized by pronounced regional disparities in economic growth and development. These disparities are themselves reflected in differences in labor market performance (Table 4.2). The Belgrade region has better labor market indicators in comparison to other

---

15 Mihail Arandarenko and Dragan Aleksić, "Not all Jobs are Created Equal: How not to Misread the Labour Force Statistics in Serbia", Ekonomika preduzeća 64, no. 3–4 (2016): 211–224; Mihail Arandarenko, Miladin Kovačević and Dragan Aleksić, Kretanje zaposlenosti u Srbiji: između tražnje za radom i ponude rada. Ekonomska politika Srbije u 2016. godini (Employment Trends in Serbia: between Labor Demand and Labor Supply. Economic Policy of Serbia in 2016), 2016, 151–175.
16 Maja Jandrić and Dejan Molnar, "Adaptability and Security: Key Aspects of the Quality of Employment in the Changing Labor Markets", Ekonomika preduzeća 66, no. 3–4, (2018): 213–225, https://doi.org/10.5937/ekopre1804213j.
17 Ministry of Labour, Employment, Veteran and Social Affairs, National Employment Action Plan 2020, http://socijalnoukljucivanje.gov.rs/wp-content/uploads/2020/02/Nacionalni_akcioni_plan_zaposljavanja_2020_eng.pdf (accessed June 14, 2020).
18 Ibid.

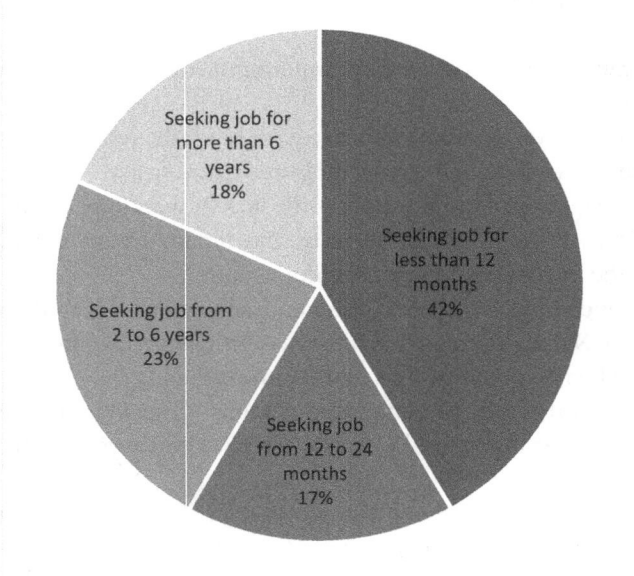

FIGURE 4.8 Length of job seeking time in 2019
SOURCE: SORS, UNEMPLOYED PERSONS BY LENGTH OF JOB SEEKING AD REGION, HTTPS://DATA.STAT.GOV.RS/HOME/RESULT/240002090301?LANGUAGECODE=EN-US (ACCESSED JUNE 6, 2020).

TABLE 4.2 Regional differences in key labor market indicators in 2019

Territory	Indicator	Working age (15–64), in %
Beogradski region	Rates of activity	70.8
	Rates of employment	64.9
	Rates of unemployment	8.4
Vojvodina region	Rates of activity	66.9
	Rates of employment	60.7
	Rates of unemployment	9.3
Šumadija i Zapadna Srbija region	Rates of activity	68.4
	Rates of employment	59.8
	Rates of unemployment	12.5
Južna i Istočna Srbija region	Rates of activity	66.2
	Rates of employment	56.9
	Rates of unemployment	14.1

TABLE 4.2 Regional differences in key labor market indicators in 2019 (*cont.*)

Territory	Indicator	Working age (15–64), in %
Kosovo and Metohija region	Rates of activity	n/a
	Rates of employment	n/a
	Rates of unemployment	n/a

SOURCE: SORS, RATES OF ACTIVITY, EMPLOYMENT, INACTIVITY AND UNEMPLOYMENT BY AREA, HTTPS://DATA.STAT.GOV.RS/HOME/RESULT/2400020102?LANGUAGECODE=EN-US& DISPLAYMODE=TABLE&GUID=E72F6780-EEC7-4740-AEFF-F46132AE02C8 (ACCESSED JUNE 6, 2020).

NUTS 2 regions, while the two southern regions (Šumadija i Zapadna Srbija and Južna i Istočna Srbija) lag behind. These differences call for stronger policy actions at the regional level and well-targeted measures in accordance with specific local labor market conditions.

There are also signs that there is a significant skills mismatch: NES reports state that fewer than 50% of vacancies are effectively filled through NES mediation on an annual basis. One of the most common reasons for failing to fulfill vacancies is that there were no persons with appropriate knowledge and skills in NES records.[19]

Aside from economic factors, the general demographic situation in Serbia raises many concerns and has serious consequences for the labor market. Like other European countries, Serbia is facing the problem of an ageing population. Data on the median age of the population shows that Serbia is one of the oldest nations in Europe (Figure 4.9). This problem is recognized in National Employment Strategy 2011–2020,[20] as well as in other strategic documents. In the last years, the Republic of Serbia significantly improved the legislative framework and introduced various measures aimed at the improvement of the demographic policy.[21]

---

[19] Ministry of Labour, Employment, Veteran and Social Affairs, National Employment Action Plan 2020.

[20] Nacionalna Strategija Zapošljavanja za period 2011–2020 (National Employment Strategy for the Period 2011–2020), http://demo.paragraf.rs/demo/combined/Old/t/t2011_06/t06_0023.htm (accessed May 10, 2020).

[21] For more details, see Government of the Republic of Serbia. Third National Report on Social Inclusion and Poverty Reduction in the Republic of Serbia. The Status of Social

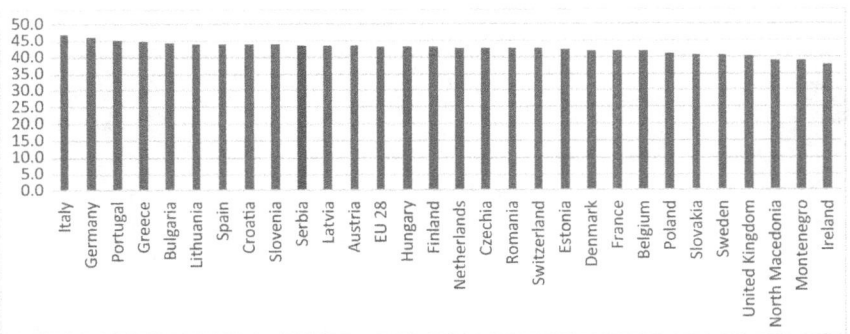

FIGURE 4.9 Median age of population in 2019
SOURCE: EUROSTAT, POPULATION: STRUCTURE INDICATORS, HTTPS://
EC.EUROPA.EU/EUROSTAT/DATABROWSER/VIEW/DEMO_R_PJANIND2/
BOOKMARK/TABLE?LANG=EN&BOOKMARKID=4BE76EAD-7B4F-450E-BF0C
-0B6F4BC4A998 (ACCESSED JUNE 8, 2020).

Workforce projections for Serbia for the period 2010–2050 show that the share of the working-age population (15–64 years) in the total population will decrease in all three observed scenarios (i.e., scenarios based on the medium, high, and low fertility) (Table 4.3).

TABLE 4.3 Changes in the share of the working-age population in the total population in Serbia in the period 2010–2050

	Medium fertility			High fertility			Low fertility		
	2010	2050	Change	2010	2050	Change	2010	2050	Change
Working age population (15–64 years) as % of total population	67.6	61.1	-6.5	67.5	59.9	-7.6	67.9	62.4	-5.5

SOURCE: РЕПУБЛИЧКИ ЗАВОД ЗА СТАТИСТИКУ, ПРОЈЕКЦИЈЕ РАДНЕ СНАГЕ РЕПУБЛИКЕ СРБИЈЕ, 2010–2050, БЕОГРАД, 2011, 10 (STATISTICAL OFFICE OF THE REPUBLIC OF SERBIA, PROJECTIONS OF THE LABOR FORCE OF SERBIA, 2010–2050, BELGRADE 2011, 10), HTTPS://PUBLIKACIJE.STAT.GOV.RS/G2011/PDF/ G20114 002.PDF (ACCESSED JUNE 8, 2020).

Exclusion and Poverty Trends in the Period 2014–2017 and Future Priorities, 14, Belgrade, December 2018, https://media.srbija.gov.rs/medeng/documents/third-national-report-on-social-inclusion-and-poverty-reduction2014-17_eng.pdf (accessed May 20, 2020).

Additionally, external migration outflows are relatively large. Eurostat data on first residence permits[22] issued in EU countries for persons who are citizens of the Republic of Serbia show that these flows have become even stronger in recent years (Figure 4.10). Heavy emigration flows can lead to important structural problems in the near future and the overall demographic situation calls for resolute and comprehensive policy action. This need has been recognized by policymakers and realized by some of the key strategic documents (i.e., in 2018 the government adopted a new Strategy for the Encouragement of Childbirth[23] and in 2020 the Economic Migration Strategy of the Republic of Serbia 2021–2027).[24]

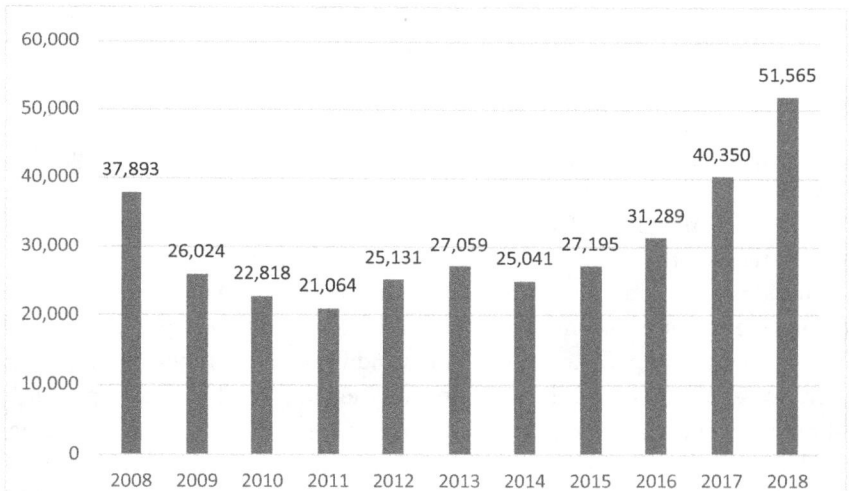

FIGURE 4.10 First permits for persons with citizenship of RS in EU 28
SOURCE: EUROSTAT, FIRST PERMITS BY REASON, LENGTH OF VALIDITY AND CITIZENSHIP, HTTPS://TINYURL.COM/2REPB67S (ACCESSED JUNE 10, 2020). DATA FOR PERIOD 2008–2012 IS BASED ON ADDING DATA EU27 AND UK.

---

22 Residence permit issued to a person for the first time.
23 Стратегија подстицања рађања, Влада Републике Србије, 2018, (Birth Promotion Strategy, Government of the Republic of Serbia, 2018), https://www.mdpp.gov.rs/doc/strategije/Strategija-podsticanja-radjanja-2018.pdf (accessed March 7, 2020).
24 Стратегија о економским миграцијама Републике Србије за период 2021–2027. године, Влада Републике Србије, 2018 (Strategy on economic migration of the Republic of Serbia for the period 2021–2027, the Government of the Republic of Serbia), 2018, https://www.minrzs.gov.rs/sr/aktuelnosti/vesti/usvojena-strategija-o-ekonomskim-migracijama-republike-srbije-za-period-2021-2027-godine (accessed June 7, 2020).

4 Economic Growth and (Un)employment

The period from the beginning of the effective transition process in the early 2000s until the economic crisis 2008/2009 is usually referred to as a period of "jobless growth".[25] During most of this period, the values of employment elasticity were negative, which means that growth in gross domestic product was accompanied by decreasing employment. This was probably the result of significant restructuring of the economy in the transition process – the negative impact of the restructuring process on employment was larger than the positive impact of growing GDP. According to Arandarenko, negative employment elasticity values also occurred in other transition countries, most often in shorter periods of at most a few years, during the middle phase of transition.[26] We can assume that in this period in Serbia positive effects of GDP growth were transmitted to the population through the growth of productivity and wages, instead of through growth in employment.[27] However, with the onset of the economic crisis in 2008/2009, we can observe a change in the sign of employment elasticity, which became positive and greater than one. This means that during the recession a decline in GDP was accompanied by an even stronger decline in employment. This effect seems to have been more pronounced in Serbia than in other Central and Eastern Europe countries (CEE) (Figure 4.11).

Arandarenko finds that although the decline in formal, non-agricultural employment was less pronounced, it was still significantly sharper than the fall in GDP. In that line, we can assume that, in addition to the impact of the crisis, there were other factors which influenced the labor market in that period.[28] After an exceptionally deep decline in employment in the period 2008–2012, the labor market began a recovery (Table 4.4). However, it should be noted that, due to the previously mentioned changes in LFS methodology, data before 2014 are not fully comparable with data after that year.[29] Still, a recovery trend in the labor market is apparent.

---

25 Dušan Pavlović and Mihail Arandarenko, "Serbia: equity and efficiency-hand-in-hand", SEER, Journal for Labour and Social Affairs in Eastern Europe 14, no. 2 (2011): 169–184.
26 Mihail Arandarenko, Tržište rada u Srbiji: trendovi, institucije, politike (Beograd: Centar za izdavačku delatnost Ekonomskog fakulteta u Beogradu, 2011), 78.
27 Gorana Krstić and Dejan Šoškić, Ekonomska statistika (Beograd: Centar za izdavačku delatnost Ekonomskog fakulteta u Beogradu, 2014), 224.
28 Mihail Arandarenko, Pomoćne strategije za oporavak iz krize u jugoistočnoj Evropi – Studija procene – Srbija, ILO, 2011, https://www.ilo.org/budapest/what-we-do/publications/WCMS_167015/lang--en/index.htm (accessed March 12, 2020).
29 According to older LFS methodology, which was previously discussed, the employment rate in 2014 was 49.6%, https://data.stat.gov.rs/Home/Result/24000100?languageCode=sr-Cyrl (accessed June 15, 2020).

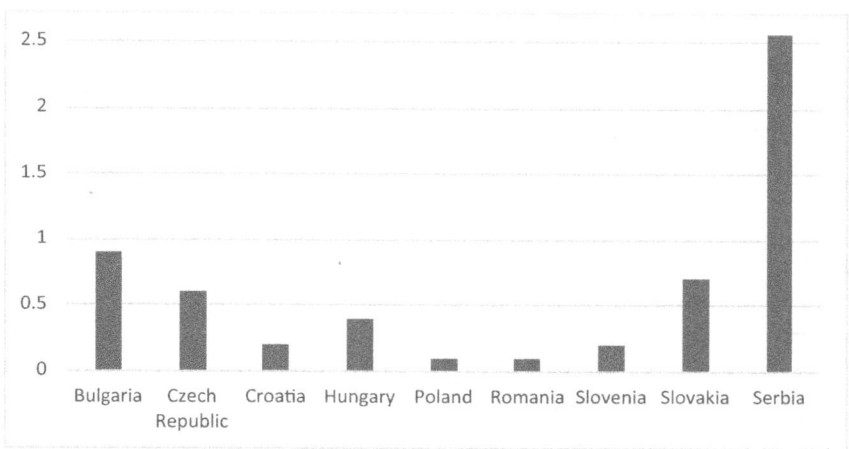

FIGURE 4.11 Employment elasticity during the recession 2008/2009
Note: Presented values are based on the cumulative fall of GDP from the beginning until the end of recession for every country and the fall in employment in the period Q1 2008–Q1 2010. This graph is based on the research conducted by Quarterly Monitor in 2010, available at https://fren.org.rs/kvartalni-monitor/kvartalni-monitor-21/ (accessed June 15, 2020)
SOURCE: BASED ON THE DATA FROM DANKO BRČEREVIĆ, "POUZDANOST ZVANIČNIH PODATAKA O BRUTO DOMAĆEM PROIZVODU U SRBIJI", QUARTERLY MONITOR NO. 24 (2011): 64–67, HTTPS://FREN.ORG.RS/KVARTA LNI-MONITOR/KVARTALNI-MONITOR-24/ (ACCESSED MARCH 12, 2020); "PAD ZAPOSLENOSTI U ZEMLJAMA CIE U PERIODU EKONOMSKE KRIZE" IN "ZAPOSLENOST I ZARADE", QUARTERLY MONITOR NO. 21 (2010): 20, HTTPS://FREN.ORG.RS/KVARTALNI-MONITOR/KVARTALNI-MONITOR-21/ (ACCESSED JUNE 15, 2020).

TABLE 4.4 Employment rates and GDP growth in 2008–2019

Year	Employment rate 15–64, %	GDP, real growth, %
2008	53.7	5.7
2009	50.4	-2.7
2010	47.2	0.7
2011	45.4	2.0
2012	45.3	-0.7
2013	47.5	2.9
2014	50.7	-1.6

TABLE 4.4 Employment rates and GDP growth in 2008–2019 (*cont.*)

Year	Employment rate 15–64, %	GDP, real growth, %
2015	52.0	1.8
2016	55.2	3.3
2017	57.3	2.1
2018	58.8	4.5
2019	60.7	4.3

SOURCES: SORS, RATES OF ACTIVITY, EMPLOYMENT, INACTIVITY AND UNEMPLOYMENT BY AREA, HTTPS://DATA.STAT.GOV.RS/HOME/RESULT/2400020102?LANGUAGECODE=EN-US&DISPLAYMODE=TABLE&GUID=E72F6780-EEC7-4740-AEFF-F46132AE02C8 (ACCESSED JUNE 6, 2020); SORS, RATE OF ACTIVITY, EMPLOYMENT, INACTIVITY AND UNEMPLOYMENT, HTTPS://DATA.STAT.GOV.RS/HOME/RESULT/24000100?LANGUAGECODE=EN-US&DISPLAYMODE=TABLE&GUID=DE2DF46F-BE1C-4AE7-97CA-36D7C82E1182, (ACCESSED JUNE 15, 2020); STATISTICAL OFFICE OF THE REPUBLIC OF SERBIA, LABOUR FORCE SURVEY IN THE REPUBLIC OF SERBIA, 2019, BULLETIN 658, BELGRADE, 2020, HTTPS://PUBLIKACIJE.STAT.GOV.RS/G2020/PDFE/G20205658.PDF (ACCESSED JUNE 15, 2020); WORLD BANK, GDP GROWTH (ANNUAL %). SERBIA, HTTPS://DATA.WORLDBANK.ORG/INDICATOR/NY.GDP.MKTP.KD.ZG?LOCATIONS=RS (ACCESSED JUNE 15, 2020).

Although general labor market indicators show a positive trend, issues like the quality and structure of new employment also need to be taken into account. The importance of the analysis of both quantitative and qualitative aspects of employment in Serbia is recognized in many other studies, namely Jandrić and Molnar,[30] Oruč and Bartlett,[31] Kovačević, Pantelić and Aleksić.[32] Another important characteristic of the labor market in Serbia, which should not be neglected in the analysis, is its duality. The duality of the labor market in Serbia is well documented and analyzed in numerous studies (e.g.,

---

30 Maja Jandrić, Molnar Dejan, Adaptability and Security: Key Aspects of the Quality of Employment in the Changing Labour Markets, Ekonomika preduzeća 66, no. 3–4 (2018): 213–225, https://doi.org/10.5937/ekopre1804213j.
31 Nermin Oruč, Will Bartlett, Labour Markets in the Western Balkans: Performance, Causes and Policy Options, Employment and Social Affairs Platform Regional Report (Sarajevo: RCC/ EU, 2018).
32 Miladin Kovačević, Vesna Pantelić, and Dragan Aleksić, Trends and Challenges in Serbian Labour Market: Change in the Nature of Jobs and Labour Underutilization. Ekonomika preduzeća 65, no. 5–6 (2017): 341–354, https://doi.org/10.5937/ekopre1706341k.

Arandarenko,[33] Tesić, Ilić and Đjelić,[34] Paunović and Kosanović).[35] According to Arandarenko,

> [...] in order to constitute elements of labor market duality, these elements must fulfill two important conditions: i) there must be serious obstacles to the transition from the lower to the higher employment segment; and ii) both segments must be relevant, rather than marginal, in volume.[36]

The main dichotomies in the Serbian labor market are those between the private and public sectors, formal and informal employment, the modern and traditional labor market, wage employment and self-employment, standard and vulnerable employment, and paid vs. unpaid work. The driving forces of changes in the primary and secondary labor market sectors may be different, as well as the impact of the usually mentioned factors such as recession or changes in the framework provided by labor market institutions. On the other hand, the relationship between economic growth and employment depends on many other factors, such as wage flexibility, employment protection legislation, adaptability of working hours, or the structure of the economy.

5   Labor Market Institutions and Unemployment

The most important formal labor market institutions are trade unions and collective bargaining, the unemployment benefit system, minimum wages,

---

33 Mihail Arandarenko, Tržište rada u Srbiji: trendovi, institucije, politike (Beograd: Centar za izdavačku delatnost Ekonomskog fakulteta u Beogradu, 2011); Mihail Arandarenko, Supporting Strategies to Recover from the Crisis in South Eastern Europe. Country Assessment Report – Serbia, International Labour Organization, 2011.

34 Aleksandra Tesić, Vladimir Ilić and Anastazija Tanja Đjelić, Labour Market in Serbia- An Opportunity or Limitation of Economic Growth. Economics of Agriculture 62, no. 4 (2015): 1117–1136, http://www.ea.bg.ac.rs/index.php/EA/article/view/267/250 (accessed March 17, 2020).

35 Sanja Paunović and Rajko Kosanović, "The Problem of Unemployment in the Republic of Serbia with Specific Regard to Informal Employment". SEER: Journal for Labour and Social Affairs in Eastern Europe, no. 4 (2011): 505–519. https://doi.org/10.5771/1435-2869-2011-4-505.

36 Mihail Arandarenko, Supporting Strategies to Recover from the Crisis in South Eastern Europe, Country Assessment Report – Serbia, 30.

employment protection legislation, labor taxation and active labor market policies. Institutional characteristics can alter the motives and incentives of participants in the labor market, and therefore have a significant influence on labor market performance. As previously described, since 2001 the labor market in Serbia has been affected by two important groups of factors: 1) processes of transition and the accompanying restructuring of firms and 2) the effects of pure macroeconomic shocks, such as the economic crisis in the period of the last quarter of 2008.[37] At the same time, the labor market in Serbia has been exposed to major institutional changes. Theoretical recommendations regarding the direction in which labor market institutions should be reformed differ widely among different macroeconomic schools. These differences arise mainly from different theoretical models describing the labor market. For example, schools that rely on a structural approach assume that there is a natural rate of unemployment (NRU) to which the economy converges, which depends only on structural factors. In that line, this stream of macroeconomic thought provides recommendations that are oriented towards deregulation and flexibilization of the labor market. The concept of a natural unemployment rate was introduced separately by Milton Friedman and Edmund Phelps in the late 1960s. NRU-based theories focus on measures that affect the long-term structure of the labor market. The basic position of the NRU-based models is that labor market flexibility is a key solution to the unemployment problem. For a long time, this was the dominant theory, which had significant consequences on the shaping of economic policy (e.g., Freeman,[38] Elmeskov and Scarpetta).[39] On the other hand, if we theoretically accept the existence of the hysteresis effect in the labor market, as the other stream of macroeconomic thought does, the role of aggregate demand becomes essential. Theories based on the concept of hysteresis place an emphasis on policy measures that positively affect employment and highlight the importance of the implementation of a policy of stabilization in order to avoid permanent negative effects caused by exogenous shocks. The hysteresis effect in the labor market, its possible presence, as well as its causes and consequences are analyzed by numerous

---

37 Maja Jandrić, Fleksibilnost i sigurnost na tržištu rada i uticaj na nezaposlenost u zemljama u tranziciji. (Flexibility and security in the labour market: influence on unemployment in transition countries). Doctoral dissertation (Belgrade: University of Belgrade, Faculty of Economics, 2014).

38 Richard Freeman, "The Limits of Wage Flexibility to Curing Unemployment", Oxford Review of Economic Policy 11, no. 1 (1995): 63–72, https://doi.org/10.1093/oxrep/11.1.63.

39 Jörgen Elmeskov, John Martin and Stefano Scarpetta, "Key Lessons for Labour Market Reforms: Evidence from OECD Countries Experience", Swedish Economic Policy Review 5, no. 2 (1998): 205–252.

authors, relying on the framework established, among others, by Blanchard and Summers,[40] Franz,[41] and Lindbeck and Snower.[42]

In the end, we can assume that both labor market institutions and economic policy measures directed towards boosting aggregate demand have significant effects on the labor market. The final effect of a single measure will depend on various interactions between macroeconomic shocks, positive or negative, and labor market institutions, but also on numerous interactions between different labor market institutions. The final impact will depend on the general institutional framework that also regulates other areas, such as the financial sector, housing markets, etc. In spite of this complex system, the flexibilization of the labor market has been often seen as a simple solution for many labor market problems. However, the vast body of empirical research does not provide a single answer to the question whether an inflexible labor market is a direct cause of high unemployment rates.[43]

Over the last two decades in Serbia, some of the key labor market institutions which set the main framework for the flexibility-security balance in the labor market have been reformed in Serbia. In spite of the European commitment to the concept of flexicurity, reforms in Serbia were mainly directed towards greater flexibility and less security. This primarily refers to the employment protection legislation and the system of unemployment benefits. In line with the neoclassical (or structuralist) point of view, one of the main motives for the flexibilization of the labor market in Serbia was reducing unemployment.

40　Olivier Blanchard and Lawrence Summers, "Hysteresis and the European Unemployment Problem", NBER Working Paper Series, no. 1950 (1986): 1–75, https://doi.org/10.3386/w1950.

41　Wolfgang Franz, Hysteresis, Persistence and the NAIRU: An Empirical Analysis for the Federal Republic of Germany, in The Fight Against Unemployment: Macroeconomic Analysis from the Centre for European Policy Studies, ed. Richard Layard and Lars Calmfors (Cambridge: MIT-Press, 1987), 91–122.

42　Assar Lindbeck and Denis Snower, The Insider-Outsider Theory of Employment and Unemployment (Cambridge: MIT Press, 1989).

43　Econometric estimates often give different conclusions about the strength, statistical significance, and even the direction of the impact of certain labor market institutions on key indicators of the labor market (unemployment rate, employment rate, activity rate, etc.). For an overview of differences in results of various empirical studies see Dean Baker, Andrew Glyn, David Howell, John Schmitt, Unemployment and Labour Market Institutions: The Failure of the Empirical Case for Deregulation. ILO Working Paper 43, 2004; David Howell, Dean Baker, Andrew Glyn, John Schmitt, Are Protective Labor Market Institutions at the Root of Unemployment? A Critical Review of the Evidence. Capitalism and Society, Berkeley Electronic Press 2, no. 1 (2007), https://papers.ssrn.com/sol3/papers.cfm?abstract_id=2206526; Tito Boeri, "Institutional Reforms and Dualism in European Labour Markets". Handbook of Labor Economics (Amsterdam: Elsevier, 2011), https://doi.org/10.1016/s0169-7218(11)02411-7.

6 Employment Protection Legislation – More Flexibility for Less Unemployment?

The labor legislation of the Republic of Serbia has undergone numerous changes in the period since 2000. Compared to previous legal solutions, the 2001 Labor Law[44] significantly increased the external numerical flexibility of the labor market. In contrast, further changes starting in 2005[45] were mainly aimed at expanding the rights of workers in comparison to solutions stipulated in earlier law, with the aim of harmonization with European Union and International Labor Organization (ILO) standards. Another important milestone was the reform which was undertaken in 2014[46] when important amendments to the Labor Law were adopted to further increase external numerical flexibility.

In a broader sense, labor legislation provides a legal framework for the functioning of the labor market. One of the most important aspects covered by labor laws refers to employment protection legislation (EPL), which is often seen as one of the main sources of the inflexibility of the labor market. For international comparison of employment protection legislation (which is mainly determined by the labor law), researchers and policymakers most often use the OECD EPL index.[47] In addition to the value of the aggregate EPL index, its structure is also extremely important – if there are significant differences in the strictness of regulations related to those employed with standard contracts on the one hand, and those with temporary contracts on the other, labor market segmentation can deepen. The values of EPL indexes in a group of selected European countries are presented in Figure 4.12. The data shows that in most European countries the value of the EPL[48] index was higher than in Serbia. In other words, only a few countries had less rigid employment protection

---

44 Zakon o radu, "Službeni glasnik RS", br. 70/2001, 73/2001.
45 Zakon o radu, "Službeni glasnik RS", br. 24/2005, 61/2005.
46 Zakon o izmenama i dopunama Zakona o radu, "Službeni glasnik RS", br. 75/2014.
47 The EPL index assumes values from 0 to 6, with higher values denoting regimes with higher strictness of the employment protection legislation. The aggregate index consists of three sub-indicators: an index for standard contracts (EPR), indices for temporary contracts (EPT) and an index showing the strictness of additional provisions related to collective redundancies (EPC).
48 Data from 2012 to 2015, depending on a country, see OCED Employment Protection Database, https://www.oecd.org/employment/emp/EPL-%20data.xlsx (accessed May 22, 2020); Maja Jandrić, "Measures of de facto Employment Protection Legislation", Management: Journal of Sustainable Business and Management Solutions in Emerging Economies 25, no. 1 (2020): 23–36, https://doi.org/10.7595/management.fon.2019.0008.

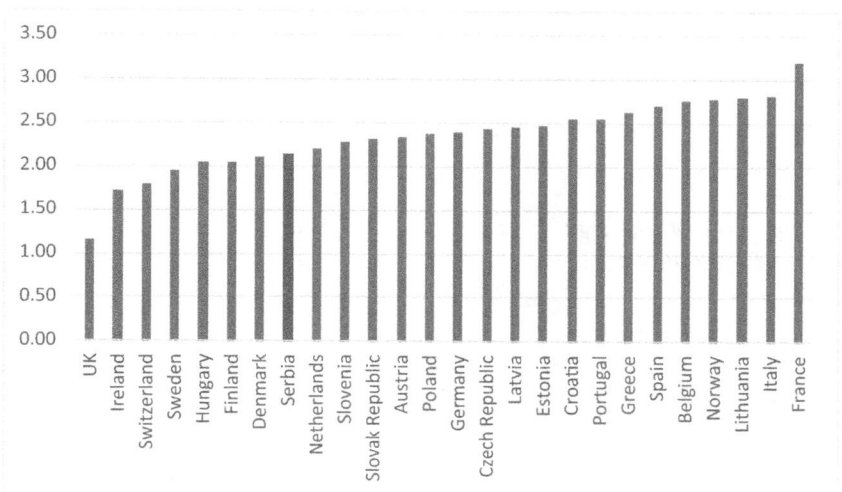

FIGURE 4.12   EPL index
SOURCE: MAJA JANDRIĆ, "MEASURES OF DE FACTO EMPLOYMENT PROTECTION LEGISLATION", MANAGEMENT: JOURNAL OF SUSTAINABLE BUSINESS AND MANAGEMENT SOLUTIONS IN EMERGING ECONOMIES 25 NO. 1(2020): 28, DOI: 10.7595/MANAGEMENT.FON.2019.0008.

legislation: traditionally more liberal countries such as Ireland and the United Kingdom, some of the Scandinavian countries (which mostly rely on the flexicurity concept) as well as Switzerland and Hungary. A similar situation is apparent when analyzing the EPT and EPR sub-indexes. The only exception is the EPC sub-index, which refers only to additional requirements in case of collective dismissals.

The changes in the EPL index in Serbia from the end of 1990s until the changes of the Labor Law in 2014 are presented in Table 4.5. Although there are some differences in the OECD methodology for the computation of the index for different time periods, the trend towards more flexibilization is clear. That means that in general, changes to the Labor Law led to lowering the stringency of employment protection legislation and to increasing the external numerical flexibility of the labor market.

The effective stringency of labor regulation, i.e., the real flexibility of the labor market, is largely dependent on the implementation of the legislation. Earlier research by Rutkowski and Scarpetta pointed out that Serbia was in the group of countries with weaker enforcement levels (Table 4.6).

This is confirmed by the more recent research, which found that *de facto* external numerical flexibility of the labor market in Serbia, adjusted for the

TABLE 4.5   Changes in the EPL index in Serbia

OECD methodology	EPL (end of 1990s)	EPL 2008	EPL 2014 after the labor law changes
Older OECD methodology	2.9	2.4	–
New OECD methodology (since 2013)	–	2.3	2.1

SOURCE: MAJA JANDRIĆ, AND DRAGAN ALEKSIĆ, "INSTITUCIJE I POLITIKE TRŽIŠTA RADA", ZAPOSLENOST I RAD U SRBIJI U XXI VEKU, SANU (2018): 197.

TABLE 4.6   Classification of the transition countries according to the strictness and the level of EPL application in 2005

Enforcement	Flexible EPL	More restrictive EPL	Very rigid EPL
Weaker enforcement	Albania, Kazakhstan	Armenia, Georgia, Russia, Serbia, Montenegro, Turkey	Azerbaijan, Belarus, Bosnia and Herzegovina, Kyrgyz Republic, Moldova, Ukraine, Uzbekistan
Intermediate enforcement	–	Bulgaria	Croatia, Macedonia, Romania
Stronger enforcement	Czech Republic, Estonia, Hungary, Poland, Slovakia	Latvia, Lithuania, Slovenia	–

SOURCE: JAN RUTKOWSKI AND STEFANO SCARPETTA, ENHANCING JOB OPPORTUNITIES: EASTERN EUROPE AND THE FORMER SOVIET UNION (WASHINGTON DC: THE WORLD BANK, 2005), 121.

measures of the implementation of labor law, is higher than when measured by the original unadjusted EPL indexes (Figures 4.13 and 4.14).[49]

---

49   Maja Jandrić, "Measures of de Facto Employment Protection Legislation", Management: Journal of Sustainable Business and Management Solutions in Emerging Economies 25,

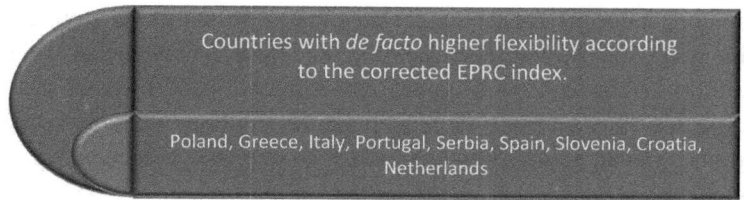

FIGURE 4.13   Countries with greater de facto relative flexibility: EPRC
Note: Adjusted indexes take into account effective implementation of legal provisions. EPRC is a sub-index which refers to the protection of permanent workers against individual and collective dismissals. It represents the weighted average of EPR and EPC sub-indices.
SOURCE: MAJA JANDRIĆ, "MEASURES OF DE FACTO EMPLOYMENT PROTECTION LEGISLATION", MANAGEMENT: JOURNAL OF SUSTAINABLE BUSINESS AND MANAGEMENT SOLUTIONS IN EMERGING ECONOMIES 25, NO. 1(2020): 23–36.

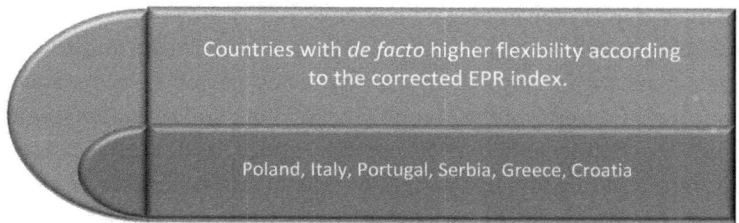

FIGURE 4.14   Countries with greater de facto relative flexibility: EPR
SOURCE: MAJA JANDRIĆ, "MEASURES OF DE FACTO EMPLOYMENT PROTECTION LEGISLATION", MANAGEMENT: JOURNAL OF SUSTAINABLE BUSINESS AND MANAGEMENT SOLUTIONS IN EMERGING ECONOMIES 25, NO. 1(2020): 23–36.

More precise assessments of the effects of labor market flexibilization on employment and unemployment levels require further sophisticated empirical research, which would allow discernment of these effects from the influence of other institutional and macroeconomic factors. Based on current knowledge from theoretical and empirical studies, caution is advised about how optimistically one can regard the degree of positive effects of reforms aimed at reducing EPL. On the other hand, reforms that are not carefully designed could

---

no. 1 (2020): 23–36, 30. Adjusted indexes take into account effective implementation of legal provisions. EPRC is a sub-index which refers to the protection of permanent workers against individual and collective dismissals. It represents the weighted average of EPR and EPC sub-indices.

lead to deepening labor market segmentation and to a decrease in the quality of employment. It is also important to mention that, besides the fact that labor market flexibility can bring some benefits to the functioning of the labor market, increasing flexibility by relatively high incidence of non-compliance with the legal norms is not an optimal strategy, since it is connected to a high degree of legal insecurity.[50]

7   Unemployment Benefit System

The main role of the system of unemployment benefits is to ensure income stability during periods of unemployment, but there is a danger that excessively generous systems may reduce incentives to leave unemployment and thus negatively affect labor market performance. The main channels of the impact of unemployment benefits are through (1) the impact on the duration of unemployment and (2) the impact on wages.[51]

Like employment protection legislation, this system in Serbia underwent numerous revisions in the period after 2000. These changes were made through several amendments of the Law on Employment and Unemployment Insurance and were mainly aimed at greater restrictions, both in terms of the maximum duration of entitlement to benefits for a certain number of years of insurance and in terms of the amount of compensation. While in some European countries unemployment benefit systems incorporate two pillars, a system based on insurance (contributory schemes) and a system based on assistance (non-contributory schemes), Serbia only has an insurance-based system. A particular problem is the extremely low coverage of unemployment benefits (Figure 4.15), which has been below 10% in most years in the last decade. In comparison to most other European countries, the share of unemployed persons receiving unemployment benefits in Serbia is relatively low.

---

50   Maja Jandrić, "Measures of de Facto Employment Protection Legislation", Management: Journal of Sustainable Business and Management Solutions in Emerging Economies 25, no. 1 (2020): 23–36, 30.

51   Maja Jandrić and Djordje Mitrović, "Sistem naknada za slučaj nezaposlenosti – mogućnosti ograničenja", in Uloga države u novom modelu rasta privrede Srbije, ed. Božidar Cerović (Belgrade: CID-Ekonomski fakultet u Beogradu, 2014), 107–123.

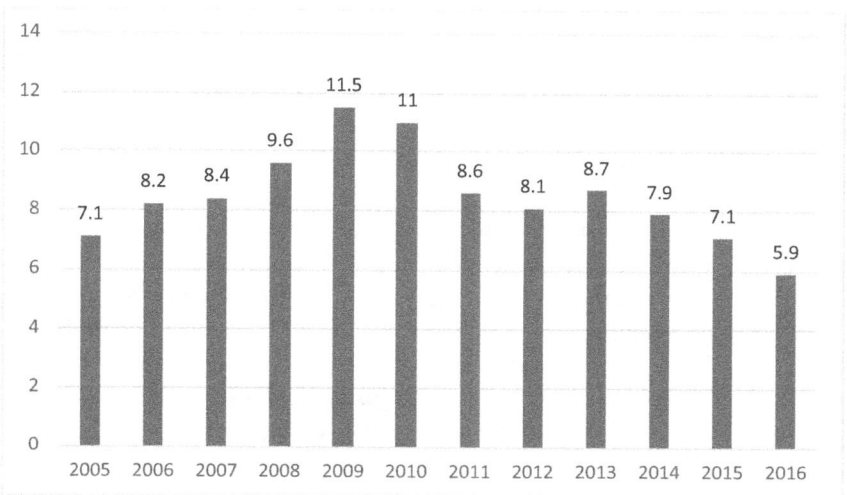

FIGURE 4.15   Share of unemployment benefit recipients in total registered unemployment (in %)
Note: Number of unemployment benefit recipients divided by number of registered unemployed persons.
SOURCE: NES, MAJA JANDRIĆ AND VESNA FABIAN, "VOĐENJE POLITIKE TRŽIŠTA RADA U REPUBLICI SRBIJI: OD NACIONALNOG DO LOKALNOG" IN STRUKTURNE REFORME I U REGULATORNA TELA U SRBIJI, EDS. MIOMIR JAKŠIĆ, ALEKSANDRA PRAŠČEVIĆ, GALJINA OGNJANOV (EKONOMSKI FAKULTET U BEOGRADU, 2017):132.

Some examples of the direction of reforms that were undertaken through several changes of the relevant law in the parts that regulate the unemployment benefit system in the last two decades are presented in Table 4.7.

Since proper international comparisons of the generosity of the system of unemployment benefits require taking various system characteristics into account (such as maximum duration of entitlement to benefit, amount of benefit, replacement rate, coverage of the system, etc.), both comparisons and quantitative assessments of the impact of this system on macroeconomic aggregates such as unemployment rates are not simple. However, considering several key features of the system in Serbia, we can conclude that this system is not overly generous, especially given the fact that its coverage is extremely low. This conclusion can be supported by findings of Anić and Krstić, who focused on the three most important benefit types in Serbia: monetary social assistance, the child allowance, and unemployment benefits. The study proved that both unemployed and inactive individuals who are able to work do not

TABLE 4.7 Key changes in the unemployment benefit system in Serbia – the rate of benefits

Years	Changes in unemployment benefit system
2001–2003	60% of the average wage earned in the last three months, increased by 2% for each year of insurance. The resulting benefit cannot be lower than 40% nor higher than 80% of the average wage in the Republic.
2003–2009	60% of the average wage earned in the six months before unemployment status was granted in the first three months, and 50% for the remaining time. The resulting benefit cannot be lower than the minimum wage nor higher than the average wage in the Republic.
2009–2015	50% of the base (the base is the average wage earned in the 6 months before unemployment status was granted). The resulting benefit cannot be lower than 80% of the minimum wage nor higher than 160% of the minimum wage in the Republic.
2015–2018	50% of the base (the base is the average wage earned in the 12-month period before unemployment status was granted). The resulting benefit cannot be lower than 80% of the minimum wage nor higher than 160% of the minimum wage in the Republic.
2018–present	*Determining factors of the benefits*: Previous earnings or contribution basis, the average wage in Serbia, a fixed amount of the daily benefit base, number of days in the month the benefit is paid for. The minimum and maximum amounts of the monthly benefit (gross) are set in fixed terms – in 2019: minimum – 22,838 RSD, maximum – 52,943 RSD. Net amounts: minimum – 14,548 RSD (27% of the average wage in Serbia in January 2019), maximum – 33,725 RSD (62% of the average wage).

SOURCE: OWN ELABORATION BASED ON DATA FROM COUNCIL OF EUROPE, HTTPS://WWW.COE.INT/EN/WEB/EUROPEAN-SOCIAL-CHARTER/MISSCEO-COMPARATIVE-TABLES (ACCESSED JUNE 15, 2020).

prefer being dependent on the safety net to working for market wages, due to low benefit coverage and the low benefit amounts.[52]

8 Active Labor Market Policy

At the same time, expenditures for active labor market policies are relatively low. If we start with the well-known "Danish triangle" of flexicurity which has three key elements, employment protection legislation, the unemployment benefit system and active labor market policies, it is clear that flexibility in employment protection legislation was not accompanied by appropriate institutional elements that could ensure an adequate level of labor market security. Jandrić compared labor market flexibility and security levels in 24 European countries and found that the level of flexibility in Serbia was slightly higher than average, while the estimated level of security was the lowest in the observed group of 24 European countries. All the elements of security that were included in the analysis affected the results in the same way: the coverage of the unemployment benefit system was among the lowest in the observed group of countries (below 10%) and labor market policy expenditures were also very low compared to other observed countries[53] (Figure 4.16).

Although the amount of funding for active labor market policy has been increasing in recent years, its share of GDP remains at relatively low levels. According to the National Employment Action Plan for 2020,[54] these funds are sufficient for the inclusion of only a quarter of the unemployed in NES records (22.4% in 2017 and 26.2% in 2018). It is also recognized that there is a need to increase the coverage of unemployed persons specifically in additional education and training measures, having in mind that in NES records one-third of unemployed persons are unqualified or low-skilled and that two-thirds of the registered unemployed are in long-term unemployment, which results in the loss of their knowledge and skills. This aspect, together with enhancing the system of recognizing employers' needs concerning the skills and knowledge of the workforce, is especially important in contemporary labor markets that are subject to continuous change triggered by technological progress.

---

52   Aleksandra Anić and Gorana Krstić, "Are the Unemployed and Inactive Financially Trapped? Evidence from Serbia", Ekonomski Anali 62, no. 214 (2017): 87–106.
53   Maja Jandrić, "Procena nivoa sigurnosti na tržištu rada primenom analize glavnih komponenata". Ekonomske ideje i praksa, no. 25 (2017): 35–50.
54   Ministry of Labour, Employment, Veteran and Social Affairs, National Employment Action Plan 2020.

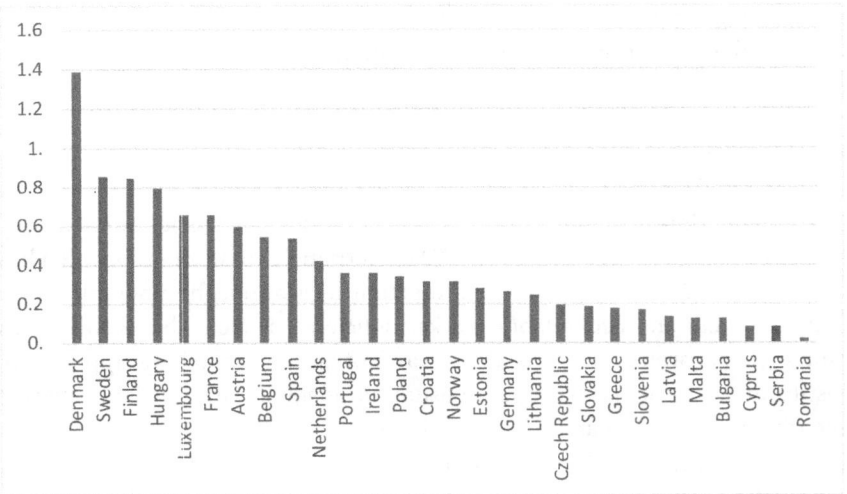

FIGURE 4.16 Public expenditure on active labor market policies (% of GDP in 2017)
SOURCE: OWN ELABORATION BASED ON EUROPEAN COMMISSION, PUBLIC EXPENDITURE ON LABOR MARKET POLICIES, BY TYPE AND ACTION, HTTPS://WEBGATE.EC.EUROPA.EU/EMPL/REDISSTAT/DATABROWSER/BOOKMARK/36B2B52E-3F36-4D33-BF4C-956D70550A96?LANG=EN (ACCESSED JUNE 21, 2020); COUNCIL OF EUROPE, EUROPEAN SOCIAL CHARTER: 9TH NATIONAL REPORT ON THE IMPLEMENTATION OF THE EUROPEAN SOCIAL CHARTER SUBMITTED BY THE GOVERNMENT OF SERBIA, APRIL 2020, 6, HTTPS://RM.COE.INT/RAP-CHA-SRB-09-2020/16809E44B3 (ACCESSED JUNE 21, 2020). MINISTRY OF LABOR, EMPLOYMENT, VETERAN AND SOCIAL AFFAIRS, NATIONAL EMPLOYMENT ACTION PLAN 2020, HTTP://SOCIJALNOUKLJUCIVANJE.GOV.RS/WP-CONTENT/UPLOADS/2020/02/NACIONALNI_AKCIONI_PLAN_ZAPOSLJAVANJA_2020_ENG.PDF (ACCESSED JUNE 14, 2020).

9 Conclusion

The Serbian labor market has been subject to the impact of various factors in the observed period: restructuring connected to transition processes, economic crisis, and significant reforms of key labor market institutions. In these circumstances, it is not easy to discern the effect of a single factor on labor market performance. At the same time, Serbia is facing significant demographic problems: both an ageing population and large emigrational flows. The current COVID-19 pandemic makes the future even more uncertain.

Some of the most prominent characteristics of the labor market in Serbia are labor market duality, large regional differences, and comparatively low quality of employment. Skills mismatch is also one of the problems that should be addressed, especially in the current dynamic environment characterized by rapid technological change. Both education policy and active labor market policies have a significant role to play in this area. However, reforms aimed at lowering the stringency of employment protection legislation were followed by decreasing or retaining at insufficient levels the generosity of key labor market institutions that ensure adequate levels of security in this market, such as the unemployment benefit system and active labor market policy. Although the importance of active labor market policy is recognized in key national strategic documents, expenditures for these measures are still insufficient and low in comparison to other European countries.

In line with the main challenges, economic policy decision-makers have made steps towards facing possible negative trends. Aside from measures aimed at mitigating the consequences of the COVID-19 crisis, key demographic challenges have been recognized, together with making strong efforts to recognize the needs for knowledge and skills in rapidly changing labor markets.

In order to fully understand the underlying mechanisms of labor market performance in Serbia, which would help in formulating adequate policy measures, future research should cover three main avenues: (i) econometric analysis of the effects of reforming specific labor market institutions on key labor market indicators; (ii) analysis of the skills mismatch and (iii) analysis of the main factors that affect migration flows, taking into account both internal and external migrations. The knowledge gained in this way would be of great importance for economic and social policy decision makers and would allow them to make adequate data-based decisions in order to face serious challenges, brought by rapid technological changes, demographic problems, and the current pandemic crisis.

To meet these challenges effectively, the cooperation of different institutional segments, as well as the provision of adequate scientific insights into the key problems present in the labor market, is more important than ever before.

Bibliography

Anić, Aleksandra, and Krstić Gorana. "Are the Unemployed and Inactive Financially Trapped? Evidence from Serbia". Economic Annals 62, no. 214 (2017): 87–106.

Arandarenko, Mihail. Pomoćne strategije za oporavak iz krize u jugoistočnoj Evropi – Studija procene – Srbija, ILO, 2011. Accessed March 12, 2020. https://www.ilo.org/budapest/what-we-do/publications/WCMS_167015/lang--en/index.htm.

Arandarenko, Mihail. Tržište rada u Srbiji: trendovi, institucije, politike. Beograd: Centar za izdavačku delatnost Ekonomskog fakulteta u Beogradu, 2011.

Arandarenko, Mihail. Supporting Strategies to Recover from the Crisis in South Eastern Europe. Country Assessment Report – Serbia, International Labour Organization, 2011. Accessed March 17, 2020. https://www.ilo.org/budapest/what-we-do/publications/WCMS_167008/lang--en/index.htm.

Arandarenko, Mihail. "The The Labour Market Crisis and the Road to Job Recovery in Serbia". SEER: Journal for Labour and Social Affairs in Eastern Europe 15, no. 2(2012): 225–252. https://doi.org/10.5771/1435-2869-2012-2-225.

Arandarenko, Mihail, and Dragan Aleksić. "Not all Jobs are Created Equal: How not to Misread the Labor Force Statistics in Serbia". Ekonomika preduzeća 64, no. 3–4 (2016): 211–224. https://doi.org/10.5937/ekopre1604211a.

Arandarenko, Mihail, and Dragan Aleksić. Influence of the Pandemic-Caused Crisis on the Serbian Labor Market. Accessed May 31, 2020. http://mons.rs/influence-of-the-pandemic-caused-crisis-on-the-serbian-labour-market.

Arandarenko, Mihail, Miladin Kovačević, and Dragan Aleksić. Kretanje zaposlenosti u Srbiji: Između tražnje za radom i ponude rada. Ekonomska politika Srbije u 2016. godini (Employment Trends in Serbia: between Labour Demand and Labour Supply. Economic Policy of Serbia in 2016), (2016): 151–175. Accessed April 28, 2020. http://ndes.ekof.bg.ac.rs/downloadsakta/zbornik2015deo2.pdf.

Baker, Dean, Andrew Glyn, David Howell, and John Schmitt. Unemployment and Labor Market Institutions: The Failure of the Empirical Case for Deregulation. ILO Working Paper 43, 2004.

Blanchard, Olivier, and Lawrence Summers. "Hysteresis and the European Unemployment Problem". NBER Working Paper Series no. 1950 (1986): 1–75. https://doi.org/10.3386/w1950.

Boeri, Tito. "Institutional Reforms and Dualism in European Labor Markets". Handbook of Labor Economics. Amsterdam: Elsevier, 4B, 2011, 1173–1236. https://doi.org/10.1016/s0169-7218(11)02411-7.

Brčerević, Danko. "Pouzdanost zvaničnih podataka o bruto domaćem proizvodu u Srbiji". Quarterly Monitor, no. 24 (2011): 64–67. Accessed March 12, 2020. https://fren.org.rs/ kvartalni-monitor/kvartalni-monitor-24/.

Council of Europe. European Social Charter: 9th National Report on the Implementation of the European Social Charter Submitted by the Government of Serbia, April 2020. Accessed June 21, 2020. https://rm.coe.int/rap-cha-srb-09-2020/16809e44b3.

Council of Europe. MISSCEO Comparative tables, ORS. Accessed June 15, 2020. https://www.coe.int/en/web/european-social-charter/missceo-comparative-tables.

Стратегија о економским миграцијама Републике Србије за период 2021–2027. године, Влада Републике Србије (Strategy on Economic Migration of the Republic of Serbia for the Period 2021– 2027, the Government of the Republic of Serbia), 2018. Accessed March 7, 2020. https://www.minrzs.gov.rs/sr/aktuelnosti/vesti/usvojena-strategija-o-ekonomskim-migracijama-republike-srbije-za-period-2021-2027-godine.

Стратегија подстицања рађања, Влада Републике Србије, 2018 (Birth Promotion Strategy, Government of the Republic of Serbia). Government of the Republic of Serbia, 2018. Accessed March 7, 2020. https://www.mdpp.gov.rs/doc/strategije/Strategija-podsticanja-radjanja-2018.pdf.

Elmeskov, Jörgen, John Martin and Stefano Scarpetta. "Key Lessons for Labor Market Reforms: Evidence from OECD Countries Experience". Swedish Economic Policy Review 5, no. 2 (1998): 205–252.

European Commission, Public Expenditure on Labor Market Policies, by Type and Action. Accessed June 20, 2020. https://webgate.ec.europa.eu/empl/redisstat/databrowser/bookmark/36b2b52e-3f36-4d33-bf4c-956d70550a96?lang=en.

Eurostat. Employment and Activity Rates by Sex, Age, and Citizenship (%). Accessed June 20, 2020. https://ec.europa.eu/eurostat/databrowser/bookmark/dd897ce1-11cc-4cb3-803e-c8f643825d8e?lang=en.

Eurostat. First Permits by Reason, Length of Validity and Citizenship. Accessed June 10, 2020. https://tinyurl.com/2repb67s.

Eurostat. Unemployment Rate by Age, Sex and Citizenship (2019, in%). Accessed June 20, 2020. https://ec.europa.eu/eurostat/databrowser/view/LFSA_URGAN_custom_2039879/bookmark/table?lang=en&bookmarkId=41886c55-12c6-4949-b039-d884c68bdf48.

Eurostat, Population: Structure Indicators. Accessed June 6, 2020. https://ec.europa.eu/eurostat/databrowser/view/DEMO_R_PJANIND2/bookmark/table?lang=en&bookmarkId=4be76ead-7b4f-450e-bf0c-ob6f4bc4a998.

Franz, Wolfgang. Hysteresis Persistence and the NAIRU: An Empirical Analysis for the Federal Republic of Germany. In The Fight Against Unemployment: Macroeconomic Analysis from the Center for European Policy Studies, edited by Richard Layard and Lars Calmfors, 91–122. Cambridge: MIT–Press, 1987.

Freeman, Richard. "The Limits of Wage Flexibility to Curing Unemployment". Oxford Review of Economic Policy 11, no. 1 (1995): 63–72. https://doi.org/10.1093/oxrep/11.1.63.

Government of the Republic of Serbia. Third National Report on Social Inclusion and Poverty Reduction in the Republic of Serbia. The Status of Social Exclusion and Poverty Trends in the Period 2014–2017 and Future Priorities, Belgrade, December 2018. Accessed May 20, 2020. https://media.srbija.gov.rs/medeng/documents/third-national-report-on-social-inclusion-and-poverty-reduction2014-17_eng.pdf.

Howell, David, Dean Baker, Andrew Glyn, and John Schmitt. "Are Protective Labor Market Institutions at the Root of Unemployment? A Critical Review of the Evidence. Capitalism and Society", Berkeley Electronic Press 2, no. 1 (2007): 1–72. https://papers.ssrn.com/sol3/papers.cfm?abstract_id=2206526.

International Labor Organization. ILO Monitor: COVID-19 and the World of Work. Third Edition – Updated Estimates and Analysis, 29 April 2020. Accessed May 17,

2020. https://www.ilo.org/wcmsp5/groups/public/@dgreports/@dcomm/docume nts/briefingnote/wcms_743146.pdf.

Jandrić, Maja. "Measures of de facto Employment Protection Legislation". Management: Journal of Sustainable Business and Management Solutions in Emerging Economies 25, no. 1(2020): 23–36. doi: https://doi.org/10.7595/management.fon.2019.0008.

Jandrić, Maja. Fleksibilnost i sigurnost na tržištu rada i uticaj na nezaposlenost u zemljama u tranziciji. Doctoral dissertation. Belgrade: University of Belgrade, Faculty of Economics, 2014.

Jandrić, Maja. "Procena nivoa sigurnosti na tržištu rada primenom analize glavnih komponenata". Ekonomske ideje i praksa, no. 25 (2017): 35–50.

Jandrić, Maja, and Dragan Aleksić. "Institucije i politike tržišta rada". Zaposlenost i rad u Srbiji u XXI veku, SANU, (2018): 191–226.

Jandrić, Maja, and Mitrović Djordje. „Sistem naknada za slučaj nezaposlenosti – mogućnosti i ograničenja". In Uloga države u novom modelu rasta privrede Srbije, edited by Božidar Cerović, 107–123. Belgrade: CID-Ekonomski fakultet u Beogradu, 2014.

Jandrić, Maja, and Dejan Molnar. Kvalitet zaposlenosti i tržište rada u Srbiji. (Quality of employment and labor market in Serbia). Beograd: Friedrich Ebert Stiftung, 2017. Accessed May 24, 2020. https://library.fes.de/pdf-files/bueros/belgrad/13589.pdf.

Jandrić, Maja, and Dejan Molnar. "Adaptability and security: Key aspects of the quality of employment in the changing labor markets". Ekonomika preduzeća 66, no. 3–4 (2018): 213–225. https://doi.org/10.5937/ekopre1804213j.

Jandrić, Maja, and Vesna Fabian. Vođenje politike tržišta rada u Republici Srbiji: od nacionalnog do lokalnog. In Strukturne reforme i uloga regulatornih tela u Srbiji, edited by Miomir Jakšić, Aleksandra Praščević, Galjina Ognjanov, Belgrade: Ekonomski fakultet u Beogradu 125–155, 2017.

Kovačević, Miladin, Vesna Pantelić, and Dragan Aleksić. "Trends and Challenges in Serbian Labour Market: Change in the Nature of Jobs and Labour Underutilisation". Ekonomika preduzeća 65, no. 5–6 (2017): 341–354. https://doi.org/10.5937/ekopre1706341k.

Krstić, Gorana, and Dejan Šoškić. Ekonomska statistika. Beograd: Centar za izdavačku delatnost Ekonomskog fakulteta u Beogradu, 2014.

Labor Force Survey – Abridged Methodology, Statistical Office of the Republic of Serbia, 2017. Accessed April 20, 2020. https://publikacije.stat.gov.rs/G2017/PdfE/G201720107.pdf.

Lindbeck, Assar, and Denis Snower. The Insider-Outsider Theory of Employment and Unemployment, Cambridge: MIT Press, 1989.

Mehran, Farhad. Preparing Consistent Time Series on Employment and Unemployment Following Change of Definitions in Serbia's LFS, final report to the ILO, 2010.

Ministry of Labor, Employment, Veteran and Social Affairs, National Employment Action Plan 2020. Accessed June 14, 2020. http://socijalnoukljucivanje.gov.rs/wp-content/uploads/2020/02/Nacionalni_akcioni_plan_zaposljavanja_2020_eng.pdf.

Nacionalna Strategija Zapošljavanja za period 2011–2020 (National Employment Strategy for the period 2011–2020). Accessed May 10, 2020. http://demo.paragraf.rs/demo/combined/Old/t/t2011_06/t06_0023.htm.

OECD. OCED Employment Protection Database. Accessed May 22, 2020. http://www.oecd.org/employment/emp/epl-data.xlsx.

Oruč, Nermin, and Will Bartlett. Labor Markets in the Western Balkans: Performance, Causes and Policy Options. Employment and Social Affairs Platform Regional Report. Sarajevo: RCC/EU, 2018.

"Pad zaposlenosti u zemljama CIE u periodu ekonomske krize". In "Zaposlenost i zarade". Quarterly Monitor, no. 21 (2010): 17–22, Accessed April 20, 2020. https://fren.org.rs/kvartalni-monitor/kvartalni-monitor-21/.

Paunović, Sanja, and Rajko Kosanović. "The Problem of Unemployment in the Republic of Serbia with Specific Regard to Informal Employment". SEER: Journal for Labour and Social Affairs in Eastern Europe 14, no. 4 (2011): 505–519. https://doi.org/10.5771/1435-2869-2011-4-505.

Pavlović, Dušan, and Mihail Arandarenko. "Serbia: Equity and Efficiency-Hand-in-Hand". SEER: Journal for Labour and Social Affairs in Eastern Europe 14, no. 2 (2011): 169–184. https://doi.org/10.5771/1435-2869-2011-2-169.

Pavlović, Dejana, Dragan Bjelica, and Ivana Domazet. "What Characteristics in the Youth Labor Market of Serbia are Likely to Result in Employment?". Stanovništvo 57, no. 2 (2019): 35–47. https://doi.org/10.2298/STNV190823006P.

Popadić, Dragan, Pavlović Zoran, and Mihailović Srećko. Mladi u Srbiji 2018/2019 (Youth in Serbia 2018/2019), Belgrade: Friedrich Ebert Stiftung, 2019. Accessed June 24, 2020. http://socijalnoukljucivanje.gov.rs/wp-content/uploads/2019/05/mladi_u_srbiji_2018-2019_fes.pdf.

Републички завод за статистику. Пројекције Радне Снаге Републике Србије, 2010–2050, Београд, 2011. (Statistical Office of the Republic of Serbia. Projections of the Labor Force of Serbia, 2010–2050, Belgrade 2011). Accessed June 8, 2020. https://publikacije.stat.gov.rs/g2011/pdf/g20114 002.pdf.

Rutkowski, Jan, and Stefano Scarpetta. Enhancing Job Opportunities: Eastern Europe and the Former Soviet Union. Washington DC: The World Bank, 2005.

SORS, Rates of Activity, Employment, Inactivity and Unemployment. Accessed June 20, 2020. https://data.stat.gov.rs/Home/Result/24000100?languageCode=en-US&displayMode=table&guid=de2df46f-be1c-4ae7-97ca-36d7c82e1182.

SORS. Rates of Activity, Employment, Inactivity, and Unemployment by Area. Accessed June 6, 2020. https://data.stat.gov.rs/Home/Result/2400020102?languageCode=en-US&displayMode=table&guid=e72f6780-eec7-4740-aeff-f46132ae02c8.

SORS. Unemployed Persons by Length of Job Seeking and Region. Accessed June 6, 2020. https://data.stat.gov.rs/Home/Result/240002090301?languageCode=en-US.

Statistical Office of The Republic of Serbia, Labour Force Survey in the Republic of Serbia, 2019, Bulletin 658, Belgrade, 2020. Accessed June 15, 2020. https://publikacije.stat.gov.rs/G2020/PdfE/G20205658.pdf.

Tesić, Aleksandra, Vladimir Ilić, and Anastazija Tanja Đjelić. Labor Market in Serbian Opportunity or Limitation of Economic Growth. Economics of Agriculture 62, no. 4(2015): 1117–1136. Accessed March 17, 2020. http://www.ea.bg.ac.rs/index.php/EA/article/view/267/250.

Torrejón, Sergio, Ignacio González-Vázquez, Marta Fana, and Enrique Fernández-Macías. The Impact of COVID Confinement Measures on EU Labour Market, European Commission, Science for Policy Briefs, 2020, https://ec.europa.eu/jrc/sites/default/files/jrc.120585_policy.brief_impact.of_.covid-19.on_.eu-labour.market.pdf (accessed May 31, 2020).

World Bank. GDP Growth (Annual %). Serbia. Accessed June 15, 2020. https://data.worldbank.org/indicator/NY.GDP.MKTP.KD.ZG?locations=RS.

Zakon o izmenama i dopunama Zakona o radu. "Službeni glasnik RS", br. 75/2014.

Zakon o radu. "Službeni glasnik RS", br. 24/2005, 61/2005.

Zakon o radu. "Službeni glasnik RS", br. 70/2001, 73/2001.

Zemniczky, Nandor, Gábor Csüllög, and Zsuzsanna Császár. "Serbia's Economy in the Context of EU Integration". Dvacáté Století, no. 2 (2015): 31–42.

PART 2

Social Security in Kosovo

∴

CHAPTER 5

The Renegotiation of Social Policy in Kosovo: Gradual Institutional Change since Independence

Artan Mustafa and Pëllumb Çollaku

1 Introduction

Kosovo remains under the military protection of the North Atlantic Treaty Organization (NATO) more than two decades after NATO's military intervention (March-June 1999) ended the war (1998–1999) between the insurgent Kosovo Liberation Army (KLA) and the forces of the Government of the remnants of former Federal Republic of Yugoslavia. Subsequently, the KLA was demilitarized, while the Yugoslav (de facto Serbian) administration and forces were withdrawn from Kosovo. Although Kosovo created a small professional army (2018), NATO's multinational force (KFOR) remains the main military actor in place.

Kosovo's political and economic administration, on the other hand, was run from June 1999 to February 2008 (when Kosovo declared its independence) by a United Nations' civilian mission (UNMIK) tasked to establish democratic self-governing institutions. This task combined with other existing conditions created a classic 'critical juncture' which, among other things, was used to influence the trajectory of social policy. In close cooperation with other major international organizations, particularly the World Bank and the International Monetary Fund (IMF), UNMIK launched a radically pro-market social policy consisting of a residual narrow government-financed basic social floor while expecting the market to produce jobs and the bulk of social welfare. It almost fully discontinued the policy of former Yugoslav self-management socialism (1952–1989) – which had grown in relevance in Kosovo especially after it gained the status of an Autonomous Socialist Province through Federal level constitutional reforms in 1974 – dominated by social insurance institutions centered on the working class and resembling to a large degree the western Bismarckian welfare states of the time. In contrast to Kosovo, most social insurance institutions in the other former Yugoslav entities were maintained in post-socialism.

This study employs the gradual institutional change theory to examine the forms and processes of change in social security since Kosovo declared independence, and to make sense of its directionality. It analyzes secondary data such as reform documents, social indicators, legislation and other parliamentary public data, and official comments on reform documents.

The findings contribute to the literature on recent social policy changes in South-eastern Europe and Kosovo by addressing the following questions:
- Why do gradual social policy changes occur instead of more radical ones?
- What is the direction of the changes observed in Kosovo in comparison to ideal social policy archetypes and what do they imply?

This, in turn, provides insights on the role of democratization and overall development of social policy trajectories in Kosovo.

2 Radical and Gradual Institutional Change of Social Policy

Institution(s) and social policy terms are here used interchangeably. Social policies are institutions in the sense that they establish formal rules of behavior for the state and individual actors towards expected performances and activities that are sanctioned by society.[1] National social policies fall under different ideal models and ideological underpinnings – e.g. most commonly in residual-liberal, conservative-Bismarckian, social democratic, and socialist models – based on the dominance of institutions, their redistributive purposes, and actual outcomes.[2] Institutions are dynamically contested over time and prone to change. Researchers have shown major interest in the timing, forms and causes of such institutional change.

A prominent example of institutional change research is the analysis of social policy trajectories in western welfare states and in the nations of South-eastern Europe (SEE) since the fall of the Berlin Wall. These trajectories have been largely analyzed from a tradition or a school of institutional change research which views institutions as broadly stable, immovable structures over long periods of time, with tendencies to reproduce themselves through path-dependence and feedback capacities, while expecting change to occur only in moments of critical junctures or exogenous shocks that provide openings for actors to make new choices which are then reinforced and reproduced through

---

1 See Wolfgang Streeck and Kathleen Thelen, Beyond Continuity (Oxford: Oxford University Press, 2005), 12.
2 Richard Titmuss, Social Policy (London: George Allen & Unwin, 1974), 87; Gøsta Esping-Andersen, The Three Worlds of Welfare Capitalism (Cambridge: Polity Press, 1990), Part one; Walter Korpi and Joakim Palme, "The Paradox of Redistribution and Strategies of Equality: Welfare State Institutions, Inequality, and Poverty in the Western Countries", American Sociological Review 63/5 (1998), 661–687.

limited alternative choice options, increasing resources for maintenance coalitions, increasing returns etc.[3] This school argues that the recent marketisation-leaning change in the western welfare states, impacted by expanding pressures of globalization and retrenchment, has been smaller in the nations with a history of a generous, sophisticated social policy either due to political interests that welfare states created in maintaining them[4] or substantial social-democratic-based power coalitions that resisted retrenchment and austerity measures,[5] thus largely preserving existing institutions. The larger change in SEE – made possible from the critical juncture created by the collapse of Soviet Union and past economic failures – was in addition to other factors strongly impacted by major international organizations such as the World Bank and IMF, which Bob Deacon has called 'political globalization'.[6] This international influence promoted a generally residual-liberal change, although with uneven results among nations depending on their contexts.[7] Yet even in SEE, despite these contingencies where more significant changes were embraced, the literature points to substantial institutional continuities, including in the Central European countries and countries that emerged from the former socialist Yugoslavia, made possible by institutional legacies and actors interested in maintaining them.[8]

---

3   See for example Paul Pierson, Politics in Time (Princeton: Princeton University Press, 2004), 18; James Mahoney, The Legacies of Liberalism: Path-Dependence and Political Regimes in Central America (Baltimore: The Johns Hopkins University Press, 2001), 6; Ruth Berins Collier and David Collier, Shaping the Political Arena: Critical Junctures, the Labour Movement, and Regime Dynamics in Latin America (Notre Dame: University of Notre Dame Press, 2002), 30; Giovanni Capoccia, "Critical Junctures and Institutional Change", in Advances in Comparative-Historical Analysis, ed. James Mahoney and Kathleen Thelen (Cambridge: Cambridge University Press, 2015), 151.
4   Paul Pierson, "Coping with Permanent Austerity: Welfare State Restructuring in Affluent Democracies", Revue Française de Sociologie 43, no. 2 (2002): 371.
5   Walter Korpi and Joakim Palme, "New Politics and Class Politics in the Context of Austerity and Globalization: Welfare State Regress in 18 Countries, 1975–95", American Political Science Review 97/3 (2003): 436.
6   Bob Deacon, "Eastern European Welfare States: The Impact of the Politics of Globalization", Journal of European Social Policy 10/2 (2000): 157.
7   Ibid; and Bob Deacon and Michelle Hulse, "The Making of Post-communist Social Policy: The Role of International Agencies", Journal of Social Policy, 26/1 (1997):54.
8   See for example: Bob Deacon and Paul Stubbs, Social Policy and International Interventions in South East Europe (Cheltenham: Edward Elgar, 2007), 10; Thomasz Inglot, Welfare States in East Central Europe, 1919–2004 (Cambridge: Cambridge University Press, 2008), 214; Marija Stambolieva, Welfare State Transformation in the Yugoslav Successor States: From Social to Unequal (New York: Routledge, 2016), 22.

However, recent literature from the gradual institutional change school of research has pointed to the fact that important and transformative institutional change also occurs gradually and endogenously,[9] that change can take place in stable, 'settled times' and not only during critical 'breakpoints'.[10] In traditional approaches, coalitions of actors and individuals as well as history are relevant, while here the emphasis is on the state institutional characteristics and the ordinary, daily political context that create chances for coalitions for action and small changes. It thus views institutions such as social policy as "distributional instruments laden with power implications".[11] We focus mainly on the impact of emerging political coalitions and existing veto powers and points (institutional characteristics)[12] in the state structure as casual mechanisms of change. During settled times, the probabilities of more veto powers or points present in an institutional context (state structure) are higher and therefore subversive rather than insurrectional forces, which favor gradual reforms, are more likely to drive change through processes such as layering (adding layers in the foundation of an original institution, with changing implications) and drift (the purposeful non-reaction of institutions to environmental change).[13] As Thelen writes, "the addition of new elements and renegotiations based on changing coalitional foundations", as well as non-action can redirect institutions toward "goals and functions completely unanticipated by the original founders".[14] According to this school, path-dependency itself should be understood as a dynamic, contested process, where the institutional outcomes do not necessarily reflect the aims

---

9   Wolfgang Streeck and Kathleen Thelen, Beyond Continuity, Chapter one.
10 Kathleen Thelen, How Institutions Evolve: The Political Economy of Skills in Germany, Britain, the United States and Japan (Cambridge: Cambridge University Press, 2004): 292–3.
11 James Mahoney and Kthleen Thelen, Explaining Institutional Change: Ambiguity, Agency and Power (Cambridge: Cambridge University Press, 2010), 8.
12 Veto powers and veto points include various institutional, state mechanisms (e.g. ministerial mechanisms and parliamentary committees) that the policy change has to pass through, but they can also include a polity's larger organisation (e.g. a presidential republic, a federation, the electoral system etc). For the role of veto powers and veto points in social policy see for example Ellen Immergut, "Political Institutions", in Oxford Handbook of the Welfare State, ed. Francis G. Castles, Stephan Leibfried, Jane Lewis, Herbert Obinger, and Christopher Pierson (Oxford: Oxford University Press): 227–240; Evelyne Huber and John D. Stephens, Democracy and the Left: Social Policy and Inequality in Latin America (Chicago, IL: The University of Chicago Press, 2012), 117.
13 James Mahoney and Kathleen Thelen, Explaining Institutional Change: Ambiguity, Agency and Power, 14–31.
14 Ibid., 293.

and expectations of the founders; furthermore, due to the limitations of their knowledge, coalitions of actors may attach different goals and meanings to the institutions by rearticulating them, endorsing new ambiguous agreements with space for differing interpretations, and blocking institutions from reacting to newly appearing risks, socio-demographic changes etc.[15] It argues that the cumulative or aggregate gradual changes across different sectors in the recent history of western welfare states have generally leaned towards liberalization,[16] whereas in developing countries the changes often moved in the contrary direction: from a small, exclusivist policy towards more ambitious, universal social policy.[17]

3 Radical Institutional Change in the Social Protection Sector under UNMIK

Kosovo's social policy has been mainly analyzed from the perspective of the traditional school of institutional change. Existing research shows that the residual, liberal policy launched after the war in Kosovo by international organizations during the UNMIK administration constituted the largest abrupt departure[18] from socialist insurance legacy among the former entities of the Socialist Federal Republic of Yugoslavia (SFRY). This major international influence was possible due to a mix of factors: favorable attitudes towards UNMIK and its international partner organizations, including NATO, the paucity of existing local policy skills, the ailing economy (including due to the legacy of the poorest self-management outcomes in comparison with other regions of Yugoslavia), and eroded labor skills as a consequence of institutional boycotts

---

15 Ibid; see also Bruno Palier, "Ambiguous Agreement, Cumulative Change: French Social Policy in the 1980s", in Beyond Continuity, ed. Wolfgang Streeck and Kathleen Thelen (Oxford: Oxford University Press, 2005), 127–144.
16 Wolfgang Streeck and Kathleen Thelen, Beyond Continuity (Oxford: Oxford University Press, 2005), 30–33; Wolfgang Streeck, Reforming Capitalism: Institutional Change in the German Political Economy (Oxford: Oxford University Press, 2009), 231.
17 Evelyne Huber and John D. Stephens, Democracy and the Left: Social Policy and Inequality in Latin America (Chicago, IL: The University of Chicago Press, 2012), 221; Huck-Ju Kwon, "Leaving behind the Developmental State: The Changing Rationale of Governance in Korean Governments", in The Korean Government and Public Policies in a Development Nexus: Sustaining Development and Tacking Policy Changes, ed. Jongwon Choi, Huck-Ju Kwon and Min Gyo Koo (Cham: Springer, 2017), 41–44.
18 Marija Stambolieva, "Welfare State Change and Social Citizenship in the Post-Yugoslav States", European Politics and Society 16/3 (2015): 383.

and conflicts during the 1990s.[19] Although the legislation that installed the post-war social protection system was voted on by the Kosovo Assembly (created in 2001), UNMIK had the sole power of promulgating legislation, and most relevant local political parties had a right-leaning ideological position anyway. The main party in the assembly at the time, the Democratic League of Kosovo (LDK), was furthermore heavily reliant on foreign endorsement and did not rigorously voice the interests of the more urban, formerly working population it represented, in contrast to what had happened in other emerging economies where the urban, middle class resisted changes.[20]

Similar to Soviet style socialism, Yugoslav self-management's social policy was centered on workers and a significant amount of welfare was distributed through work organizations (enterprises) in the form of stringent work contracts, work counselling, in-kind subsidies etc. However, most relevant institutions were not like those in the Soviet Union. Social insurance was directly organized and managed by Self-Governing Communities of Interest (involving workers, communities, and syndicates) including pay-as-you-go (PAYG) pensions, health insurance, social protection insurance for children and adults etc. Self-management even maintained a small unemployment insurance program and a highly targeted cash poverty transfer managed through municipal Centers of Social Work (CSWs). This Bismarckian legacy of Yugoslav self-management (1952–1989) is well acknowledged in literature.[21] These institutions

---

19   For information on this conjuncture see Fred Cocozzelli, War and Social Welfare (New York: Palgrave McMillan, 2009), 61–90; Marija Stambolieva, "Kosovo – from State of Welfare Emergency to Welfare State?", in Economic Development and Political Transition in Kosovo, Conference, 12–13 October. (Prishtina, American University in Kosovo, 2012), 2–5; Nathalie Duclos, "The DDR in Kosovo: Collision and Collusion among International Administrators and Combatants", Peacebuilding 4/1 (2016), 41–53; Artan Mustafa, "The Politics of Citizenship, Social Policy, and Statebuilding in Kosovo", in Unravelling Liberal Interventionism: Local Critiques of State-Building in Kosovo, ed. Gëzim Visoka and Vjosa Musliu (London: Routledge, 2019): 162–177.

20   Ibid. For former urban, working cleavages that resisted market solutions elsewhere in transitioned economies see Ethan B. Kapstein and Branko Milanovic, Income and Influence: Social Policy in Emerging Market Economies (Michigan: W.E. Upjohn Institute for Employment Research, 2003), 38, 45.

21   References to the Bismarckian legacy of Yugoslav self-management are made for example in Bob Deacon and Paul Stubbs, "Social Policy and International Interventions in South East Europe: Conclusions", in Social Policy and International Interventions in South East Europe, ed. Bob Deacon and Paul Stubbs (Cheltenham: Edward Elgar, 2007), 221–242; Vlado Puljiz, "Social Policy of the Post-Yugoslav Countries: Legacy, Transition Problems, Perspectives", in Reframing Social Policy: Actors, Dimensions and Reforms, ed. Maja Gerovska-Mitev (Skopje: University "Ss Cyril and Methodius" and Friedrich Ebert Stiftung, 2008), 77, 81; Marija Stambolieva, Welfare State Transformation in the Yugoslav Successor States: From Social to Unequal (New York: Routledge, 2016).

were introduced in Kosovo like in other entities of SFRY and they were developed in particular during 1970s when it gained the autonomous status through federal reforms.

After the war (1999), UNMIK and its partner organizations did not continue the self-management insurance institutions. Soon after UNMIK's deployment, in October 1999, the World Bank launched an eighteen-month Transitional Support Strategy (TSS) for Kosovo and a Trust Fund to support its implementation. The strategy called for a liberal market economy, private sector growth and the privatization of former social enterprises as an adequate and sustainable approach to "quickly provide jobs for the population".[22] The TSS at the same time prescribed a "well-targeted system of social protection" to replace the immediate post-war humanitarian relief.[23] Drawing on TSS and co-financing it together with The United Kingdom Department for International Development (DFID), the World Bank subsequently launched a specific five-year long program which created Kosovo's contemporary social protection system. The general transitional strategy and the specific social protection programs were two typical instruments of influence from the World Bank that were also applied elsewhere in South-Eastern Europe.[24] Two important goals of the World Bank were to install restrained social wage budgetary commitments and to discontinue various forms of institutions from socialism, especially pensions and similar work-related insurances.[25] As a result, UNMIK and its partners installed a basic government-financed social floor consisting of flat cash social transfers and last resort public care (services) for persons in need. The transfers included:
- a targeted cash social assistance covering families with fully disabled or dependent members and single parent families with a child under five years old, cancellable upon employment or other income;
- a basic pension for all citizens over 65 years of age;
- a pension covering persons with permanent work disability in the amount of the basic pension;

---

22 World Bank, "Transitional Strategy for Kosovo", http://documents.worldbank.org/curated/en/796841468270619562/pdf/multi-page.pdf (accessed May 1, 2019).
23 Ibid., 8.
24 Bob Deacon and Michelle Hulse, "The Making of Post-Communist Social Policy: The Role of International Agencies," Journal of Social Policy 26, no. 1 (1997): 55.
25 World Bank, "Project Appraisal Document on a Proposed Trust Fund Grant in the Amount of US$ 4.20 million to UNMIK for the Benefit of Kosovo, Republic of Yugoslavia (Kosovo) for a Social Project", https://documents1.worldbank.org/curated/en/934781468772459727/pdf/multiopage.pdf (accessed May 27, 2020).

– and a benefit for the disabled (with 40% or more disability) resulting from war and the next of kin of those who died in war. The payments were all flat and minimal, reflecting the costs of 2,100 calories of food per day, which was the equivalent of the official extreme consumption-based poverty line instituted by the World Bank. The purpose of this connection was made clear by the World Bank: it foresaw that in time the cost of the programs would increase at a lower rate than the growth of the economy.[26]

The last-resort public care system, covering cases where families and the market failed to protect individuals in need – such as through residential care for old age, residential care for the mentally ill, and welfare counselling for victims of human trafficking and family violence – was also slowly initiated, but it developed with considerably less success since it required more skills from the bureaucracy, and international organizations continually promoted sub-contracting services to the third sector (non-governmental institutions). This and a subsequently added small, flat pension for early retirees of the Trepça mine was the entire public social protection. No minimum wage in the market, no unemployment or public health insurance was launched.

The absolute share of income maintenance, pension income maintenance, health insurance, other care and welfare were expected to be found on the market. All workers were mandatorily expected to contribute a minimum (5% employees + 5% employers) amount of their gross wages to pension savings managed by the Kosovo Pension Savings Trust (KPST), similarly designed by the World Bank and its partners.[27] KPST, an autonomous body, was legally obligated to finance savings in the international financial market through a conservative investment policy, which represents another major binding of local welfare with the global economy (globalization of welfare). In most other Yugoslav entities and neighboring Albania, in addition to continuity in most social insurance institutions, pay-as-you-go (PAYG) pensions were continued after 2000, whereas mandatory Second Pillar (pension savings) were introduced only in Croatia and Macedonia as a smaller addition to PAYG.[28] The

---

26 World Bank, Kosovo Poverty Assessment: Promoting Opportunity, Security, and Participation for All, https://openknowledge.worldbank.org/handle/10986/8650 (accessed May 2, 2019).

27 World Bank, The Kosovo Pension Reform: Achievements and Lessons, https://socialprotection.org/discover/publications/kosovo-pension-reform-achievements-and-lessons (accessed May 20, 2019).

28 Marija Stambolieva, Welfare State Transformation in the Yugoslav Successor States: From Social to Unequal, chapters on Croatia and Macedonia.

legislation further opened the door for voluntary pension contributions in the third pillar (private pension insurance programs).

In its entirety, this was a typical residual, liberal social policy predisposed to cover for the 'failures' of the market and the family. Future social stratifications would be market-originated, that is, persons doing well in the market would reproduce their situation in old age income or in sickness insurance (in the market)[29] and in similar risks etc. Since it contained such minimal rights, Kosovo's policy resembled in fact 'a caricature'[30] of the ideal liberal welfare state regime.

Indeed, as foreseen by the international designers, the basic social floor expenditure financed by government revenues – itself financed predominantly through consumption taxation – remained low prior to independence compared to Kosovo's growing Gross Domestic Product (GDP) or compared to expenditures in the other countries in the region.[31] As Korpi and Palme argue,[32] this social protection system was poorly positioned to reduce growing market income poverty and inequality since the public social floor was designed to target extreme consumption poverty.[33] Yet, this system reduced considerably more poverty and market inequality than self-management did (during its best years in Kosovo), because self-management's insurance institutions concentrated on workers and pensioners who had been previously in work relation and their families. Since Kosovo had an unusually low rate of employment during self-management (maximum 23% in 1986), and the existing non-work-related small poverty program covered less than 20,000 individuals, self-management created massive exclusion from state benefits, leaving large portions of society dependent on small scale agriculture, craft, and remittances. The new, post-war system – in particular due to the basic pensions and

---

29 For expectations and outcomes of residual, liberal regimes see Richard Titmuss, Social Policy (London: George Allen & Unwin, 1974); Gøsta Esping-Andersen, The Three Worlds of Welfare Capitalism (Cambridge: Polity Press, 1990).
30 Fred Cocozzelli, Kosovo, in Social Policy and International Interventions in South East Europe, ed. Bob Deacon and Paul Stubbs (Cheltenham: Edward Elgar, 2007): 218.
31 World Bank, Rebalancing for a Stronger Growth, https://openknowledge.worldbank.org/bitstream/handle/10986/24399/South0East0Eur00for0stronger0growth.pdf?sequence=1&isAllowed=y (accessed May 20, 2019).
32 As Walter Korpi and Joakim Palme say: "Final redistribution is a function of degree of low-income targeting x [multiplied by] redistributive budget size", see Walter Korpi and Joakim Palme, "The Paradox of Redistribution and Strategies of Equality: Welfare State Institutions, Inequality, and Poverty in the Western Countries", American Sociological Review 63, no. 5 (1998): 672.
33 Artan Mustafa, "Kosovo's Social Policy during Self-management, UNMIK and Independence", International Journal of Social Welfare 29 (2020): 96–108.

more generous social assistance – reduced significantly more market poverty because these transfers were not related to prior market earnings.[34]

4   Gradual Short-Term Institutional Change since Independence

As soon as the World Bank-financed Social Protection Support program ended and UNMIK began transferring more significant power into the hands of the self-governing institutions of Kosovo from 2006 onwards, important local claims were immediately brought forward to the Kosovo Assembly. The government proposed a health insurance law financed by payroll taxation; the League of Pensioners of Kosovo, a union of pensioners consisting of former workers under self-management socialism, proposed a law on pension and disability insurance resembling the former generous, defined benefit PAYG pensions of self-management socialism; and the Democratic Party of Kosovo (PDK), then in opposition, proposed a law to differentiate between the Kosovo Liberation Army disabled veterans and the next of kin of KLA soldiers killed in the war on one side, and the civilian disabled and families of civilian victims on the other side. All claims were made in 2006; all were rejected by UNMIK which maintained the power to promulgate legislation. But following Kosovo's declaration of independence in February 2008 and with the PDK – the main party that arose from former KLA structures – assuming leadership of the government, the government revenue-financed social floor soon began seeing new layers. During the year independence was achieved (2008), the law differentiated the social status and (significantly) the level of benefits between KLA and civilian victims,[35] introduced rights to custodians of the disabled, as well as in-kind rights in the form of recreation subsidies as well as education and tax privileges for KLA-related beneficiaries. Within the same year, it created a generous cash benefit issued regardless of other current or future employment income for former members of the Kosovo Protection Corps (KPC), which consisted of around 5,000 former KLA members, when the KPC was dissolved to open the way for the Kosovo Security Force (KSF) which transformed to a small army later in 2018. In late 2010, the PDK-led parliamentary majority voted on a law introducing a social status which guaranteed access to similar in-kind

---

34   Ibid.
35   For example, in 2009, the highest paid KLA war-disabled person received a benefit worth €182 in comparison to a highest paid civilian war disabled, who received €117, see Kosovo Agency of Statistics, "Annual Social Welfare Statistics", http://ask.rks-gov.net/media/2692/social-welfare-statistics-2009.pdf (accessed May 21, 2019).

privileges with KLA "categories of war" and a one-time compensation for each day spent in jail for around 12,000 former political prisoners of Yugoslavia as well.[36] All these groups were the base voters of the PDK and of the Alliance for the Future of Kosovo (AAK) – the smaller party that emerged from the former KLA structures. However, the PDK shared a broad governing coalition in the first government after independence with the Democratic League of Kosovo (LDK), which had led parliamentary majorities during the UNMIK period and was more popular among the former urban, self-management working population. In negotiating the benefits for the KLA related categories, former political prisoners as well as government-financed investments and job distribution to the formerly poorer, more rural areas, as well as in an effort to enlarge its voter base, the PDK agreed with LDK-backed pensioner unions to introduce another layer to the government financed floor adding €30 to the existing €45 basic pensions for former workers under socialism with the condition of proven fifteen years of contributions to the former self-management PAYG scheme. The pensioner unions in addition used as an argument the fact that the former workers of self-management who had also managed to work for a period after the war received very low pension payments from the mandatory savings made into the KPST, which represented a poor outcome of the pension design installed under UNMIK.

Following the 2010 snap elections, the PDK gained fuller control of the executive, as the governing coalition did not include the LDK for the first time in the post-war period. Thereafter, the PDK continuously revisited the benefits for "KLA categories". By increasing payments, it routinely increased public sector wages (especially around election dates), and it introduced a major law creating cash benefits for around 60,000 war veterans covering former KLA soldiers and their logistical support.[37] In addition, various transfers targeting specific groups such as pensions for blind persons and persons with

---

36   The compensation was worth €15 for every day in jail, provided that the person had 60 or more days in jail for political reasons prior to 1999; for example, the prominent former Kosovo Albanian political prisoner in the former Yugoslavia, Adem Demaçi, alone received around €150,000 in compensation for 28 years in jail.

37   By 2019, these rights ensured that around 44,500 individuals and more than 2,000 other families were beneficiaries of transfers for "categories of war" and many more were expected to be included; during the same year, the highest paid KLA war disabled received a monthly benefit worth €448, the highest-paid civilian war disabled received €152, former KPC members received an average €803 benefit, the KLA veteran received €170 (equal to the statutory minimum wage), see Kosovo Agency of Statistics, Social Welfare Statistics – Three First Months of 2019, http://ask.rks-gov.net/media/4769/statistikat-e-mir%C3%ABqenies-sociale-tm1-2019.pdf (accessed May 25, 2019).

paraplegia were added to the system either in an effort to legitimize the KLA particularistic transfers or to cover for new social needs (e.g. early retirement pensions for members of the military and police). In total, the government-financed social floor consisted of 10 more new official specific layers of social transfers approved as compared to pre-independence[38] and more claims for similar rights were addressed to the government. The LDK returned shortly to government in a PDK-dominated majority (2015–2017) and led the Ministry of Labor and Social Welfare, where it backed the differentiation in status among former self-management workers (pensioners), resulting in differentiated income, with a view of backing the former, more educated workers – its voting base.[39] However, after new snap elections in 2017, the LDK returned to opposition and the PDK-dominated majority included other main parties that emerged from the KLA, the Alliance for the Future of Kosovo (AAK) and the Social Democratic Initiative (NISMA), the latter being a former PDK breakaway faction. It maintained the particularistic rights and distributions, accepting and negotiating even more claims in the same fashion.

As this dynamic layering through particularistic social transfers and rights was taking place, there was no parallel major political interest in the social care services and general poverty protection. These institutions were decentralized beginning in 2009 based on the UN Envoy's Comprehensive Status Proposal[40] and both care and poverty management were delegated to municipal Centers for Social Work (CSWs), which became less monitored by the central government and more vulnerable due to an unclear financing formula. The care services did not see any significant consolidation,[41] while eligibility

---

[38] Ibid. Compensation for victims of rape during the war was approved pending implementation, a claim for adding pension amounts to the pensions of former teachers was approved by the Parliament, and the Parliament approved budget for an early retirement pension for members of the police – all increasing the layers in the government-financed social floor.

[39] A former self-management worker with higher education receives a €230 pension; one with elementary education a €158 pension.

[40] Martti Ahtisaari, "Comprehensive Proposal for the Kosovo Status Settlement", UN Envoy Report, 2007, https://www.kuvendikosoves.org/common/docs/Comprehensive%20 Proposal%20.pdf (accessed May 24, 2019).

[41] For example, the government reported in late 2018 that most social services are provided by the third sector – nongovernmental organisations (NGOs); however, of the 31 licenced NGOs, 16 work in biggest cities Prishtina and Prizren, and as a result several services are not provided at all in practice in many municipalities: Ministry of Labour and Social Services, Concept Document on Social and Family Services. Reform Document, 2018, http://konsultimet.rks-gov.net/viewConsult.php?ConsultationID=40521 (accessed May 26, 2019).

conditions for cash social assistance established by the World Bank were not updated and were kept rigorous and highly targeted, thus effectively excluding around 10,000 families within a decade after independence. Since the institutions were not updated to cover new social needs, such as those resulting from income deprivation and demographic change, this constitutes a significant change through policy drift.[42]

As a result of the dynamic layering in the rest of the public financed floor and the inertia in social assistance and social care, the entire system began displaying results unanticipated by its founding designers, namely, the government-financed transfers covered increasingly more citizens and not necessarily the poor; since most transfers were status related (categorical), they discouraged employment;[43] and general government expenditure grew considerably relative to Gross Domestic Product. The international organizations, such as the World Bank and IMF, maintained a close, powerful presence, and continually discouraged electorally-motivated particularistic benefits,[44] and an International Civilian Office (ICO) – representing the major Western Powers and the EU – monitored Kosovo institutions for the first five years of independence. However, they did not offer strong opposition to the layering since it did not challenge the foundations of the residual, liberal system, as most of the changes created short-term rights that were set to expire in a few decades. Although the LDK was an important parliamentary party and won some small distributional battles, it similarly did not commit to seriously opposing or blocking the KLA-related particularistic transfers. This is perhaps related to its war legacy: the LDK had not participated in the war (1998–1999), which represented the key dividing issue between political ruptures in the years that followed, and it probably chose to reconcile with and not further antagonize the 'war wing'. However, the institutional changes might have a lasting impact

---

42 For drift as another gradual institutional change, see James Mahoney and Kthleen Thelen, Explaining Institutional Change: Ambiguity, Agency and Power; Jacob S. Hacker, Paul Pierson and Kathleen Thelen, "Drift and Conversion: Hidden Faces of Institutional Change", in Advances in Comparative – Historical Analysis, ed. James Mahoney and Kathleen Thelen (Cambridge: Cambridge University Press, 2015), 180–204.

43 For example, a KLA veteran, receiving a compensation on the amount of minimum wage, loses the benefit upon employment; similarly, a social assistance beneficiary family loses the benefit upon a member's employment.

44 See for example World Bank, Kosovo Public Finance Review Report, https://openknowledge.worldbank.org/bitstream/handle/10986/20756/ACS93510WP0P130IC00Final0 Kosovo0PFR.pdf?sequence=1&isAllowed=y (accessed May 26, 2019); International Monetary Fund, Kosovo: Enhancing Social Protection Cash Benefits, https://www.imf.org/external/pubs/ft/scr/2016/cr16123.pdf (accessed May 27, 2019).

since they have served as electoral resources in support of parties that emerged from the KLA. They have helped promote a certain historical narrative of war that benefits this coalition of parties for their role in the independence movement while minimizing the role of other forces such as LDK. Such particularistic rights have not contributed to a citizenship of shared rights and ways of life, and women and minorities have been left out.[45] Therefore, the first post-independence decade has primarily benefited those working in the bureaucracy, the beneficiaries of particularistic rights and the top business elite, and social inequality has grown in Kosovo. This was one of the main factors behind high outmigration in particular from 2015 onwards – amounting to around 15% of the population the country had in 2011.

5 Gradual Longer-Term Changes: Social Insurance

Longer-term changes in the social protection system were recently articulated and initiated, essentially seeking to launch social insurance institutions. Here again, the international organizations remained relevant agencies either by proposing solutions or monitoring policy developments. For example, the World Bank ran a health sector-financing study in 2008 and proposed a health insurance model for Kosovo that would be financed by employers and employees, national revenues and patient co-payments, and would be managed from an autonomous body based on the example of the Kosovo Pension Savings Trust.[46] The World Bank's proposal – again designing a major institution – was made law by the Kosovo Parliament in 2014, but as of 2019, the government had not implemented it. The European Union, which is becoming increasingly perceptible in its influence as well, signed a Stabilization and Association Agreement with Kosovo in 2016, which called for a social protection system promoting employment, inclusive growth and protection of citizens from

---

45 For further see also Nathalie Duclos, "The DDR in Kosovo: Collision and Collusion among International Administrators and Combatants", Peacebuilding 4, no. 1 (2016): 41–53; Isabelle Ströhle, "Kosovo Liberation Army Veteran's Politics and Contentious Citizenship in Post-War Kosovo", in Transcending Fratricide, ed. Srda Pavlović and Marko Zivkovic (Baden-Baden: Nomos, 2013), 243–264; Artan Mustafa, "The Politics of Citizenship, Social Policy, and State-Building in Kosovo", in Unravelling Liberal Interventionism: Local Critiques of State-Building in Kosovo, ed. Gëzim Visoka and Vjosa Musliu (London: Routledge, 2019), 162–177.

46 World Bank, Kosovo Health Financing Reform Study, https://openknowledge.worldbank.org/bitstream/handle/10986/8121/431830ESW0P10717397B01OFF0USE0ONLY1.pdf?sequence=1&isAllowed=y (accessed May 27, 2019).

health threats.[47] Since social insurance institutions are a backbone of social policy in continental Europe, the EU might be expected to support the development of social insurance as Kosovo and the region move closer to integration into the bloc. However, Kosovo's public bureaucracy (with improved skills compared to immediately post-war) and especially the rise of the left-leaning parties were the crucial factors impacting the recent development trends in social insurance institutions, despite international agencies such as the World Bank, IMF and EU remained close to social policy developments and provided regular comments and alternatives to local initiatives.

If not in major macro-economic indicators, there was visible change in Kosovo's political context, as illustrated in Figure 5.1. The number of elected representatives running for seats with left-leaning programs has gradually increased since 2010, reaching 1/3 of the 120-seat parliament in 2017 from insignificance a decade ago. The Social Democratic Initiative (NISMA) gained control of the Ministry of Labor and Social Welfare (MLSW) and, since it was part of a small majority government (2017–2019), its votes and positions mattered, even if the state structure remained under the dominance of right-leaning political coalitions. Although close to the KLA division of voters, as a former breakaway fraction of PDK, and often resembling the wider political style of the PDK and the AAK (the larger parties in the government), NISMA backed non-particularistic reform initiatives of the ministry's bureaucracy. For example, in 2018, the NISMA-led MLSW proposed a major document of reforms to launch a Social Insurance Fund[48] financed from employer and employee contributions. The Fund was proposed to manage new pay-as-you-go (PAYG) pensions, work disability pensions, unemployment and health insurance, sick leave insurance etc. In February 2019, an ad-hoc parliamentary committee, led by the Social Democratic Party (PSD), was created to formulate legislation. The PSD, whose parliamentary group parted with the left-leaning Vetëvendosje (*self-determination*) following the 2017 elections, gained the leadership of the reform committee as a political compromise in negotiations with the government: as it looked to connect with labor and the related electorate, the small majority government needed PSD to not support any opposition

---

47   See Article 116 of Stabilisation and Association Agreement Between the European Union and the European Atomic Energy Community, of the One Part, and Kosovo, of the Other Part, https://data.consilium.europa.eu/doc/document/ST-10728-2015-REV-1/en/pdf (accessed May 28, 2019).

48   Ministry of Labour and Social Welfare, Concept Document on Regulating and Managing Pensions and other Social Insurance Benefits, https://konsultimet.rks-gov.net/viewConsult.php?ConsultationID=40521 (accessed May 28, 2019).

motions. This was because the largest Serbian party in the parliamentary majority boycotted the government due to disputes between Kosovo and Serbia over on-going normalization negotiations mediated by the EU. In addition to refining MLSW's reform proposals focused on insurance institutions, the PSD-led committee supported a National Health Service model (rather than the model proposed by the World Bank) financed from general taxes and conditional on citizenship only. While the International Monetary Fund (IMF) expressed its preference for a policy of the status-quo in social protection, both the World Bank and the European Commission supported various dimensions of reforms, crucially, such as a small PAYG.[49]

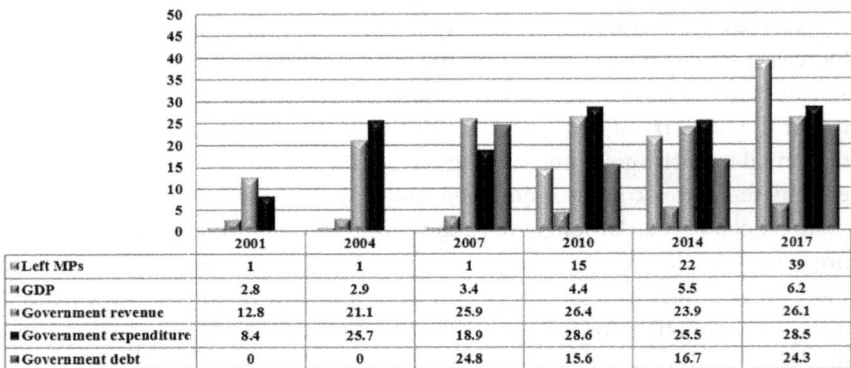

	2001	2004	2007	2010	2014	2017
Left MPs	1	1	1	15	22	39
GDP	2.8	2.9	3.4	4.4	5.5	6.2
Government revenue	12.8	21.1	25.9	26.4	23.9	26.1
Government expenditure	8.4	25.7	18.9	28.6	25.5	28.5
Government debt	0	0	24.8	15.6	16.7	24.3

FIGURE 5.1 Number of left-wing MPs, GDP, and government revenue, expenditure, and debt, 2001–2017
Notes: Members of the Parliament elected by competing with a left-leaning program include MPs from Vetëvendosje (VV), Social Democratic Party (PSD), Social Democratic Initiative (NISMA), The Unification Movement (LB) and Socialist Party of Kosovo (PSK) see Kosovo Parliament, Archive of Legislatures, https://kuvendikosoves.org/?cid=1,158&legid=5&secid=107 (accessed May 28, 2019). Gross Domestic Product (GDP) in billons and current prices; Government revenue, expenditure and debt as percentage of GDP see International Monetary Fund, World Economic Outlook Database, https://www.imf.org/external/pubs/ft/weo/2016/01/weodata/weoselser .aspx?c=967&t=1 (accessed May 28, 2019).

These institutional changes advanced and articulated by the bureaucracy and the left should launch a major, transformative layer with long-term

---

49 Comments to the MLSW document sent by the World Bank, International Monetary Fund (IMF) and EU Commission in 2018.

implications, creating for the first time in Kosovo's history a mixture of social policy consisting of social insurance, government-financed redistribution, and private market institutions. As shown above, under self-management socialism, Kosovo's policy was dominated by social insurance combined with a very small amount of government-financed poverty protection; after the war its social protection was designed to provide for a minimum floor of government-financed safety-net, while expecting the private sector to provide the rest of the welfare. Both policies had crucial shortcomings. As illustrated in Figure 5.2, the changes launching social insurance are projected to lead to a social protection financing mixture in which social insurance will become increasingly important.

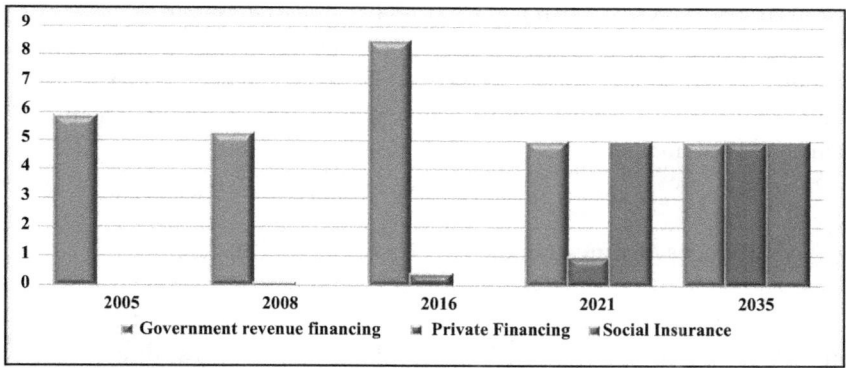

FIGURE 5.2   Current structure (2008–2016) of social protection expenditure as % of GDP and the prognosis of social protection expenditure
SOURCE: OWN ELABORATION BASED ON SOCIAL EXPENDITURE DATA FROM ARTAN MUSTAFA AND AMIR HAXHIKADRIJA, "KOSOVO: FINANCING SOCIAL PROTECTION", ESPN REPORT 2019, 8.

The change would curb the continuous claims for government revenue-financed particularistic and categorical rights by installing universal institutions and by correcting the existing weak protection provided by the market. Kosovo's private health insurance covers only around 15% of the population (the rest remaining uncovered), while most pensioners reaching old age exhaust their mandatory pension savings in the KPST (paid out in the amount of the minimum wage) within an average of four years, thereafter ending up with only the government-financed basic pension (around 90€). The changes should ensure a better protected pension income in the entire period of old-age and full coverage with public health insurance. In addition, the changes aim to provide better income maintenance in cases of work disability (currently attainable only in cases of full disability and financed by government revenues), in cases of early retirement and unemployment (both currently nonexistent programs). In addition, the changes articulate a universal child benefit (the existing child benefits are financed by the government and target only children under community care and fully disabled children) and a social-insurance financed parental leave where the leave would include a mandatory shorter (compared to the mother) period for the father of the child as well. The current existing maternity leave is financed by employers (six months) and the government (three months at the level of 50% of the replacement rate). As a whole, the reform seeks to increase social solidarity by increasing the financing burden on the labor force or middle class as opposed to current financing originating generally from consumption taxation, and by moving the current social contract towards a better generational balance compared to the existing design which targets the aged, the poor and other particularistic social groups through government financed transfers, while in the longer term expecting the major burden to be shifted to private jobs, private pension savings and private pension health insurance.

6   Changes Advanced in the Poverty Protection System

The Ministry of Labor and Social Welfare (MLSW) proposed another important reform in 2019 concerning Social Assistance, the largest direct poverty protection institution,[50] after many years of ignoring the sector. The MLSW requested a study from the World Bank, which again informed the proposed reform.[51] It in essence aims to make cash poverty protection more generous through ending the categorization of social assistance beneficiaries and through relaxing the means-test to allow for other income from one or more family members as long as the total disposable income remains under the poverty threshold (thus to encourage employment as well). As shown above, over a long period of time the number of social assistance beneficiaries continually declined due to high targeting and un-updated eligibility criteria;

---

50   Ministry of Labour and Social Welfare, "Concept-Document on Social Assistance Scheme", http://konsultimet.rks-gov.net/viewConsult.php?ConsultationID=40521 (accessed May 28, 2019).

51   World Bank, Kosovo Social Assistance Scheme Study: Assessment and Reform Options, 2019, https://documents1.worldbank.org/curated/en/994991557470271998/pdf/Kosovo-Social-Assistance-Scheme-Study-Assessment-and-Reform-Options.pdf (accessed May 2, 2019).

once the new approach is applied, the number of families covered by the program should rise, which would mean not only that more families would receive a better social assistance payment, but more families would have access to in-kind rights such as reimbursement of electricity bills, primary and secondary health care services, free books for pupils, tuition fee waivers for students, and municipal tax waivers.[52]

Despite the improvements, the MLSW's reform of Social Assistance designed by the World Bank remains strongly connected to the initial design, in that the calculation of the Social Assistance payment remains tied to the value of the extreme consumption poverty line (basic food basket). The World Bank continues to calculate the regular official absolute and extreme poverty indicators of Kosovo together with the Kosovo Agency of Statistics based on a so-called "objective" formula that the bank installed after the war, applied to consumption data, which has been widely criticized (eg. by Bradshaw and Mayhew)[53] among other reasons for downplaying important social differentiations and deprivations in time. All other former Yugoslav entities and most European Union countries apply EUROSTAT's at-risk-of-poverty rate measurement, applied to disposable income-based survey data. In this, usually equivalized families falling under 60% of the median income poverty line are considered poor. If social assistance were tied to such measurements, it would provide higher benefit levels for beneficiaries in Kosovo. In addition, the measurement would be relative rather than absolute, and therefore able to narrow the differentiations between income groups. In general, the consumption-based poverty line shows smaller social differentiations than income-based indicators, especially in economies that are doing well. As depicted in Figure 5.3, this is the case in Kosovo as well as the country's economy improves, "objective" poverty is declining, whereas relative income-based poverty is higher than the consumption-based poverty (2015).

This reality has inspired discussions within the left parties, most prominently articulated by the Social Democratic Party, for a relative measurement of poverty to protect the population from the new forms of deprivation what would make social assistance more generous and turn it to essentially a minimum guaranteed living standard sensitive to changes in overall level of disposable income in society. The change in the poverty

---

52   Ibid., 24.
53   Jonathan Bradshaw and Emese Mayhew, "The Measurement of Extreme Poverty in European Union", http://www.york.ac.uk/inst/spru/research/pdf/measurementExtreme .pdf (accessed May 29, 2019).

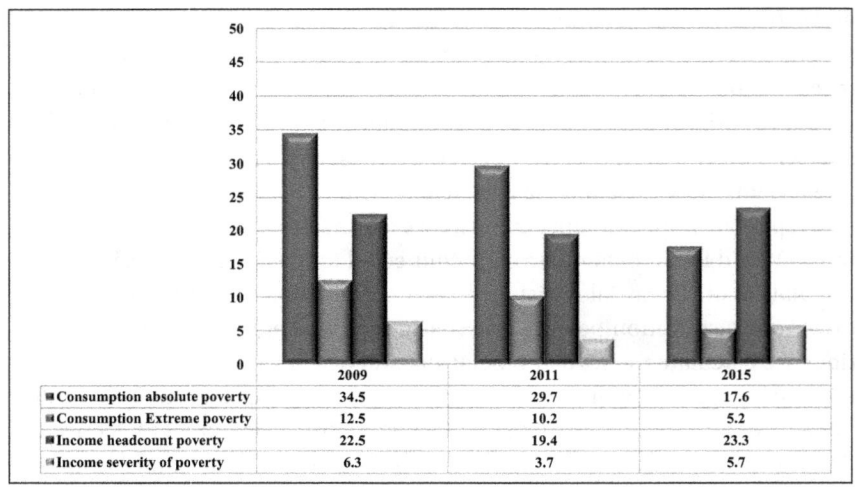

FIGURE 5.3 Consumption and income poverty rate, 2009–2015 (in %)
SOURCE: FOR REGULAR CONSUMPTION BASED POVERTY INDICATORS SEE THE KOSOVO AGENCY OF STATISTICS AND THE WORLD BANK REPORTS HTTP://ASK.RKS-GOV.NET/SQ/AGJENCIA-E-STATISTIKAVE-TE-KOSO VES/SOCIALE/KUSHTET-E-JETESES (ACCESSED MAY 29, 2019); INCOME BASED POVERTY INDICATORS SEE ARTAN MUSTAFA, "KOSOVO'S SOCIAL POLICY DURING SELF-MANAGEMENT, UNMIK AND INDEPENDENCE", INTERNATIONAL JOURNAL OF SOCIAL WELFARE, 29 (2020): 101.

formula would not only change the way the country thinks about poverty, but it is also well-timed with the move of the Kosovo Agency of Statistics to begin the implementation of the European Union Statistics on Income and Living Conditions (EUSILC) survey starting in 2018, which is well suited to the relative and multidimensional measurement of poverty. The KAS will now run the Household Budget Survey (HBS) – which informs the current official poverty indicators – only once in five years; this will effectively make an association between social assistance benefits and official poverty measurement.

7   Gradual Change in Employment and Wage Protection

When UNMIK and its partner institutions launched the residual, liberal model of social protection discussed above – parallel to the start of the privatization of former social enterprises which was directed from an UNMIK pillar (department) led by the European Commission – they also sought to establish a highly flexible labor market,[54] then widely considered by such agencies as a necessary precondition of moving from a poor, stagnant economy towards one that would thrive in the future, in which social welfare hopes are linked to the private market and individual initiative as its central institutions. As in the case of social protection, other entities of former Yugoslavia had maintained more of the self-management legacy of considerable labor burdens and employment stringency in post-socialism.[55] Although the sector maintains the features installed by the international organizations, there has been gradual change over time here as well, including in employment protection, labor costs, wage protection, the inclusion of unions in industrial relations, etc.

In employment protection, UNMIK's regulation on labor for example foresaw no limitation in terms of the length of contracts concluded for definite periods of time; no defined number of days notification prior to termination of contracts; no definition of unfair dismissal; no definition of collective dismissals; no limitations on repeated contracts signed for definite periods of time[56] etc. Usually the policies that seek stronger labor protection, found in conservative and social-democratic models, create stricter limits for defined period contracts compared to the more liberal economies, longer notice periods based on work experience, more generous definitions and protection from unfair and collective dismissals.[57] When a new Labor Law was adopted by the right-leaning dominated Kosovo Parliament in 2010, two years after independence was declared, it made several changes, but still the rules maintained weak employment protection. The law regulated that the contracts for definite periods of time could be concluded for no longer than 10 years, that the termination of contracts required 30 (for open-ended contracts) to 15 (other contracts) days of prior notification, that the contract of an employee absent due to maternity leave and special child care could not be terminated etc.[58] In 2018,

---

54 The main legislation that regulated employment protection included UNMIK regulations on Essential Labour Law (2001), https://unmik.unmissions.org/sites/default/files/regulations/03albanian/A2001regs/RA2001_27.pdf (accessed May 23, 2019); Labour Inspectorate Law (2003), https://unmik.unmissions.org/sites/default/files/regulations/03albanian/A2003regs/RA2003_04.pdf (accessed May 23, 2019); and on the Occupational Safety, Health and Working Environment Law (2003), https://unmik.unmissions.org/sites/default/files/regulations/03albanian/A2003regs/RA2003_33.pdf (accessed May 23, 2019).
55 Mihail Arandarenko, "International Advice and Labour Market Institutions in South-East Europe", Global Social Policy 4/1 (2004): 27–53.
56 UNMIK Regulation on Essential Labour Law, 2001.
57 See for example the differences between Germany, Sweden, and United Kingdom: OECD, "Indicators of Social Protection", https://stats.oecd.org/Index.aspx?DataSetCode=HEALTH_PROT (accessed May 23, 2019).
58 Law No. 03/L–212 on Labour, Official Gazette of the Republic of Kosovo.

the Ministry of Labor and Social Welfare (MLSW) proposed a new law[59] which foresees changing the limitation of defined period contracts to a maximum three years, extending the termination notification period to two months, defining collective dismissals as the dismissal of 10 to 30 employees within 30 to 90 days. The law has been challenged by various veto powers (such as parliament committees), but left-wing opposition parties, and especially the Social Democratic Party of Kosovo, have proposed amendments to further improve the draft law, including clarification of the way employers are to account for contract renewals/extensions so that they do not amount to more than the minimum defined period contracts, providing a more inclusive definition of unfair dismissal (such as dismissal due to union activity, whistleblowing due to health concerns, requests for payments at least as high as the minimum wage, and after efforts to find another job by the employee at the same work place are exhausted), considering 10 dismissals within 30 days as collective dismissals, creating a special court department for handling labor law cases etc. All of these changes represent significant movement towards stronger employment protection.

There is a similar trend of gradual layering when it comes to typical labor costs with even more transformative potential. Under UNMIK, the mandatory payroll charges on employers as mandatory private pension savings were limited to 5%, and this practice has not changed at any point in time, since the health insurance law (which was expected to charge employers another 3.5% in contributions) has not been implemented. The payroll charges on employers might however increase initially up to 10%[60] with the addition of social insurance institutions advanced recently by the left, which would still be among the lowest rates in the continent. In addition, UNMIK foresaw the right of employees to their regular wage (charged to employers) during sick leave, but it did not define the maximum length of sick leave, which in 2010 was defined as a maximum of 90 days. The MLSW and PSD have now proposed through social insurance initiatives that sick leave – like income replacement in unemployment, which remains non-existent – should be financed by social insurance contributions. This has been done with the aim of easing the burden on employers and strengthening the protection of employees in longer sick leave cases due to illness longer than 90 days. In reality, all 90+ day leaves currently are the personal burden of workers unless they become fully disabled, in which case they qualify for a flat, government-financed disability

---

59 Draft Law on Labour, Ministry of Labour and Social Welfare, 2018.
60 Based on PSD and MLSW proposals.

pension. The same agents have proposed converting the existing maternity leave – which early on during the UNMIK period covered three months of paid leave upon the birth of a child, financed by employers, later extended to a maximum of six months of paid leave by employers and three more months financed by the government – to a parental leave to be financed through social insurance contributions, again with the aim of easing the burden on employers, but also to reduce the burden on consumption taxation and to improve the gender balance in child care. All these dimensions represent a gradual change and signal more layering towards increased contribution charges, but not necessarily in the form of conservative increased employer costs. In addition, while UNMIK spent around €300,000 annually in active labor measures, the government expenditure after independence, in particular after 2015, grew to around five million euros covering the registration of the unemployed, professional training, registration of open vacancies etc., although the activation policies remain generally poorly maintained and unsophisticated.

UNMIK legislation mentioned a minimum wage, but it was not instituted in practice. The first minimum wage was set by the Kosovo government in 2011 at 170 euros for adult workers (130 for young workers). The government still did not show how it calculated the minimum wage and it never increased it again, despite growing wage disparities in the market. The Kosovo Parliament, however, approved a resolution on increasing the minimum wage on May 30, 2019, after public debates on widespread working poverty sparked by frequent deaths among low earners, often informal workers in the construction sector – forced to work in unsafe conditions due to family poverty and absence of employment choices.[61] The resolution, advanced by the Social Democratic Party, called upon the Social Economic Council – a tripartite forum advising the Government on social and economic legislation and policy – to propose a new minimum wage. The Union of Independent Syndicates, which represents employees in the tripartite council, proposed a minimum wage set as a defined percentage of average wages, which would resemble models used in France and the United Kingdom;[62] on the other hand several politicians, including the Prime Minister, proposed tying the minimum wage to the lowest salary paid in the public sector. Based on both ideas, the minimum wage would be around

---

61   Amir Haxhikadrija, Artan Mustafa, and Artan Loxha, "In-work Poverty in Kosovo", European Social Policy Network, European Commission Report 2019.
62   International Labour Organisation, "Social Justice and Growth: The Role of the Minimum Wage", https://www.ilo.org/public/libdoc/ilo/P/09238/09238(2012-1).pdf (accessed May 30, 2019).

250 euros. But the government has nonetheless not been able to use its tools to force implementation of the minimum wage in the private market, due to low union density and low union inclusion in industrial relations, especially prior to 2014. The MLSW's new draft law and PSD amendments foresee the formation of work councils at places of employment for the first time and more union inclusion in minimum wage and contract relations. The PSD even argued for stronger worker rights in naming board members of enterprises as well.

As shown in Figure 5.4, despite following low employment protection and low labor costs, employment realities did not radically change in Kosovo. These measures were not enough to spark a thriving economy. Since government revenues are predominantly (75%) financed from consumption taxation, the government has not been strongly interested in raising formal labor figures – including through dynamic activation mechanisms – and thus direct, more progressive revenue.

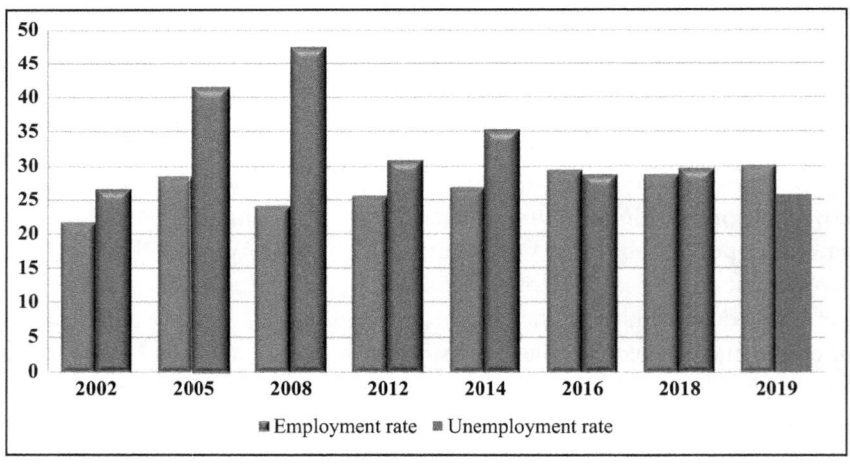

FIGURE 5.4 Employment and unemployment rate, 2002–2019
SOURCE: KOSOVO AGENCY OF STATISTICS (KAS), ANNUAL LABOUR FORCE SURVEYS, REGULAR REPORTS, 2002–2018, HTTPS://ASK.RKS-GOV.NET/SQ/AGJENCIA-E-STATISTIKAVE-TE-KOSOVES/SOCIALE/TREGU-I-PUNES (ACCESSED MAY 29, 2019); KOSOVO AGENCY OF STATISTICS, LABOR FORCE SURVEY IN KOSOVO, 2019, HTTPS://ASK.RKS-GOV.NET/EN/KOSOVO-AGENCY-OF-STATISTICS/ADD-NEWS/LABOR-FORCE-SURVEY-IN-KOSOVO-2019 (ACCESSED NOVEMBER 18, 2020).

The capital-owning elite might simply fancy a high unemployment rate and informal workforce to avoid strong commitments towards employees. By the same token, workers have not had many reasons (rational interest) to enter into formal employment, since in the absence of well-developed social insurance and employment protection, formalization would not change their income maintenance realities. These conditions make significant change unavoidable, especially since the rise of the left leads necessarily to frequent public outcry and class consciousness among workers and the poor.

8 The Theoretical and Political Implications of Gradual Institutional Changes

8.1 *Clientelistic Policy Allowed by International Veto Powers*

The declaration of independence of Kosovo in February 2008 did not amount to a typical critical juncture that would have created opportunities for radical institutional change. The declaration was read and signed by political forces that were ideologically right-leaning and satisfied with the institutional design of social policy established after the war by international organizations. In addition, the West supported the declaration of independence only under the condition that the Parliament adopts a package of legislation and policy that proceeded from the UN envoy's comprehensive status proposal, which reiterated that Kosovo was to pursue an open, market economy. The International Civilian Office (ICO), the body functioning on behalf of western powers and the European Union, was created to monitor the implementation of the conditions and government policy for a period of five years. The ICO – which even had a role in the selection process of members of the Constitutional Court – therefore served as an important, unusual veto power[63] inserted in the state structure, which would have been difficult to bypass even if there had been significant forces in support of policy options not in accordance with the internationally-backed liberal, market-oriented economy. However, there has been significant institutional change taking place in Kosovo since independence in a dynamic and gradual, rather than an abrupt manner, with short-term and longer-term implications.

Most short-term, intensive changes in the form of layering took place in the period of "conditional independence" and soon thereafter. Layering was driven by political forces emerging from the former Kosovo Liberation Army and especially the main one, the PDK. The PDK led governments continually increased the salaries of bureaucratic workers and created particularistic, categorical benefits financed by national revenues. While most relevant benefits

---

63 For regular veto powers see Ellen Immergut, "Political Institutions", 232; Evelyne Huber and John D. Stephens, "Democracy and the Left: Social Policy and Inequality in Latin America", 216.

targeted social categories related to former KLA and former political prisoners – the PDK's electoral base – the practice was used for similar claims from various other social groups including those supported by the Democratic League of Kosovo (LDK), the party that received the most votes during the UNMIK period. There were also important cases of policy drift for a long period of time, in the sector of social care services and direct poverty protection, that arose due to inaction and the absence of coverage of new social needs.

Continuous, short-term changes impacted the design of the initial basic social floor financed by government revenues in significant ways. The international organizations had expected that in time the expenditure on basic social floor would remain low as the economy grew, while most citizens would find solutions in the market; the layering increased the level of government-financed expenditure and more and more social groups were claiming similar rights. Furthermore, against initial expectations, most government-financed benefits did not necessarily target the poor; being categorical in nature, they were not related to prior work earnings and discouraged beneficiaries from seeking employment. The layering targeted the male Albanian population, going against early expectations of wider, inclusive institutions and inherently encouraging a divisive rather than an expansive and inclusive citizenship. Most layers were electorally motivated, usually taking place around election dates, or were used to legitimize the former layers, eventually leading to a situation in which the aggregate policy became financially unsustainable, regressive and at the service of a clientelistic and asymmetric redistribution resembling the post-war experiences of Croatia[64] or experiences in the more distant history of developed countries.[65]

The ICO and major international organizations expressed concern regarding these changes, but they did not strongly oppose or block the dynamic changes, as long as the changes were generally short-term (expiring in time with generational change), they did not alter the foundations of the initial post-war design in the long-term, and the major KLA parties engaged in other market-oriented policies, such as in accelerating the privatization of former social enterprises, prioritizing infrastructure investments etc. The LDK's resources to offer resistance seemed to have been limited by its history, namely its position of non-participation during the war. These changes, in addition to widespread corruption and the considerably better employment conditions of public workers compared to those working in the private market, are liable

---

64   Paul Stubbs and Sinisa Zrinščak, "Citizenship and Social Welfare in Croatia: Clientelism and the Limits of 'Europeanisation'", European Politics and Society 16, no. 3 (2015): 395–410.
65   Theda Skocpol, Protecting Mothers and Soldiers: The Political Origins of Social Policy in the United States (Cambridge: Harvard University Press, 1995), 120–124.

to have a major negative future impact on the way citizens think about public transfers, public goods and citizenship[66] and in consolidating the political power of the KLA parties through public distribution that impacts the future resources based on the balance of political conflict as well as public narratives and discourses (path-dependence).[67]

8.2 Left-Wing Agents Using Market Failures and Weak Majority Governments for Policy Renegotiation

Longer-term changes and reform initiatives have proved to require more complex negotiation between parties of the left and social policy bureaucrats on the one hand and the international organizations and the right-leaning dominant political coalitions in major political parties and within the state structure on the other hand. These changes improve employment conditions, social solidarity, and universal coverage. The change agents have articulated them in the context of increased social inequality and new needs. As theory predicts, there is always limited knowledge on the side of the institutional founders.[68] In the case of Kosovo, the designers of the residual, liberal-leaning policy failed in their expectations that the market would be able to produce a satisfactory level of social welfare in terms of social care, extensive employment, pension income, and health insurance. As employment remained low (Figure 5.4) most former workers reaching old age faced low mandatory pension saving income (exhaustible in a few years) while only a small part of the population was covered by private health insurance. As the workers in public bureaucracy and beneficiaries of categorical social transfers benefited from the particularistic layering, the remaining citizens faced low employment income and high social inequality. This inequality and the state of public funds and institutions has inspired substantial economic emigration since 2015. The agents of long-term change – a circle of experts within the public bureaucracy and the growing parties of the left, again as theory predicts[69] – used this lack of foresight on

---

66   Ibid.
67   For such distributional impacts see Paul Pierson, Politics in Time (Princeton: Princeton University Press, 2004); Peter Hall, "Historical Institutionalism in Rationalist and Sociological Perspective", in Explaining Institutional Change: Ambiguity, Agency and Power, ed. James Mahoney and Kthleen Thelen (Cambridge: Cambridge University Press, 2010), 204–220.
68   See for example Paul Pierson, Politics in time; Wolfgang Streeck and Kathleen Thelen, Beyond Continuity.
69   For the impact of the left parties towards social-democratic leaning, consolidated welfare states see for example Walter Korpi, The Democratic Class Struggle (London: Routledge & Kegan Paul, 1983), 187; and Gøsta Esping-Andersen, The Three Worlds of Welfare Capitalism. For the role of the left parties towards more comprehensive and redistributive

the part of the founders, the danger of unsustainable growth in public expenditure, and outmigration as a result of inequality and lack of employment opportunities, to argue for changes towards better employment protection, more solidarity, and more universal institutions.

The expertise pool within the bureaucracy improved compared to the situation immediately after the war. The left-leaning parties in addition saw the policy changes as opportunities to create connections with a larger electorate and to promote solutions corresponding to their social-democratic oriented ideology. They grew in popularity despite the left's fragmentation, which hinders the chances of a coalition across the left. Still, change continually faced multiple veto points within the right-leaning dominance of state structures backed by international organizations. The World Bank and IMF remain important and close to policy dynamics, although not with monetary conditionality, which has not been used as a major influence mechanism since Kosovo maintains a low level of government debt compared to other countries. Despite this difficult conjuncture, changes are taking place because they occur in single, separate moves (e.g., employment policy) rather than as a set of major reforms at a single point in time, or as a result of political compromises made with the parties of the left (social insurance). Since Kosovo's electoral system has produced weak majorities in recent years, the latter use concessions towards the reform initiatives of the left-wing opposition parties (most prominently the Social Democratic Party and NISMA) to avoid motions of no-confidence and government instability.

Therefore, the initial effects of democracy after independence did not create new social rights that would improve citizenship by creating conditions for more equal use of civil and political rights[70] and did not contribute, as social policy might do,[71] to a thriving democratization understood as the fuller political participation and civic engagement of increasingly equal citizens. Still, despite the unfinished process of state-building on the international stage (for example, two UN Security Council members - Russia and China, and five EU countries, Cyprus, Greece, Romania, Slovakia and Spain, do not recognize

---

welfare states in developing nations see Evelyne Huber and John D. Stephens, Democracy and the Left: Social Policy and Inequality in Latin America.

[70] Thomas Marshall defined citizenship as consisting of civil, political, and social rights where social rights would make "possible the enjoyment of a full life according to prevailing social standards", see Thomas H. Marshall, Citizenship and Social Class (London: Cambridge University Press, 1950), 11.

[71] For literature on how social policy can contribute to democratisation see Olli Kangas and Joakim Palme, "Making Policy Work for Economic Development: The Nordic Experience", International Journal of Social Welfare 18, no. 1 (2009): 62–72.

Kosovo) and the strong presence of international organizations, democracy has created a political context in which parties compete over (re)distribution and as theory predicts,[72] left-leaning parties articulate and drive changes towards a more sophisticated, solidaristic and universal institutional setting. In the West, the recent cumulative silent and gradual change has generally leaned towards liberalization,[73] that is towards more space for the market in producing social welfare while dismantling[74] the welfare state. Short-term changes in Kosovo since 2008 have leaned in directions that are specific (in form and timing) but also have similarities with the clientelistic post-war experiences of countries in the region, while the recent longer-term changes bear resemblance to trends in the wider world of developing countries with calls towards more universal and solidaristic institutions.[75]

9   Conclusion

The results of this study have shown that since independence, there has been a significant gradual, institutional change in the social protection and employment policy in Kosovo. By providing a comprehensive analysis of the policy changes the findings from this study make important contributions to the current literature. The main generalisable points are the following:
– if particularistic layering within the government-financed social floor benefiting certain social groups is initiated, it can be difficult to stop its expansion, since social groups will claim rights won by other groups in similar forms and parties will back them due to the need to legitimize particularism;
– such layering can take place even with the presence of powerful veto-powers, such as bodies working on behalf of international powers that allow the layering as long as the policy does not alter their main pro-market ideological solutions;

---

72   See for example Walter Korpi, The Democratic Class Struggle; Gøsta Esping-Andersen, The Three Worlds of Welfare Capitalism; Evelyne Huber and John D. Stephens, Democracy and the Left: Social Policy and Inequality in Latin America.
73   For literature review on recent institutional change in Western capitalism see for example Wolfgang Streeck and Kathleen Thelen, Beyond Continuity; Wolfgang Streeck, Reforming Capitalism: Institutional Change in the German Political Economy.
74   The term is used by Paul Pierson, "The New Politics of the Welfare State", World Politics 48/2(1996): 143–179.
75   Evelyne Huber and John D. Stephens, Democracy and the Left: Social Policy and Inequality in Latin America, 221; Jongwon Choi, Huck-Ju Kwon and Min Gyo Ko, The Korean Government and Public Policies in a Development Nexus: Sustaining Development and Tacking Policy Changes (Cham: Springer, 2017), 40.

- the parties of the left can initiate change not only through assuming leadership of crucial government sectors, but also by using moments of instability in parliamentary majorities (caused by the electoral system) to negotiate avoidance of motions of no-confidence in exchange for institutional compromises and by articulating policy failures;
- drift resulting from non-action to cover new social needs through social services and social assistance can help exacerbate a policy of increasing inequality and material deprivation.

Long-term change in a solidaristic and universal direction is however very difficult to take place in a context where powerful international organisations, such as the World Bank, are continuously active in the background. Based on the findings of this paper, it is recommended that Kosovo engage in the following social policy reforms if it aims to achieve more social equality, comprehensive citizenship, and a balanced generational social contract:

- continue the reform on launching and consolidating social insurance institutions based on the most sustainable European examples (e.g., pension, health, unemployment, sick leave insurance etc.) and, at the same time, continue to negotiate the removal of the majority of particularistic institutions established after independence;
- show greater focus on extending and consolidating universal public social services, such as childcare and long-term care for persons in need, and prioritize the employment of women in these sectors;
- establish a universal cash transfer system for children;
- use tax incentives, government-guaranteed jobs, and activation policies as measures to improve the employment rate;
- subsidize urban housing for families currently living in remote rural areas;
- raise the progressivity of income and wealth taxation;
- measure poverty and inequality based on EUROSTAT standards.

Bibliography

Ahtisaari, Martti. "Comprehensive Proposal for the Kosovo Status Settlement". UN Envoy Report. Accessed May 24, 2019. https://www.kuvendikosoves.org/common/docs/Compre hensive%20Proposal%20.pdf.

Arandarenko, Mihail. "International Advice and Labour Market Institutions in South-East Europe". Global Social Policy 4, no. 1 (2004), 27–53.

Bradshaw, Jonathan and Emese Mayhew. The Measurement of Extreme Poverty in the European Union, Report 2010. Accessed May 29, 2019, http://www.york.ac.uk/inst/spru/research/pdf/measurementExtreme.pdf.

Capoccia, Giovanni. "Critical Junctures and Institutional Change". In Advances in Comparative – Historical Analysis, edited by James Mahoney and Kathleen Thelen, 147–179. Cambridge: Cambridge University Press, 2015.

Choi, Jongwon, Huck-Ju Kwon, and Min Gyo Ko. The Korean Government and Public Policies in a Development Nexus: Sustaining Development and Tacking Policy Changes. Cham: Springer, 2017.

Cocozzelli, Fred. Kosovo. In Social Policy and International Interventions in South East Europe, edited by Bob Deacon and Paul Stubbs, 203–220. Cheltenham: Edward Elgar, 2007.

Cocozzelli, Fred. "War and Social Welfare". New York: Palgrave McMillan, 2009.

Collier, Ruth Berins, and David Collier. Shaping the Political Arena: Critical Junctures, the Labour Movement, and Regime Dynamics in Latin America. Notre Dame: University of Notre Dame Press, 2002.

Deacon, Bob. "Eastern European Welfare States: The Impact of the Politics of Globalization". Journal of European Social Policy 10/2 (2000), 146–161.

Deacon, Bob, and Michelle Hulse. "The Making of Post-communist Social Policy: The Role of International Agencies". Journal of Social Policy 26, no. 1 (1997): 43–62.

Deacon, Bob, and Paul Stubbs. "Social Policy and International Interventions in South East Europe: Conclusions". In Social Policy and International Interventions in South East Europe, edited by Bob Deacon and Paul Stubbs, 221–242. Cheltenham: Edward Elgar, 2007.

Duclos, Nathalie. "The DDR in Kosovo: Collision and Collusion among International Administrators and Combatants", Peacebuilding 4, no. 1 (2016): 41–53.

Esping-Andersen, Gøsta. The Three Worlds of Welfare Capitalism. Cambridge: Polity Press, 1990.

European Union and World Bank. Comments to the MLSW's Concept Document on Regulating and Managing Pensions and Other Social Insurance Benefits, 2018.

European Union and Kosovo. "Stabilization and Association Agreement". Access May 24, 2009. http://data.consilium.europa.eu/doc/document/ST-10728-2015-REV-1/en/pdf.

Hacker, Jacob S., Paul Pierson and Kathleen Thelen. "Drift and Conversion: Hidden Faces of Institutional Change". In Advances in Comparative-Historical Analysis, edited by James Mahoney and Kathleen Thelen, 180–210. Cambridge: Cambridge University Press, 2015.

Hall, Peter. "Historical Institutionalism in Rationalist and Sociological Perspective". In Explaining Institutional Change: Ambiguity, Agency, and Power, edited by James Mahoney and Kathleen Thelen, 204–220. Cambridge: Cambridge University Press, 2010.

Haxhikadrija, Amir, Artan Mustafa, and Artan Loxha. "In-work Poverty in Kosovo," European Social Policy Network. European Commission Report 2019.

Huber, Evelyne and John D. Stephens. Democracy and the Left: Social Policy and Inequality in Latin America. Chicago, IL: The University of Chicago Press, 2012.

Immergut, Ellen. Political Institutions. In Oxford Handbook of the Welfare State, edited by Francis G. Castles, Stephan Leibfried, Jane Lewis, Herbert Obinger, and Christopher Pierson, 227–240. Oxford: Oxford University Press, 2010.

Inglot, Thomasz. Welfare States in East Central Europe, 1919–2004. Cambridge: Cambridge University Press, 2008.

International Labour Organisation. Social Justice and Growth: The Role of the Minimum Wage. Accessed May 29, 2019. https://www.ilo.org/public/libdoc/ilo/P/09238/09238(2012-1).pdf.

International Monetary Fund. Kosovo: Enhancing Social Protection Cash Benefits, Report, 2016. Accessed May 27, 2019, https://www.imf.org/external/pubs/ft/scr/2016/cr16123.pdf.

International Monetary Fund. World Economic Outlook Database. Accessed May 28, 2019. https://www.imf.org/external/pubs/ft/weo/2016/01/weodata/weoselser.aspx?c=967&t=1.

International Monetary Fund. Comments to the MLSW's Concept Document on Regulating and Managing Pensions and Other Social Insurance Benefits, 2018.

Kangas, Olli, and Joakim Palme. "Making Policy Work for Economic Development: The Nordic Experience". International Journal of Social Welfare 18, no. 1 (2009): 62–72.

Kapstein, Ethan B., and Branko Milanovic. Income and Influence: Social Policy in Emerging Market Economies. Michigan: W.E. Upjohn Institute for Employment Research, 2003.

Korpi, Walter. The Democratic Class Struggle. London: Routledge & Kegan Paul, 1983.

Korpi, Walter, and Joakim Palme. "The Paradox of Redistribution and Strategies of Equality: Welfare State Institutions, Inequality, and Poverty in the Western Countries". American Sociological Review 63, no. 5 (1998), 661–687.

Korpi, Walter, and Joakim Palme. "New Politics and Class Politics in the Context of Austerity and Globalization: Welfare State Regress in 18 Countries", American Political Science Review 97, no. 3 (2003): 425–446.

Kosovo Agency of Statistics. Annual Labour Force Surveys, Regular Reports, 2002–2018. Accessed May 29, 2019. https://ask.rks-gov.net/en/kosovo-agency-of-statistics/social/labour-market.

Kosovo Agency of Statistics. Annual Social Welfare Statistics. Accessed May 21, 2019. http://ask.rks-gov.net/media/2692/social-welfare-statistics-2009.pdf.

Kosovo Agency of Statistics. Statistics of Social Welfare Reports for 2009 and 2019. Accessed May 21, 2019. http://ask.rks-gov.net/sq/agjen cia-e-statistikave-te-kosoves/sociale/shendetesia-dhe-mireqenia-sociale.

Kosovo Agency of Statistics. Social Welfare Statistics – Three First Months of 2019. Accessed May 25, 2019. http://ask.rks-gov.net/media/4769/statistikat-e-mir%C3%ABqenies-sociale-tm1-2019.pdf.

Kosovo Agency of Statistics. Labor Force Survey in Kosovo, 2019. Accessed November 18, 2020. https://ask.rks-gov.net/en/kosovo-agency-of-statistics/add-news/labor-force-survey-in-kosovo-2019.

Kosovo Agency of Statistics and the World Bank. Regular Consumption-based Poverty Indicators, 2009–2015. Accessed May 29, 2019. https://ask.rks-gov.net/sq/agjencia-e-statistikave-te-kosoves/sociale/kushtet-e-jeteses.

Kosovo Parliament 2019. Archive of Legislatures, Public Information. Accessed May 28, 2019. https://kuvendikosoves.org/?cid=1,158&legid=5&secid=107.

Kwon Huck-Ju, "Leaving behind the Developmental State: The Changing Rationale of Governance in Korean Governments". In the Korean Government and Public Policies in a Development Nexus: Sustaining Development and Tacking Policy Changes, edited by Jongwon Choi, Huck-Ju Kwon and Min Gyo Koo. Cham: Springer, 2017.

Labour Inspectorate Law (2003), Accessed May 23, 2019. https://unmik.unmissions.org/sites/default/files/regulations/03albanian/A2003regs/RA2003_04.pdf.

Law No. 03/L–212 on Labour. Official Gazette of the Republic of Kosovo.

Mahoney, James. The Legacies of Liberalism: Path-Dependence and Political Regimes in Central America. Baltimore: The Johns Hopkins University Press, 2001.

Mahoney, James and Kathleen Thelen. Explaining Institutional Change: Ambiguity, Agency, and Power. Cambridge: Cambridge University Press, 2010.

Marshall, Thomas H. Citizenship and Social Class. London: Cambridge University Press, 1950.

Ministry of Labor and Social Welfare. Concept Document on Regulating and Managing Pensions and other Social Insurance Benefits, Reform Document, 2018. Accessed May 28, 2019. https://konsultimet.rks-gov.net/viewConsult.php?ConsultationID=40521.

Ministry of Labor and Social Welfare. Concept Document on Social and Family Services, a Reform Document, 2018. Accessed May 26, 2019. https://konsultimet.rks-gov.net/viewConsult.php?ConsultationID=40521.

Ministry of Labor and Social Welfare. Draft Law on Labour, 2018.

Ministry of Labor and Social Welfare. Concept Document on Social Assistance Scheme, Reform Document 2019. Accessed May 28, 2019. https://konsultimet.rks-gov.net/viewConsult.php?ConsultationID=40521.

Ministry of Labor and Social Welfare. Report from the Meeting of the ad-hoc Parliamentary Committee in Prizren, June 26, 2019.

Mustafa, Artan. "The Politics of Citizenship, Social Policy, and State-Building in Kosovo". In Unravelling Liberal Interventionism: Local Critiques of State-Building in Kosovo, edited by Gëzim Visoka and Vjosa Musliu, 162–177. London: Routledge, 2019.

Mustafa, Artan. "Kosovo's Social Policy during Self-Management, UNMIK and Independence". International Journal of Social Welfare, no. 29 (2020): 96–108.

Mustafa, Artan, and Amir Haxhikadrija. "Kosovo: Financing Social Protection". Brussels: European Social Policy Network, 2019.

Occupational Safety, Health and Working Environment Law (2003). Accessed May 23, 2019, https://unmik.unmissions.org/sites/default/files/regulations/03albanian/A2003regs/RA2003_33.pdf.

OECD. "Indicators of Social Protection". 2013. Accessed May 29, 2019. https://www.oecd.org/els/emp/All.pdf.

OECD. "Indicators of Social Protection". Accessed May 23, 2019. https://stats.oecd.org/Index.aspx?DataSetCode=HEALTH_PROT.

Palier, Bruno. "Ambiguous Agreement, Cumulative Change: French Social Policy in the 1980s". In Beyond Continuity, edited by Wolfgang Streeck and Kathleen Thelen, 127–144. Oxford: Oxford University Press, 2005.

Pierson, Paul. "The New Politics of the Welfare State", World Politics 48/2 (1996): 143–179.

Pierson, Paul. "Coping with Permanent Austerity: Welfare State Restructuring in Affluent Democracies", Revue Française de Sociologie 43/2 (2002): 369–406.

Pierson, Paul. Politics in Time. Princeton: Princeton University Press, 2004.

Puljiz, Vlado. "Social Policy of the Post-Yugoslav Countries: Legacy, Transition Problems, Perspectives". In Reframing Social Policy: Actors, Dimensions and Reforms, edited by Maja Gerovska-Mitev, 64–85. Skopje: University "Ss Cyril and Methodius" and Friedrich Ebert Stiftung, 2008.

Skocpol, Theda. Protecting Mothers and Soldiers: The Political Origins of Social Policy in the United States. Cambridge: Harvard University Press, 1995.

Stabilisation and Association Agreement Between the European Union and the European Atomic Energy Community, of the One Part, and Kosovo, of the Other Part. Accessed May 28, 2019. https://data.consilium.europa.eu/doc/document/ST-10728-2015-REV-1/en/pdf.

Stambolieva, Marija. "Kosovo – from State of Welfare Emergency to Welfare State?", Economic Development and Political Transition in Kosovo – Conference, 12–13 October. Prishtina: American University in Kosovo, 2012.

Stambolieva, Marija. "Welfare State Change and Social Citizenship in the Post-Yugoslav States", European Politics and Society 16/3 (2015): 379–394.

Stambolieva, Marija. "Welfare State Transformation in the Yugoslav Successor States: From Social to Unequal". New York: Routledge, 2016.

Streeck, Wolfgang, and Kathleen Thelen. Beyond Continuity. Oxford: Oxford University Press, 2005.

Streeck, Wolfgang. Reforming Capitalism: Institutional Change in the German Political Economy. Oxford: Oxford University Press, 2009.

Ströhle, Isabelle. "Kosovo Liberation Army Veteran's Politics and Contentious Citizenship in Post-War Kosovo". In Transcending Fratricide, edited by Srda Pavlović and Marko Zivkovic, 243–264. Baden-Baden: Nomos, 2013.

Stubbs, Paul and Sinisa Zrinščak, "Citizenship and Social Welfare in Croatia: Clientelism and the Limits of 'Europeanisation'", European Politics and Society 16, no. 3 (2015): 395–410.

Thelen, Kathleen. How Institutions Evolve: The Political Economy of Skills in Germany, Britain, the United States. Cambridge: Cambridge University Press, 2004.

Titmuss, Richard. Social Policy. London: George Allen & Unwin, 1974.

UNMIK Regulations on Essential Labour Law (2001). Accessed May 23, 2019. https://unmik.unmissions.org/sites/default/files/regulations/03albanian/A2003regs/RA2003_04.pdf.

World Bank. Transitional Strategy for Kosovo. Accessed May 1, 2019. https://documents1.worldbank.org/curated/en/796841468270619562/pdf/multi-page.pdf.

World Bank. Project Appraisal Document on a Proposed Trust Fund Grant in the Amount of US$ 4.20 million to UNMIK for the Benefit of Kosovo, Republic of Yugoslavia (Kosovo) for a Social Project. Accessed May 27, 2020. http://documents1.worldbank.org/curated/en/934781468772459727/text/ multiopage.txt.

World Bank. Kosovo Poverty Assessment: Promoting Opportunity, Security, and Participation for All. Accessed May 27, 2020. https://openknowledge.worldbank.org/handle/10986/8650.

World Bank. The Kosovo Pension Reform: Achievements and Lessons. Accessed May 20, 2019. https://socialprotection.org/discover/publications/kosovo-pension-reform-achievements-and-lessons.

World Bank. Kosovo Health Financing Reform Study. Accessed May 27, 2019. https://openknowledge.worldbank.org/bitstream/handle/10986/8121/431830ESW0P10717397B01OFF0USE0ONLY1.pdf?sequence=1&isAllowed=y.

World Bank. Kosovo Public Finance Review. Report. Accessed May 26, 2019. https://openknowledge.worldbank.org/bitstream/handle/10986/20756/ACS93510WP0P130IC00Final0Kosovo0PFR.pdf?sequence=1&isAllowed=y.

World Bank. Rebalancing for a Stronger Growth. Accessed May 20, 2019. https://openknowledge.worldbank.org/bitstream/handle/10986/24399/South0East0Euro0for0stronger0growth.pdf?sequence=1&isAllowed=y .

World Bank. Comments on the MLSW's Concept Document on Regulating and Managing Pensions and Other Social Insurance Benefits, 2018.

World Bank. Kosovo Social Assistance Scheme Study: Assessment and Reform Options. Accessed May 2, 2019. https://documents1.worldbank.org/curated/en/994991557470271998/pdf/Kosovo-Social-Assistance-Scheme-Study-Assessment-and-Reform-Options.pdf.

CHAPTER 6

Developments and Challenges in the Kosovo Pension System

Remzije Istrefi and Ruzhdi Morina

1   Introduction[1]

Kosovo society has undergone dramatic changes in its political, cultural, economic, and social levels due to the overall processes of transition and the long lasting repressive Serbian regime.[2] The legacies of the past have affected all groups of society and the category of elderly people has not been spared either. Nearly all workers and pensioners were deprived of their pension benefits in what were called "special measures" taken by the repressive Milosevic regime at the time, and this issue remains unresolved yet.[3] Pensions in general are intended to ensure that people have sufficient steady income to maintain a standard of living throughout retirement and reduce the risk of poverty among older people.[4] Public pension schemes contain several features that make social exclusion and poverty less or more likely to occur. Therefore, it is highly important for pension systems to be sustainable, both fiscally and politically, in order to achieve the objective of overall support. While much research has been done on the concept, modalities and pension schemes, economic

---

1   The views expressed in this chapter by Remzije Istrefi and Ruzhdi Morina are their personal academic opinions and do not represent any official standpoint. Ruzhdi Morina's elaboration was part of her doctoral research conducted under the mentorship of Professor R. Istrefi at the Faculty of Law, International Law Department, University of Prishtina.
2   On the casualties and repression in Kosovo see Lavinia Stan and Nadia Nedelsky eds., Encyclopedia of Transitional Justice 2 (New York: Cambridge University Press, 2013), 266–279; Independent International Commission on Kosovo, The Kosovo Independent Report: Conflict, International Response, Lessons Learned (Oxford: Oxford University Press, 2004).
3   Paulina Nushi and Laura Nimani, Kosovo Pensioners' 17 years struggle for Serbian Compensation, Prishtina Insight, https://prishtinainsight.com/kosovo-pensioners-17-year-struggle-serbian-compensation-mag/ (accessed October 20, 2020).
4   Andreas Hoff, Tackling Poverty and Social Exclusion of Older People – Lessons from Europe, Working Paper 308 (Oxford: Oxford Institute of Aging, 2008), 1–76.

development, and its impact on pension funds,[5] the functioning of pension schemes and their impact on pensioners in the processes of state system transition still remains an unexplored field.[6] The case of the Kosovo pension system and its peculiarities due to the overall systemic transition, repressive regime and war-related events exemplifies these challenges. The Kosovo pension system prior to the 1999 war was instituted after the Second World War. In 1945 The Law on Implementation of Social Security in the Socialist Federal Republic of Yugoslavia (SFRY) was enacted. This Law had created the central organ of social security at the federal level and the local organs at the level of federal units.[7] Until the 1980s, several other laws had been enacted including the Law on Retirement of State Clerks 1945; Law on Social Security of Employees and Clerks 1946; Law on Social Security of Employees and Clerks and their Families 1950; Law on Health Security 1954, Law on Pension Security 1958, and Law on Disability Security in 1958.

With decree No. 51/56 of SFRY, voluntary security along with the mandatory security was established as well. With the constitutional reforms of 1970, the decentralization of competencies in the field of social security was accepted. The 1972 Law on Basic Rights to Pension and Disability Security defined the basic rights and provided for general principles, whereas federal units had authority to enact their detailed laws and depending on their financial possibilities could provide more favorable conditions. In 1982, at the federal level, a new Law on Pension and Disability Security was approved. This Law provided for harmonization of the laws of federal units, including Kosovo. In the 1980s, the area of social and disability security in Kosovo was regulated mainly by the Law on Pension and Disability Security (Official Gazette of KSAK, no. 26/83, 26/86, 11/88)

---

5 On the concept and understanding of the pensions see Martin Sullivan, Understanding Pensions (New York: Rutledge, 2004), 5–43. On developments and restructuring of the pension funds see Anusic Zoran, "Administrative Charges of Private Mandatory Pension Funds", Presentation for ILO Tripartite Conference on "Recent Developments on Pension Restructuring in Central and Eastern Europe", Budapest, December 2004; Agnieszka Chlon-Dominczak, Funded Pensions in Transition Economies in Europe and Central Asia: Design and Experience, Kiev, Ukraine, International Federation of Pension Funds Association (FIAP) and World Bank, 2003.

6 See however, Isabel Ortiz, Fabio Durán-Valverde, Stefan Urban and Veronika Wodsak eds., Reversing Pension Privatizations: Rebuilding Public Pension Systems in Eastern Europe and Latin America (Geneva: International Labour Organization, 2018), 33–36; Nicolae Balteş and Jimon Ştefania Amalia, "Considerations Regarding the Pension Systems in Countries of Central and Eastern Europe", "Ovidius" University Annals, Economic Sciences Series 18, no. 2 (2018), 94–99.

7 Adil Fetahi, Qerim Zariqi, Monograph of the Kosovo Pensioners League (Prishtinë: Editor Kosovo League of Pensioners and Occupational Invalids, 2013), 12.

and the Statute of the self-governing association of the interest of pension and disability security (Official Gazette of KSAK, no. 44/83 and 6/88). These two laws defined the rights, liabilities, terms, and criteria to benefit from the pension system. The Pension System in Kosovo, by the 1990s, had reached a quite high social and human standard. It was a pension system based on PAYG (generation financing generation) concept, and it also had many other social components. However, it lacked a universal character, because it did not cover all citizens who reached retirement age, but only those pensioners who had a minimum period of pension contribution payments (at least 15 years). In 1998 prior to the war, the overall number of evidenced pensioners in Kosovo was 88,901.[8]

From the 1990s up to the end of the 1999 war, in Kosovo the pension system in reality did not function because it was understaffed; in fact, few Albanian employees worked during this period. They were expelled by the then repressive Serbian regime due to discriminatory policies toward Albanian workers along with those from other communities who did not agree with the repressive regime.[9] Consequently, pension contributions were not paid at all, even if individuals had been working.[10] In this period, the payment of pensions was interrupted and later the European Court for Human Rights, adjudicating over an individual case of a Kosovar, ascertained that the arbitrary interruption of pension payments was done in contradiction to international conventions and laws in force and also constitutes a human rights violation.[11]

With the end of war, in June 1999, Kosovo was placed under the international administration of United Nations Mission in Kosovo (UNMIK), according to UNSC Resolution 1244.[12] With UNMIK regulation 1999/1, the entire legislative and executive powers, as well as the administration of justice, were exercised

---

8   Ibid., 24–38.
9   Richard Nelsson, How Milosevic Stripped Kosovo's Autonomy – Archive, 1989, "The Guardian", March 20, 2019, https://www.theguardian.com/world/from-the-archive-blog/2019/mar/20/how-milosevic-stripped-kosovos-autonomy-archive-1989 (accessed October 20, 2020). On the detailed account of Kosovo war see Mark Weller, Contested Statehood: Kosovo's Struggle for Independence (Oxford University Press, 2009); Noel Malcolm, Kosovo: A Short History (New York: New York University Press, 1999).
10 Adil Fetahi, Qerim Zariqi, Monograph of the Kosovo Pensioners League, 49.
11 During the 90s, Serbia had interrupted payment of pensions with the justification of not collecting pension contributions and being unable to pay them. This interruption of pension payments by the Court of Strasbourg (the case of Lutfije and Mahmut Grudiqi, former residents in Mitrovicë, Kosovo) has been ascertained that it presents violation of human rights. In this case the Court has obliged the state of Serbia to pay pensions and compensate the inflicted damages. See European Court for Human Rights, Grudic v Serbia: ECHR 17 April 2012, 31925/08, [2012] ECHR 708, https://tinyurl.com/2p987vf2 (accessed October 15, 2020).
12 UN Security Council Resolution 1244, 1999, https://unmik.unmissions.org/sites/default/files/old_dnn/Res1244ENG.pdf (accessed September 21, 2020).

by the Special Representative of the Secretary General (SRSG).[13] Under UNMIK regulation 2001/35 the Pension System in Kosovo was established as a new and unique pension system[14] and unbound from the previous system (PAYG) applicable in Kosovo up to 1999.[15] The provisions of UNMIK regulation 2001/35 continue to be implemented, and has been complemented with Kosovo legislation approved by Kosovo institutions, after the declaration of Kosovo's independence on February 17, 2008.[16] Currently, the Pension System in Kosovo consists of three basic pillars and pensions for specific categories, which are regulated by particular laws. The Pension System in Kosovo, by the nature of its funding, is separated into schemes funded by the state, which in theory are non-funding schemes as they are not self-funding, and the second and third pillar, which are funded schemes as they are foreseen to be self-funded. As such, the pension system can be separated into the first pillar that is funded from taxes, known as the pension scheme, funded by the state (for research purposes it is noted as the first pillar); the second mandatory pillar (where the Pension Savings Fund of Kosovo functions); and the third voluntary pillar (where private pension funds can operate) that are funded by pension contributions. In the next sections of this study, we shall explain the functioning of these schemes that form the multi-pillar pension system in Kosovo with an analytic approach through focusing on the main challenges, and its advantages and disadvantages.

The aim of the chapter is to reveal and critically examine peculiarities of the Kosovo pension system introduced by the UN administration and the main challenges in its implementation in practice by the Kosovo authorities. The main question addressed by this research is: Is the newly established multi-pillar pension system – based on modern principles – adequate for a post-war setting such as Kosovo? Through answering this question, we aim to propose an adequate pension model that will provide a social standard and the inclusion of all categories of pensioners in Kosovo.

The study employs a comparative methodology carefully analyzing the theoretical and legal framework governing the pension schemes, EU standards related to the pension schemes, information, and data available on institutional reports, various books and articles, and other reports by international organizations.

---

13 UNMIK Regulation 1999/1 dated 25/06/1999 for Authorizations of Interim Administration in Kosovo, https://unmik.unmissions.org/sites/default/files/regulations/02english/E1999regs/RE1999_01.htm (accessed October 19, 2020).
14 John Gubbels, David Snelbecker and Lena Zezulin, The Kosovo Pension Reform: Achievements and Lessons, SP Discussion Paper 707 (Washington, DC: World Bank Group, 2007).
15 On Pensions in Kosovo, Regulation 2001/35 dated 22 December 2001.
16 UNMIK Regulation 2001/35, UNMIK Regulation 2005/20, and Law No. 04/ L-131 on Pension Schemes Funded by the State (LSPFSH), LFPK, Chapter II, III, IV and V.

2   Breaking with the Past – Effectiveness of the Pension System in Kosovo

With the end of the 1999 war, UNMIK introduced a new pension system in Kosovo unbound entirely from the previous system (PAYG), and based on practices and ideas promoted by the World Bank for a pension system with multi pillars, as a global trend.[17] The first pension pillar, or as it is otherwise known as the basic pension funded by the state, introduces a general pension scheme with social elements, aiming to protect persons reaching 65 years of age from poverty. All Kosovo residents who have reached the retirement age and meet the terms and criteria set by Law No. 04/L-131on Pension Schemes Financed by the State (LPSFS) can benefit from this scheme.[18] The basic pension scheme is based on the Beveridegean concept of social welfare and is entirely funded by the state budget. The pensions based on this pillar are funded by the state, otherwise known as non-funded pensions.[19] This pillar is universal in character and the beneficiaries of this scheme are all persons who reach 65 years of age, and also meet the criteria stipulated by the Law on Pension Scheme Financed by the State.[20] This scheme funds the basic state pension, contributory age pensions,[21] disability pensions, early pensions, family pensions and occupational invalid pensions, pensions of categories that emerged out of war and other schemes that can be created.[22] At the outset this pension system did not provide a sustainable solution for all pensioners mainly due to low pensions and the lack of a relation between these pensions and the pension contributions paid before 1999.[23]

---

17   Adil Fetahi, Qerim Zariqi, Monograph of the Kosovo Pensioner's League, 56.
18   Law No. 04/L-131 on Pension Schemes Financed by the State (LPSFS), https://gzk.rks-gov.net/ActDetail.aspx?ActID=9517%20 (accessed September 11, 2020).
19   Non-funded schemes are pension schemes funded by the state budget – so they are not self-funded for more information see European Commission, Classification of Funded Pension Schemes and Impact on Government Finance, 4 (Luxembourg: Publications of the European Communities, 2004), 4, https://ec.europa.eu/eurostat/documents/3859598/5884325/KS-BE-04-002-EN.PDF/ccfc8b5a-a45e-4444-b467-3d2e1cab8d7e (accessed April 25, 2020).
20   Law No. 04/L-131 on Pension Scheme Financed by the State, Supra note 17, Articles 7–12.
21   Contributory age pensions are pensions related to pension contribution before 1999, Beneficiaries of this pension can be citizens who have at least 15 years of paid pension contributions. Contributory pensions prior to 1999 have been paid since 2012.
22   Law No. 04/L-131 on Pension Scheme Financed by the State, Supra note 17. Article 1, paragraph 1.
23   The discrimination and the violation of the pensioner's rights continued even after the war, with the new pension system. See Adil Fetahi, Qerim Zariqi, Monograph of Pensioners League of Kosovo, 56.

In general, the first pillar introduces a model of pension schemes that in terms of financing modality (only by state budget) is not very widespread in the European Union (EU). Public pension schemes in the EU and the region are mainly contributive and part of pension contributions goes to finance the basic pensions of the first pillar and part goes to second or the third pillar, as obligatory or voluntary individual pension contributions/ savings.[24] In contrast, in cases of the basic pension systems, financed only by the state, the first and the second pillars are related to a pension general income of 60–70% of the salary.[25] Therefore, placement of a contributive system creates a pension fund that finances pensions and usually only the deficit is covered by the state.

In Kosovo, there are considerable varieties of pensions for special categories, such as categories that emerged out of the 1998/99 war and other special categories, due to the processes of transformation in the country.[26] These schemes are placed to financially support special categories, conditioned by their (un)employment status, since the benefits from these pensions are possible only when members of these categories are unemployed (an exception are disabled veterans, who receive a pension even if they are employed).[27] Inclusion of these categories in the pension system of the country complicated the reform of the pension system. A clear legal and fiscal separation in terms of social expenses and benefits of different categories and pensions that result from the work relation is needed in Kosovo. In this context, a sustainable pension plan could easily be designed for everyone that works, whereas social expenses and other benefits of different categories would be covered by the state budget without implicating pension contributions.

---

24 European Commission, Pension Schemes and Pension Projections in the EU-27 Member States – 2008–2060, 1. Occasional Papers 56, October 2009, https://ec.europa.eu/economy_finance/publications/pages/publication16034_en.pdf (accessed October 15, 2020).

25 Ibid, on the different models of financing pension schemes in different EU member states.

26 In Kosovo there are pensions for categories that emerged out of the Kosovo Liberation Army (KLA) war of 1998/99, former members of the Kosovo Protection Corps (KPC) after its transformation and former employees of the 'Trepça' mine facility.

27 Law No. 04/L-054 on the Status and Rights of Martyrs, Invalids, Veterans, Members of Kosovo Liberation Army, Civilian Victims and their Families, https://gzk.rks-gov.net/ActDetail.aspx?ActID=2793 (accessed October 19, 2020); Law No. 04/L-261 on Kosovo Liberation Army War Veterans, https://gzk.rks-gov.net/ActDetail.aspx?ActID=14581 (accessed October 19, 2020); Law No. 03/L-100 on the Pensions for Kosovo Protection Corps Members, https://tinyurl.com/2p97m3sw (accessed October 25, 2020).

Placing a universal age pension system in the first pillar was followed with the establishment of a second pillar with a mandatory pension scheme, with the concept of defined contributions as its basis (Defined Contribution), which is administered by the Pension Savings Fund of Kosovo[28] and the third pillar, as a voluntary scheme for supplementary pensions. The third pillar was also a novel concept for employees and Kosovo society in general, and due to the lack of information on its functioning a number of dilemmas as well as much debate arose, which continues to date.[29] Placement of a new market-based pension system has not been supported by education programs for employees on the functioning of these pension schemes and their relevance for each individual. Another shortcoming is the lack of clarity on which age groups the second pillar applies to and for which age groups it is not applicable. Hence, clarity should have been provided because individuals need to contribute for a period of about 30 years before a realistic return is generated from second pillar Pension Funds. Non-implementation of the provision which defined that only individuals under 46 years of age were required to be part of the second pillar, led to discrimination against the middle generation, which had not reached a required period of contributions (30 years) before retirement age and do not meet the criteria to benefit from the contributory pension of the first pillar. Furthermore, they are discriminated against in relation to the older generation (which meet their contributory criteria of 15 years before the war) and the new generations, which might manage to contribute to the Kosovo Pension Savings Trust (KPST) for around 30 years or more. The practice of defining modalities on how the second pillar is applied for certain age groups has been applied in almost all the reform of pension systems processes throughout the EU and region, and a broadly similar definition should have been undertaken in Kosovo as well.

In contrast to Kosovo, countries like Croatia, Macedonia and Slovenia put a multi-pillar pension system in place but preserving the PAYG system, whereas countries like Serbia, Montenegro and Bosnia and Herzegovina preserved the PAYG system and created legal preconditions for the third voluntary pillar (Table 6.1).[30]

28　The Kosovo Pension Savings Trust is a public independent non-profit institution, established in 2001, with UNMIK regulation 2001/35 of 2001. KPST is established according to the concept of defined pension contributions, which means that each contributor saves for his pension in a personal account. See UNMIK Regulation 2001/35, https://www.atk-ks.org/wp-content/uploads/2017/11/Regulation_2001_35.pdf (accessed September 21, 2020).

29　Fazli Kajtazi, Crossroads of Kosovo Pensioners (Prishtinë: BSPK 2010), 101–103, 145–150; Adil Fetahi, Qerim Zariqi, Monograph of the Kosovo Pensioners League, 56.

30　Expert Group on Gender Equality and Social Inclusion, Health and Long-Term Care Issues (EGGSI), "The Socio-Economic Impact of Pension Systems on the Respective Situations

TABLE 6.1 Pension systems in the region

Country	Pension system	First pillar	Second pillar	Third pillar	Pension contribution	First pillar	Second pillar
Croatia	Multi-pillar	PAYG	Mandatory	Voluntary	20%	15%	5%
North Macedonia	Multi-pillar	PAYG	Mandatory	Voluntary	18%	12%	6%
Montenegro	PAYG + Voluntary	PAYG	NA	Voluntary	21.5%	21.5%	NA
Serbia	PAYG + Voluntary	PAYG	NA	Voluntary	26%	26%	NA
Albania	PAYG + Voluntary	PAYG	NA	Voluntary	21.6%	21.6%	NA
Kosovo	Multi-pillar	Universal	Mandatory	Voluntary	10%	NA	10%

SOURCE: OWN ELABORATION BASED ON MILIVOJE RADOVIĆ, ROGIC SUNCICA AND BOŽO CEROVIĆ, "INFLUENCE OF DEMOGRAPHIC TRENDS AND EMPLOYMENT ON THE FINANCIAL SUSTAINABILITY OF THE MONTENEGRIN PENSION SYSTEM", ZBORNIK RADOVA EKONOMSKOG FAKULTETA U ISTOCNOM SARAJEVU 15 (2017): 39–47; HABIL MUSTAFAI, "PENSION SYSTEM REFORM IN THE REPUBLIC OF MACEDONIA", INTERNATIONAL REFEREED SCIENTIFIC JOURNAL VISION 2, NO. 1 (2017): 69–78, HTTP://VISIONJOURNAL.EDU.MK/WP-CONTENT/UPLOADS/2017/07/IRSJV_V2I1_HABIL.PDF;EDU. MK/WP-CONTENT/UPLOADS/2017/07/IRSJV_V2I1_HABIL.PDF (ACCESSED SEPTEMBER 25, 2020); SOCIAL INSURANCE INSTITUTE OF ALBANIA, HTTP://WWW.ISSH.GOV.AL/?PAGE_ID=6814&LANG=EN (ACCESSED OCTOBER 25, 2020); ESPN THEMATIC REPORT: ASSESSMENT OF PENSION ADEQUACY IN SERBIA 2017, HTTPS://TINYURL.COM/P58BTXPZ (ACCESSED OCTOBER 25, 2020); LAW NO. 04/L-101 ON PENSION FUNDS IN KOSOVO, ARTICLE 6, HTTPS://WWW.ATK-KS.ORG/WP-CONTENT/UPLOADS/2017/11/LAW-NO.-04-L-101.PDF (ACCESSED OCTOBER 23, 2020). HTTP://VISIONJOURNAL.EDU.MK/WP-CONTENT/UPLOADS/2017/07/IRSJV_V2I1_HABIL.PDF.

It can be concluded that the lack of awareness in the area of pensions, (particularly for market-based concepts, such as DC Pension Funds), the previous pension practice during the existence of FRY, familiarity with the previous

---

of Women and Men and the Effects of Recent Trends in Pension Reforms", Synthesis Report, May 9, 2011, http://www.praxis.ee/wp-content/uploads/2014/03/2011-Socio-economic-impact-of-pension-systems-of-women-and-men.pdf (accessed September 25, 2020); IOPS, "Country Profiles – FYRO Macedonia", http://www.iopsweb.org/principles guidelines/40561423.pdf (accessed September 25, 2020); Milivoje Radović, Rogic Suncica and Božo Cerović, "Influence of Demographic Trends and Employment on the Financial Sustainability of the Montenegrin Pension System", Zbornik radova Ekonomskog fakulteta u Istocnom Sarajevu 15 (2017): 39–47; Law No. 04/ L-101 on Pension Funds in Kosovo, Article 6, https://gzk.rks-gov.net/ActDetail.aspx?ActID=13269 (accessed October 23, 2020).

PAYG pension system as well as the period of around 10 years without a functioning pension system have contributed to societal expectations for a pension system similar to the one of former Yugoslavia just as most of the other former federation countries have adopted.

3   The Mandatory Second Pillar Pension and Its Impact on Pension Value

In a few aspects the second pillar pension, a mandatory scheme according to the defined contribution concept implemented in Kosovo, is in line or even ahead of other EU member states. In EU member states defined benefit (DB) continues to dominate the pension schemes concept, however in recent years there has been an increasing trend towards defined contribution schemes (DC).[31] In both DB and DC concepts, the accumulated pension contributions are invested aiming to generate a return (increase) from investment. Investment of these means indicates that these means are exposed to the risk of financial markets.

These two concepts, apart from others, differ in who should bear the risk from investments, the employee or the employer. In defined contribution schemes, the risk from investments and shifts in financial markets is borne by the employee, whereas in defined benefit schemes the risk from investments and shifts in financial markets is borne by the employers (founders of pension fund).[32] Indeed, the level of contributions and returns from investments are the parameters which determine the pension value.

These elements are more relevant when salaries are at a low level, such as in the case of Kosovo, where low salaries are characteristic for both the public and private sector. Therefore, employees and trade unions must be encouraged continuously to aim for a contribution level in order not to remain only at the necessary minimum, but to achieve a contribution that would guarantee employees welfare after retirement. Pension contributions accumulated in a Pension Fund according to applicable legislation must be invested aiming to provide a return on investments. Risks that result from exposure to financial markets are one of the factors that must be assessed fairly and professionally

---

31   See more at Willis Towers Watson, "Global Pension Assets Study 2016", https://tinyurl.com/2p9ddyd4 (accessed September 09, 2020).

32   EFAMA, Define-Contribution pension schemes, 2008, 48–49, https://www.efama.org/Publications/Public/Long-Term_Savings_and_Pension_Steering_Committee/oxera_report.pdf (accessed September 19, 2020).

by the Pension Fund in order to provide an adequate return on investment. Apart from financial risks, Pension Funds (particularly mandatory public ones) also face legal and political risks due to frequent and continuous changes of legislation and policies.

This aspect, apart from positive impacts, can also have negative impacts, by creating uncertainty for contributors and by the constant possibility of nationalization of the fund through systemic changes. This is a continuous risk which can only be managed by active citizens. Examples of state interference by nationalizing the Fund entirely or partially have already occurred in Poland in 2011, where the Fund was partially nationalized and in Hungary in 2010,[33] where the Fund was entirely nationalized.

The results of pension funds are viewed over the long-term, and are characterized not only by continuous fluctuations, drops in periods of financial crisis (the crisis of 2008) but also financial markets in general and KPST in particular have resulted in a positive performance. KPST, since its establishment has had a positive performance of 41.41%. These results, apart from short-term fluctuations in financial markets (such as the case with global crisis of 2008/9 and also the difficulties of 2011 and the end of 2018) remain the strongest argument that in the long term the financial markets show continuous growth and consequently the investment of pension funds also generating positive results. However, due to strong public pressure and a large number of regulations in many cases (such as in the case of KPST) quite conservative investment strategies are made, and they exceed inflation only with difficulty. Pension Funds according to the DC concept aim to invest accumulated pension contributions in a manner that allows for greater security (low or moderate risk) to generate the highest possible return from investments. Diversification of investments (classes, products, financial instruments, and geographic diversification), aims to reduce exposure to risks and can only be achieved by accepting a lower return on investments.[34]

Countries regulate or define principles and limits with respective legislation on the way that pension contributions are invested.[35] Investment

---

33 Martin T. Bohl, Judith Lischewski and Svitlana Voronkova, "Pension Funds' Performance in Strongly Regulated Industries in Central Europe: Evidence from Poland and Hungary" Emerging Markets Finance and Trade 47 (2010), 80–94.
34 EFAMA, Define-Contribution Pension Schemes, 48–49.
35 Law on KPST, Article 9. In compliance with legislation and regulations applied, KPST makes investments through the managers of means (asset managers), who are selected in an international public procedure. The Steering Board priory decides in relation to classes and instruments where it wants to invest. After this decision, the public procedure

of pensions, through the greatest possible diversification, should result in improved security and a reasonable return on investment. All this also fulfills the principle for the fund to have adequate liquidity. In general, these are also internationally accepted and applied principles for pension fund investment.[36] EU Directives, but also Kosovo legislation require that the responsible officials who take decisions must be professional, credible and responsible (prudent person principle).[37] Figure 6.1 shows the change to unit price over the span of 20 years.

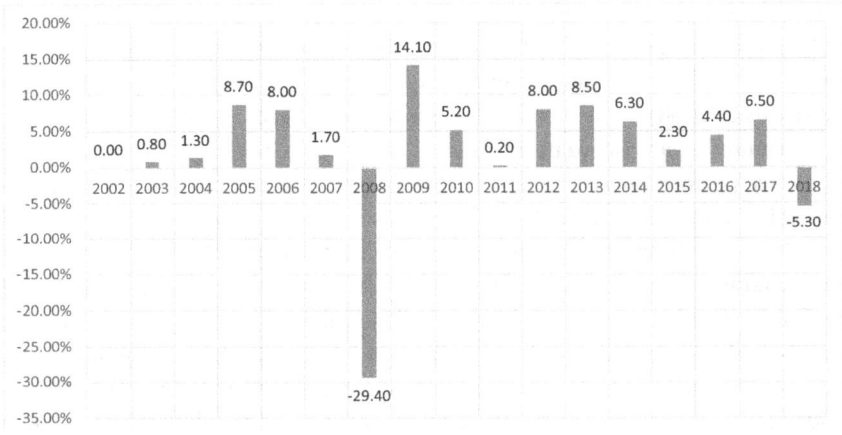

FIGURE 6.1 Annual changes to unit price 2002–2018 (in %)
SOURCE: KOSOVO PENSION SAVING TRUST, ANNUAL RETURNS AND CASH-FLOWS 2002–2020, HTTP://HTTPS://TINYURL.COM/MS9DUVPB (ACCESSED SPETEMBER 19, 2020).

is developed to obtain the most favourable and secure offer. Before taking the decision to select the asset manager, all risk assessments are made according to the investment manual and not only, the performance shown, and other aspects are analysed to fulfil the principles and legal limitation completely. Principles of investments are mainly focused but not limited to: "Security of pension fund, variety of investments, maximal profit in compliance with security of maximal fund and maintenance of adequate liquidity." KPST is obliged to build the strategy of investments in compliance with these principles and with limits set by legislation, as in the aspect of classes where they can be invested and also in limitations concerning one single issuer.

36 EFAMA, Define-Contribution Pension Schemes, 49–50.
37 For more information, refer to Article 18, of Directive 2003/41/EC of the European Parliament and of the Council of 3 June 2003 on the Activities and Supervision of Institutions for Occupational Retirement Provision go to https://tinyurl.com/bdhd4dye (accessed August 19, 2020); Law on KPST, Article 4, paragraph 4.3 and 4.4, https://gzk.rks-gov.net/ActDetail.aspx?ActID=13269 (accessed October 23, 2020).

In the figure above it can be seen that the performance of KPST since its establishment is positive, but in various periods it had strong oscillations. The value of pensions contributions suffered a significant decrease from the effects of the 2008 economic crisis which affected persons retiring in that period. It took the KPST almost six years to recover back to its position before the 2008 crisis. After the crisis of 2008, the value of contributions also suffered a decrease in 2018 by around 5% that can be dissipated also in depreciation results of around two years of operation. It can be concluded that for over 15 years of operation, almost half of the period went on recovering from negative movements in the value of pension contributions. Whilst the annual return of KPST since its establishment is around 43.32% inflation or the consumer price index in Kosovo is 36.21% reducing the value of this gain. Thus, despite positive figures from returns on investments, taking the crisis of 2008 as a reference point and the inflation for this period into consideration, it can be concluded that KPST has mostly preserved the value of pension contributions rather than realized or is in the process of realizing an increase in the value of pension contributions. Therefore, pension funds must have a strategy and policies that protect their value from short-term fluctuations and thereby protect individuals as they approach retirement age from the risk of sudden large decreases in the value of their pensions, such was the case with the crisis of 2008 and market falls at the end of 2018.

It should be emphasized that in contrast to the second pillar, the third pillar pension scheme provides for the pension funds of an employer and an individual, as complementary pensions. Both these pension models can function as DC or DB, depending on what pension model is licensed. These pension funds are supervised by the Central Bank of Kosovo (CBK) and they function according to applicable legislation and regulations drafted by CBK. The development of the pension funds in this pillar, to date, has not been satisfactory. This is the result of the low average income level in the country. Additional contributions in excess of the legal minimum of 5% that an employee or institution might wish to make can be placed in the second pillar KPST.[38]

In the third voluntary pillar there is the Slovenian–Kosovan Pension Fund (SKPF), licensed to manage the complementary funds of employer and also to

---

38   Law No. 04/L-101 on Pension Funds in Kosovo, Article 6, https://gzk.rks-gov.net/ActDetail.aspx?%20ActID=13269 (accessed October 23, 2020).

provide individual complementary pensions.[39] The value of assets under the management of SKPF on December 31, 2018 was about EUR 7 million in value, with about 4,000 contributors.[40] SKPF administers pension means according to the DC concept, in compliance with regulations of management and supervision, set by CBK, as the competent authority for licensing, supervision and setting regulations for investments.[41] Positive legislation in Kosovo regulates the way investments are made in the third pillar pension. Invested means are exposed to similar financial risks to the pension savings in SKPF. As pension funds or operators of the third pillar are licensed by CBK, they are subject to more strict supervision by the CBK since in this case the entire responsibility falls on CBK, as the regulator and supervisory authority. Apart from risks in financial markets (possible negative returns) these means should not face other legal risks or risks of another nature, as they are voluntary savings.[42]

4 A New Pension Model in Kosovo and the Problems It Should Address

Pension reforms must focus on the following factors, specifically demographic projections, the high unemployment rate, informality, the level of salaries, and emigration. Certainly, the pension reforms must initially aim to make a clear separation of pensions and other benefits for different categories in society. Pension reforms must also relate the role of state and market, by placing a contributory pension which would stimulate longer work periods and the highest payment of contributions. Above all, the pension system should be modelled having the individual and their role as its basis. Placement of a basic NDC scheme followed with a DC mandatory scheme in the second pillar as well as by developing more active policies which prompt development of the third voluntary pillar would have the individual in a key role. Along with institutional reform, the education of citizens related to their role in projection of their social future is a prerogative. Citizens should expect that the state creates the preconditions, legislation, and an adequate policy, but the role of

---

39 Law No. 04/l-10 on Pension Funds in Kosovo, Chapter IV, https://gzk.rks-gov.net/ActDetail.aspx?ActID=13269 (accessed October 23, 2020).
40 Fondi Slloveno Kosovar i Pensioneve, http://www.fondipensional.com/english/index_eng.html (accessed October 24, 2020).
41 Law No. 04/l-10 on Pension Funds in Kosovo, Chapter IV (Articles 13–24), https://gzk.rks-gov.net/ActDetail.aspx?ActID=13269 (accessed October 23, 2020).
42 Law No. 04/l-101 on Pension Funds in Kosovo, https://gzk.rks-gov.net/ActDetail.aspx?ActID=13269 (accessed October 23, 2020).

the individual is crucial as well. The individuals' active role is expressed by working continuously, working longer than the legal retirement age, when possible, by paying more contributions than the legal minimum and being part of voluntary pension schemes. This concept of an active citizen is a global trend, and institutions and social partners must engage continuously in education and raising awareness of the importance of pension systems. The demographic transition in Kosovo is presented in Table 6.2.

TABLE 6.2   Kosovo population according to age groups and year

Years	Population by age				Population by age in %			
	Total	0–14	15–64	65+	Total	0–14	15–64	65+
2017	1,783,531	446,633	1,192,181	144,718	100	25	67	8
2021	1,809,458	431,526	1,211,592	166,341	100	24	67	9
2031	1,818,674	364,294	1,217,592	236,787	100	20	67	13
2041	1,759,492	290,436	1,150,779	318,277	100	17	65	18
2051	1,652,090	247,855	1,034,147	370,088	100	15	63	22
2061	1,492,192	199,518	892,803	399,871	100	13	60	27

SOURCE: OWN ELABORATION BASED ON KOSOVO AGENCY STATISTICS, KOSOVO POPULATION PROJECTION 2017–2061, 2017, 21, HTTPS://ASK.RKS-GOV.NET/MEDIA/3925/PARASHIKIMI-I-POPULLSIS%C3%AB-2017-2061.PDF (ACCESSED AUGUST 18, 2020).

The above analysis reveals that the current Kosovo pension system encounters several deficiencies: it fails to address appropriately contributive pensions; it fails to address appropriately the impact of "the age – contribution period" factor; it does not provide security to the second pillar; and it does not have sufficient active policies to prompt development of the third pillar.

In this context and to address the issue of pensions in Kosovo clearly and in the long-term, a multi pillar system should be implemented that first of all has a separation from the social protection scheme, a pension system that provides funds for current pensions and is related to the role of the individual (individualized) and market based. A pension model that enhances the role of the state and strengthens the role of individual is in accordance with modern trends, with demographic developments and can be a long-term solution.

In the scheme below (Table 6.3), we present a model of the pension system that we believe addresses the problems encountered by the current pension

TABLE 6.3 Pension system model recommended to be applied in Kosovo

Social protection	Pension system		
	Contributive pension scheme		Third pillar
I. Contributive pensions for persons that have worked before 1999 II. Universal age-related benefits for citizens that have not worked after 1999 III. Other benefits for other categories	First pillar NDC I. Contributive pensions for persons that have worked after 2000 II. Other pensions e.g. disability, family related to pension contributions after 2000	Second pillar DC Organized according to DC principle with a minimum guaranteed return	I. Pension funds of employers II. Individual pension plans provided by licenced operators
Funding	**Funding**	**Funding**	**Funding**
From state budget 100%	From pension contributions and the applied growth rate	From pension contribution and return from investments	From pension contribution and return from investments

SOURCE: THE MODEL PROPOSED BY AUTHORS.

scheme and provides a sustainable solution in the long-term context. Initially, the new pension system should be separated from pensions that are not generated from the employment relations as a basis or did not contribute to the current pension system. Thus the pension system would address the long-term needs of employees that contribute and consequently the social burden that creates instabilities on the pension system will be eliminated.

The model proposed above is based on international trends and practices, which continuously combine the role of the state and the market, and the role of companies and individuals. A relation of these factors emerges mainly due to lessons from the past. The economic crisis of 2008 demonstrated that we cannot have a pension system depending only on market-based pension models, since such a crisis can significantly harm groups of citizens, who retire in crisis periods and we can easily reach a moment when, even the category of people who had worked and contributed for years, become a burden on social schemes. On the one hand, a pension system based only on PAYG contributions or state funding lacks financial sustainability, and the state must redistribute pension contributions to citizens who are not receiving the benefits they deserve, or to specific groups determined on the basis of the redistribution principle.

This remains dependent on the 'political will' of different governments, which depending also on political orientations, might change the pension systems, since the pension system depends on state subsidy. On the other hand, the development of an active prompting policy might have an impact on the development of the Pension Funds of employers and encourage citizens to be a part of individual pension plans. In this context, inevitably there is a need for two reform processes. The first is systemic reform by changing the institutional structure and the pension and parametric system, by setting adequate values of pension contributions and by distributing adequately to first, second and eventually to the third pillar. The second reform is to appropriately address the transitional period of certain age groups.

An aspect that must be addressed is the clear separation between social protection and the responsibility of the state for different social categories (categories that emerged from war, contributive pensioners before 1999 etc.) and the pension system. The pension system must be related only to benefits that result from work relation and pension contributions. Other benefits, of those who did not work, categories that emerged from war and other categories must be treated as social protection and as benefits due to their contribution and institutional transformations that have occurred. These benefits must be exclusively covered by the state budget only and not to be even a competence of institutions that deal with pensions. The universal system of old-age pensions, which is designed to provide protection from poverty, as well as a considerable number of pension schemes, which do not have any relation to work relation and contributions, should be grouped under the social protection scheme of other benefits. The categories that emerged from the war and other categories of benefits that are provided for former Kosovo Protection Corps members, former pensioners of the 'Trepça' mines and other similar categories could also be considered here. Benefits from this category should be recognized as social benefits and benefits for special categories and the term pension avoided, because it does not have any relation to contribution and the work relation. Also included in this category can be the scheme for protection from unemployment, care toward family and children and other similar categories. Inserted into this category must also be contributive pensioners, as the current pension system does not have any fund financed by their contributions. While the matter of pension contributions prior to 1999 remains a political issue, expenses for this category should be covered only by the state.

The voluntary Pension Funds of employers and licensed operators that can provide individual pension plans could operate in the third pillar. Aiming to prompt the development of this scheme, it is preferable to review and analyze the possibility that at least 2% of contributions go in this scheme, leaving the possibility for employees to decide within a year if they wish to be part of any Pension Fund or to be a part of any individual pension plan. Nonetheless, in order not to encroach on the voluntary character of this scheme, the possibility must exist for the employee to declare within a year if they do not want to be a part of any scheme provided in this pillar by deciding that the mandatory contribution of 2% should go either into the first or into the second pillar of the mandatory contributive scheme. This element could give individuals the possibility to decide for themselves which scheme they wish to be their basic pension scheme: the contributive one with the PAYG element or the NDC. The proposed 2% pension contribution in the third pillar aims to enable social partners through collective contracts or other forms, along with the employer and voluntarily, to contribute to this scheme up to a maximum of 5%. At the same time, the Pension Funds as well as other operators could play an active role by promoting these pension schemes so that they would have a guaranteed initial capital.

5   Contributive Schemes, First and Second Pillar

The implementation of a contributive scheme with pillars within it would be a novelty to the Pension System of Kosovo and broadly speaking captures positive elements of PAYG schemes, schemes funded by the state, schemes following the DC concept and DC market-based schemes, by providing a relation between these two elements to ensure a sustainable pension over the entire life. The basic reason why there is a necessity to relate these two schemes lies in the security level required to eliminate risks that could emerge from financial markets and the balanced role of the state and the individual. With this scheme, the state bears the risk for a sustainable pension and the guaranteed return on investments, whereas on the other hand the state is allowed to utilize and redistribute the accumulated means in the Pension Fund of first pillar in order to cover the needs for pensions in the social protection scheme. In order for this scheme to function, the level of pension contributions in Kosovo should be harmonized with regional practices and it should be increased from 10% as it is today to at least 15% with a possibility of increase up to 17%, similarly to countries in the region and EU practices.[43] Only with this increase of the contribution level, will our pension system regain a similar level to the region and EU countries. In this context, then essential reform must include placement of a contributive system for the first and second pillar, with a pension contribution rate of at least 15%. This rate of pension contribution is to be distributed with 7.5% to go in the first pillar and 7.5% to go in the second pillar. The first pillar is to function according to the National Defined Contribution (NDC) principle,[44] whereas the second pillar is to be organized according to the DC concept, with hybrid elements and a guaranteed return, respectively increasing the value of pension contributions. The retirement age should show an increasing trend, and to allow the possibility that with the consent of employers, individuals will be able to work even beyond this age. This would decrease time (lifespan) after retirement (and hence the number of years a pension would be paid for), and thereby guarantee a more sustainable pension. Both of these pillars must be related on appointment of the pension level, by taking the average salary as a basis along with the employment period, level of contribution and both of

---

43 The average of pension contribution levels in OECD countries is 15.4% in public schemes, whereas it is 10.7% in voluntary schemes. This indicates that on average in public and voluntary schemes employees in OECD countries pay over 20%. See more at OECD, Pensions at a Glance 2017 (Paris: OECD, 2017), 140–141, http://dx.doi.org/10.1787/pension_glance-2017-en (accessed October 20, 2020).

44 NDC National Defined Contributions are pension systems that introduce a relation between the PAYG and DC pension systems. In these systems, pension contributions go to a national account and personal evidence is kept for contributions paid by the employee. Accumulated contributions can be utilized by State for its needs to pay current pensions or similar, but unlike PAYG systems, for these contributions a level of increase is applied according to a defined formula where usually economic growth is taken into account. On reaching retirement age, the employee's contribution is verified, the amount is adjusted accordingly, and an individualized pension is defined. This pension model prompts employment and motivates employees to pay as much pension contributions as the same reflects the level of pension. For more information about NDC schemes see Axel Borsch-Suppan, What Are NDC Pension Systems? What do they Bring to Reform Strategies strategies (Munich: Max Planck Institute, 2004): http://mea.mpisoc.mpg.de/uploads/user_mea_discussionpapers/fu66wudcl4okogdk_dp42.pdf (accessed October 15, 2020). Robert Holzmann, "The ABCs of Nonfinancial Defined Contribution (NDC) Schemes", International Social Security Review 70, no. 3 (2017), https://www.iza.org/publications/pp/130/the-abcs-of-nonfinancial-defined-contribution-ndc-schemes (accessed October 30, 2020).

these pillars should jointly aim at least to guarantee a pension of 60 to 70% of the average salary of the employee.

The first contributive pillar is expected to function according to the NDC principle, where the contributions of current employees that are part of this scheme will go to a personal account within a national account. These means might be used to cover the expenses of current pensions in this pillar or social protection and accumulated contributions to obtain a guaranteed return. It emerges from comparative research, analysis of current contributions being paid, analysis of the number of employees that are expected to retire and the demographic trends, as well as the large potential for an increase in employment, that this scheme may achieve financial sustainability if a 7.5% pension contribution goes into this scheme. According to the 2017 KPST annual report, with a contribution level of 7.5%, cashed pension contributions have reached the value of around 160 million euro.[45] From this data we can conclude that a 7.5% pension contribution value would be sustainable for the current number of pensioners who would be part of this pillar, and this would help in covering expenses for the benefits of the social protection scheme. The contribution in the second pillar of 7.5% would guarantee a supplement of the basic pension and thus a pension of around 60–70% of the average salary in Kosovo could be secured for the initial period of 10 years, whereas after this period the pension should reach 60%–70% of the employee's salary. Surely, employees who had a high income during their employment period should not be harmed as the same might obtain a pension from KPST, depending on their accumulated amount. Regardless, an important transition role should be played by current pension means accumulated by KPST as well. For all employees, who did not accumulate at least EUR 25,000 and are not beneficiaries of contributive pensions before 1999, their means shall be carried over to the Pension Fund of the first pillar and the same shall be beneficiaries of the contributive pension over their entire life. All employees who are beneficiaries of the pre-1999 contributive pension system shall become a part of the contributive system upon retirement since at that time around 60% of the accumulated pension means shall be transferred into the first pillar, whereas 40% of means shall be provided to them from the second pillar. Surely, this would not be implemented for employees who have accumulated an amount of such means that the use of only the second pillar would be more favorable to them. In this case the most favorable form for the contributor would/should be applied. However, at least for another 10 to 15 years, the state should cover any eventual deficit in the first

---

45   Kosovo Pension Saving Trust, Annual Report of Year (2017), http://www.trusti.org/wp-content/uploads/2017/12/AR21017_eng.pdf (accessed October 30, 2020).

pillar, since those pensioners who have contributed less after 1999 are placed in this pillar, and the Pension Fund obtained little or no income from this category.

One of the basic arguments on why NDC should apply is also based on global trends. Every individual should contribute to secure a pension for themselves by working actively and contributing as much as possible.[46] Starting from this premise, we shall have an individualized pension but simultaneously we shall obtain a reasonable increase because the state utilizes and operates with accumulated pension contributions. In these schemes, the Government usually (after negotiations with social partners) defines the growth formula that is applied, but usually the annual economic growth is taken as a barometer. However, there are different practices of defining the formula for calculating pensions and reasonable growth, whereas a key element is usually the pension contribution related also to the period of contribution and economic growth.[47] An individualization of pensions should also be done because Kosovo is currently facing a very high unemployment rate of around 30%[48] and also there is a trend for emigration abroad.[49] Both these factors have a fundamental impact on the provision of the necessary means for pensions. It is not a solution for pension contributions to be utilized to settle problems with liquidity of the pension scheme, which results from a high level of unemployment and/or emigration. In this context, the solution is achieved by the

---

[46] NDC with different specifications and modalities is applied in Sweden, Italy, Poland and there is a trend toward enhancement of this model. See more at Axel Borsch-Suppan, "What Are NDC Pension Systems? What do they Bring to Reform Strategies" (Munich: Max Planck Institute 2004), http://mea.mpisoc.mpg.de/uploads/user_mea_discussion papers/fu66wudcl4okogdk_dp42.pdf (accessed October 15, 2020).

[47] See more about NDC schemes at Robert Holzmann, "The ABCs of Nonfinancial Defined Contribution (NDC) Schemes": 53–77.

[48] The unemployment rate in Kosovo decreased to 25.30 percent in the second quarter of 2019 from 26.90 percent in the first quarter of 2019. The unemployment rate in Kosovo averaged 35.39 percent from 2001 until 2019, reaching an all-time high of 57 percent in the fourth quarter of 2001 and a record low of 25.30 percent in the second quarter of 2019. See Trading Economists, "Unemployment Rate in Kosovo", https://tradingeconomics.com/kosovo/unemployment-rate (accessed October 15, 2020); Kosovo Agency for Statistics Labour Force Survey, 2018, https://ask.rks-gov.net/en/kosovo-agency-of-statistics/add-news/labour-force-survey-in-kosovo-2018 (accessed October 15, 2020). The data are taken for the year 2019, which show the data under a "stable trend" while the employment rates for 2020 are subject to the COVID-19 conditions.

[49] In the period from 2008 to 2018, a total of 203,330 Kosovo citizens left the country and filed asylum applications in the EU; for more information see Blerta Begisholli, "Leaving Kosovo: Legal Migration Upsurge Causes Depopulation Fears" (Pristina: Balkan Insight, 2019), https://balkaninsight.com/2019/04/25/leaving-kosovo-legal-migration-upsurge-causes-depopulation-fears/ (accessed October 15, 2020).

separation of pensions that are secured from work relation, from the benefits or payments on another basis that are not related to work relation and pension contributions, just as we have recommended above.

Concerning the second contributive pillar, which functions as a market-based scheme and is a mandatory scheme, similar to regional countries such as Croatia and North Macedonia, the novelty that is proposed in this scheme relates to two aspects with a common purpose. From the research and analysis, we come to the conclusion that the current DC scheme faces many risks such as financial risks (economic crisis, other moves in financial markets), and also legal and political risks (possible legal changes up to nationalization of the fund). In this context and based on the fact that the scheme is mandatory, we propose two versions which would mitigate these risks for the citizen by transferring them to the state. The basic premise is that it is not right to legally obligate citizens to pay pension contributions, which will be placed in financial markets, with the risk to be borne by the citizen.

In this context, the reform will have to foresee that the current scheme remains similar to the DC, but to have a guaranteed return on investments. Return on investments should include preservation of the purchasing power of contributions (to cover inflation) and to guarantee an annual minimum return on investments, starting from 0.05% up to 0.30%. By supposing that through a social dialogue, the agreed value would be at least around 0.15%, on average around 4.50% over inflation to be the guaranteed return from investment, respectively the growth of the value of pension contributions over the entire contribution period (that is supposed to be at least 30 years). Surely the level of return might also be related to the contribution period, e.g., the value of 4.50% guaranteed return could be obtained only by pensioners that have contributed over 30 years and thus an increase of the benefit rate would be made. This would have several effects on the costs of the fund, and it would settle a benefit principle to be distributed in the fairest way possible. Other positive aspects of this model would be that there would be no more citizen and media pressure on KPST every time it does not perform well in a given year, and it would increase its credibility among citizens, as the state is assuming the risk. The only negative effect of this model is that it would put KPST under pressure to achieve results and in extremely urgent situations, such as the economic crisis of 2008, a short-term subsidy would have to be made by the state to cover any eventual loss. Regardless, of the current practice, the likelihood of this occurring is very low (with exclusion of cases like the economic crisis of 2008), even in cases when a subsidy is introduced then its value is not unaffordable.

In general, this pension system model introduces one of the strongest modern market-based systems, with individualized pensions and provision of an interest rate, as well as growth of pension means that are utilized by the state to cover other social expenses. This is unlike a PAYG system, which does not provide any interest rate for utilization of accumulated pension means. This pension model must also be followed with a reform of the retirement age, indicating a growth trend, and also leaving the possibility that with the employer's consent a person may work full time or part time even beyond this age (maximally up to 70 years). On the other hand, a DC scheme (with hybrid elements) with a market-based guaranteed return represents one of the global trends, by combining it with good practices, such as those of Switzerland that has a guaranteed return.[50] In general, this pension scheme gives a basic role to the state in mandatory schemes and it also gives a proactive role to citizens themselves, who by making the highest possible pension contribution, a longer possible period of employment, as well being a part of voluntary schemes, can significantly influence their future welfare by having a pension that is as high as possible after reaching retirement age.

6   Conclusions

The pension system established in Kosovo after 1999, with UNMIK regulations and later through legislation enacted by Kosovo institutions, is a new pension system, unbound from the previous PAYG system. This pension system was put into place without societal debate and without consultation with social partners and consequently brought discontent and many dilemmas as to the purpose and mission of the pension system. The new pension system applied in Kosovo has been mostly considered as a social program rather than a pension system. This pension system did not respond appropriately to the social situation of pensioners and the capacities of employees to understand and take the risk for their pension contributions. The concept of pension funds with defined contributions (DC) was not a concept known to the contributors and even today, contributors are not ready to bear the risk of financial markets. The global crisis of 2008 has shown that pension funds can be affected, and as a consequence, social problems can be created. Nevertheless, despite all the fluctuations and economic crisis, current trends of the pension fund since its establishment are positive but followed by constant uncertainty. The lack of relation of the first and second pillar means that after an average period of around four years, an individual pensioner's fund accumulated from pension

---

50   OECD, Pensions at a Glance 2017 (Paris: OECD, 2017), 140–141.

contributions saved in the Kosovo Pension Saving Trust (KPST) is exhausted. Consequently, they remain a burden only on the first pillar – the basic pension, which is very low. Reform of Kosovo legislation, apart from placement of a new pension model that foresees the separation of the pension system from other benefits which do not have work relation and pension contributions as a basis, should address problems of sustainable pensions for people who are to retire in the next 10 to 15 years. These future retirees are unlikely to be able to be beneficiaries of pension contributions in Kosovo. In addition, the future pension reform should better address the individualization of pensions through placement of the NDC model in the first pillar, payment of contributions in the first and second pillar as well as addressing the conveyance of risk by finding a solution to guarantee pension contributions, a shift of the second mandatory pillar towards a DC scheme with hybrid elements (preservation of the value of contributions or a guaranteed return on investment), which would be regarded as more appropriate in the context of Kosovo. At the same time, there must be public prompting policies and engagement by social partners as well as the development of voluntary pension schemes.

Bibliography

Åslund, Anders, and Simeon Djankov, eds. The Great Rebirth: Lessons from the Victory of Capitalism over Communism. Washington: Peterson Institute of International Economics, 2014.

Balteș, Nicolae, and Jimon Ștefania Amalia. "Considerations Regarding the Pension Systems in Countries of Central and Eastern Europe." "Ovidius" University Annals, Economic Sciences Series 18, no. 2 (2018): 94–99.

Begisholli, Blerta. "Leaving Kosovo: Legal Migration Upsurge Causes Depopulation Fears." Pristina: Balkan Insight, 2019. Accessed October 15, 2020. https://balkan insight.com/2019/04/25/leaving-kosovo-legal-migration-upsurge-causes-depopula tion-fears/.

Bohl, Martin T., Judith Lischewski, and Svitlana Voronkova. "Pension Funds' Performance in Strongly Regulated Industries in Central Europe: Evidence from Poland and Hungary". Emerging Markets Finance and Trade 47, 2011: 80–94.

Borsch-Suppan, Axel. "What Are NDC Pension Systems? What do they Bring to Reform Strategies". (Munich: Max Planck Institute 2004). Accessed October 15, 2020. https:// www.mpisoc.mpg.de/fileadmin/user_upload/datapool/publications/fu66wudcl4 okogdk_dp42.pdf.

Chlon-Dominczak, Agnieszka. Funded Pensions in Transition Economies in Europe and Central Asia: Design and Experience. Kiev, Ukraine, International Federation of Pension Funds Association (FIAP) and World Bank, 2003.

Clark, Gordon L. Pension Fund Capitalism. Oxford: Oxford University Press, 2011.
EFAMA. Define-Contribution Pension Schemes. 2008. Accessed September 19, 2020. https://www.efama.org/Publications/Public/LongTerm_Savings_and_Pension_Steering_Committee/oxera_report.pdf.
ESPN Thematic Report: Assessment of Pension Adequacy in Serbia 2017. Accessed October 25, 2020. https://tinyurl.com/p58btxpz.
European Commission. Classification of Funded Pension Schemes and Impact on Government Finance (Luxembourg: Publications of the European Communities, 2004), 4. Accessed April 25, 2020. https://ec.europa.eu/eurostat/documents/3859598/5884325/KS-BE-04-002-EN.PDF/ccfc8b5a-a45e-4444-b467-3d2e1cab8d7e.
European Commission. Pension Schemes and Pension Projections in the EU-27 Member States – 2008–2060, 1. Occasional Papers 56, October 2009. Accessed October 15, 2020. https://ec.europa.eu/economy_finance/publications/pages/publication16034_en.pdf.
European Court for Human Rights. Grudic v Serbia: ECHR 17 April 2012, 31925/08, [2012] ECHR 708. Accessed October 15, 2020. https://tinyurl.com/2p987vf2.
Expert Group on Gender Equality and Social Inclusion, Health and Long-Term Care Issues (EGGSI). "The Socio-Economic Impact of Pension Systems on the Respective Situations of Women and Men and the Effects of Recent Trends in Pension Reforms" Synthesis Report, May 9, 2011. Accessed June 25, 2020. http://www.praxis.ee/wp-content/uploads/2014/03/2011-Socio-economic-impact-of-pension-systems-of-women-and-men.pdf.
Fetahi, Adil, and Fetahi Qerim Zariqi. Monograph of Pensioners League of Kosovo. Prishtinë: Kosovo League of Pensioners and Occupational Invalids, 2013.
Fondi Slloveno Kosovar i Pensioneve. Accessed October 24, 2020. http://www.fondipensional.com/english/index_eng.html.
Gubbels, John, David Snelbecker, and Lena Zezulin. The Kosovo Pension Reform: Achievements and Lessons, SP Discussion Paper 707. Washington, DC: World Bank Group, 2007.
Hoff, Andreas. Tackling Poverty and Social Exclusion of Older People – Lessons from Europe, Working Paper 308. Oxford: Oxford Institute of Aging, 2008.
Holzmann, Robert. "The ABCs of Nonfinancial Defined Contribution (NDC) Schemes". International Social Security Review 70, no. 3 (2017): 53–77. Accessed October 30, 2020. https://www.iza.org/publications/pp/130/the-abcs-of-nonfinancial-defined-contribution-ndc-schemes.
Independent International Commission on Kosovo. The Kosovo Independent Report: Conflict, International Response, Lessons Learned. Oxford: Oxford University Press, 2000.
IOPS. Country Profiles – FYRO Macedonia. Accessed September 25, 2020. http://www.iopsweb.org/principlesguidelines/40561423.pdf.

Kajtazi, Fazli. Crossroads of Kosovo Pensioners. Prishtinë: BSPK, 2010.

Kosovo Agency for Statistics Labour Force Survey, 2018. Accessed October 15, 2020. https://ask.rks-gov.net/en/kosovo-agency-of-statistics/add-news/labor-force-survey-in-kosovo-q4-2018.

Kosovo Agency Statistics. Kosovo Population Projection 2017–2061, 2017. Accessed August 18, 2020. https://ask.rks-gov.net/media/3925/parashikimi-i-popullsis%c3%ab-2017-2061.pdf.

Kosovo Pension Saving Trust. Annual Report of Year, 2017. Accessed October 30, 2020. http://www.trusti.org/wp-content/uploads/2017/12/AR21017_eng.pdf.

Kosovo Pension Saving Trust. Annual Returns and Cash-flows 2002-2020. Accessed Spetember 19, 2020. http://www.trusti.org/wp-content/uploads/2020/02/KPST_key_annual_information_2020eng.pdf.

Law No. 03/L-100 on the Pensions for Kosovo Protection Corps Members. Accessed October 25, 2020. https://tinyurl.com/2p97m3sw.

Law No. 04/L-101 on Pension Funds in Kosovo. Accessed October 23, 2020. https://www.atk-ks.org/wp-content/uploads/2017/11/Law-No.-04-L-101.pdf .

Law No. 04/L-261 on Kosovo Liberation Army War Veterans. Accessed October 19, 2020. https://gzk.rks-gov.net/ActDetail.aspx?ActID=14581.

Law No. 04/L-054 on Status and the Rights of Martyrs, Invalids, Veterans, Members of Kosovo Liberation Army, Civilian Victims and their Families. Accessed October 19, 2020. https://gzk.rks-gov.net/ActDetail.aspx?ActID=2793.

Law No. 04/L-131 on Pension Schemes Financed by State. Accessed September 11, 2020. https://gzk.rks-gov.net/ActDetail.aspx?ActID=9517.

Malcolm, Noel. Kosovo: A Short History. New York: New York University Press, 1999.

Muir, Dana M., and John A. Turner. Imagining the Ideal Pension System: International Perspectives. Kalamazoo: W.E. Upjohn Institute for Employment Research, 2011.

Mustafai, Hrabil. "Pension System Reform in the Republic of Macedonia." International Refereed Scientific Journal Vision 2, no. 1 (2017): 69–78. Accessed September 25, 2020. http://visionjournal.edu.mk/wp-content/uploads/2017/07/irsjv_v2i1_habil.pdf.

Nelsson, Richard. How Milosevic Stripped Kosovo's Autonomy – Archive, 1989. The Guardian, March 20, 2019. Accessed October 20, 2020. https://www.theguardian.com/world/from-the-archive-blog/2019/mar/20/how-milosevic-stripped-kosovos-autonomy-archive-1989.

Nushi, Paulina, and Laura Nimani. "Kosovo Pensioners' 17 Years Struggle for Serbian Compensation." Prishtina Insight, October 20, 2016. Accessed October 20, 2020. https://prishtinainsight.com/kosovo-pensioners-17-year-struggle-serbian-compensation-mag/.

OECD. Pensions at a Glance 2013 OECD and G20 indicator. OECD Publishing, 2013 Accessed September 31, 2020. https://www.oecd.org/pensions/public-pensions/OECDPensionsAtAGlance2013.pdf.

OECD. Pensions at a Glance 2017. Paris: OECD Publishing, 2017. Accessed September 31, 2020. http://dx.doi.org/10.1787/pensionglance-2017-en.

Ortiz, Isabel, Fabio Durán-Valverde, Stefan Urban and Veronika Wodsak eds. Reversing Pension Privatizations: Rebuilding Public Pension Systems in Eastern Europe and Latin America. Geneva: International Labour Organization, 2018.

Radović, Milivoje, Rogic Suncica, and Božo Cerović. "Influence of Demographic Trends and Employment on the Financial Sustainability of the Montenegrin Pension System". Zbornik radova Ekonomskog fakulteta u Istocnom Sarajevu 15 (2017): 39–47.

Regulation 1999/1 dated 25/06/1999 for Authorizations of Interim Administration in Kosovo. Accessed October 19, 2020. https://unmik.unmissions.org/sites/default/files/regulations/02english/E1999regs/RE1999_01.htm.

Regulation 2001/35 dated 22 December 2001, on Pensions in Kosovo. Accessed October 19, 2020, https://www.atk-ks.org/wp-content/uploads/2017/11/Regulation_2001_35.pdf.

Social Insurance Institute of Albania. Accessed October 25, 2020. https://www.issh.gov.al/?page_id=6814&lang=en.

Stan, Lavinia, and Nadia Nedelsky eds. Encyclopedia of Transitional Justice 2. New York: Cambridge University Press, 2013.

Stiglitz, Joseph. "Whither Reform? Ten Years of Transition." In the Rebel Within, edited by Ha-Joon Chang, 127–171. London: Anthem Press.

Sullivan, Michael. Understanding Pensions. New York: Routledge, 2004.

Trading Economists. "Unemployment Rate in Kosovo." Accessed October 15, 2020. https://tradingeconomics.com/kosovo/unemployment-rate.

UNMIK Regulation 2001/35. Accessed September 21, 2020. https://www.atk-ks.org/wp-content/uploads/2017/11/Regulation_2001_35.pdf.

UNMIK Regulation 2005/20. Accessed September 21, 2020. https://tinyurl.com/y3x9x7d7.

UN Security Council Resolution 1244, 1999. Accessed September 21, 2020. https://unmik.unmissions.org/sites/default/files/old_dnn/Res1244ENG.pdf.

Weller, Mark. Contested Statehood: Kosovo's Struggle for Independence. Oxford: Oxford University Press, 2009.

Willis Towers Watson. Global Pension Assets Study, 2016. Accessed September 09, 2020. https://tinyurl.com/2p9ddyd4.

Zoran, Anusic. "Administrative Charges of Private Mandatory Pension Funds." Presentation for ILO Tripartite Conference on "Recent Developments on Pension Restructuring in Central and Eastern Europe." Budapest, December 2004.

CHAPTER 7

Buying Social Peace: Lessons from Kosovo

Besnik Fetahu and Marzena Żakowska

1 Introduction

Beginning in 1974, Kosovo had its own social protection system, which provided social care through social work centers. As part of the former Yugoslavia and one of the federal units, Kosovo adopted a socialist approach to social security with the state having a strong role in providing various social services. Child benefits, education, health care, employment benefits, a low rate of unemployment, housing, very strong syndicates, pensions, and different social services were all supported with public funds. The main tenet of socialism is that all resources must be distributed equally to everyone in society. At that time, general state policies minimized the role of the free market and tried to build a collective system in which everything is 'ours' and nothing 'yours'. With the suppression of Kosovo's autonomy in the 1990s, social protection in Kosovo failed. It was later developed as a selective social security system that completely excluded the Albanian population. This made the Albanians build a parallel system of providing basic health care, education, and a few forms of support such as food packages for poverty-stricken families. On the other hand, the public fund was suppressed by Serbia, and especially the contributions of pensioners, and bank deposits.[1] After the end of the war (1999), the United Nations Mission in Kosovo (UNMIK) found a system totally devastated by a lack of human, professional, and financial resources. In this emergency phase with thousands of people without shelter, food, or work, the UNMIK administration decided to rebuild social work centers throughout the country, with the aim of providing forms of social assistance.[2] With the strong support

---

1 Besnik Pula, "The Emergence of the Kosovo "Parallel State" 1988–1992", Nationalities Papers 32, no 4 (2004): 813–815. Flamur Keqa, "Serbia përmend borxhet ndaj kursimtarëve devizorë nga republikat e ish-Jugosllavisë, 'harron' Kosovën", Koha, July 15, 2019, https://www.koha.net/arberi/174116/serbia-permend-borxhet-ndaj-kursimtareve-devizore-nga-republikat-e-ish-jugosllavise-harron-kosoven/ (accessed August 5, 2019).
2 United Nation Security Council, Report of the Secretary-General of the United Nations Interim Administration Mission in Kosovo (S/2000/1196), 15 December 2000, 8–10. Besnik Fetahu, "Applying Esping-Andersen Typology of Welfare State in Western Balkan Countries", The International Journal of Interdisciplinary Civic and Political Studies 12, no. 2 (2017), 20–21, 24.

of international nongovernmental organizations, social security was determined to be a fundamental and distinctive feature of Kosovo following the European social model. Building a liberal model of social security was more reasonable due to the restrictions of public finance. However, Kosovo was facing tremendous economic and social upheavals, and it was very challenging to adapt to the new social security system. Without public funds, and only with the support of international donors, the UNMIK administration decided to build a free market system, with few social schemes and strong support of international nongovernmental organizations providing social assistance in food, shelter, and human capacity development. This kind of development with the main focus on the free market, and with minimal public funds in the area of social security was very challenging for Kosovo in the post-war period. Restrictions were introduced due to lack of finance. Therefore the new welfare system continued to display the weaknesses. The policy and social policy became widely neo-liberal in an expanded general setting of crony-capitalism, clientelistic political mobilization and captured public resources.[3]

In addition, it was closely related to the Kosovo policy to become an EU member. The desire to have stable political, economic, and social systems drives the states to the implementation of various reform programs. Due to political circumstances, Kosovo still faces many social difficulties on its way to European integration. The achievement of social cohesion is very challenging because of the high rates of unemployment, poverty, corruption, and the difficulties in international recognition as the state.[4] Facing social pressures from various social groups, Kosovo has now extended social expenses to different social groups. This growth of expenditures is not the result of a long-term strategic plan but an ad hoc response to protests and strikes by various social groups. This policy of buying social peace has placed Kosovo in a difficult financial position with a real chance of financial collapse in the coming years.

Kosovo has been identified as the poorest country in the region, with fragile social protection systems, where unemployment, poverty and inequality

---

[3] Marija Stambolieva, Kosovo from State of Welfare Emergency to Welfare State? (October 12, 2012), SSRN Electronic Journal, doi: 10.2139/ssrn.2687677, 6-7; Artan Mustafa, "Welfare Politics in Kosovo: Growing Role for the State and Benefit Disproportionality", in Innovative Approaches in Labour Market Policy and Health and Long-Term Care in Eastern Europe ed. Anette Scoppetta, Kai Leichsenring and Willem Stamatiou (European Centre Vienna, 2017), 25–26.

[4] For more details about poverty, corruption and unemployment see European Commission, Kosovo 2018 Report (Brussels: EC, 2018); European Commission, Kosovo 2019 Report (Brussels: EC, 2019); regarding problem of the international recognition and integration see Ramesh Jaura, "Kosovo Looks Forward To UN Membership, IDN – In Depth News", https://www.indepthnews.net/indexphp/the-world/eu-europe/2032-kosovo-looks-forward-to-un-membership (accessed August 3, 2019).

are constantly increasing. The lack of recognition of its independence by five European Union states[5] has been an impediment in the EU integration process. In addition integration difficulties have emerged for Kosovo and other Western Balkan countries, in recent years as a result of the COVID-19 pandemic, the financial crisis in the euro area, the migration crisis, BREXIT, the conflict in Ukraine, sanctions against Russia, and terrorist attacks by the Islamic State. All these are challenges for the European Union in its unclear future. The financial cost of managing these crises is extremely high, so there are voices calling for the revision of various social programs.

Today, the main functions of social security in Kosovo cannot be met in full either by the market or by the family. Fulfilling these functions is an essential part of what can be considered a modern and democratic society. Therefore, a complex social policy reform needs to be urgently implemented to resolve the problem. Its reform is something that needs to be a top priority. In Kosovo, there has been an increase in funds for social schemes with the state offering cash to a considerable number of its citizens from these vulnerable categories. However, employment centers and vocational training, despite financial support from the European Union, are still inefficient and experience many operational problems. In a study published by the Institute for Development Policy on vocational training in Kosovo, of 28 modules/profiles provided by employment centers, only five of them have been validated by the National Qualifications Authority.[6] This reflects the lack of long-term plans in relation to the issue of employment.

The purpose of this chapter is to identify the determinants of social changes in Kosovo, occurring mainly after 1999. Therefore, the study focuses on the current situation of social security in Kosovo, social protection, and what mechanisms are used to deal with social problems. A comparative methodology is used to address social security issues in Kosovo, utilizing available data, provided by the Kosovo Agency of Statistics (KAS), the European Social Survey (ESS), the Organization for Development and Cooperation (OECD), the World Bank (World Bank), the International Monetary Fund (IMF), the International Labour Organization (ILO), and the European Commission (EU Commission). The comparative perspective used as the framework for this study allowed us to present social security in Kosovo at an early stage under the socialist model, with the post-war situation developed under the liberal model. This framework points out not only variations between individuals and social groups, but

---

5   Euractiv, The EU Parliament calls on all EU countries to recognise Kosovo, https://tinyurl.com/46c3zh3r (accessed August 5, 2019).
6   Gent Ahmetaj et al., Aftësimi Profesionalnë Kosovë: Specifikat, Marrëdhëniet dhe Problemet (Pristhinë: Institute for Development Policy, 2016), 22.

also the differences between countries in their process of transition. Therefore, a micro-level analysis (variations between individuals, groups, etc.) has been combined with a macro-level analysis (between countries) to gain a better understanding of the standard of living of households, work mobility and social expenditure. These data reflect citizens' perceptions of the efficiency of social security, various social protection schemes, worker mobility, income levels and social inequalities in the respective countries. The research seeks to answer the following questions: What types of social security system should Kosovo develop, taking into account its internal social issues? What lessons can be drawn from Kosovo's social system transformation by states aspiring to join the EU?

2 Social Security through Left and Right Perspectives

Our most general understanding of social security is facilitated through theoretical perspectives, within which the basic concepts of social security are established. These theoretical perspectives have their strengths and weaknesses in their approach to social security. The left addresses social security by emphasizing adaptation of the capitalist economy to the demands of the working class, while the right perspective demands the free market and a weak role of government in providing various social security services.[7]

The 'social' element of the left perspective is based on collective action, which can be understood either as mutual aid or as action with a common purpose. According to Offe, de-codification is necessary to reproduce society and legitimize the system.[8] Mutual assistance is expressed through a network of rights and responsibilities in society. Typical examples of this include both informal family and community networks, and formal arrangements such as workplace wellbeing and a friendly society. Action with a common purpose or joint action is usually favored in the form of cooperative agreements or interactions. In continental Europe, this type of approach is often associated with 'corporatism', in which the state strives to co-ordinate and foster co-operation between different groups of interest.[9] Corporatism can be seen as an attempt to control different factions, but it can be understood as a system for securing

---

7 Christopher Pierson, Francis G. Castles and Ingela K. Naumann eds., The Welfare State Reader (Cambridge: Polity Press, 2015).
8 For further information about Claus Offe's approach see Mullard Maurice and Paul Spicker, Social Policy in Changing Society (New York: Routledge, 1998), 38.
9 Ibid., 79.

the representation of their interests and promoting collaborative efforts.[10] The market excludes some people in the form of 'negative selection'. This is due to high levels of social need and relatively low income as well as geographic location; for these reasons services cannot be offered to some people. The main opposition to the left perspective comes from the liberals who believe that the acceptance of the collective premise and state intervention is seen as dangerous for the rights of the individual.

If the right to social security is based on being a member of the community, then there are those who are not members of the community and who are not nationals. Often, these are people of different races, nationalities, or (as in many countries of Europe) migrant workers. Social security rights in many European countries are unique; they are earned through special contributions and directly linked to the work records of each person.[11] The left perspective is concerned that this redistribution should be progressive, which means that wealthier people must pay more than the poorest people.[12] The position of the right perspective in terms of well-being is a double-sided coin. On the one hand, the right perspective favors universal human rights and opposes discrimination. On the other hand, state intervention is viewed with considerable skepticism. According to the right perspective, the state's role in providing social security should be small, at a minimum, in order to protect individual freedom and avoid abuses from government activities. Privatization has been a key pillar of liberal politics. It is seen as a boon for individual choice because it privatizes public sector monopolies. Privatization takes different forms, including out-of-service contracting, denationalization of public services, liberalization of occupations, liberalization of labor markets and removal of artificial barriers from the outset.[13] The right perspective has also been strongly associated with equal opportunities and the idea of broad access to employment opportunities for all. The presence of income inequality may mean that the level of income determines which individuals are more able to capitalize on their potential: lack of income acts as a barrier to entry to higher education.[14]

---

10   Ibid., 79
11   John Hassler, Jose V. Rodriguez Mora, Kjetil Storesletten and Fabrizio Zilibotti, "The Survival of the Welfare State" The American Economic Review 93, no. 1 (2003): 87.
12   Robert Skidelsky, Beyond the Welfare State (London: The Social Market Foundation 1997).
13   Mullard Maurice, Paul Spicker, Social Policy in Changing Society, 62.
14   Milton Friedman, Capitalism and Freedom (Chicago: University of Chicago Press, 2002), 16–17, 162, 164, 195; Melissa S. Kearney and Phillip B. Levine, Income Inequality, Social Mobility, and the Decision to Drop Out of High School, Brookings Papers on Economic Activity, Spring 2016, 333–380.

This is linked to the fact that children from low-income groups tend to leave school at an early age.

3 From the Old to the New Model of Social Security in Kosovo

In the former Yugoslavia, Kosovo as a federal unit, applied the social security model based on inter-generational solidarity. Active forces in employment contributed to the pension fund for current pensioners. During the 1990s, Kosovo built a parallel system with high solidarity of citizens to help feed and clothe the most vulnerable social groups. The destruction of Yugoslavia has opened up a clear prospect of European integration for Kosovo. Generally, fragile social peace and a certain level of democracy prevail in Kosovo. To an extent, Kosovo has made some real economic progress, but the process of privatization has turned industrial factories into commercial warehouses, raising the high level of unemployment and poverty.[15]

Therefore, Kosovo and other countries aspiring to join the European Union need to align their social policies with the priority areas defined by the EU, as presented in Table 7.1 and Table 7.2.

TABLE 7.1 Forms of social policy in the European Union

	Matters by field	Relations EU – member states
Regulation of standards and social rights.	**Mainly:** Labor Law, health and safety at work, equal treatment policies.	Common competencies, the EU increased its importance from 1970 to 1990.

---

15 Besnik Fetahu, "Applying Esping-Andersen Typology of Welfare State in Western Balkan Countries", 24; Rita Augestad Knudsen, "Privatization in Kosovo: 'Liberal Peace' in Practice", Journal of Intervention and Statebuilding 7, no 3 (2013): 299–300.

TABLE 7.1   Forms of social policy in the European Union (cont.)

	Matters by field	**Relations EU – member states**
Expenditures for social purposes.	**Mainly:** European Social Fund, Globalization Fund, Agricultural Fund, and Regional Fund.	Low EU spending compared to national social welfare systems, but within the EU budget, it is important.
Coordination to promote voluntary harmonization in the social field.	**Mainly:** Employment policies, pensions, social assistance, and education.	The impact of the EU depends on internal readiness.
Liberalization of public services in general, including "social services" (as a result of EU economic policy).	**Mainly:** Employment services, energy, transport, postal services, but also part of the healthcare industry. Economic policies affect "outer ring" of social protection.	Member States cannot discriminate against private actors in the market or exclude them outside certain narrow, controversial areas of public interest.

SOURCE: GERDA FALKNER, EUROPEAN UNION IN THE OXFORD HANDBOOK OF THE WELFARE STATE ED. FRANCIS G. CASTLES, STEPHAN LEIBFRIED, JANE LEWIS, HERBERT OBINGER AND CHRISTOPHER PIERSON (OXFORD: OXFORD UNIVERSITY PRESS, 2010), 299.

European integration is beneficial for Kosovo because it promotes the development of economies through the opening of the labor market, social security, joint coordination of social policies, tax harmonization and free competition. The European Union is active in promoting social dialogue in order to develop close cooperation between social actors, and in building a sustainable system of social spending in all member states and candidate countries. Moreover, the EU recognizes the value of social cohesion, which can be promoted through income distribution, employment levels, standards, social policies related to quality of life. Therefore, the process of European integration is essential for the European Union in order to reinforce social cohesion throughout its territory and to reduce polarizations in terms of economic and social system development.

TABLE 7.2 Impact of European integration on social expenditure of Member States

	Effect	EU policies	Assessment arguments
Impact on costs	Direct	Opening borders and social security systems for citizens of other EU countries: – social transfers were now no longer limited to their "own citizens"; – not consumed within the territory of the respective state.	From the perspective of member states, this may be costly. But the situation in other countries is similar, reciprocity is possible. If not the European Court of Justice (ECJ) provides (some) protection of the financial stability of social security systems. From a civic perspective, this offers new social rights.
Impact on budgetary resources	Direct	The European Monetary Union (EMU) defines the limits of the expenditure deficit.	Short-term: the restrictive effect on potential social costs, although the state is free to make reductions, where they consider it to be of benefit. Long-term: not limiting budget deficits may have a negative effect on social budgets due to debt overload.
	Indirect	Partial tax harmonization at EU level, space for competition in taxation between member states.	The de facto pressure on states to lower taxes (including social security contributions) in mobile economic actors. But this remains to be decided at the national level.

SOURCE: GERDA FALKNER, EUROPEAN UNION IN THE OXFORD HANDBOOK OF THE WELFARE STATE ED. FRANCIS G. CASTLES, STEPHAN LEIBFRIED, JANE LEWIS, HERBERT OBINGER AND CHRISTOPHER PIERSON (OXFORD: OXFORD UNIVERSITY PRESS, 2010), 301.

On the other hand, due to poor integration in the international financial markets, Kosovo was not significantly affected by the EU financial crisis (so-called the Great Recession of 2008 through 2012). This does not mean, however, that Kosovo enjoys immunity from these financial crises in the EU member states because of the presence of a large Kosovar diaspora in Germany and Switzerland. Kosovo receives considerable amounts each year from the remittances of its expatriates. These funds play an important role in the domestic economy, especially in households, given that many families survive through remittances from their family members abroad. Any reduction in these remittances directly affects the living standards of households. It also affects economic development and increased economic worries.[16] In response to these external and internal challenges, Kosovo has built up different social schemes aimed at providing economic assistance, social assistance, and social service delivery.[17] However, EU member states with their social security policies continue to be more attractive to many Kosovar citizens. Although only declared a safe place in 2015, Kosovars have been identified as the largest group of asylum seekers in the European Union, even ahead of Syrians.[18]

The process of integrating potential member states into the European Union is accompanied by closer cooperation with them and with a particular emphasis on regional development. Kosovo is relying on the progress of various reforms and approximation of legislation through expertise and various financial instruments adopted over the years. All this support aims at building democracy and the rule of law. This is achieved through the strengthening of political stability, economic development, and social dialogue. Kosovo is benefiting from EU support to build institutional and administrative capacity, as well as developing a free market economy through regional cooperation. According to Fetahu, the EU integration process is proceeding slowly for Kosovo and other Balkan countries, which results in the problems the EU is facing, such as eurozone crisis, migration, Brexit crisis and Ukraine conflict.[19] On the other hand, over the last years Kosovo

---

16 Amir Haxhikadrija, Diaspora as a Driving Force for Development in Kosovo: Myth or Reality?, Summary, Swiss Agency for Development and Cooperation - Forum for Democratic Initiatives, June 2009.

17 Besnik Fetahu, "Applying Esping-Andersen Typology of Welfare State in Western Balkan Countries", 23.

18 Plator Avdiu, Largimi drejt shteteve anëtare të BE-së (Prishtinë: Qendra Kosovare për Studimetë Sigurisë, 2015), 13.

19 Besnik Fetahu, "Applying Esping-Andersen Typology of Welfare State in Western Balkan Countries", 24; Desmond Dinan, Neill Nugent, William E. Paterson eds., The European Union in Crisis (London: Red Globe Press 2017); Peter A. Hall, The Euro Crisis and the Future of European Integration, https://www.bbvaopenmind.com/en/articles/the-euro-crisis-and-the-future-of-european-integration/ (November 15, 2020).

has expended considerable effort to accelerate the EU membership path, including: (i) negotiation of a Stabilization and Association Agreement (SAA), which was signed in 2015; (ii) increased cooperation with the European Commission (EC) regarding questions of governance and economic policies, which includes submitting an Economic Reform Program; and (iii) continuing to play the role of a constructive partner in bilateral talks with Serbia, moderated by the EU, which strive for the normalization of relations between the two countries.[20]

However, realistically Kosovo is not ready at this moment to join the European Union. Kosovo has not completed the transition, has fundamental international disagreements about the future of the state and, according to the US State Department and the European Commission, is challenged with high rates of corruption and organized crime. Kosovo's current capacities are inadequate to meet EU requirements as they are undoubtedly weaker compared to other countries in the region.[21] This situation is exacerbating social insecurity, political turmoil, and sluggish economic development; especially for young people who do not have good employment opportunities. Nonetheless Kosovo has been slowly increasing its GDP and employment rate and reducing poverty and inflation (Table 7.3). Furthermore, it has defined other development priorities by making a sort of bypass and still not showing due interest in social issues. The greatest paradox is the desire to adopt the social policies of other countries by applying them without study and in discord with internal factors.

TABLE 7.3 Macroeconomic indicators in Kosovo

Indicators in %/ Years	2006	2007	2008	2009	2010	2011	2012
Annual real growth of GDP	4.5	7.3	6.3	3.6	3.3	4.4	2.8
Employment rate by years	29	26.5	24.3	26.4	–	–	25.6
Extreme poverty	16.7	16.8	18	12.5	8.2	10.2	7.8
General poverty	45.1	45.4	42	34.5	29.2	29.7	23.7
Inflation rate	0.6	4.4	9.4	-2.4	3.5	7.3	2.5
Unemployment rate	41.4	44.9	43.6	45.5	45.4	45	30.9

20 World Bank, Kosovo - Country Snapshot (World Bank, 2015), 2.
21 Venera Hajrullahu, Fatmir Curri. Gjendja aktuale dhe sfidat kryesore të Kosovës në rrugën e anëtarësimit në Bashkimin Europian (Prishtinë: Fondacioni për shoqëritë hapur, 2006), 5, European Commission, Kosovo 2019 Report (Brussels, 2019), 4, 19.

TABLE 7.3 Macroeconomic indicators in Kosovo (cont.)

Indicators in %/ Years	2013	2014	2015	2016	2017	2018	2019
Annual real growth of GDP	3.4	1.2	4.1	4.1	4.2	3.8	4.9
Employment rate by years	25.5	28.4	26.9	25.2	30.4	29.8	29.8
Extreme poverty	5.7	6.9	5.1	5.8	5.1	–	–
General poverty	17.8	21.5	17.6	16.8	21.6	19.8	21
Inflation rate	1.8	0.4	-0.5	0.3	1.5	1.05	2.7
Unemployment rate	30	30	35.3	32.9	30.6	30.7	31.4

SOURCE: OWN ELABORATION BASED ON STATISTICAL OFFICE OF KOSOVO, RESULTS OF THE LABOUR FORCE SURVEY 2009, 16, HTTPS://ASK.RKS-GOV.NET/MEDIA/1691/RESULTS-OF-THE-LABOUR-FORCE-SURVEY-2009.PDF (ACCESSED NOVEMBER 19, 2020); MINISTRY OF ECONOMIC DEVELOPMENT, RAPORTI I INDIKATORËVE MAKROEKONOMIK TË KOSOVËS 2013–2017 (DEVELOPMENT, 2018), 12; MACROTRENDS, KOSOVO GDP GROWTH RATE, HTTPS://WWW.MACROTRENDS.NET/COUNTRIES/XKX/KOSOVO/GDP-GROWTH-RATE (ACCESSED NOVEMBER 19, 2020); TRADING ECONOMICS, KOSOVO EMPLOYMENT RATE, HTTPS://TRADINGECONOMICS.COM/KOSOVO/EMPLOYMENT-RATE (NOVEMBER 19, 2020); KOSOVO AGENCY OF STATISTICS, RESULTS OF THE KOSOVO LABOUR FORCE SURVEY 2012, SEPTEMBER 2013, 19, 28, HTTPS://ASK.RKS-GOV.NET/MEDIA/1671/RESULTS-OF-THE-KOSOVO-2012-LABOUR-FORCE-SURVEY.PDF (ACCESSED NOVEMBER 19, 2020); KOSOVO AGENCY OF STATISTICS, RESULTS OF THE KOSOVO LABOUR FORCE SURVEY 2013, JULY 2014, 3, 10, HTTPS://OPENKNOWLEDGE.WORLDBANK.ORG/HANDLE/10986/21042 (ACCESSED NOVEMBER 19, 2020); WORLD BANK, INFLATION, CONSUMER PRICES (ANNUAL %) – KOSOVO, HTTPS://DATA.WORLDBANK.ORG/INDICATOR/FP.CPI.TOTL.ZG?LOCATIONS=XK (ACCESSED NOVEMBER 20, 2020); KOSOVO AGENCY OF STATISTICS – WORLD BANK, CONSUMPTION, POVERTY IN THE REPUBLIC OF KOSOVO IN 2011, 3, 11, HTTPS://ASK.RKS-GOV.NET/MEDIA/2737/CONSUMPTION-POVERTY-IN-THE-REPUBLIC-OF-KOSOVO-IN-2011.PDF (ACCESSED NOVEMBER 20, 2020); KOSOVO AGENCY OF STATISTICS, CONSUMPTION POVERTY IN THE REPUBLIC OF KOSOVO 2019, 5, HTTPS://DOCUMENTS1.WORLDBANK.ORG/CURATED/EN/210201560762490515/PDF/CONSUMPTION-POVERTY-IN-THE-REPUBLIC-OF-KOSOVO.PDF (ACCESSED NOVEMBER 21, 2020); STATISTICAL OFFICE OF KOSOVO, KOSOVO POVERTY ASSESSMENT. VOLUME I: ACCELERATING INCLUSIVE GROWTH TO REDUCE WIDESPREAD POVERTY, REPORT, NO. 39737-XK, 13, HTTPS://ASK.RKS-GOV.NET/MEDIA/2725/KOSOVO-POVERTY-ASSESSMENT-VOLUME-I.PDF (ACCESSED NOVEMBER 21, 2020); WORLD BANK. KOSOVO. POVERTY & EQUITY, 2019. ACCESSED NOVEMBER 27, 2020. HTTPS://TINYURL.COM/2P999ZS2; WORLD BANK, KOSOVO, HTTPS://PUBDOCS.WORLDBANK.ORG/EN/993701492011106034/MPO-KSV.PDF (ACCESSED NOVEMBER 21, 2020); WORLD BANK, CONSUMPTION POVERTY IN THE REPUBLIC OF KOSOVO, 5 HTTP://DOCUMENTS1.WORLDBANK.ORG/CURATED/EN/210201560762490515/PDF/CONSUMPTION-POVERTY-IN-THE-REPUBLIC-OF-KOSOVO.PDF (ACCESSED NOVEMBER 21, 2020) WORLD BANK, INFLATION. CONSUMER PRICES (ANNUAL %) – KOSOVO, HTTPS://TINYURL.COM/YCKZUZ6P (ACCESSED NOVEMBER 21, 2020).

As far as social protection is concerned, Kosovo inherited from the former Yugoslavia some of the social protection system and non-governmental activities during the parallel system in the 1990s, mainly the activities of the humanitarian organization "Mother Teresa".[22] The parallel system of the 1990s was characterized by high solidarity among citizens helping the most vulnerable social groups with food and clothing. Now, Kosovo is building social security (Figure 7.1), with a large number of social schemes and higher financial costs.

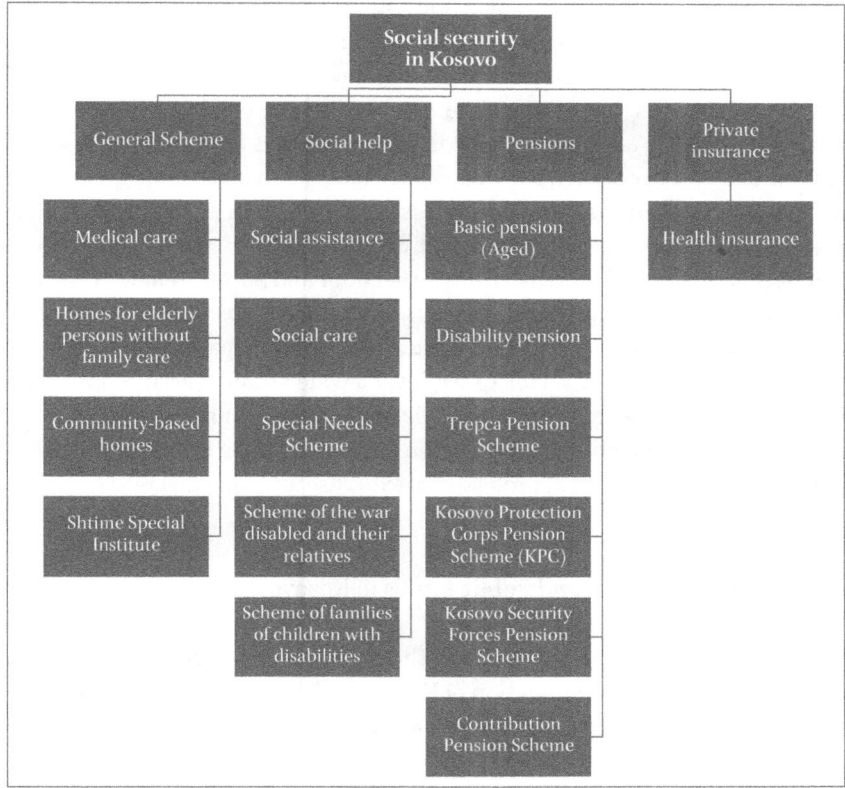

FIGURE 7.1   Social security system in Kosovo
SOURCE: OWN ELABORATION.

---

22   The Mother Teresa charitable society was founded in 1990 as part of the parallel society established in Kosovo in response to the Serbian government repression of the Albanian majority in Kosovo. Albanians were dismissed from their jobs and evicted from their homes; their institutions were closed down in a thoroughgoing effort to expunge them from the social and political life of Kosovo. Gani Demolli, The Mother Teresa Society and the War in Kosovo, https://odihpn.org/magazine/the-mother-teresa-society-and-the-war-in-kosovo/ (accessed November 21, 2020).

The design and implementation of social policies and the institutionalization of social and pension assistance were directly influenced by the UNMIK. The transfer of these responsibilities to local institutions was made in recent years, although it must be recognized that the involvement of international consultants continues to play a key role. They have built a liberal model of social protection, giving priority to combating poverty through social assistance schemes, by making payments to poorer families with public funds (direct from the state budget).[23] Kosovo social protection expenditure is slowly growing; but, in comparison to European and regional levels, remains low. From 2005–16, total expenditure grew by 4 percentage points, but remained below 9% GDP (8.9% in 2016). This expenditure is mostly financed by government revenues with a large part of social protection expenditure being on senior citizens' pensions. The remaining costs are covered by individual contributions both legally mandated and voluntary and by foreign aid.[24] Moreover, family benefit spending is low, and the expense of the means-tested social assistance program is steadily declining. However, in recent years, expenditure on 'categories of war' and former political prisoners has increased with the Ministry of Labor and Social Welfare absorbing the largest amount of state financial costs. Nonetheless Kosovo is making progress decentralizing the social services provided by municipal Centers for Social Work (CSW) and the third sector. CSWs cover a wide array of services, including primary care and advice for victims of violence in the family; case oversight of shelters (orphans and abandoned children); and care for the ill and disabled. But they still suffer from a lack of professional expertise and financial resources.[25]

4 Social Problems and Public Funds in Kosovo

Kosovo has the highest poverty rate in the region. This was roughly similar in previous years when the population of Kosovo had worse living conditions than any other part of Yugoslavia. Poverty in Kosovo dropped from 44.4% in 1978 to 39.8% in 1983, but then increased to 81.9% in 1989, which is high compared to the Yugoslav average (23.5% at that time) and was reflected during the suppression of autonomy by the Serbian government.[26] After the war in Kosovo, three poverty assessments were made by the World Bank and the Kosovo Agency of

---

23 Artan Mustafa, Amir Haxhikadrija, ESPN Thematic Report on Financing Social Protection, European Social Policy Network (ESPN), Brussels: European Commission, 2019, 6.
24 Ibid., 6, 8.
25 Ibid., 9–11. For more information about decentralization of social services see Rahel Kahlet, Sonila Danaj, Decentralization of Social Services in Kosovo – Policy Challenges and Recommendations, Policy Brief 2018/5, Vienna: European Centre, 2018, 1–11.
26 Ardiana Gashi, Amir Haxhikadrija, Social Impact of Emigration and Rural-Urban Migration in Central and Eastern Europe. Final Country Report – Kosovo, April 2012, 5.

Statistics. Based on the annual results of the Household Budget Survey from the post-war period up to 2006, approximately 45% of the population of Kosovo lives below the level of the consumer poverty line.[27] As a result of the increase in social inequality in Kosovo, it is estimated that one-fifth of Kosovo's population experienced a loss of up to 10% of their purchasing power during this period. The level of poverty has fallen in urban areas but has increased in rural areas. There is tendency toward regional differences regarding poverty and exclusion, where according to the level of human development, municipalities in the north and east of Kosovo have the highest level of human development. The groups most vulnerable to poverty appear to be the largest families – especially those with six or more members; families with dependent persons; families in which a woman is the head of household; the unemployed; although both self-employed and those working in the mining sector are at risk; and those endangered who have not finished elementary school.[28] Improving opportunities in less developed regions, better access to high schools and job creation, seem to be the best combination to reduce poverty over the medium to long term. In the short term, increasing funding for the social assistance scheme would be a very important measure. It is also essential to have clear policies and strategies to target interventions to alleviate poverty and social exclusion in Kosovo in line with European Union policies. In particular, the voice of the poor should be systematically integrated within national policies.

At the end of the war in Kosovo, data on contributors to the pension insurance system were taken over by the Serbian government. Faced with this situation, the UNMIK mission created a new pension scheme, laying the foundation for a basic pension for all residents of Kosovo, older than 65 years of age. However, the basic pension is not directly linked to work contributions and is considered a kind of 'social pension' in order to control the widespread poverty in this vulnerable group. Its initial value in 2002 was 28 euros per month, set to reach 75 euros in 2016. What is characteristic of this basic pension is that it is funded directly from the Kosovo budget and administered by the Ministry of Labor and Social Welfare. There are over 132 thousand Kosovo residents who are entitled to this basic pension by right.[29] Nevertheless between 2015-2019, Kosovo increased the total value of its social spending public funds, which included spending on pensions, social welfare, and labour and employment issues and implementing pensions for veterans (Table 7.4).

---

27 World Bank – Statistical Office of Kosovo, Kosovo Poverty Assessment. Volume I, Report No. 39737-XK, October 2007, 18, https://tinyurl.com/47vj5dx3 (accessed November 21, 2020).
28 Ibid., 17–25.
29 UNMIK, Basic Pensions, UNMIK/PR/794, 31 July 2002; IMF, Kosovo, IMF Country Report No. 16/123, May 2016, 10, https://tinyurl.com/yc48ccny (accessed November 21, 2020).

TABLE 7.4 Kosovo budget funds for social expenditures (in euro)

Kosovo	2015	2016	2017	2018	2019
Total budget	1,682,486,849	1,726,757,887	2,001,020,477	2,080,480,837	2,378,231,797
Social transfers	417,000,000	452,000,000	468,000,000 e	475,000,000 e	477,000,000 e
Pensions	264,979,437	321,743,867	328,355,170	257,628,435	309,612,050
Social welfare (schemes, services, institutions)	35,822,816	37,322,176	38,890,170	44,925,710	45,876,013
Veterans pensions	–	32,000,000	38,000,000	58,750,000	57,911,776
Labor and employment issues	6,521,105	5,772,995	7,272,311	7,333,604 e	7,297,628 e

e – estimated

SOURCE: OWN ELABORATION BASED ON LAW NO. 05/L-001, ON BUDGET OF REPUBLIC OF KOSOVO FOR YEAR 2015, HTTPS://MF.RKS-GOV.NET/DESK/INC/MEDIA/E2A5414A-D99D-4A1C-B43E-326D83BC0 134.PDF (ACCESSED NOVEMBER 23, 2020); LAW NO. 05/L-109 ON AMENDING AND SUPPLEMENTING THE LAW NO. 05/L-071 ON BUDGET OF REPUBLIC OF KOSOVO FOR THE YEAR 2016, HTTPS://MF.RKS-GOV.NET/DESK/INC/MEDIA/76C7CA43-368A-4340-9DBF-020B371886D0.PDF (ACCESSED NOVEMBER 23, 2020); LAW NO. 05/L–125 ON BUDGET OF REPUBLIC OF KOSOVO FOR YEAR 2017, HTTPS://MF.RKS-GOV.NET/DESK/INC/MEDIA/319C5CEF-38CF-4E34-A1F3-A581FC1DE627.PDF (ACCESSED NOVEMBER 23, 2020); LAW NO. 06/L-020, 2018 ON BUDGET OF REPUBLIC OF KOSOVO FOR YEAR 2018, HTTPS://MF.RKS-GOV.NET/DESK/INC/MEDIA/ED82668F-DF99-42A3-A3ED-DE85125C56BC.PDF (ACCESSED NOVEMBER 23, 2020); LAW NO. 06/L–133 ON THE BUDGET APPROPRIATIONS FOR THE BUDGET OF THE REPUBLIC OF KOSOVO FOR YEAR 2019, HTTPS://MF.RKS-GOV.NET/DESK/INC/MEDIA/6DD9224D-9C40-448E-B71F-06284B8E810C.PDF (ACCESSED NOVEMBER 23, 2020).

The basic pension for the disabled (disability pension) was created in July 2004 and is pegged to the level of the basic pension. To qualify for this pension, the beneficiary should have a total and permanent disability declared by the Medical Commission Ministry of Labor and Social Welfare. When these individuals reach the age of 65, the disability pension is replaced by the basic pension. Under the same criteria, those within the compulsory savings scheme will receive the annual pension after being classified as having a total and permanent disability. In case of death, the annual pension is transferred to the closest relative, who is determined in advance.[30] Kosovo also allocates funds for the various classes of veterans and their families (see Table 7.5).

---

30 Law on Pension Schemes of 2014, https://mpms.rks-gov.net/wpdm-package/ligji-nr-04-l-131-per-skemat-pensionale-te-finacuar-nga-shtetei-pdf/ (accessed September 15, 2019).

TABLE 7.5 Pension scheme for families of martyrs disabled veterans by categories (in number)

Category	Q4 2015	Q4 2016	2017[a]	2018[a]	2019[a]
Disabled veterans	3,444	3,423	3,405	4,149	3,798
Families of missing civilians	365	363	358	339	255
Carers of disabled civilians	36	33	31	32	23
Civil war disabled veterans	2,096	1,975	1,901	1,784	1,370
Families of civilian victims	4,693	4,573	4,469	4,116	2,917
Families of KLA martyrs	1,985	1,964	1,943	2,341	1,805
Guardians of disabled veterans	75	73	73	77	68
Families of KLA missing veterans	20	20	20	20	14
Families of disabled veterans after death	138	153	167	176	161
Families of disabled civilians after death	99	103	105	104	82

a Data recorded in December of the given year

SOURCE: OWN ELABORATION BASED ON KOSOVO AGENCY OF STATISTICS, SOCIAL WELFARE STATISTICS 2015, 29, HTTPS://ASK.RKS-GOV.NET/MEDIA/2649/MIREQENIA-ANGLISHT-2015.PDF (ACCESSED NOVEMBER 24, 2020); KOSOVO AGENCY OF STATISTICS, SOCIAL WELFARE STATISTICS 2016, 28, HTTPS://ASK.RKS-GOV.NET/MEDIA/3204/SOCIAL-WELFARE-STATISTICS-2016.PDF (ACCESSED NOVEMBER 24, 2020); KOSOVO AGENCY OF STATISTICS, SOCIAL WELFARE STATISTICS 2017, 27, HTTPS://ASK.RKS-GOV.NET/MEDIA/4066/SOCIAL-WELFARE-STATISTICS-2017.PDF (ACCESSED NOVEMBER 24, 2020); KOSOVO AGENCY OF STATISTICS, SOCIAL WELFARE STATISTICS 2018, 32, HTTPS://ASK.RKS-GOV.NET/MEDIA/4884/SOCIAL-WELFARE-STATISTICS-2018.PDF (ACCESSED NOVEMBER 24, 2020); KOSOVO AGENCY OF STATISTICS, SOCIAL WELFARE STATISTICS 2019, 31, HTTPS://ASK.RKS-GOV.NET/MEDIA/5839/SOCIAL-WELFARE-STATISTICS-IN-Q4-2019.PDF (ACCESSED NOVEMBER 24, 2020).

The most complex issues about the sustainability of the pension scheme relate to individual savings accounts and the decision that all funds saved be invested outside of Kosovo and be administered by a single company. The issue of acceptance of the pension system by society is complicated. The system seems quite unfair since it makes no distinction in terms of the amount of contributions and their duration. Additionally, the current scheme is perceived as an outbound scheme.

Kosovo continues to operate a centralized medical system that functions according to the model of direct delivery of medical services, which is financed directly from the state budget.[31] In recent years, efforts have been made to introduce health insurance and initially, in 2015, the government of Kosovo provided financial support to kick start the first phase of the operation of the Joint Health Insurance Fund. However, this health insurance has not yet come into effect and there are still many debates about the financial cost and benefits of this system. Most of the funds in the area of social welfare are allocated to the categories listed in Table 7.6.

TABLE 7.6 Distribution of funds within social welfare in Kosovo (in euro)

Year	2015	2016	2017	2018	2019
Social welfare in Kosovo	35,822,816	37,322,176	38,890,170	44,925,710	45,876,013
Social assistance scheme	28,148,125	30,594,956	27,427,080	31,426,880	29,602,854
Social services	4,760,388	4,718,697	4,760,937	4,730,485	4,326,326
Institutions	2,557,270	1,761,854	2,048,865	4,106,527	6,400,498
Institutions of social policies	134,077	149,207	137,401	143,198	147,355
General Council for Social Services	37,151	25,514	15,887	18,620	18,980
Labor and employment issues	6,521,105	5,772,995	7,272,311	7,333,604 e	7,297,628 e
Employment division	4,435,653	4,100,948	5,095,669	5,201,502 e	5,282,066 e
Labor Inspections	567,952	566,583	610,716	613,341 e	615,966 e
Professional training	1,517,500	1,105,463	1,565,926	1,132,287	1,183,206

e - estimated

SOURCE: OWN ELABORATION BASED ON LAW NO. 05/L-001, ON BUDGET OF REPUBLIC OF KOSOVO FOR YEAR 2015, HTTPS://MF.RKS-GOV.NET/DESK/INC/MEDIA/E2A5414A-D99D-4A1C-B43E-326D83BC0 134.PDF (ACCESSED NOVEMBER 25, 2020); LAW NO. 05/L-109 ON AMENDING AND SUPPLEMENTING THE LAW NO. 05/L-071 ON BUDGET OF REPUBLIC OF KOSOVO FOR THE YEAR 2016, HTTPS://MF.RKS-GOV.NET/DESK/INC/MEDIA/76C7CA43-368A-4340-9DBF-020B371886D0.PDF (ACCESSED NOVEMBER 25, 2020); LAW NO. 05/L-125 ON BUDGET OF REPUBLIC OF KOSOVO FOR YEAR 2017, HTTPS://MF.RKS-GOV.NET/DESK/INC/MEDIA/319C5CEF-38CF-4E34-A1F3-A581FC1DE627.PDF (ACCESSED NOVEMBER 25, 2020); LAW NO. 06/L-020, 2018 ON BUDGET OF REPUBLIC OF KOSOVO FOR YEAR 2018, HTTPS://MF.RKS-GOV.NET/DESK/INC/MEDIA/ED82668F-DF99-42A3-A3ED-DE85125C56BC.PDF (ACCESSED NOVEMBER 25, 2020); LAW NO. 06/L-133 ON THE BUDGET APPROPRIATIONS FOR THE BUDGET OF THE REPUBLIC OF KOSOVO FOR YEAR 2019, HTTPS://MF.RKS-GOV.NET/DESK/INC/MEDIA/6DD9224D-9C40-448E-B71F-06284B8E810C.PDF (ACCESSED NOVEMBER 25, 2020).

---

31 Law on Health Insurance of 2014, Article 14, https://gzk.rks-gov.net/ActDetail.aspx?ActID=9450 (accessed September 15, 2010).

Kosovo offers relief from premium payments, co-financing and other benefits to individuals who are identified as poor according to official test criteria, as defined by sub-legal acts of the Kosovo government. These categories are old-age pensioners and contributors; Trepca pensioners; KPC Pensioners and the KSF; close family members of martyrs; war invalids, war veterans and their close family; former political prisoners and close family; close family members of civilian victims of war; victims of sexual violence during the war; persons with disabilities; as well as students. As Table 7.7 shows in 2015–2019 social spending on some of the groups increased which resulted in a heavy burden on the state budget.

TABLE 7.7   The distribution of pensions in Kosovo (in euro)

Year	2015	2016	2017	2018	2019
Pensions	264,979,437	321,743,867	328,355,170	257,628,435	309,612,050
Basic pensions	119,083,713	119,550,488	114,274,807	116,226,788	140,087,706
Pensions for persons with disabilities	15,117,200	18,315,000	19,700,000	19,700,000	17,100,000
Pensions for disabled veterans	40,829,837	37,833,691	38,155,675	38,160,325	39,664,269
Early pensions (Trepca)	4,100,000	4,610,000	4,610,888	4,300,000	5,300,000
KPC early pensions	2,000,000	2,506,000	2,600,000	2,600,000	2,785,000
Pensions of KSF members	800,000	800,000	800,000	1,300,000	1,403,000
Contributing basic pensions	68,633,800	91,683,800	89,713,800	89,891,647	111,121,647

SOURCE: OWN ELABORATION BASED ON LAW NO. 05/L-001 ON BUDGET OF REPUBLIC OF KOSOVO FOR YEAR 2015, HTTPS://MF.RKS-GOV.NET/DESK/INC/MEDIA/E2A5414A-D99D-4A1C-B43E-326D83BC0134.PDF (ACCESSED NOVEMBER 26, 2020); LAW NO. 05/L-109 ON AMENDING AND SUPPLEMENTING THE LAW NO. 05/L-071 ON BUDGET OF REPUBLIC OF KOSOVO FOR THE YEAR 2016, HTTPS://MF.RKS-GOV.NET/DESK/INC/MEDIA/76C7CA43-368A-4340-9DBF-020B371886D0.PDF (ACCESSED NOVEMBER 26, 2020); LAW NO. 05/L-125 ON BUDGET OF REPUBLIC OF KOSOVO FOR YEAR 2017, HTTPS://MF.RKS-GOV.NET/DESK/INC/MEDIA/319C5CEF-38CF-4E34-A1F3-A581FC1DE627.PDF (ACCESSED NOVEMBER 26, 2020); LAW NO. 06/L-020 ON BUDGET OF REPUBLIC OF KOSOVO FOR YEAR 2018, HTTPS://MF.RKS-GOV.NET/DESK/INC/MEDIA/ED82668F-DF99-42A3-A3ED-DE85125C56BC.PDF (ACCESSED NOVEMBER 26, 2020); LAW NO. 06/L-133 ON THE BUDGET APPROPRIATIONS FOR THE BUDGET OF THE REPUBLIC OF KOSOVO FOR YEAR 2019, HTTPS://MF.RKS-GOV.NET/DESK/INC/MEDIA/6DD9224D-9C40-448E-B71F-06284B8E810C.PDF (ACCESSED NOVEMBER 26, 2020).

It is traditionally thought that the need for long-term health care in Kosovo should be covered by the wider family and especially by close family members. This means that in Kosovo over the years there have been fewer institutions offering long-term health care than in other countries in the region. In a way, this gives Kosovo a special advantage in modernizing long-term care services, as in most cases when long-term care is required in Kosovo, this is provided by the family in combination with home care services that are available in some of the larger cities in Kosovo. However, there are some concerns about this system. Firstly, partly as a result of the crisis of the 1980s, extended families are dispersed and have fewer members, mainly due to the large migration out of Kosovo. Secondly, economic and demographic trends are extinguishing the tradition of care from extended family, and more importantly, they are reducing the family's ability to take care of the old and the disabled. Thirdly, especially

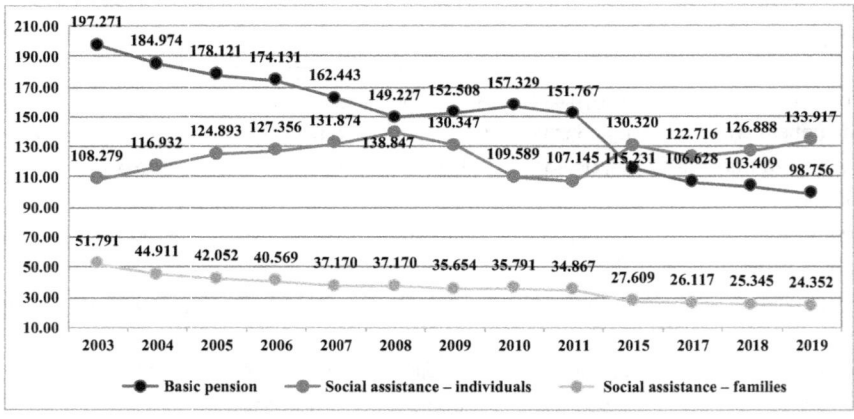

FIGURE 7.2 Beneficiaries of social assistance in Kosovo, 2003–2019
SOURCE: OWN ELABORATION BASED ON ARBËRESHA LOXHA, PENSION SYSTEM IN KOSOVO: REVIEW OF CURRENT STATE, MAIN CHALLENGES AND GAPS, POLICY REPORT 06/2012, (GROUP FOR LEGAL AND POLITICAL STUDIES, DECEMBER 2012), 8; VALON MURATI, QERKIN BERISHA, SOCIAL POLICIES IN KOSOVO: SOCIAL SCHEMES AND THEIR CONFORMITY WITH THE KOSOVO REALITY, FRIEDRICH-EBERT-STIFTUNG, PRISHTINA 2010, 12; KOSOVO AGENCY FOR STATISTICS, HTTPS://ASK.RKS-GOV.NET/SQ/AGJENCIA-E-STATISTIKAVE-TE-KOSOVES/ADD-NEWS/STATISTIKAT-E-MIREQENIES-SOCIALE-TM3-2015 (ACCESSED NOVEMBER 27, 2020); WORLD BANK, KOSOVO SOCIAL ASSISTANCE SCHEME STUDY. ASSESSMENT AND REFORM OPTIONS, 14, HTTP://DOCUMENTS1.WORLDBANK.ORG/CURATED/EN/994991557470271998/PDF/KOSOVO-SOCIAL-ASSISTANCE-SCHEME-STUDY-ASSESSMENT-AND-REFORM-OPTIONS.PDF (ACCESSED NOVEMBER 27, 2020); KOSOVO AGENCY OF STATISTICS, SOCIAL WELFARE STATISTICS 2018, 14, HTTPS://ASK.RKS-GOV.NET/MEDIA/4884/SOCIAL-WELFARE-STATISTICS-2018.PDF (ACCESSED NOVEMBER 27, 2020); KOSOVO AGENCY OF STATISTICS, SOCIAL WELFARE STATISTICS Q4 2019, 14, HTTPS://ASK.RKS-GOV.NET/MEDIA/5839/SOCIAL-WELFARE-STATISTICS-IN-Q4-2019.PDF (ACCESSED NOVEMBER 27, 2020).

with regard to disabled children, family care may not always be in the best interest of the child due to socio-cultural taboos where the feeling of shame and the tendency of concealment and the exclusion of the child from many social activities prevail. Figure 7.2 above shows long-term trends of declining number of both pension beneficiaries and families receiving social assistance with an increase in the number of individual beneficiaries of social assistance.

5   Challenging Factors for Social Policy

In order to join the European Union, Kosovo must harmonize its social policies during the accession process. Harmonization of social security is complicated by the structural and institutional differences in social security that exist among the European Union member states. These structural differences vary considerably in their budget allocations for social programs, social assistance, health care, pensions, and unemployment benefits.

Institutional challenges include the various social support mechanisms that exist for the redistribution of social security. The respective European Union member states use a combination of different methods to support their social state programs, such as offering social services, social coupons, cash, and transfer payments. Kosovo pursues such practices by harmonizing its social system with related regional systems. Harmonization of social security at the European level, in addition to the unique definition of special benefits, would also require necessary fundamental structural and institutional changes in the social state of the member and candidate countries. This can potentially create serious social instability and may provoke a hostile public reaction by affecting other important sectors within member and candidate countries. Kosovo clearly lacks the financial means to become comparable with EU member states regarding the generosity of redistributing social spending. The high degree of inequality in Kosovo, somewhat mitigated by the considerable inflow of remittances from abroad, represents a weak base in the development of production and poor international competitiveness. In Kosovo, the labor market is characterized by low turnout and high unemployment rates.[32]

A difficult situation occurs when the majority of the unemployed are young people between 17 and 24 years of age, who fall into the category of the

---

32   Artan Haziri, "Characteristics of the Labor Market in Kosovo and Europe", European Journal of Economics and Business Studies 1, no 3 (2015): 192–198; World Bank – Vienna Institute for International Economic Studies, Western Balkans Labor Market Trends 2020, March 2020, 22, https://wiiw.ac.at/western-balkans-labor-market-trends-2020-dlp-5300.pdf (accessed November 28, 2020).

long-term unemployed and who are unqualified according to market demand, making this issue structurally rigid. Kosovo faces a widespread informal economy, with weak rule of law and the absence of fiscal predictability, which are genuine obstacles to improving competitiveness and productivity in society. While the definitions of groups in need of social protection may change in any country in the world, the case of Kosovo and its post-war history makes the list of the most complex social risks. This includes a large number of specific groups in need of protection such as children without parental care, children with anti-social behavior, children in conflict with the law without criminal liability, children with disordered family relationships, deferred persons, persons with physical illness, disability or mental disability, neglected and ill-treated children, children at risk or victims of exploitation or abuse (e.g. women who are survivors of rape in war), victims of domestic violence, victims of human trafficking, persons who are dependent on alcohol or drugs as well as war veterans, invalids, martyrs, civilian victims of war and their families.[33]

A disastrous situation continues in Kosovo, and the country's social protection schemes have a limited impact on poverty reduction due to budget constraints. Kosovo is faced with poor coordination between state resources and a lack of the resource allocation needed to provide effective social services. As far as the health care system is concerned, Kosovo remains last in the region and has practically not yet begun to offer this social service. However, the funds provided for health insurance have not yet been implemented in practice, with the justification that they are insufficient for the introduction of health insurance for the citizens of Kosovo. Such challenges are not seen just in Kosovo, but also in the EU member states themselves. They continuously regulate labor market policies, improve education, and reform their social protection systems.

With the exception of the social assistance scheme for families, the two schemes of the basic (old age) and disabled veterans have grown over the last few years, further increasing their financial cost to the Kosovo budget. In addition, in 2016, Kosovo has established another social fund of 25 million euro for war veterans (who are not in employment) and has expressed the readiness to also allocate funds in the near future to female survivors of sexual violence during the war in Kosovo (the number of whom is about 20,000), which together place a heavy burden on the Kosovo budget and on its economic development.

---

33   Law No. 02/L-17 on Social and Family Services, Article 1.3 (e), https://childhub.org/sites/default/files/library/attachments/369_430_EN_original.pdf (accessed November 27, 2020); Law No. 04/L-054 on the Status and the Rights of the Martyrs, Invalids, Veterans, Members of Kosova Liberation Army, Civilian Victims of War and their Families, https://tinyurl.com/y43ksyad (accessed November 27, 2020).

However, Kosovo does not allocate substantial funds to social spending, but in recent years, due to pressures from various social groups, the country has begun to increase social spending with the sole purpose of maintaining its fragile internal stability. In other words, this increase in spending is not the result of a process planned years ago, nor the result of courage, but is entirely the result of social pressure and of seeking to maintain social peace. Nevertheless, compared to some of the EU countries, social expenditure in Kosovo is low with GDP and poverty remaining at a high level (Table 7.8).

TABLE 7.8 Macroeconomic indicators and social expenditure in Kosovo and selected EU countries

Country	GDP [per capita, €]		Poverty scale [%]		GINI coefficient [%]		Social expenditure [% GDP]	
	2010	2018	2010	2018	2010	2018	2010	2018
Austria	35.390	37.720	14.5	13.3	28.3	26.8	29.0	28.9
Croatia	10.610	12.200	20.9	18.3	31.6	29.7	22.7	23.2
Denmark	43.840	48.450	12.1	12.5	26.9	27.8	38.6	36.2
Czechia	15.020	17.990	9.7 (2014)	9.7	24.9	24.0	19.9	19.9
Finland	35.080	36.740	13,7	11.6	25.4	25.9	31.7	30.8
France	30.690	32.820	14.0	13.6	29.8	28.5	32.2	34.3
Kosovo	2.480	3.746	29.2	19.8	33.3	29.0 (2017)	5.9	29.0 (2017)

SOURCE: OWN ELABORATION BASED ON EUROSTAT, REAL GDP PER CAPITA, HTTPS://EC.EUROPA.EU/EUROSTAT/DATABROWSER/BOOKMARK/97639A48-DC97-4C34-9790-3F4DECF67972?LANG=EN (ACCESSED NOVEMBER 28, 2020); KOSOVO AGENCY OF STATISTICS, GROSS DOMESTIC PRODUCT 2008-2019, SEPTEMBER 2020, 7, HTTPS://TINYURL.COM/T3745YS9 (ACCESSED NOVEMBER 28, 2020); WORLD BANK, POVERTY HEADCOUNT RATIO AT NATIONAL POVERTY LINES (% OF POPULATION) – AUSTRIA, CROATIA, DENMARK, CZECH REPUBLIC, FINLAND, FRANCE (PERIOD 2010-2018), HTTPS://TINYURL.COM/42X4RT7N (ACCESSED NOVEMBER 28, 2020); KOSOVO AGENCY OF STATISTIC - WORLD BANK, CONSUMPTION. POVERTY IN THE REPUBLIC OF KOSOVO IN 2011, MARCH 2013, 3, HTTPS://ASK.RKS-GOV.NET/MEDIA/2737/CONSUMPTION-POVERTY-IN-THE-REPUBLIC-OF-KOSOVO-IN-2011.PDF (ACCESSED NOVEMBER 27, 2020); WORLD BANK, KOSOVO. POVERTY & EQUITY BRIEF (OCTOBER, 2019), HTTPS://TINYURL.COM/2P999ZS2 (ACCESSED NOVEMBER 27, 2020); EUROSTAT, GINI COEFFICIENT OF EQUIVALISED DISPOSABLE INCOME - EU-SILC SURVEY, HTTPS://EC.EUROPA.EU/EUROSTAT/DATABROWSER/BOOKMARK/56E7011A-C54D-418E-90F4-C9240B600C7A?LANG=EN (ACCESSED NOVEMBER 27, 2020); WORD BANK, GINI INDEX – KOSOVO (2003-2017), HTTPS://DATA.WORLDBANK.ORG/INDICATOR/SI.POV.GINI?LOCATIONS=XK (ACCESSED NOVEMBER 27, 2020); EUROSTAT, RECEIPTS BY TYPE, HTTPS://EC.EUROPA.EU/EUROSTAT/DATABROWSER/BOOKMARK/EFD8D67F-E057-4161-824B-B323A7F59262?LANG=EN (ACCESSED NOVEMBER 28, 2020); ARTAN MUSTAFA, AMIR HAXHIKADRIJA, ESPN THEMATIC REPORT ON FINANCING SOCIAL PROTECTION, EUROPEAN SOCIAL POLICY NETWORK (ESPN), BRUSSELS: EUROPEAN COMMISSION, 2019, 8.

In Kosovo, low levels of education and permanent unemployment are also factors, which contribute to poverty. The size of the family, especially in the case of Kosovo, is another factor. The privatization of many state and public enterprises was a failure, causing many of these industries to turn into storage facilities, which further contributed to a high level of unemployment, increased the level of corruption and lack of satisfaction with social life. One of the factors that influenced the increase of poverty in Kosovo was the privatization process of public enterprises.

In the case of Kosovo, poverty-related studies began in the year 2000, mainly by international organizations that had a strong presence in the country. In 2001, about 12% of individuals lived in extreme poverty, defined by the World Bank as people who could not afford a minimum food basket that provides 2,100 calories for adults. This extreme poverty line is estimated to be the equivalent of about $ 0.813 per adult per day. The other measure is the complete poverty line, which is defined as the amount where a family income is not able to meet its basic needs, i.e. $1.60 per day in Kososvo. The extreme poverty gap (the average distance that divides the population from the extreme poverty line) is only 2.5%. This is important because it means that the cost of social assistance needed to move these people over the extreme poverty line is relatively low at 1.7% of GDP in Kosovo, according to World Bank and IMF estimates.[34]

In a survey of 2,880 families, the World Bank Living Standard Measurement Study (LSMS) examined poverty in Kosovo in detail in 2001. Working in cooperation with the Kosovo Agency of Statistics (KAS), the study estimated the poverty line at €53.67 income per month. Subsequently between 2002-2006 KAS produced four Household Budget Surveys (HBS) based on 2400 families. On the basis of the 2002/2003 survey, the World Bank reported the estimated poverty line at €43.12. Estimates reported from the subsequent HBS surveys showed an unchanging estimated poverty line of just over €43 per month.[35]

The UNDP also conducted its own study of poverty in Kosovo, in 2004. This study made use of two types of Human Poverty Indicators (HPI) – HPI-1 and HPI-2. The first indicator being a measure of indicators of extreme poverty, whereas the second is designed to assess poverty that is not extreme. According to the resulting 2004 Human Development Report, there was a decline in the rate of extreme poverty in Kosovo from 17.6% of the population in 2001 to 9.7% in 2003. This was accompanied by an increase in the share of the population

---

34 World Bank, Kosovo Poverty Assessment. Volume I, Report No. 23390-KOS, December 20,2001 (Washington DC, 2001), Executive Summary (viii), 8.
35 Ibid, 6, 9; World Bank – Statistical Office of Kosovo, Kosovo Poverty Assessment. Volume II, Report No. 39737-XK, October 2007, 32.

unable to meet their daily needs: from 11.9% in 2001 to 13% in 2003. Other indicators such as the unemployment rate and the number of people living on less than $2 a day also show that poverty has been reduced, these indicators nonetheless remain at a high level.[36]

Kosovo, on account of the challenging economic situation the country faces, lacks the resources to provide adequate social protection, in particular for vulnerable groups. The World Bank and Statistical Office of Kosovo report on poverty from 2007 stated that social schemes in Kosovo have not significantly improved social welfare, owing to the combination of poor coverage and low benefits. As a result of its high rates of unemployment and poverty, Kosovo ranks last in Southeastern Europe in terms of the Human Development Index and is among the least developed societies in Europe.[37] The main factors characterizing the structure of poverty in Kosovo are:
- the poverty rate in households with more than seven members is 7% higher than in households smaller than four;
- the percentage of female-headed households receiving family support is 4% higher than that of male-headed households;
- the poverty rate of the unemployed is 50% higher than that of employed persons. Between the 32 and 35% of the employed are poor, most of whom are casual workers and miners;
- poverty in rural areas is 5 to 10% higher than in urban areas. The Mitrovica and Ferizaj/ Uroševac regions have the highest rates of poverty in Kosovo;
- in addition, almost 8% of the population live in multidimensional poverty. They are materially poor, without water in their homes or access to health and sanitary services. The vulnerable groups most at risk of poverty are ethnic minorities, women, and individuals with disabilities.[38]

An important factor in reducing poverty is the large number of migrant workers (abroad) and their transfers. It is estimated that about 20% of Kosovar families have a family member living abroad. Therefore, the poverty rate in families with at least one member abroad is 7% lower than the average.[39] The political circumstances of recent decades have contributed to the lack of investment, the low level of business expansion and the limited number of new business startups. On the other hand, over the years, Kosovo has seen an increase in average wages, although they remain low compared to other countries in the region.

---

36 United Nations Development Program, Human Development Report Kosovo 2004, Pristina: UNDP 2004, 7, 18, https://tinyurl.com/3hy5ahsb (accessed November 29 2020).
37 World Bank – Statistical Office of Kosovo, Kosovo Poverty Assessment. Volume I, Executive Summary.
38 Ibid.
39 Ibid.

Kosovo had a slow increase in the average wage from 2000 until 2008 when it was under the international administration of the United Nations. Under this administration, Kosovo developed favorable economic policies for foreign investors. One of these economic policies was to keep the average wage at a low rate to attract foreign investors who would see the economic potential of Kosovo's young population, and low employment costs. Kosovo has seen an increase in the average net wage since its declaration of independence in 2008 (Figure 7.3).

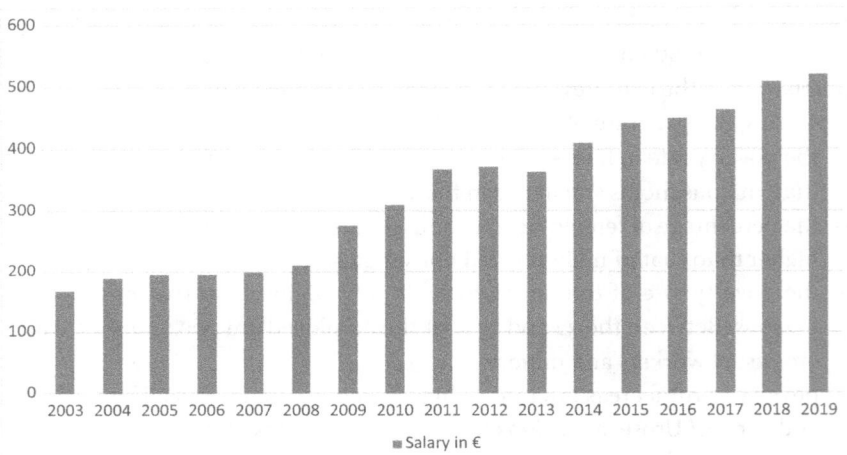

FIGURE 7.3 Kosovo average net wages in the budget sector, 2003–2019 (in euro)
SOURCE: KOSOVO AGENCY OF STATISTICS, KOSOVO IN FIGURES 2010, 33, HTTPS://ASK.RKS-GOV.NET/MEDIA/2901/KOSOVO-IN-FIGURES-2010.PDF (ACCESSED NOVEMBER 28, 2020); KOSOVO AGENCY OF STATISTICS, KOSOVO IN FIGURES 2013, 40, HTTPS://ASK.RKS-GOV.NET/MEDIA/2898/KOSOVO-IN-FIGURES-2013.PDF (ACCESSED NOVEMBER 28, 2020); KOSOVO AGENCY OF STATISTICS, KOSOVO IN FIGURES 2017, 43, HTTPS://ASK.RKS-GOV.NET/MEDIA/ 4404/KOSOVO-IN-FIGURES-2017.PDF (ACCESSED NOVEMBER 28, 2020); KOSOVO AGENCY OF STATISTICS, LEVEL OF WAGE IN KOSOVO, 2012–2018, HTTPS://ASK.RKS-GOV.NET/EN/KOSOVO-AGENCY-OF-STATISTICS/ADD-NEWS/LEVEL-OF-WAGE-IN-KOSOVO-2012-2018 (ACCESSED NOVEMBER 28, 2020); KOSOVO AGENCY OF STATISTICS, KOSOVO IN FIGURES 2019, 43, HTTPS://ASK.RKS-GOV.NET/MEDIA/5821/KOSOVO-IN-FIGURES-2019.PDF (ACCESSED NOVEMBER 28, 2020).

There have been two recent significant increases in the value of wages, one of which was over 25%, both of these were associated with electoral campaign promises by political parties and not as a result of sustainable economic development. These increases have been criticized by international organizations which stressed that any increase in the average wage should come as a result of overall economic growth and not as a result of political campaigns. Today, a significant part of the public budget is used to pay the salaries of public sector employees.

The establishment of the system and structure of salaries, allowances and bonuses for civil servants is determined by Law No. 03/L-149 on the Civil Service of Kosovo and Law No. 03/L-147 on Salaries of Civil Servants.[40] In accordance with the provisions of these laws, the salary system for civil servants in Kosovo is defined. In addition, there are public employees, who are not civil servants, and their wages are not regulated by this law. These public employees, not included in the civil service are paid directly from the Kosovo budget. The law establishes a system and structure of salaries, allowances, and bonuses only for civil servants and not for the above group of public servants. For some of the above group, salaries are regulated by special laws (a law on salaries for political appointees is being drafted), while others are regulated by secondary legislation. This has created wage sub-systems that are inconsistent and incoherent, including some where wages and other forms of compensation are regulated by sublegal acts without an adequate legal basis. The lack of a legal framework for salaries in these categories has led to the situation in which specific legal and sub-legal acts regulate the operation of the affected institutions. This particular legislation contains provisions regulating the salaries and competences of the institution for the approval of staff salaries. This practice has led to the creation of a system of incoherent payments, income inequality, ungrounded in the institutional hierarchy pyramid and which is financially inadequate and demotivating for certain categories of employees. In certain sectors of public administration, such as non-civilian institutions, the legal framework for the payroll system is incomplete and fragmented. Payment system management in non-civil service institutions is very difficult due to the lack of a legal framework.[41]

---

40 Law No. 03/L-149 on Civil Service of Kosovo of 2012, https://gzk.rks-gov.net/ActDetail.aspx?ActID=2679 (accessed September 15, 2020); Law No. 03/L-147 on Salaries of Civil Servants, http://old.kuvendikosoves.org/common/docs/ligjet/2010-147-eng.pdf (accessed September 15, 2020).

41 Rreze Hoxha Zhuja, The New Law on Salaries in Kosovo: What is Missing, and What is Needed to Ensure an Equal, Efficient and Non-discriminatory Salary Policy, Policy Analysis 02/2021, Group for Legal and Political Studies, January 2021.

6 Criticism from External Players

Despite significant effort to build good social security institutions and practices, the social situation in Kosovo, is fragile. The poverty rate decreased about six percentage points between 2012–2017 but remains high. In 2018 – 19.8 percent of its approximately 1.8 million population was considered poor. Kosovo has a relatively low Gini index and flat consumption distribution, with poverty rates declining gradually.[42] Pensions, social assistance, health care and housing for the poorer sections of society do not meet vital needs. Even though growth averaged 3,6 percent over 2009-2019 it did not translate into more jobs and the employment rate stayed almost constant between 2017-2019. In 2019, 21 percent of the population still lived on less than $5.5 per person per day (in 2011 PPP).[43]

While Kosovo has a substantial trade deficit, with much higher imports than exports, it is quite paradoxical that the largest source of imports into the country is Serbia, with which it was recently at war and with which relations remain tense. The persistence of poverty in Kosovo results in part from this difficult social situation. Society in Kosovo, however, is quite cohesive, and this has allowed many poor families to survive not only because of the financial minimum they receive from the state through social assistance schemes, but also because of solidarity within the community has meant helping people and families in need. Frequent cases of assistance are provided by various immigrant associations, businessmen, religious communities, or even successful individuals. It is believed that without this financial support, the rate of poverty and the extreme poverty rate would be even higher. However, evaluation reports drafted by the International Monetary Fund are highly influential in determining government policies in Kosovo. The International Monetary Fund has stressed its concerns regarding social schemes. The basis of social schemes in Kosovo, which includes old age pensions, contributors, other social categories, various war-related benefits, are burdening Kosovo's budget, even small ones. The International Monetary Fund has been critical in recent years of efforts to increase spending on social schemes. Raising the biggest concern was the increase in state spending to provide war-related benefits.[44] These

---

42 World Bank. Kosovo. Poverty & Equity, 2019. Accessed November 27, 2020.

43 World Bank, Kosovo, https://pubdocs.worldbank.org/en/993701492011106034/mpo-ksv.pdf (accessed September 15, 2020); World Bank, Kosovo Country Snapshot, April 2020, https://thedocs.worldbank.org/en/doc/501051589122470465-0080022020/original/KosovoSnapshotApr2020.pdf (accessed September 15, 2020).

44 International Monetary Fund, Republic of Kosovo. IMF Country Report No. 16/123, March 2016, https://tinyurl.com/b6u4jmhr (accessed September 16, 2020); International

expenditures are placing ever greater pressure on the state budget because the efforts of state authorities are being jeopardized to maintain fiscal sustainability. In other words, the completion of many capital projects and other priority expenditures remains hostage to rising social costs for different schemes.

However, at the behest of the International Monetary Fund the state of Kosovo is preparing a package of measures aimed at better structuring and calibration of these schemes, keeping the respective related expenditures within 1 to 1.25 percent of GDP per year. IMF chief Ruud Vermeulen said the current schemes and potential reforms should be revised not only to generate the savings needed to bring spending down to more affordable levels, but also to make the schemes fairer and less distorting. For example, the war veterans' scheme now allows a skilled veteran of the age of 30 or 40 to receive a retirement pension for the rest of his life. This discourages veterans from finding jobs or holding down the jobs they have. It also encourages concealment of income, as well as fraudulent practices to qualify for retirement.[45]

There is strong political pressure for spending in non-vital areas from powerful interest groups such as former political prisoners and veterans, civil servants and pensioners, as well as from a number of foreign partners. As the IMF has indicated, expenditures of this nature threaten to starve investments that could increase economic growth and reduce poverty, such as in education, health care, and other capital projects. The 170 euro sum that KLA veterans receive as retirements for their contribution to the war must be reduced. If this is to be done according to the requirements of the International Monetary Fund, then it will be necessary to amend the law for veterans, as it stipulates that a war veteran must receive a pension not lower than the minimum wage in the country, which in Kosovo is 130 euros for people under the age of 35, and 170 for those over this age.[46] However, war veterans' associations have warned that if such a change occurs, there will be revolt and widespread opposition in every way.

Despite the creation of a legal framework and institutional mechanisms, the fight against organized crime and corruption remains an overwhelming challenge. Under the pressure of European integration, Kosovo has taken some legal and institutional steps to combat this phenomenon. The following laws

---

Monetary Fund, Republic of Kosovo. IMF Country Report No. 17/68, March 2017, 8–12, https://tinyurl.com/yc8xnxs7 (accessed September 16, 2020).

45 Rud Vermeulen, "Kosova mund të shkojë drejt krizës fiskale", Koha, October 16, 2018, https://www.koha.net/arberi/123108/vermeulen-kosova-mund-te-shkoje-drejt-krizes-fiskale/ (accessed July 20, 2019).

46 International Monetary Fund, Republic of Kosovo. IMF Country Report No. 17/68, March 2017, 9–11; International Monetary Fund, Republic of Kosovo. IMF Country Report No. 18/31, February 2018, 29-30, https://tinyurl.com/ypfsxf9k (accessed September 16, 2020).

have been drafted: The Law on Declaration, Origin and Control of Assets as well as Official Gifts; the Law on Prevention of Conflict of Interest in Public Functions; and the Law on the Anti-Corruption Agency. In an effort to meet these obligations on paper, Kosovo drafted two strategies and action plans for combating corruption for 2009–2017. However, the results are minimal: the rate of corruption remains high in Kosovo. This complicated situation has also hindered the ability of the EULEX international mission to combat organized crime and corruption. In fact, this mission was often part of various scandals. The European Commission report for Kosovo (period 2016–2020) mentions that corruption remains a negative aspect of Kosovo that is endangering the well-being of citizens. Kosovo is at an early stage in the fight against organized crime.[47] The visa liberalization process with Kosovo was also on hold for a long time as Kosovo failed to meet two conditions, one of which has to do directly with the fight against organized crime and corruption.

Taking advantage of the European integration process, Kosovo can benefit from European experience in using an open method of co-ordination for the exchange of experiences in a selection of various socio-economic problems. The signing of the Stabilization and Association Agreement between the EU and Kosovo guarantees and respects social rights through economic cooperation, free movement of people, goods, services and free labor forces, and free trade. The European integration of the Western Balkan countries has imposed the development of related social policies at the regional level. These policies require a sustainable social system and guaranteed social rights for all citizens, wherever they live. Kosovo needs to unify the terminology in the area of social security, to develop the most effective and efficient intervention methods, and to build the standards of its social security system. Kosovo needs to take advantage of its partners' experience in developing social security and in developing social protection instruments by dividing their best financing and sustainability practices and their relationship between the state, market, and social partners.

7   Conclusion

There have been many developments in Kosovo in the period after the war. The process of transition toward capitalism and liberalism has helped greatly

---

47   European Commission, Kosovo 2016 Report (Brussels: EC, 2016), 5, 17, 20; European Commission, Kosovo 2018 Report (Brussels: EC, 2018), 3, 4, 13, 18; European Commission, Kosovo 2019 Report (Brussels: EC, 2019), 4,12,19; European Commission, Kosovo 2020 Report (Brussels: EC, 2020), 5, 24, 39. Regarding the corruption rate see also Transparency International, The Global Coalition against Corruption. Washington: TI, 2013.

when it comes to political and civil rights, and improvement of the standard of living. Yet at the same time, it has created some grievances among certain segments of society that have not been able to keep up with the changes and the transition. There are elements that feel left behind, and those transformative trends have created what is generally considered to be social anxieties. In the process of European integration, we are facing a clash between the desire to build strong liberal institutions and those social anxieties.

Kosovo has failed to build a comprehensive social system under the international administration. During this period, social support was offered to some groups, while excluding others. Replacing a system that once provided social support for different social categories with a system that offered minimal support only to the most vulnerable categories, created a broad range of problems. Moreover, Kosovo had just emerged from war with widespread critical infrastructure damage and human losses. The process of European integration was very slow, with stagnation where the exchange of experiences on social security was weak. As countries in the region underwent the gradual transition of their social systems, Kosovo had a completely different perspective. The process was ad-hoc, without proper planning and not based on internal factors. Kosovo still does not have clear social protection instruments, financing methods, or defined roles of the state, market, and other social partners. Kosovo has to manage numerous social schemes with high financial costs. Most of these schemes stem directly from the consequences of the war. Kosovo is facing criticism of the overwhelming number of public funding recipients on the veterans list, while it does not yet provide benefits for children, unemployment benefits, security for workers in their workplaces, nor health care. Therefore, Kosovo should draw on different social security models in European countries, with the aim of adopting a more sustainable and more appropriate model for the country's internal social factors. The conservative model which is applied in most European countries would be a good model to develop social security in Kosovo.

Countries in transition, like Kosovo, that are facing persistent social problems such as poverty and unemployment, should develop best practices for mitigating them through the exchange of proven methods and the adoption of standards and technical assistance from the developed countries. They should reform the state mechanisms responsible for the development and implementation of social policies in order to avoid corruption and improve the financing and targeting of social security. The basic philosophy of social security systems is solidarity between generations. In order to create financial sustainability, countries in transition can apply funding methods based on this principle. The social protection systems need to be adapted to meet the challenge of the regional aging population trends by reorganizing the labor market, family structure, increasing regional cooperation and a reduction in the flight of qualified staff. Right now, Kosovo can benefit greatly from the socio-demographically favorable conditions in which the majority of the population is young.

Taking advantage of the European integration process, Kosovo can benefit from the European experience in using an open method of co-ordination for the exchange of experiences on a selection of various socio-economic problems. The signing of the Stabilization and Association Agreement with Kosovo guarantees the respect of social rights through economic cooperation, free movement of people, goods, services and free labor forces, and free trade. Since the free movement of labor is guaranteed, states need to coordinate their social policies in order to present themselves more efficiently to these challenges.

Bibliography

Ahmetaj, Gent, Burim Ejupi, Dardan Abazi, and Learta Hollaj. Aftësimi Profesionalnë Kosovë: Specifikat, Marrëdhëniet dhe Problemet. Pristhinë: Institute for Development Policy, 2016.

Augestad Knudsen, Rita. "Privatization in Kosovo: 'Liberal Peace' in Practice". Journal of Intervention and Statebuilding 7, no 3 (2013): 287–307.

Avdiu, Plator. Largimi drejt shteteve anëtare të BE-së. Prishtinë: Qendra Kosovare për Studimetë Sigurisë, 2015.

Budget Law of Kosovo of 2015. Accessed September 15, 2020. https://gzk.rks-gov.net/ActDetail.aspx?ActID=10606.

Castles, Francis. The Oxford Handbook of the Welfare State. UK: Oxford University Press, 2010.

Central Bank of Kosovo. Annual Report 2018. Prishtinë: CBK, 2018.

Demolli, Gani. The Mother Teresa Society and the War in Kosovo. Accessed November 21, 2020. https://odihpn.org/magazine/the-mother-teresa-society-and-the-war-in-kosovo/.

Dinan, Desmond, Neill Nugent and William E. Paterson eds., The European Union in Crisis. London: Red Globe Press 2017.

European Commission. Kosovo 2016 Report. Brussels: EC, 2016.

European Commission. Kosovo 2018 Report Brussels: EC, 2018.

European Commission. Kosovo 2019 Report. Brussels: EC, 2019.

European Commission. Kosovo 2020 Report. Brussels: EC, 2020.

Eurostat. At-risk-of-poverty Rate by Poverty Threshold, Age and Sex – EU-SILC and ECHP Surveys. Accessed November 28, 2020. https://ec.europa.eu/eurostat/databrowser/view/ILC_LI02/bookmark/table?lang=en&bookmarkId=110b8efe-4430-4a32-b6d2-3e4304fe66e3.

Eurostat. Gini Coefficient of Equivalised Disposable Income – EU-SILC Survey. Accessed November 18, 2020. https://appsso.eurostat.ec.europa.eu/nui/show.do?dataset=ilc_di12.

Eurostat. Real GDP per Capita. Accessed November 28, 2020. https://ec.europa.eu/eurostat/databrowser/view/sdg_08_10/default/table?lang=en.

Eurostat. Receipts by Type. Accessed November 28, 2020. http://appsso.eurostat.ec.europa.eu/nui/show.do?dataset=tps00108&lang=en.

Falkner, Gerda. European Union. In The Oxford Handbook of the Welfare State edited by Francis G. Castles, Stephan Leibfried, Jane Lewis, Herbert Obinger, and Christopher Pierson. Oxford: Oxford University Press, 2010.

Fetahu, Besnik. "Applying Esping-Andersen Typology of Welfare State in Western Balkan Countries". The International Journal of Interdisciplinary Civic and Political Studies 12, no. 2 (2017): 17–26. https://doi.org/10.18848/2327-0071/CGP/v12i02/17-26.

Flander, Praprotnik. Legal Assessment and Sectorial Comparative Analysis of the Wage Ratio in the Current Salary Subsystems of the Republic of Kosovo. Prishtina: UNDP – Riana, 2013.

Friedman, Milton. Capitalism and Freedom. Chicago: University of Chicago Press, 2002.

Gashi, Ardiana, and Amir Haxhikadrija. Social Impact of Emigration and Rural-Urban Migration in Central and Eastern Europe. Final Country Report – Kosovo, April 2012.

Hajrullahu, Venera, and Fatmir Curri. Gjendja aktuale dhe sfidat kryesore të Kosovës nërrugën e anëtarësimit në Bashkimin Europian. Prishtinë: Fondacioni për shoqëritë hapur, 2006.

Hall, Peter A. The Euro Crisis and the Future of European Integration. November 15, 2020. https://www.bbvaopenmind.com/en/articles/the-euro-crisis-and-the-future-of-european-integration/.

Hassler, John, Jose V. Rodriguez Mora, Kjetil Storesletten, and Fabrizio Zilibotti. "The Survival of the Welfare State." The American Economic Review 93, no. 1 (2003): 87–112. https://doi.org/10.2307/3132163.

Haxhikadrija, Amir. Diaspora as a Driving Force for Development in Kosovo: Myth or Reality?, Summary. Swiss Agency for Development and Cooperation – Forum for Democratic Initiatives, June 2009.

Haziri, Artan. "Characteristics of the Labor Market in Kosovo and Europe". European Journal of Economics and Business Studies 1, no 3 (2015): 192–198.

Hoxha Zhuja, Rreze. The New Law on Salaries in Kosovo: What is Missing, and What is Needed to Ensure an Equal, Efficient and Non-discriminatory Salary Policy, Policy Analysis 02/2021. Group for Legal and Political Studies, January 2021.

IMF. Kosovo, IMF Country Report No. 16/123, May 2016. Accessed November 21, 2020. https://tinyurl.com/yc48ccny.

International Monetary Fund. Republic of Kosovo. IMF Country Report No. 16/123, March 2016. Accessed September 16, 2020. https://tinyurl.com/b6u4jmhr.

International Monetary Fund. Republic of Kosovo. IMF Country Report No. 17/68, March 2017. Accessed September 16, 2020. https://tinyurl.com/yc8xnxs7.

International Monetary Fund. Republic of Kosovo. IMF Country Report No. 18/31, February 2018. Accessed September 16, 2020. https://tinyurl.com/ypfsxf9k.

Jaura, Ramesh. "Kosovo Looks Forward To UN Membership". IDN – In Depth News". Accessed September 3, 2019. https://www.indepthnews.net/index.php/the-world/eu-europe/2032-kosovo-looks-forward-to-un-membership.

Kahlet, Rahel, and Sonila Danaj. Decentralization of Social Services in Kosovo – Policy Challenges and Recommendations. Policy Brief 2018/5. Vienna: European Centre, 2018.

Kearney, Melissa S., and Phillip B. Levine. Income Inequality, Social Mobility, and the Decision to Drop Out of High School. Brookings Papers on Economic Activity, Spring 2016: 333–380.

Keqa, Flamur. "Serbia përmend borxhet ndaj kursimtarëve devizorë nga republikat e ish-Jugosllavisë, 'harron' Kosovën". Koha, Jul 15, 2019. Accessed September 15, 2020. https://www.koha.net/arberi/174116/serbia-permend-borxhet-ndaj-kursimtareve-devizore-nga-republikat-e-ish-jugosllavise-harron-kosoven/.

Korpi, Walter. Faces of Inequality: Gender, Class, and Patterns of Inequality in Different Types of Welfare States. New York: Social Politics, 2000.

Kosovo Agency of Statistics – World Bank. Consumption. Poverty in the Republic of Kosovo in 2011. Accessed November 28, 2020. https://ask.rks-gov.net/media/2737/consumption-poverty-in-the-republic-of-kosovo-in-2011.pdf.

Kosovo Agency of Statistics – World Bank. Consumption Poverty in the Republic of Kosovo 2019. Accessed November 21, 2020. https://documents1.worldbank.org/curated/en/210201560762490515/pdf/Consumption-Poverty-in-the-Republic-of-Kosovo.pdf.

Kosovo Agency of Statistics. Gross Domestic Product 2008 – 2019, September 2020. Accessed November 28, 2020. https://tinyurl.com/t3745ys9.

Kosovo Agency of Statistics. Kosovo in Figures 2010. Accessed November 28, 2020. https://ask.rks-gov.net/media/2901/kosovo-in-figures-2010.pdf.

Kosovo Agency of Statistics. Kosovo in Figures 2013. Accessed November 28, 2020. https://ask.rks-gov.net/media/2898/kosovo-in-figures-2013.pdf.

Kosovo Agency of Statistics. Kosovo in Figures 2017. Accessed November 28, 2020. https://ask.rks-gov.net/media/4404/kosovo-in-figures-2017.pdf.

Kosovo Agency of Statistics. Kosovo in Figures 2019. Accessed November 28, 2020. https://ask.rks-gov.net/media/5821/kosovo-in-figures-2019.pdf.

Kosovo Agency of Statistics. Level of Wage in Kosovo, 2012–2018. Accessed November 18, 2020. https://ask.rks-gov.net/en/kosovo-agency-of-statistics/add-news/level-of-wage-in-kosovo-2012-2018.

Kosovo Agency of Statistics. Results of the Kosovo Labour Force Survey 2012, September 2013. Accessed November 19, 2020. https://ask.rks-gov.net/media/1671/results-of-the-kosovo-2012-labour-force-survey.pdf.

Kosovo Agency of Statistics. Results of the Kosovo Labour Force Survey 2013, July 2014. Accessed November 19, 2020. https://openknowledge.worldbank.org/handle/10986/21042.

Kosovo Agency of Statistics. Social Welfare Statistics 2015. Accessed November 24, 2020. https://ask.rks-gov.net/media/2649/mireqenia-anglisht-2015.pdf.

Kosovo Agency of Statistics. Social Welfare Statistics 2016. Accessed November 24, 2020. https://ask.rks-gov.net/media/3204/social-welfare-statistics-2016.pdf.

Kosovo Agency of Statistics. Social Welfare Statistics 2017. Accessed November 24, 2020. https://ask.rks-gov.net/media/4066/social-welfare-statistics-2017.pdf.

Kosovo Agency of Statistics. Social Welfare Statistics 2018. Accessed November 27, 2020. https://ask.rks-gov.net/media/4884/social-welfare-statistics-2018.pdf.

Kosovo Agency of Statistics. Social Welfare Statistics 2019. Accessed November 24, 2020. https://ask.rks-gov.net/media/5839/social-welfare-statistics-in-q4-2019.pdf.

Kosovo Agency of Statistics, Statistical Yearbook of the Republic of Kosovo 2018. Pristina: KAS, 2018. Accessed November 21, 2020 https://ask.rks-gov.net/media/4369/statistical-yearbook-2018.pdf.

Law No. 05/L-001 on Budget of Republic of Kosovo for Year 2015. Accessed November 23, 2020. https://mf.rks-gov.net/desk/inc/media/E2A5414A-D99D-4A1C-B43E-326D83BC0134.pdf.

Law No. 05/L-109 on Amending and Supplementing the Law no. 05/l-071 on Budget of Republic of Kosovo for the Year 2016. Accessed November 23, 2020. https://mf.rks-gov.net/desk/inc/media/76C7CA43-368A-4340-9DBF-020B371886D0.pdf.

Law No. 05/L-125 on Budget of Republic of Kosovo for Year 2017. Accessed November 23, 2020. https://mf.rks-gov.net/desk/inc/media/319C5CEF-38CF-4E34-A1F3-A581FC1DE627.pdf

Law No. 06/L-020 on Budget of Republic of Kosovo for Year 2018. Accessed November 23, 2020. https://mf.rks-gov.net/desk/inc/media/ED82668F-DF99-42A3-A3ED-DE85125C56BC.pdf.

Law No. 06/L-133 on the Budget Appropriations for the Budget of the Republic of Kosovo for Year 2019. Accessed November 23, 2020. https://mf.rks-gov.net/desk/inc/media/6DD9224D-9C40-448E-B71F-06284B8E810C.pdf.

Law on Civil Service of Kosovo of 2012. Accessed September 15, 2019. https://gzk.rks-gov.net/ActDetail.aspx?ActID=2679.

Law on Health Insurance of 2014. Accessed September 15, 2020. https://gzk.rks-gov.net/ActDetail.aspx?ActID=9450.

Law on Pension Schemes of 2014. Accessed September 15, 2019 https://mpms.rks-gov.net/wpdm-package/ligji-nr-04-l-131-per-skemat-pensionale-te-finacuar-nga-shtetei-pdf/.

Law No. 02/L-17 on Social and Family Services, Article 1.3 (e). Accessed November 27, 2020. https://childhub.org/sites/default/files/library/attachments/369_430_EN_original.pdf.

Law No. 04/L-054 on the Status and the Rights of the Martyrs, Invalids, Veterans, Members of Kosova Liberation Army, Civilian Victims of War and their Families. November 27, 2020. https://tinyurl.com/y43ksyad.

Loxha, Arbëresha. Pension System in Kosovo: Review of Current State, Main Challenges and Gaps. Policy Report 06/2012. Group for Legal and Political Studies, December 2012.

Macrotrends. Kosovo GDP Growth Rate. Accessed 19 November 2020. https://www.macrotrends.net/countries/XKX/kosovo/gdp-growth-rate.

Maurice, Mullard, and Paul Spicker. Social Policy in Changing Society. New York: Routledge, 1998.

Ministry of Economic Development. Raporti i indikatorëve makroekonomik të Kosovës 2013–2017. Prishtinë: MED, 2018.

Murati, Valon, and Qerkin Berisha. Social Policies in Kosovo: Social Schemes and their Conformity with the Kosovo Reality. Friedrich-Ebert-Stiftung, Prishtina 2010.

Mustafa, Artan. "Welfare Politics in Kosovo: Growing Role for the State and Benefit Disproportionality". In Innovative Approaches in Labour Market Policy and Health and Long-Term Care in Eastern Europe edited by Anette Scoppetta, Kai Leichsenring and Willem Stamatiou. European Centre Vienna, 2017.

Mustafa, Artan, and Amir Haxhikadrija. ESPN Thematic Report on Financing Social Protection, European Commission – European Social Policy Network (ESPN). Brussels: European Commission, 2019.

Pula, Besnik. "The Emergence of the Kosovo "Parallel State," 1988–1992". Nationalities Papers 32, no 4 (2004): 797–826.

Pestieau, Pierre. The Welfare State in the European Union. New York: Routledge, 2006.

Pierson, Christopher, Francis G. Castles and Ingela K. Naumann eds., The Welfare State Reader. Cambridge: Polity Press, 2015.

Riinvest Institute for Development Research. Public-Sector Wages in Kosovo and Likely Implications on the Macro-Fiscal Stability and Social Cohesion. Accessed November 18, 2020. https://www.riinvestinstitute.org/uploads/files/2020/June/04/Pagat_e_sektorit_publik_ne_Kosove_Anglisht1591264843.pdf.

Skidelsky, Robert. Beyond the Welfare State (London: The Social Market Foundation 1997).

Stambolieva, Marija. Kosovo from State of Welfare Emergency to Welfare State? (October 12, 2012). SSRN Electronic Journal. doi: 10.2139/ssrn.2687677.

Statistical Office of Kosovo. Results of the Labour Force Survey 2009. Accessed November 19, 2020. https://ask.rks-gov.net/media/1691/results-of-the-labour-force-survey-2009.pdf.

Trading Economics. Kosovo Employment Rate. Accessed November 18, 2020. https://tradingeconomics.com/kosovo/employment-rate.

Transparency International. The Global Coalition against Corruption. Washington: TI, 2013.

United Nation Development Program. Human Development Report Kosovo 2004. Pristina: UNDP 2004. Accessed November 29, 2020. https://tinyurl.com/3hy5ahsb.

United Nation Security Council. Report of the Secretary-General of the United Nations Interim Administration Mission in Kosovo (S/2000/1196), 15 December 2000.

Vermeulen, Rud. "Kosova mund të shkojë drejt krizës fiskale". Koha, October 16, 2018, https://www.koha.net/arberi/123108/vermeulen-kosova-mund-te-shkoje-drejt-krizes-fiskale/.

World Bank. Kosovo. Country Snapshot. World Bank, 2015.

Word Bank. Gini Index – Kosovo. Accessed November 27, 2020. https://data.worldbank.org/indicator/SI.POV.GINI.

World Bank. Inflation. Consumer Prices (annual %) – Kosovo. Accessed November 21, 2020. https://tinyurl.com/yckzuz6p.

World Bank. Inflation, Consumer Prices (annual %) – Kosovo. Accessed November 21, 2020. https://data.worldbank.org/indicator/FP.CPI.TOTL.ZG?locations=XK.

World Bank. Kosovo. Accessed November 21, 2020. https://pubdocs.worldbank.org/en/993701492011106034/mpo-ksv.pdf.

World Bank. Kosovo Country Snapshot, April 2020. September 15, 2020. https://thedocs.worldbank.org/en/doc/501051589122470465-0080022020/original/KosovoSnapshotApr2020.pdf.

World Bank. Kosovo Poverty Assessment. Volume I, Report No. 23390-KOS, December 20,2001. Washington DC, 2001.

World Bank. Kosovo. Poverty & Equity, 2019. Accessed November 27, 2020.

World Bank. Kosovo Social Assistance Scheme Study. Assessment and Reform Options. Accessed November 27, 2020. http://documents1.worldbank.org/curated/en/994991557470271998/pdf/Kosovo-Social-Assistance-Scheme-Study-Assessment-and-Reform-Options.pdf.

World Bank. Poverty Headcount Ratio at National Poverty Lines (% of population) – Austria, Croatia, Denmark, Czech Republic, Finland, France. Accessed November 28, 2020. https://tinyurl.com/42x4rt7n.

World Bank – Statistical Office of Kosovo. Kosovo Poverty Assessment. Volume I, Report No. 39737-XK, October 2007. Accessed November 21, 2020. https://tinyurl.com/47vj5dx3.

World Bank – Statistical Office of Kosovo. Kosovo Poverty Assessment. Volume II, Report No. 39737-XK, October 2007. Accessed November 21, 2020. https://tinyurl.com/mtbcu7vr.

World Bank - Vienna Institute for International Economic Studies. Western Balkans Labor Market Trends 2020, March 2020. Accessed November 28, 2020. https://wiiw.ac.at/western-balkans-labor-market-trends-2020-dlp-5300.pdf.

CHAPTER 8

Kosovo Society: Coexistence, Challenges and Opportunities

Dritero Arifi and Ngadhnjim Brovina

1   Introduction

The majority of Kosovo's society (the Albanians) felt disadvantaged in the latter part of former Yugoslavia's history and therefore there were always demands from the Albanian side for equal rights particularly after the removal of Kosovo's autonomy by the Serb government. Following the end of the war in 1999, the United Nations Mission in Kosovo,[1] authorized by the United Nations Security Council, helped establish self-governing institutions in Kosovo. However, these provisional institutions did not have real power because the UNMIK mission was effectively in control.[2] As with any society that has emerged from war,

---

1   Resolution 1244 adopted by the UN Security Council authorised the establishment of the United Nations Mission in Kosovo (UNMIK) as an international civilian and military presence in the post-conflict area. In fulfilling its duties under UNSC 1244, the Special Representative of Secretary General (SRSC) is empowered to enact laws in the form of directives and ancillary instruments (administrative directives), see Security Council Resolution 1244 (1999), http://unscr.com/en/resolutions/doc/1244 (accessed July 30, 2019).

2   The operational framework or UNMIK institutions were divided into four pillars led by various international organizations that for the first time acted as part of the government and enjoyed a high level of autonomy in the creation and implementation of policy principles. The humanitarian pillar was led by the UNHCR which completed its task in June 2000. In the fall of 2002, the pillars were: (I) Police and Justice, under the direct leadership of the United Nations; (II) Civil Administration (UN); (III) Democratization and Institution Building (OSCE); and (IV) Reconstruction and Economic Development (EU). Also, within UNMIK was the Office for Support of Communities. See Reshat Nurboja, "International Civil Administration and State Building Process in Kosovo", European Scientific Journal 11, no. 13: 344, May 2015; UNMIK, "Zyra per perkrahje ne komuniteteve", https://unmik.unmissions.org/sq/zyra-p%C3%ABr-p%C3%ABrkrahje-komuniteteve (accessed August 15, 2019). UNMIK is still active in Kosovo, even after Kosovo's 2008 Declaration of Independence, and it reports to the Security Council every three months, because UN Security Council Resolution 1244 is still active, and the UN, namely the Security Council, has not recognized the statehood of Kosovo due to Russia and China. See Serbeze Haxhiaj, "A ka skaduar misioni i UNMIKU-ut ne Kosove", Balkan Insight, https://balkaninsight.com/2018/12/18/has-the-un-s-kosovo-mission-become-obsolete-12-17-2018/?lang=sq%20%28 (accessed August 15, 2019).

Kosovo had major challenges in terms of its relations with other communities especially the relationship of the Albanian majority with the minority Serb community. The March 2004 riots showed that there is a great tension between these communities in Kosovo.³ Therefore, the creation of the provisional institutions was intended to encourage cooperation between the ethnic groups and enhance the security and wellbeing of all of Kosovo's citizens. Initially, the decentralization of local self-government and municipalities in Kosovo allowed the Serbs and other ethnic groups to become part of the local policy-making process. This was also supported by the establishment of central institutions such as the Ministry of Communities and Return, which exclusively deals with the return and integration of non-majority communities.

After Kosovo's declaration of independence in 2008, state-building began to take place alongside various institutions, both locally and centrally, with institutions dealing with the education, healthcare, welfare, and employment of Kosovo citizens. A legal and constitutional basis was also created for the integration of society and identification with Kosovo state symbols and institutions. For instance, the Law on Civil Servants of the Republic of Kosovo, in particular Article 11 paragraph 3, explicitly states that at least 10% of positions should be reserved for non-majority communities that meet the specific employment criteria.⁴ This includes courts, the prosecutor's office, police, municipalities, the military and central-level institutions. In this regard, all relevant institutions in the Republic of Kosovo, which are responsible for social and societal security, are striving to create Kosovar unity and identity.

The aim of this study is to examine inter-ethnic relations, social integration, and their impact on societal security in Kosovo and Kosovar institutional identity. The focus is on the following objectives:
- exploring the possibility of intensifying the cooperation and integration of Kosovo citizens in institutions and the social and education system which are interrelated at the local and central levels;
- identifying the reasons and main challenges caused by the non-integration of some part of Kosovo's citizens into relevant public institutions, and its impact on social security.

The theoretical approach of this research is based on the concept of comprehensive security, with an emphasis on social security. That is adopting Buzan, Waever, and De Wilde's approach of understanding security in a broad way and

---

3   Kohanet, "15 vite nga trazirat e Marsit", https://www.koha.net/arberi/150981/15-vjet-nga-trazirat-e-marsit (accessed August 14, 2019).
4   Law No.03/L –149 on the Civil Service of the Republic of Kosovo, 2010. Official Gazette of the Republic of Kosovo.

stating that institutions and actors all the way down to the individual – everything is security.[5] In this regard, security is no longer just a military problem, as in the case of realists and neo-realists, but also a political, social and economic problem. In essence, the concept emphasized as the main role of security – the protection of the population both for the population and the individual from various threats (military, political, economic, social, and environmental). This way security is understood in a comprehensive manner in terms of space, time, and content. From this broader viewpoint, comprehensive security is characterized by five sectors:

- the military sector – is about military doctrine, armed forces, state capacities, etc. and is also called 'the hard power sector';[6]
- the political sector – concentrates on state stability, system of governance, legitimacy, and sovereignty;[7]
- the societal sector – entails the identity of society or collective identity, which may exist independently of the state (e.g., people, religion, such as Albanians in the former Yugoslavia, Kosovo, Macedonia, etc.);[8]
- the economic sector – is about resources (e.g., energy, water), finance, market, social welfare, etc;[9]

---

[5] Barry Buzan and Ole Waever, Regions and Powers: Structure of International Security (Cambridge: Cambridge University Press, 2003), 71.

[6] This is mainly about preserving state order against internal military threats (social order, revolutionary militant groups, territorial integrity, etc.) and external threats (foreign armies, saboteur groups, etc.), particularly after the Cold War, from threats of a non-military nature, such as migration, ideologies-nationalists spread throughout countries, terrorism, organized crime, etc. in this sense, one should be "putting security first", meaning it's impossible to defend civilians and the state without maximum security. This explicitly implies that this sector on principle entails state self-protection in total.

[7] This sector is about threats of a non-military nature against sovereignty, because only full sovereignty defines a state (according to Jean Bodin). Therefore, political and ideological threats like transnational movements: ethnic (Palestinians, or Communism/Socialism, etc.), religious, etc., may endanger the existence of a state. This sector entails and protects/defends political and social relations, and the existence of state itself.

[8] Barry Buzan views migration as a threat to the society itself, rather than to the state, because in this manner, the society may change from the inside, because "[...] community will not be what it used to be", e.g. 40% of Estonians are Russians, while there are around 20% foreigners living in Switzerland, more than 10% in Austria, Slovakia has over 11%, Slovenia around 6.9%, Bulgaria over 14%, Romania over 9%, Macedonia around 27%. A primary task of this sector is protection of common identity. See also Dritero Arifi, Umfassende Sicherheit als Wiederaufbau-Konzept für das Kosovo, (Wien: Institution: Universität Wien, Dipl.-Arb, 2006), 56–57.

[9] Risks at this point are uncontrolled growth of population (or migration from neighboring countries, which may aim to destabilize the country), which may come down to the "battle for jobs", threats from global markets, which implies the instability of the financial

– the environmental sector – is about the preservation of natural resources (e.g., energy, water, forests, etc.), flora and fauna – the 'human environment'.[10] This comprehensive security framework is the main surface for the broad analysis of the identity of a society, and the circumstances of the population's acceptance of and integration into state institutions. With this in mind the societal sector will be explored in this study. This format allows the examination of the identity and cohesion of Kosovo society from a few different perspectives: (i) the historical aspects of the development of interethnic relations, (ii) the development of the identity Kosovo Albanians as the majority of the Kosovo population, (iii) the identification of the positions and views of the other ethnic communities of Kosovo on the establishment and functioning of institutions and state symbols. The challenges of deploying and integrating Kosovar (citizens of Kosovo) society into system institutions, with an emphasis on the issue of educational structures will be also explained.

To conduct this research a qualitative content analysis has been used. Through this method the following questions are to be answered: How does the identity of the communities influence the building of cohesion in society, including the collective institutional identity and social security? What are the challenges posed during this process of integrating ethnic communities into the public institutions of Kosovo? What kind of measures are and should be implemented to intensify the process of building "moderate civilian institutionalism"?

---

system, unemployment, poverty (there are around 1.8 billion people in the world living on less than 1 dollar per day), and organized crime. The primary task of this sector are "basic human needs", e.g. nutrition, or according to Jean Ziegler "food security". See Jean Ziegler, Globalisierung. Das Imperium der Schande. Der Kampf gegen Armut und Unterdrückung (München: C. Bertelsmann, 2005), 238. Consider also factors such as emancipation/ education of society for a facilitated integration in the labor market and preservation of workplaces, free movement of goods, capital and labor, use of resources based on interest.

10 Hence, the environment as well as the livelihood of citizens are of great importance. It is the only sector in which it may be stated that there are threats without enemies, e.g. earthquakes, volcanoes, natural/climatic disasters, and human-made activities, e.g. nuclear military industries. This sector is of particular importance in terms of the strategic resource of water, because it is thought that in the short-term future, water will be more expensive than gold and more strategic than oil, often termed "the fight for blue gold." The environmental sector deals with the so-called "disaster scenarios". For example, the explosion of the nuclear plant in Chernobyl, pandemics such as bird flu, tsunamis, volcanic ashes more recently in Iceland which blocked flights for several days in Europe, etc. the primary goal of this sector remains the protection of environment in local, regional and global aspects. See Barry Buzan, Ole Waever, and Jaap De Wilde, Security: A New Framework for Analysis (Colorado: Lynne Rienner Pub, 1998), 81, 85.

2 Societal Security, Social Identity, and Social Security – Relations and Challenges

In the societal sector, Buzan et al. recognize a broad collective identity that can exist independently of the state, such as religion and nation, as the object of reference of the existential threat. From this identity, they understand the ideas and practices that make individuals stand out as members of a social group. As a result, social security refers to a large, self-supported, group identity: "Threats to identity are thus always a question of the construction of something as threatening some 'we' – and often thereby actually contributing to the construction or reproduction of 'us'".[11] Buzan, Waever, and De Wilde find that this particular reference object makes it problematic to draw clearly defined boundaries to distinguish existential and less powerful threats. According to them, collective identities arise and change in response to internal and external developments. However, given the conservative nature of identity, it is always possible for challenges and changes to appear as threats to them "because we will no longer be us".[12] So it depends on those who claim to represent the collective identity of a society whether, migration or rival identities will be securitized or not. Ultimately, one could add here: "Society is about identity […]".[13]

Since the principle of nationality is firmly rooted in international relations and among the general public, loyalty to national identity or the state is often perceived as a positive attitude. Nevertheless, it may be very difficult to differentiate nationalism from patriotism. However, for any form of social organization, the development of a sense of belonging and collective identity among members is extremely important. In principle, identification always occurs with the social differentiation between 'us' and 'others.'[14] In this process of identity creation there is an emphasis on the 'us-group' itself. This is done by differentiating and defining "the others". Anthony Smith has this reinforcement of unity and "us-feeling" described by definition and differentiation from "the others" as follows:

> The members of a particular group are alike in just those respects in which they differ from non-members outside the group. Members dress and eat in similar ways and speak the same language; in all these respects they differ

---

11   Barry Buzan, Ole Waever and Jaap De Wilde, Security: A New Framework for Analysis, (Colorado: Lynne Rienner Pub, 1998), 119.
12   Ibid., 23.
13   Ibid., 119.
14   Rolf Eickelpasch and Claudia Rademacher, Identität (Bielefeld: Transcript, 2004), 68.

from non-members, who dress, eat, and speak in different ways. This pattern of similarity-cum-dissimilarity is one meaning of national 'identity'.[15]

In order to mobilize the mass of the population and increase their self-confidence, nationalism sometimes poses a threat to the existence of national values and national awareness. On the other hand, Ernest Gellner describes nationalism as an ideological approach for the creation and enhancement of the national identity.[16] He further states that this identity is the result of a long social process and of the efforts toward linguistic standardization and cultural homogenization (high culture) of the population in the newly formed states.[17] An important precondition for building a national identity is the adaptation and integration of the population into state institutions, in other words, the "institutionalization of citizens" within the borders of the state. Smith argues that national identity is a multidimensional social phenomenon and contains five basic attributes that one must possess: "a nation can therefore be defined as a named human population sharing a historic territory, common myths and historical memories, a mass, public culture, a common economy and common legal rights and duties for all members".[18]

With this understanding, for instance Anthony Smith described national identity as a pattern of similarity, where members of a group eat and dress in an equivalent manner and speak the same language.[19] Ernest Gellner emphasized that, national identity occurs or is formed as a result of a long social process, and especially with language standardization efforts.[20]

The other aspect of national identity is the psychological dimension. Here national identity arises from the consciousness of the educated group, based on 'sentimental' closeness. The process of identifying with a particular culture also implies an emotional connection between members and encourages a sense of solidarity between them. The identity of a person is determined by the role he or she has within the limited territory. However, without a particular union, no community can develop. Hence, the similarity (or similarities) that may be constitutive to modern national identity is very difficult to understand, as it is or will be different in different situations and from one case to the next. Likewise, the fundamental question of what national identity really is or what

---

15 Anthony D. Smith, National Identity (Harmondsworth: Penguin, 1991), 75.
16 Ernest Gellner, Nationalismus und Moderne (Berlin: Rotbuch, 1995), 45–50.
17 Ibid., 83.
18 Anthony D. Smith, National Identity, 14.
19 Ibid., 75.
20 Ernest Gellner, Nationalismus und Moderne, 82–83.

constitutes it remains unclear, as it constantly looks like an altered and differentiated category.

In this complex framework of national identity, the existential threats of the social sector are varied from different actors and in disparate regions. First, as migration grows, identity is threatened by the numerical displacement of the population and so, as Buzan states: "[...] community will not be what it used to be".[21] The causes of migration are numerous. They may be political, economic, or religious. It may also be caused by political programs or actions to change the population in other cities,[22] (e.g., Russians in Central Asia and the Baltic States, where the Russian minority accounts for more than 40% of Estonia's total population).

From Buzan's standpoint population migration is a threat to society and not to the state. Migration poses a potential threat to societal security. In this context, Waever emphasizes the problem as follows: "if a state loses sovereignty, it has not survived as a state, if a society loses its identity, it has not survived as itself".[23] As examples, he cites the indigenous culture in Australia, which had no chance of 'survival', and the Indigenous peoples of the US. In general, this means that in today's world system, the most important societal security reference objects are tribes, clans, peoples, civilization, religion, and race. Martin van Creveld believes that from the early 2000s until now, the EU is one of the areas most affected by a wave of migration from a wide range of cultures.

Another issue of societal security is when a population straddles the borders of more than one state e.g., the Albanian population in the former Yugoslavia, Northern Macedonia, Kosovo, Serbia, Montenegro, and Albania. It is difficult for minorities to practice their culture in these cases, because the majority can use the state structures more easily and effectively.[24] Therefore, minorities have one of three basic options:

- first, a system of institutionalized autonomy is implemented to form a government of its own (Slovenes), or to be left alone;[25]
- second, horizontal competition to take place at each level. Communities within a country (like the Welsh, the Québécois) are wary of the dominant

---

21 Barry Buzan, Ole Waever and Jaap De Wilde, Security: A New Framework for Analysis, 121.
22 Michael Sheehan, International Security. An Analytical Survey, (London: Lynne Rienner Publishers 2005), 90.
23 Ibid. 96.
24 Barry Buzan, Ole Waever and Jaap De Wilde, Security: A New Framework for Analysis, 122.
25 Franz Nuscheler, "Migration als Konfliktquelle und internationales Ordnungsproblem", in Friedens – und Konflikt. Eine Einführung, eds. Peter Imbusch and Ralf Zoll (Wiesbaden: VS Verlag für Sozialwissenschaften, 2005), 276–279.

culture (e.g., the English, Anglo-Canadians). Smaller countries (Albania, Malaysia) face the massive impact of a larger neighboring country (Italy, Greece, China) and migration to neighboring countries (e.g., Mexicans in the US);[26] at the global level, Muslim and Asian countries are concerned about the influence of Americanization and Westernization;[27]
- third, vertical competition is the most intensive tool when it comes to the project of political integration. Such as, for example, the attempt to create a federal multinational republic of Yugoslavia.[28]

Volatile political and economic integration is represented by the EU.[29] Fragmentation and integration can be developed together, with the promotion of sub-state identity in Western Europe within the context of the EU (e.g., Catalonia, Scotland, Corsica, Northern Italy).[30] In general, for all of these reasons, in the social sector, society needs minimum agreements for commonly accepted norms and values. As far as the "world society" is concerned, Buzan refers to individuals, non-governmental organizations, and the global population as a whole as the focus of global social identities and orders. He further argues that an international society cannot develop further without parallel development in the corresponding world society.[31] In this regard, the protection of group or collective identity in the social sector plays a key role against risks and non-culpable impairments to their lifestyle. The concept of existence and risk prevention has a high priority here. Therefore, the existential threats to the social sector are very difficult to distinguish from those of the political sector.[32] To sum up in one sentence, – the security task of the social sector

---

26   Michael Sheehan, International Security. An Analytical Survey, 89.
27   Barry Buzan, Ole Waever and Jaap De Wilde, Security: A New Framework for Analysis, 125–126.
28   The consequences of this are now known to have occurred in the 1990s in the former Yugoslavia, beginning with the conflict in Slovenia, Croatia, the several years of war and the cruellest to remember only the case of Srebrenica, where Serbian forces for a short time killed over 8,000 Bosniak Muslims in Bosnia and Herzegovina 1991–1995, where NATO had to intervene against Serbian targets (with the authorization of the Security Council). Then, the war in Kosovo, where NATO intervened (1999) against the former Federal Republic of Yugoslavia, to stop the ethnic cleansing on the Albanian civilian population. See Viktor Meier, Jugoslawiens Erben: die neuen Staaten und die Politik des Westens (München: Beck, 2001), 84–87.
29   Michael Sheehan, International Security. An Analytical Survey, 89.
30   Barry Buzan, Ole Waever and Jaap De Wilde, Security: A New Framework for Analysis, 125.
31   Barry Buzan, From International to World Society? English School Theory and the Social Structure of Globalization (Cambridge, England: Cambridge University Press, 2004), 30–79.
32   Barry Buzan, People, States and Fear. An Agenda for International Security Studies in the Post-Cold War Era (Colorado: Lynne Rienner Pub, 1991), 122.

is to preserve the common identity. Two types of institution have a primary role that is directly related to the development and preservation of social identity: political institutions (ranging from government, central ministries, local institutions that are related to the political development of social identity) and legal institutions (such as the constitution, judiciary and laws), as is the case in the Republic of Kosovo.

Regarding the nation, the analysis of the historical processes of building a nation that has lived/lives almost in the same space and has undergone complex processes and various social and political movements gives us a truly clear picture of what a nation was and what it is.[33] History has a significant role in contributing towards building a certain image of a nation, and it is an instrument which can create and forge the national consciousness. Benedict Anderson pointed out the issue of the nation needs to be considered more as a political community.[34] He proposes the following definition of a nation: "it is an imaginary political community – presented as limited and sovereign".[35] In this case population is an important factor because society is the constitutive element that leads everything.[36] Furthermore, in this context, the significance of "country or geography" should be expressed as "the space where a whole society has lived, functioned or functions". According to Goran Therborn, there are two very strong distinctive elements to a country such as a country as something fixed in space, and also with continuity.[37] This means that a country is a social space where people interact with each other and with others.

Because of the fact that 90% of the population is ethnic Albanian / Kosovar, to maintain / preserve a consistent development of society, following Kosovo's independence, under the Constitution of the Republic of Kosovo in Article 3 paragraph 1,[38] Kosovo emphasizes the multiethnic composition of the state. Furthermore, to reinforce the civic-institutional link, as far as social services

---

33   Charles Tilly, "Why and How History Matters", in The Oxford Handbooks of Political Science, ed. Gooding E. Robert, Tilly Charles (New York: Oxford University Press Inc., 2006), 417–430.

34   Benedict Anderson, Die Erfindung der Nation. Zur Karriere eines erfolgreichen Konzepts, (Berlin: Ullstein, 1998), 14.

35   Ibid.

36   David Levine, "Why and How Population Matters", in The Oxford Handbooks of Political Science, ed. Gooding E. Robert, Tilly Charles (New York: Oxford University Press Inc., 2006), 615–616.

37   Göran Therborn, "Why and How Place Matters", in The Oxford Handbooks of Political Science, ed. Gooding E. Robert, Tilly Charles (New York: Oxford University Press Inc., 2006), 510–511.

38   Constitution of the Republic of Kosovo, Article 3, paragraph 1.

are concerned, institutions of all levels are based on collective benefits, especially for general human needs, e.g., health, education, security, employment, and agriculture.

3 Kosovo Albanians – the Problem of Developing Identity and Statehood

Historically, there was no Kosovar identity, but Kosovo traditionally referred to a territory. Kosovo has been and remains predominantly Albanian-inhabited; however, the Constitution of the Republic of Kosovo guarantees a culturally multi-ethnic society.[39] According to many researchers, Albanians are the only descendants of "Illyrians", starting with a language that is very distinct from those of other peoples in the Western Balkans. One can also note from the names (Teuta, Agron, Genc, Liburn, Taulant, Dardan, Alban, etc.) that these Ilyro-Albanian names are still present. The geographic extent of Illyrian tribes was along the Adriatic Sea and deeper in the Balkan territories.[40] As Aleksander Stipqeviç says in his Balkan research, every story about the Balkans begins with the Illyrians.[41] Georges Castellan, clearly states that Illyrian Albanians and Greeks are among the oldest populations in the Balkans.[42] On the other hand, Aleksander Stipqeviç concludes that: "[...] the Albanians are the oldest Balkan race" and "they form a solid block, differing in language and customs from their neighbors".[43] The first denomination "Albanian" dates back to the 2nd century BC (Ptolemy of Alexandria) referring to the Illyrian tribe Albani, or in Latin Albus, that is, the people dressed in white.[44] Hence, Albanians are named as people with many designations like Arbër, Arvanitas, Albani, etc., but with the same identity.[45] At the end of the 4th century, the separation of the Western Roman Empire-Rome from the Eastern Roman Empire-Byzantium, is otherwise known as "Theodosius line". This separation of zones of influence

---

39 Kosovo under the Constitution is a multi-ethnic state. Constitution of the Republic of Kosovo, Article 3, paragraph 1.
40 Lisen Bashkurti, Diplomacia Shqiptare (Tirana: Geer, 2005), 16–17.
41 Ibid., 18.
42 Georges Castellan, Histori e Ballkanit (Tiranë: Çabej, 1991), 21. See also Ismail Kadare, Identiteti evropian i shqiptarëve (Tiranë: Onufri, 2006), 20.
43 Bejtullah Destani and Tomes Jason, Albanian's Greatest Firend. Aubrey Herbert and Making of Modern Albania. Diaries and papers 1904–1923 (London: I.B. Taurius, 2010), 232.
44 Lisen Bashkurti, Diplomacia Shqiptare, 20.
45 Ibid.

happened precisely in the territories inhabited by Illyrians (later by Albanians) and made the integration of Illyrians even more difficult. The arrival of Slavic peoples in the Balkans occurred in the 7th century, where most of them settled in the Eastern Roman Empire – the Byzantine Empire with Constantinople as its center. At the beginning of the Ottoman conquest of the Balkans, the Kosovo Polje battle in 1389 was fought between the Ottoman army under Sultan Murad I, and an army, or rather an alliance of peoples of the region[46] under the leadership of the Serbian Prince Lazar. His army consisted of all the Balkan nations such as Serbs, Albanians, Croatians, Hungarians, Bulgarians, etc.[47] The Ottoman army won this battle, but it is immortalized in Serbian culture. After the fall of Constantinople/ Istanbul in 1453, the Ottoman Empire gradually conquered the entire Balkan region. Despite the Ottoman occupation over many centuries and the mass Islamization of Albanians, the preservation of national identity played a decisive role in the survival of the nation. The poet Pashko Vasa in the 19th century cites the thesis: "the religion of the Albanians is Albanianism",[48] which implies that the identity of the Albanians is not defined by religion, as is the case with the other nations in the Balkans.

Albania, supported by the Austro-Hungarian Empire, declared its independence on November 28, 1912.[49] It was officially acknowledged for the first time in 1913 at the Ambassadors Conference in London, where the Albanian state borders were defined, but without Kosovo and other parts of the Albanian territories.[50] At this very conference Kosovo was split between Serbia and Montenegro, while Macedonia came under Serbia's jurisdiction.[51] After the Second World War, Kosovo's territory remained under the jurisdiction of the former Yugoslavia.

In terms of population structure and ethnic identity, since the 1981 census in Kosovo, the majority population in Kosovo has been ethnic-Albanian, (Table 8.1)[52] and has remained so to this day (Table 8.2). The structural ratio of the ethnic populations in Kosovo has not changed.

---

46 Vladislav Marjanovic, "Sind Albener und Serben zum ewugen gegen seitigen haβ verurteilt?", in Aus der Geschichte Kosovas, ed. Skënder Gashi (Wien: Dardania, 1999), 274.
47 Reinhold Trautman, Slawisch – Baltische Quellen und Forschung (Leipzig: Verlag Market & Petters, 1937), 30–34.
48 Tim Judah, Kosovo. What Everyone Needs to Know (New York: Oxford University Press, 2008), 9.
49 Afrim Krasniqi, Sistemet politike në Shqipëri 1912–2008 (Tirana: AIPS, 2009), 17.
50 Emine Arifi-Bakalli, "Shqiptarët besojnë në ardhmërinë e tyre", in Kombi. Rrugët e bashkimit kombëtar, ed. Dino Asanaj and Bruno Selimaj (Tirana: Onufri, 1997), 145.
51 Noel Malcolm, Kosovo: a Short History (London: Macmillan Publishers, 1998), 210–218.
52 Enti i Statistikes se Kosoves, "Ndryshimet demografike të popullsisë së Kosovës në periudhën 1948–2006", https://ask.rks-gov.net/media/1834/ndryshimet-demografike-te-popullsise-se-kosoves-ne-periudhen-1948-2006.pdf (accessed July 28, 2019).

TABLE 8.1 Structural change of the ethnic population in Kosovo 1981–1999

Year	Albanians	Serbs	Turks	Roma	Others
1981 (registration year)	1,226,736	209,798	12,513	34,126	101,267
1982	+37,363	+2,453	+163	+668	+1,739
1983	+33,899	+2,195	+127	+559	+1,825
1984	+39,155	+2,514	+189	+928	+1,884
1985	+37,404	+1,913	+242	+751	+1,789
1986	+39,268	+2,051	+234	+825	+1,695
1987	+40,966	+2,069	+230	+934	+1,715
1988	+41,293	+1,846	+188	+964	+1,735
1989	+39,172	+1,588	+170	+901	+1,644
1990	+42,025	+2,021	+225	+936	+1,754
1991	+38,881	+2,044	+212	+859	+1,741
1992	+32,473	+1,62	+176	+716	+1,429
1993	+32,376	+1,632	+176	+714	+1,43
1994	+31,888	+1,61	+173	+704	+1,409
1995	+33,073	+855	+159	+644	+1,374
1996	+34,436	+959	+179	+724	+1,35
1997	+30,706	+1,427	+164	+676	+1,322
1998	+29,874	+1,168	+233	+912	+1,442
1999	+28,947	+1,237	+225	+870	+1,172

SOURCE: ENTI STATISTIKES SE KOSOVES (STATISTICAL OFFICE OF KOSOVO), HTTPS:// ASK.RKS-GOV.NET/MEDIA/1834/NDRYSHIMET-DEMOGRAFIKE-TE-POPULLSISE-SE-KOSOVES-NE-PERIUDHEN-1948-2006.PDF (ACCESSED JULY 28, 2019).

However, with the end of the Cold War and the changes that followed in the 1990s, the former Yugoslavia would experience painful and bloody conflicts. The dissolution of the former Yugoslavia was accompanied by a nearly 10-year war between Serbia and other republics. The most hostile and extreme cases were the conflict in Bosnia and Herzegovina and the one in Kosovo. The intervention of the United Nations and NATO was needed, to end the civil war and ethnic cleansing in Bosnia. After 1989, Serbia suppressed Kosovo's autonomy, which was guaranteed by the 1974 Constitution of SFRJ. With this action, the Serbian regime of Slobodan Milosevic left the Albanians, though a majority, totally isolated from the public system. Therefore, Kosovo Albanians were forced to create a parallel system of services, such as schools, hospitals, etc.[53] From 1989 to 1997, Ibrahim Rugova the Kosovo Albanian leader (from 1991 the president of the parallel state of the First Republic of Kosovo) led a peaceful resistance,[54] but because of the warlike circumstances that were created in the territory of the former Yugoslavia, this did not produce the needed result.[55] Following the Dayton Agreement (1995), where Kosovo political issues were left unresolved, the first stirrings of armed resistance began with the formation of the Kosovo Liberation Army (KLA, al. Ushtria Çlirimtare e Kosovës). After bloody fighting starting in 1998 and the atrocities committed by Serbian forces, the international community-initiated negotiations between the parties in the conflict.[56] Following the failure of negotiations and the increase in the intensity of Serbian military operations in Kosovo, on 24 March 1999 NATO launched an air strike campaign ("Operation Allied Forced") to stop the bloody Serbian crackdown against ethnic Albanians in Kosovo. In response, the Serbian regime expelled nearly 1,000,000 Kosovo Albanians to Macedonia and Albania.[57] This was the largest influx of refugees at the end of 20th century. The Kumanovo Agreement (Macedonia, 9 June 1999) signed between the International Security Force ("KFOR") and the Governments of the Federal Republic of Yugoslavia, and the Republic of Serbia started the process of withdrawal of Serbian forces from Kosovo. Agreement was also reached in the Security Council, namely Resolution 1244, where Kosovo's territory would maintain a high degree of autonomy whilst being administered by UNMIK-United Nation Mission in Kosovo but remain part of Serbia.[58] This Resolution consequently ended the armed conflict in Kosovo.[59] The role of UNMIK was to facilitate a political process designed to determine Kosovo's future status, in accordance with

---

53   Denis MacShane, Why Kosovo still Matters (London: Haus Publishing Ltd., 2011), 40–44.
54   Christiane Prorok, Ibrahim Rugovas Leadership. Eine Anlyse der Politik des kosovarischen Präsidenten (Frankfurt am Main: Peter Lang, 2004), 93.
55   Viktor Meiner, Jugoslawiens Erben: die neuen Staaten und die Politik des Westens, 84–87.
56   Jandl Gerhard, "Der Kosovokonflikt – mögliche und wahrscheinliche Verhandlungslösungen", in Der Kosovokonflikt – Bestandsaufname und Lösungsszenarien, ed. Riegler Henriette (Wien: Österreichisches Institut für Internationale Politik, 2000), 10.
57   Michael Ignatieff, Die Politik der Menschenrechte (Hamburg: Europäische Verlagsanstalt, 2002), 70.
58   Helmut Kramer and Vedran Dzihic, Die Kosovo Bilanz. Scheitert die internationale Gemeinschaft? (Wien: Lit Verlag, 2005), 22.
59   The term which is used very often is Kosovo conflict. Last but not least, it should not be forgotten that this is a unique victory, because it means that no one really looked forward to this victory, you could not really call it victory, because, nobody really did call it war. See Wesley K. Clark, Waging Modern War: Bosnia, Kosovo, and the Future of Combat (New York: Public Affairs, 2002), 413.

KOSOVO SOCIETY   237

the Rambouillet Accords.⁶⁰ At that time, Kosovo was also referred to as a
'United Nations Protectorate'.⁶¹ After the end of the war the international

---

60   Resolution 1244 (1999) adopted by the Security Council at its 4011th meeting, on 10 June
     1999 stated in point 10 that the Security Council, "Authorizes the Secretary-General,
     with the assistance of relevant international organizations, to establish an international
     civil presence in Kosovo in order to provide an interim administration for Kosovo under
     which the people of Kosovo can enjoy substantial autonomy within the Federal Republic
     of Yugoslavia, and which will provide transitional administration while establishing and
     overseeing the development of provisional democratic self-governing institutions to
     ensure conditions for a peaceful and normal life for all inhabitants of Kosovo"; point
     11 states, "Decides that the main responsibilities of the international civil presence will
     include: (a) Promoting the establishment, pending a final settlement, of substantial
     autonomy and self-government in Kosovo, taking full account of annex 2 and of the
     Rambouillet accords (S/1999/648); (b) Performing basic civilian administrative functions
     where and as long as required; (c) Organizing and overseeing the development of provi-
     sional institutions for democratic and autonomous self-government pending a political
     settlement, including the holding of elections; (d) Transferring, as these institutions are
     established, its administrative responsibilities while overseeing and supporting the con-
     solidation of Kosovo's local provisional institutions and other peacebuilding activities;
     (e) Facilitating a political process designed to determine Kosovo's future status, taking
     into account the Rambouillet accords (S/1999/648); (f) In a final stage, overseeing the
     transfer of authority from Kosovo's provisional institutions to institutions established
     under a political settlement; (g) Supporting the reconstruction of key infrastructure
     and other economic reconstruction; (h) Supporting, in coordination with international
     humanitarian organizations, humanitarian and disaster relief aid; (i) Maintaining civil
     law and order, including establishing local police forces and meanwhile through the
     deployment of international police personnel to serve in Kosovo; (j) Protecting and pro-
     moting human rights; (k) Assuring the safe and unimpeded return of all refugees and
     displaced persons to their homes in Kosovo forces and meanwhile through the deploy-
     ment of international police personnel to serve in Kosovo; (j) Protecting and promoting
     human rights; (k) Assuring the safe and unimpeded return of all refugees and displaced
     persons to their homes in Kosovo". See Security Council Resolution 1244 (1999), http://
     unscr.com/en/resolutions/doc/1244 (accessed July 30, 2019). The settlement of the final
     status of Kosovo adjusted in Rambouillet Accords (S/1999/648) Article 1: Amendment
     and Comprehensive Assessment point 3: "Three years after entry into force of this
     Agreement, an international meeting shall be convened to determine a mechanism for
     a final settlement for Kosovo, on the basis of the will of the people, opinions of relevant
     authorities, each Party's efforts regarding the implementation of this Agreement, and
     the Helsinki Final Act, and to undertake a comprehensive assessment of the implemen-
     tation of this Agreement and consider proposal by any Party for additional measures."
     See Rambouillet Accords (S/1999/648), https://www.securitycouncilreport.org/atf/
     cf/%7B65BFCF9B-6D27-4E9C-8CD3-CF6E4FF96FF9%7D/Kos%20S%201999%20648
     .pdf (accessed July 30, 2019).
61   Java News, "Rruga e gjatë dhe e përgjakshme e Kosovës, nga një vilajet Osman nëpër ter-
     rorin serb te pavarësia", https://javanews.al/rruga-e-gjate-dhe-e-pergjakshme-e-kosoves
     -nga-nje-vilajet-osman-neper-terrorin-serb-te-pavaresia/ (accessed August 28, 2019).

state building project began in Kosovo. Kosovo's economy was shattered and very difficult to revive. Although there was a lot of assistance to every area of life from many countries considered Kosovo's friends it did not match the needs of recovery[62] especially in the societal aspect. The idea that states can or should in some cases be (re)built by international entities are ideas of the post-Cold War era, and mainly these ideas have occurred because of globalization and changes in the autonomy of states.[63]

In 2006, negotiations began for an agreement between Kosovo and Serbia under the leadership of the UN-Security Council and diplomat Martti Ahtisaari, the former President of Finland. Given the ethnic composition of Kosovo, negotiations concluded with Ahtisaari's proposal for conditional indepenence for Kosovo. Based on this Kosovo declared independence on February 17, 2008.[64] So far, Kosovo has been recognized by 116 UN member states. Two SC members, Russia, and China, deny recognition of Kosovo,[65] and also five EU member states (Spain, Greece, Cyprus, Slovakia, Romania) have not yet recognized the independence of Kosovo.[66]

4 Kosovo Communities: Different Approaches to Build Society

There are several national and religious groups in Kosovo, which are divided into different ethnic, religious, and political groups. Based on the last 2011 census (Table 8.2),[67] the Republic of Kosovo is made up of 90% ethnic Albanians, the rest being non-majority communities. The remaining 10% of the population comprises of Serb, Turkish, Bosnian, Montenegrin, Roma, Ashkali and

---

[62] Ngadhnjim Brovina and Adnan Hoxha, "The Potentials for Political and Economic Development of Kosovo", ILIRIA International Review 2, no. 2 (2013): 319–323.

[63] Jonuz Abdullai and Ngadhnjim Brovina, "Peace-building and State-building Challenges in the Republic of Kosovo", Revista de Stiinte Politice, no. 47 (2015): 142.

[64] Agjencia e Statistikave të Kosovës, "Aatllasi i regjistrimit të popullsisë 2011", https://ask.rks-gov.net/media/2009/kosovo-census-atlas-2011.pdf (accessed June 26,2019).

[65] Republic of Kosovo Ministry of Foreign Affairs, List of Recognitions, https://www.mfa-ks.net/politika/484/lista-e-njohjeve/484 (accessed August 26, 2019).

[66] Krenar Shala, Rajoni i Ballkanit Perëndimor dhe konteksti gjeopolitik. Ndikimi Rus, Friedrich Ebert Stiftung, 9/22/2015, http://www.civilsocietylibrary.org/CSL/1773/Rajoni-i-Ballkanit-Perndimor-dhe-konteksti-gjeopolitik (accessed July 28, 2019).

[67] Kosovo Agency of Statistics, Census Population. Census 2011: Population by Ethnic/Cultural background, Sex and Municipality 2011, https://askdata.rks-gov.net/PXWeb/pxweb/en/askdata/askdata__Census%20population/?rxid=6c75a9aa-627c-48c6-ae74-9e1b95a9c47d (accessed August 26, 2019).

TABLE 8.2   Population by ethnicity in Kosovo, according to the last census from 2011

Ethnicity	Total
Albanian	1,616,869
Serb	25,532
Turkish	18,738
Bosniak	27,533
Roma	8,824
Ashkali	15,436
Egyptian	11,524
Goran	10,265
Not available	1,840
Other (specify)	2,352
Prefer not to answer	912
Total	1,739,825

SOURCE: KOSOVO AGENCY OF STATISTICS, CENSUS POPULATION. CENSUS 2011: POPULATION BY ETHNIC /CULTURAL BACKGROUND SEX AND MUNICIPALITY 2011, HTTPS://ASKDATA .RKS-GOV.NET/PXWEB/PXWEB/EN/ASKDATA/ASKDATA__CENSUS%20POPULATION/? RXID=6C75A9AA-627C-48C6-AE74-9E1B95A9C47D (ACCESSED AUGUST 26, 2019).

Egyptian communities. It needs to be noticed that some of the Serb community refused to participate in the census.[68] The Roma community living in municipalities led by the Serb community also refused to participate in the census.[69]

Each group within the territory of Kosovo has its own desires and ambitions for the future, which makes it challenging to build Kosovo's identity, social security, and implementing social policy among society/citizens of this territory. That is because without mutual understanding no community (society) can develop. Different approaches for future existence make it almost a "mission impossible" for the Republic of Kosovo to create a really engaged

68 Të dhënat e regjistrimit të popullsisë dhe ndikimi i tyre në politikat publike, GAP Politike Analizash, https://www.institutigap.org/documents/67092_GAPanalizepertedhenateASK .pdf (accessed August 20, 2019).
69 Dashamir Berxulli, Dritero Arifi and Ngadhnjim Brovina, "Roma Community in Kosovo: Between Reality and the European Dream", Journal of Identity & Migration Studies 12, no. 2 (2018): 40–49.

multi-ethnic society. The Kosovo Albanians, who make up the majority of the Kosovo population (90% Muslims,[70] and a small minority of Catholics)[71] dream of a Pan-Albanian community and aspire to an Albanian national identity.[72] Perhaps this has to do with the "unresolved Albanian question".[73] However, on the Kosovo-Albanian side, there is already a "moderate institutionalization of citizens" (that is, a Kosovar society). This Kosovar society is also slowly, but surely developing among other communities such as Roma,[74] Turks, Bosnians, Egyptians, and Montenegrins who consider their homeland to be Kosovo. They are represented in the Parliament of Kosovo, and thus protect their rights in a legitimate manner, and directly or indirectly support the independence of Kosovo. These actions manifest "moderate civilian institutionalization".

The situation regarding the participation of the Serb community in Kosovo institutions is more complex. The Serbs are the second largest ethnic group (5% of the population) and practise the Christian Orthodox religion. This community does not share a common view on building Kosovo society. Most Serbs in the northern part of Kosovo (Mitrovica region) refuse to participate in the establishment of administrative institutions i.e., the four northern municipalities (North Mitrovica, Leposaviq, Zvecan and Zubin Potok) would prefer to join Serbia. This lack of established institutions creates insecurity in this region where problems of increased crime due to smuggling are manifest. It should be noted that from the financial point of view the majority Serb municipalities

70 The Albanian nation itself is made up of two religions, Islam and Christianity. Party attitudes regarding this subject, even according to party functionaries, have been based on the idea that religion is considered a national treasure for Albanians, based on the fact that amongst Albanians there never was or is any inter-religious conflict. Therefore, it is understandable that when it comes to the subject of religion, all parties are unanimous, but at the same time they are proud of the tolerance and religious diversity that exists in Kosovo, and not only, because the intention is also to respect the belief of other ethnicities. This is a very significant point that characterizes Kosovo/ ethnic Albanians. See Dritero Arifi and Ylber Sela, "Kosovar Society through Secularism and Religion.", ILIRIA International Review 3, no. 1 (2013): 310–317.

71 Agjencia e Statistikave të Kosovës, "Aatllasi i regjistrimit të popullsisë 2011", https://ask.rks-gov.net/media/2009/kosovo-census-atlas-2011.pdf (accessed June 26, 2019).

72 Dritero Arifi, "The Concept of 'Comprehensive Security' as a Draft for Reconstructing Security in a System of International Relations", ILIRIA International Review 1, no. 1 (2011): 21–35.

73 Marie-Janine, Calic, "Südosteuropa – Vom Sukzessionskrieg zur Stabilität", in Internationale Politik im 21. Jahrhundert, ed. Mir A. Ferdowsi (München: Fink, 2002), 408–409.

74 Dasmir Berxulli, Dietro Arifi and Ngadhnjim Brovina, "Roma Community in Kosovo: Between Reality and the European Dream", 40–49.

in the north are financed from the Kosovo central budget. The courts are integrated into the Kosovo legal system which leaves only the political sphere where there is still a gap.

The Serb community living in southern Kosovo (over 80,000),[75] who constitute the majority of Serbs in Kosovo present both active and passive engagement behavior with institutions: (i) are active in the newly established institutions (integration into political institutions at local and national level); (ii) in a silent way accept Kosovo as a state, at least they do not disregard the institutions and symbols of Kosovo (i.e., identity cards, the flag, vehicle identification "KS", etc.). Just like the Serbs in the south, those in the north of Kosovo (about 30,000)[76] are part of Kosovo's institutions, the only difference is that they do not want to accept the reality created after 2008, with Kosovo effectively functioning as an independent state.

The political party Srpska Lista (Serbian List), with its headquarter in North Mitrovica, has a significant influence on Serb perception of society and the state. It is currently the dominant Serb party in Kosovo politics retaining close links to the government of Serbia. The ideology of this party is focused on Serb minority politics, national conservativism, right-wing populism, and Euroscepticism. Its political position may be described as center-right to right-wing. In the public the representatives of the Serbian List deny Kosovo statehood although the party is present in the Parliament of the Republic of Kosovo and is also a partner in the current Coalition Government. Likewise, in the registration documents the party accepts "the Republic of Kosovo", which is described in the statute of the Serbian List in Article 1: "The Serbian List has been registered in accordance with the Law on General Elections No.03- L /073 of the Republic of Kosovo".[77] The party has notably stronger support among Serbs in the North Kosovo. However, a large part of the Serbian community in the South, represented by various other Serbian parties, is against the ideology of the Serbian List. This should be considered as a significant indicator for the future development of the process of "moderate civilian institutionalization". Moreover, the policy and actions of the party are the subject of broad discussion among Serb representatives, mainly from liberal social and political platforms. Rada Trajkovic, the head of the European Movement for Kosovo

---

75 Ron Synovitz, "Tales From Mitrovica: Life In A Divided Kosovo Town", 2013, Radio Free Europe, https://www.rferl.org/a/kosovo-mitrovica-divided-town/24903007.html (accessed June 20, 2019).
76 Ibid.
77 Statut, Serpska Lista Webpage, http://srpskalista.net/wp-content/uploads/2018/04/Statut-CIRILICNO-final.pdf (accessed June 20, 2019).

Serbs, claims that the "Serbian List has no moral credibility" to protect Serbs with its dubious policies, mainly because of the following points: the policy of the party predominantly concentrates on protecting the Serbian population in the north of Kosovo[78] and the leadership of the party has questionable credibility.[79] Additionally, Slobodan Petrovic, who is the Serbian Liberal Party representative of the Serb community in the Republic of Kosovo Parliament, is opposed to the way the Serbian List does politics in the Kosovo Parliament. According to him, boycotting the institutions of the Republic of Kosovo does not improve the lives of Serbian citizens in Kosovo. The President of Serbia, Alexander Vucic, has declared Slobodan Petrovic a traitor to the Serbian people for voting in support of the motion "Platform for Dialogue with Serbia" in the Kosovo parliament.[80] In opposition to this action Serbian parties led by Nenad Rasic, the Democratic Progressive Party, Rada Trajkovic from the European Movement of Serbs in Kosovo, Dragisa Miric, the New Kosovo Party and Branislav Markovic signed a pre-election coalition agreement in preparation for the early parliamentary elections on October 6, 2019.[81] The purpose of this political initiative was to improve the lives of Serbs in Kosovo, both economically and politically. The politicians openly resisted formal cooperation with the Serbian List due to its broad focus on maintaining relations with the Serbian government which is not an effective response for the needs of all Serbs living in Kosovo. Hence, the party is viewed more as a tool of Serbian government policy in Kosovo than a forum representing the interests of Kosovo Serbs.[82] Paradoxically, the pressure of Serbian government on Serbs in Kosovo to not integrate into Kosovo institutions has not been successful because Serbs have become part of almost all the state institutions (such as police, justice, municipalities – where the Serbian community currently run 10 out of the 38

---

78 Gazeta Metro, "Rada Trajkovic Lista Serpska nuk ka kredibilitet moral", https://gazetametro.net/rada-trajkovic-lista-sprska-nuk-ka-kredibilitet-moral/ (accessed August 28, 2019).

79 Milan Radojiciq, The Vice President of the Serbian List, is wanted by Kosovo law enforcement for allegedly killing the moderate politician Oliver Ivanovic in North Mitrovica, see Radio Evropa e Lire, "Leshohet urdher-arrest per Millan Radoiciqin," 2019, https://www.evropaelire.org/a/29728943.html (accessed August 28, 2019).

80 Gazeta Periskopi, "Vuciq e shpallë tradhëtar deputetin e Kuvendit të Kosovës", https://www.periskopi.com/vuciq-e-shpalle-tradhetar-deputetin-e-kuvendit-te-kosoves/ (accessed August 28, 2019).

81 Gazeta Express, "Nenshkruhet koalicion para zgjedhorn gadisa perfaqesues te serbeve ne Kosove", https://www.gazetaexpress.com/nenshkruhet-koalicion-parazgjedhor-nga-disa-perfaqesues-te-serbeve-ne-kosove-11/ (accessed August 29, 2019).

82 Gazeta Metro, "Rashiq: Nuk bashkëpunojmë me Listën Serbe janë instrument të Serbisë", https://gazetametro.net/rashiq-nuk-bashkepunojme-me-listen-serbe-jane-instrumente-te-serbise/ (accessed August 29, 2019).

municipalities in the Republic of Kosovo including the military where there was also more hesitation / threats).[83]

The other factor which influences the level of Serb engagement in Kosovo institutions and building a multiethnic society is the position of the Serbian Orthodox Church regarding the Kosovo-Serbia political dialog on the existence of Kosovo as a state. The Serbian Orthodox Church pleaded with the government of Serbia not to recognise Kosovo's independence or to agree to any exchange of territory with the Pristina authorities.[84] This narration automatically promotes discord,[85] and creates an unfavorable climate for all communities living in Kosovo, and beyond.[86] The framework for this portrayal is the view of Kosovo shared by the Serbian Orthodox Church. Holm Sundhaussen points out that the Serbian Orthodox Church regards Kosovo as "the sacred land" or "the heart of Serbia". These sentiments were also invoked by Serbian politicians in the 80s and 90s (for political reasons) as propaganda tools increasing ethnic hate and tensions.[87] Therefore, both ideas are still often used in public debates. It needs to be noticed that all the communities living in Kosovo can practice their rituals or religious customs, without exception.[88]

There is also the opinion that the reason for the Serb community distancing itself from full engagement with Kosovo institutions is its willingness to

---

83 KIPRED, "Administrimi dhe qeverisja ne Kosove. Mesimet e mesuara dhe ato qe mbete per tu mesuar", http://www.kipred.org/repository/docs/Rehabilitimi_i_Shoq %C3%ABrive_t%C3%AB_shkat%C3%ABrruara_nga_lufta_607584.pdf (accessed August 15, 2019).

84 "Synod of the Serbian Orthodox Church: No Recognition and no Partition of Kosovo," Kosovo Sever Portal, https://kossev.info/synod-of-the-serbian-orthodox-church-no-recognition-and-no-partition-of-kosovo/ (accessed June 20, 2019).

85 Zeri Info, "Ky eshte qendrimi i Kishes serbe ne thirrjen e Vuciqit per dialog per Kosoven", https://zeri.info/aktuale/154857/ky-eshte-qendrimi-i-kishes-serbe-ne-thirrjen-e-vuciqit-per-dialog-per-kosoven/ (accessed June 20, 2019).

86 Likewise, the approach of Azem Ibrahim and Hikmet Karacic that "The Balkan Wars created a generation of Christian terrorists" shows how the invasion of the former Soviet Union in Afghanistan created the global radicalization of Islamic radicalism, followed by other conflicts in the Middle East. And the same happened with the Balkan wars when the various Christian extremists from Europe were lined up either in the Croatian Catholic side or on the Serbian Orthodox side. See Azem Ibrahim and Hikmet Karacic, "The Balkan Wars Created a Generation of Christian Terrorists. War Radicalized the far-right and Nobody Stopped them at Home", Foreign Policy, https://foreignpolicy.com/2019/05/24/the-balkan-wars-created-a-generation-of-christian-terrorists/ (accessed June 23, 2019).

87 Java News, "Rruga e gjatë dhe e përgjakshme e Kosovës, nga një vilajet Osman nëpër terrorin serb te pavarësia", https://javanews.al/rruga-e-gjate-dhe-e-pergjakshme-e-kosoves-nga-nje-vilajet-osman-neper-terrorin-serb-te-pavaresia/ (accessed August 28, 2019).

88 Religious freedoms are guaranteed by the Constitution of Kosovo, Article 38-2, 2008.

receive benefits from two income streams – Kosovo and Serbian institutions. In this understanding, part of the Serbian community deliberately remains separate from Kosovo society, especially in the social aspect of education and nurseries.[89] For instance, in North Mitrovica (a Serb-majority municipality) the University of Prishtina offers services in the Serbian language only to Serbian students, including South Kosovo Serbs, and the Main Hospital Center, which is visited mainly by the Serbian community.[90] The other communities are already part of the public school system.

The participation of ethnic communities in the education system remains the main challenge for institutionalizing Kosovo, particularly highlighting the difference in approach to this problem by the Serbs and Albanians. Serbian schools in Kosovo exclusively follow the curriculum of the Republic of Serbia,[91] with the Serbian Orthodox Church organizing a parallel school system assisted by the parallel Serbian administration that exists in Kosovo, and paid for from both the Kosovo and Serbia budgets.[92] Perhaps for political reasons, in most public schools in Kosovo, Albanian and Serbian pupils are divided inside the schools, school names are different, textbooks portray different histories of Kosovo, even games or competitions take place only within and not between the communities. This happens almost in the entire territory of Kosovo, solely depending on who is the majority in which municipality. For example, in the village of Rubovc in the municipality of Lipjan, with a majority Albanian community and a small Serbian community there is a school with two names – for Albanians, the school is called "Drita", and for Serbs "Braca Aksic". A major conflicting problem in this complicated education context is the different curricula. There is general disagreement on how to harmonize the curriculum within the didactic society. Albanian teachers have emphasized that the Constitution of the Republic of Kosovo and the Laws on Education allow the harmonization of curricula in the Serbian language as well. Whereas, Serbian professors are of the opposite opinion, and insist Serbian children are taught from the curricula of the Republic of Serbia.[93] This is further evidence that

---

89 Balkans Policy Research Group, Integrimi i Serbëvenë Kosovë. Pas Marrëveshjessë Brukselit. Prishtine: Balkans Policy Research Group, 2015: 7–8, 10–11.
90 Ibid., 7.
91 Radio Evropa e Lire, "Shkollat serbe në Kosovë preferojnë vetëm plan-programet e Serbisë", https://www.evropaelire.org/a/28142199.html (accessed September 01, 2019).
92 Bota Sot, "Mesim-Besimi zbatohet ne shkollat serbe ne Kosove", https://www.botasot.info/politika-lajme/558067/mesim-besimi-zbatohet-ne-shkollat-serbe-ne-kosove/ (accessed September 01, 2019).
93 Radio Evropa e Lire, "Shkolla me dyemra", https://www.evropaelire.org/a/1980896.html (accessed September 01, 2019).

Kosovar politics still faces a major obstacle to integrate the Serb community as a whole into all local institutions. Differences are also visible in the other fields such as culture and sport important for young people. The "Mokra Gora" football team from Zubin Potok (one of the municipalities in the North of Kosovo) has announced that as of August 2019, it will play football in Serbia's third league.[94] This creates a confusing situation, where football will be played in Kosovo, but not organized by the Football Federation of Kosovo but by that of Serbia.

5   Measures to Build Institutionalization of Citizens

A cohesive Kosovo society, collective identity and the institutionalization of citizens have been built upon the principles ensuring the rights of ethnic minorities, tolerance, respect of fundamental freedom, and ensuring freedom of participation in socio-political life, which are enshrined in the Constitution of Kosovo.[95] The minorities have ensured representation in the government

---

94   Gazeta Periskopi, "Serbia po vazhdon të organizojë gara në Kosovë, edhe pas ankesës së FFK- së në UEFA FIFA", 2019, https://www.periskopi.com/serbia-po-vazhdon-te-organizoje-gara-ne-kosove-edhe-pas-ankeses-se-ffk-se-ne-uefa-e-fifa/ (accessed August 25, 2019).

95   Chapter III of the Constitution includes a total of six articles that directly affect community rights: general principles (Article 57); State responsibilities (Article 58); the rights of communities and their members (Article 59); the Consultative Council for Communities (Article 60); representation in employment in public institutions (Article 61); representation in local government bodies (Article 62). Article 57 outlines General Principles, which include special rights, in addition to human rights and fundamental freedoms, and then highlights freedom of community identity, etc. Article 58 includes State Responsibilities, which include ensuring the development of community identity by the state, offering security in the event of threats or any discriminatory action on a national, ethnic, cultural, linguistic or religious identity basis. Also, within this article it is emphasised that the state has a duty to preserve the cultural and religious heritage of communities. Article 59 of the Constitution of the Republic of Kosovo directly defines the Rights of Communities and Their Members, i.e., the right to express, maintain and develop their culture; to receive public education in one of the official languages; to use their language and alphabet in private and public life; to use the community symbols; to have guaranteed access and special representation in the public media, etc. Article 60 relates to the Consultative Council for Communities, which acts under the authority of the President of the Republic of Kosovo, where all communities are represented. Article 60 relates to the Consultative Council for Communities, which acts under the authority of the President of the Republic of Kosovo, where all communities are represented. Article 61 relates to Employment Representation in Public Institutions. This Article provides equal representation in employment in public

institutions. According to Article 62, Representation in Local Government Bodies in municipalities where at least 10% of residents belong to minority communities and where they are not the majority, minorities are entitled to the position of deputy mayor for the communities in that municipality.[96] The Constitution on the structure of the Assembly of the Republic of Kosovo guarantees 20 of the 120 representative seats in the Assembly to minority communities.[97] Furthermore, the Serbian community is guaranteed at least ten of these 20 seats.[98] The remaining ten seats are guaranteed to the other communities: the Roma community one seat; the Ashkali community one seat; the Egyptian community one seat; and the remaining seat will be allocated to whichever of these three communities has the highest number of general votes. Then, the Bosniak community has three seats; the Turkish community two seats, and the Goran community one seat.[99] This is a process that has not yet been completed. It is also noticeable that the focus of Kosovo (Albanian) political parties and program policies has been toward improving human rights, gender equality, cultivating ethnic and inter-religious tolerance, and improving ethnic relations, which are a prerequisite for sustainable economic development and the preservation of peace. These parties follow comprehensive policies, addressing all citizens regardless of ethnicity and simultaneously keeping on the course of the European integration process.[100]

Following Kosovo's declaration of independence in 2008, all the institutions needed to meet the needs of citizens were established at the local and central level (including healthcare, education, social welfare, and labor).[101] There has also been a decentralization of municipalities, with the sole purpose of creating new municipalities in order to integrate the Serb community into Kosovo. The main ministries that provide every citizen with services in the social and health spectrum are the Ministry of Labor and Social Welfare, and the Ministry of Health. There are eleven social welfare schemes in Kosovo in

---

bodies and enterprises, particularly in the police service in the areas inhabited by the respective communities.
96 Republic of Kosovo Constitution, Chapter III Article 61, points 1–5.
97 Ibid., Chapter IV (Assembly of Republic of Kosovo), Article 64, point 2.
98 Ibid., Article 64, point 2, paragraph 1.
99 Ibid., Article 64, point 2, paragraph 2.
100 Dritero Arifi and Fjolle Nuhiu, "Kosovo Political Party Attitudes Towards European Integration", European Journal of Social Science Education and Research 5, no. 1 (2018): 142–149.
101 "Intitucionet Qendrore", Portali Shteterori Republikes se Kosoves, https://www.rks-gov.net/AL/f321/linqet/institucionet-qendrore (accessed August 28, 2019).

total which apply to all communities that live in Kosovo and are its citizens.[102] The basis of the social policies in Kosovo consists mainly of the social assistance scheme, pensions' scheme (which includes old-age and contributory pensions), early retirement from some enterprises, war veterans' benefits, as well as other social welfare categories.[103] This also applies to health services that are free throughout the territory of the Republic of Kosovo.[104] All communities use these services. In 2018 alone, the number of families in a very difficult financial situation receiving social assistance from the Kosovo budget reached about 25,000, comprising about 110,000 individuals. Last year this cost the budget of Republic of Kosovo more than 416 million euro, or 20% of the total budget. By law, these families, as part of social schemes, receive a payment of 50 to 150 euros per month, depending on the number of members in a family.[105] However in the case of the Serbian community there are some exceptions which differentiate into three groups: (i) the first group are Serbs in the north, who prior to the Brussels Agreement,[106] had parallel systems of health (Medical Center-Hospital), education (University of Prishtina North Mitrovica), social needs, etc.;[107] (ii) the second group comprises the Serbs of six municipalities in southern Kosovo,[108] who in principle accept the Kosovo authorities, but also those of Serbia in a tacit way; (iii) the third group are those who live in villages of municipalities that are inhabited by an Albanian

---

102   Zyra e Kryeministrit dhe Agjencia e Statistikave te Kosoves: Seria 5: Statistikat sociale. Statistikat e Mireqenies Sociale TM2 2019 (Prishtine: Agjencia e Statistikave te Kosoves, 2019), 56.
103   Kohanet, "Asistenca sociale për 25 mijë familje në Kosovë, vetëm për të mbijetuar", https://www.koha.net/arberi/180614/asistenca-sociale-per-25-mije-familje-ne-kosove-vetem-per-te-mbijetuar/ (accessed August 29, 2019).
104   Law No.04/L-125 on Healthcare, 2013. Official Gazette of the Republic of Kosovo.
105   Kohanet, "Asistenca sociale për 25 mijë familje në Kosovë, vetëm për të mbijetuar", https://www.koha.net/arberi/180614/asistenca-sociale-per-25-mije-familje-ne-kosove-vetem-per-te-mbijetuar/ (accessed August 29, 2019).
106   Kohanet, "Katër vjet nga marrëveshja e pare Kosovë-Serbi në Bruksel" https://www.koha.net/arberi/12964/kater-vjet-nga-marreveshja-e-pare-kosove-serbi-ne-bruksel/ (accessed August 29, 2019).
107   Balkans Policy Research Group, Integrimi i Serbëve në Kosovë. Pas Marrëveshjes së Brukselit (Prishtine: Balkans Policy Research Group 2015), 7. The Brussels Agreement was signed in 2013, one of the highlights being the formation of an Association of Serb Majority Municipalities, but it has not yet been implemented due to the non-normalisation of relations between Kosovo and Serbia. Nonetheless, there are also elements that have been respected by the agreement, such as the police commander, the activation of the courts and their functioning under the laws of Kosovo, the abolition of the financing of parallel institutions by the Republic of Serbia, the abolition of parallel structures, etc.
108   Balkans Policy Research Group, Integrimi i Serbëve në Kosovë, 9.

majority, who at the same time benefit from Serbia's services by working in both administration systems and receiving two salaries[109] (from Kosovo's and Serbia's respective budgets). Schools and medical services provide the majority of jobs and those are supported from the government in Prishtina, as well as from donors in Belgrade (Serbia) too.[110]

These legal rights of non-Albanian communities in Kosovo are proof that state institutions such as local government, central government, as well as various agencies responsible for social affairs, social assistance, pension schemes, state employment agencies, health services, education, police, law enforcement, etc. have made and are making significant efforts to integrate all communities into a social coexistence. Another way of increasing the confidence of ethnic communities in building Kosovo society is preserved by respecting their languages. The Constitution based on article 5 paragraph 1 guarantees the Serb language at national level and paragraph 2 of the same article gives the Turkish, Bosnian and Roma languages official status at the municipal level. This allows minority communities to participate at both the central and local levels, increasing their engagement with the institutionalization process. Additionally, measures to improve ethnic relations are established in the Public Radio Television of Kosovo a Serbian language channel (RTK 2) as well as channels in the languages of other non-Albanian communities.

6   Conclusion

The multiethnic makeup of Kosovo society presents multiple challenges to building a cohesive community in one country and modern civilian institutionalism. These result from the diverse aspirations within the ethnic communities that at the same time collide with the reality of functioning within one state. On the one hand there are the Albanians, Roma, Turks, Bosnians, Egyptians, and Montenegrins (total 95% Kosovar society) who actively engage in the institutions of state and on the other hand there is the Serb community who have a split vision of Kosovo divided between "dreams and reality". The Serbs from the South who are the larger part of the Serb community living in Kosovo and in some ways are participating and identifying with the institutions of Kosovo, and the northern Serbs who are more distanced from the Kosovo state institutions and some of them feel closer to Serbia. Thus, it can

---

109   Ibid., 11.
110   Ibid.

be suggested that a comprehensive integration of Kosovo society with the institutions of the Republic of Kosovo has begun, starting with social schemes, pension schemes, healthcare, security, legal issues, etc. This implies that most of society, regardless of ethnicity and religion, feels a sense of development of a common Kosovar society, in order to build their future and their life into Kosovo institutions. Hence, a large part of Kosovar society and a good part of the Serbian community have begun to live a "common dream" in reality. This means that, in this regard, there is already a "moderate institutionalization of citizens".

The analysis of the constitution as well as various laws and strategies on non-Albanian communities shows that the institutions of the Republic of Kosovo are making efforts to integrate non-Albanian communities into Kosovo society. This is also demonstrated by the very fact that everyone can participate in institutions of government at local and central levels and in municipal and parliamentary elections. As a product of building tolerance, all political parties in Kosovo have included the promotion of tolerance in their electoral platforms. However, it takes time for these aspirations to take effect within society. The success of this process depends on many factors, starting with the engagement of all the communities to support what the constitution and the laws guarantee.

The following recommendations are made to help overcome the social division between the communities: (i) Kosovo institutions should, as soon as possible, create a more open society. Schools, nurseries, universities should be more mixed, and open to everyone. Institutional integration should be reflected in the integration of all communities in everyday life, not just 'some exclusive rights' that exist only on paper; (ii) only a model of peaceful coexistence can eliminate fear of others and increase confidence in institutions and in Kosovo's society; (iii) the Serb community, especially in the northern municipalities, needs a 'new agreement' that would make use of the Serbs of the south as mediators. This implies perhaps some legal mitigation that may have to be done in cooperation with Serbia, but always respecting the State and the Constitution of the Republic of Kosovo. This issue will certainly take time, but the other option would be much more adverse; (iv) therefore, if a 'new agreement' for co-existence is not reached, Kosovo society, and in fact the security of this society will always be uncertain. This situation does not present an impression of community, at least institutionally, and can therefore lead to very undesirable prospects for the very existence of the state of Kosovo. For these and many other reasons, the Kosovo Force (KFOR) is still present in the territory of Kosovo and is responsible for the security of all citizens.

Bibliography

Abdullai, Jonuz, and Ngadhnjim Brovina. "Peace-building and State-building Challenges in the Republic of Kosovo." Revista de Stiinte Politice, no. 47 (2015): 135–145.

Agjencia e Statistikave të Kosovës, "Aatllasi i regjistrimit të popullsisë 2011", https://ask.rks-gov.net/media/2009/kosovo-census-atlas-2011.pdf (accessed June 26, 2019)

Anderson, Benedict. Die Erfindung der Nation. Zur Karriere eines erfolgreichen Konzepts. Berlin: Verl. Ullstein, 1998.

Arifi, Dritero. "The Concept of "Comprehensive security" as a Draft for Reconstructing Security in a System of International Relations". ILIRIA International Review 1, no. 1 (2011): 21–35.

Arifi, Dritero. Umfassende Sicherheit als Wiederaufbau-Konzept für das Kosovo. Wien: Institution: Universität Wien, Dipl.-Arb, 2006.

Arifi, Dritero, and Fjolle Nuhiu. "Kosovo Political Party Attitudes Towards European Integration" European Journal of Social Science Education and Research 5, no. 1 (2018): 142–149.

Arifi, Dritero, and Shendim Oxha. "The Difficult Relationship between the Kosovo Political Parties and Conservatism." ILIRIA International Review 8, no. 1 (2018): 89–101.

Arifi, Dritero, and Ylber Sela. "Kosovar Society through Secularism and Religion". ILIRIA International Review 3, no. 1 (2013): 305–317.

Arifi-Bakalli, Emine. "Shqiptarët besojnë në ardhmërinë e tyre e tyre". In Kombi. Rrugët e bashkimit kombëtar edited by Dino Asanaj and Bruno Selimaj, 145–147. Tiranë: Onufri, 1997.

Balkans Policy Research Group: Integrimi i Serbëvenë Kosovë. Pas Marrëveshjessë Brukselit. Prishtine: Balkans Policy Research Group, 2015.

Bashkurti, Lisen. Diplomacia Shqiptare. Tiranë: Geer, 2005.

Berxulli, Dashamir, Dritero Arifi, and Ngadhnjim Brovina. "Roma Community in Kosovo: Between Reality and the European Dream". Journal of Identity & Migration Studies 12, no. 2 (2018): 40–49.

Brovina, Ngadhnjim, and Adnan Hoxha. "The Potentials for Political and Economic Development of Kosovo". ILIRIA International Review 2, no. 2 (2013): 319–328.

Buzan, Barry. From International to World Society? English School Theory and the Social Structure of Globalisation. Cambridge: Cambridge University Press, 2004.

Buzan, Barry. People, States and Fear. An Agenda for International Security Studies in the Post-cold War Era. Colorado: Lynne Rienner Pub, 1991.

Buzan, Barry, and Ole Waever. Regions and Powers: Structure of International Security. Cambridge: Cambridge University Press, 2003.

Buzan, Barry, Ole Waever, and Jaap De Wilde. Security: A New Framework for Analysis. Colorado: Lynne Rienner Pub, 1998.

Calic, Janine-Marie. "Südosteuropa – Vom Sukzessionskrieg zur Stabilität." In Internationale Politik im 21. Jahrhundert, edited by Mir A. Ferdowsi, 405–421. München: Fink, 2002.

Castellan, Georges. Histori e Ballkanit. Tiranë: Çabej, 1991.

Clark, Wesley K. Waging Modern War: Bosnia, Kosovo, and the Future of Combat. New York: Public Affairs, 2002.

Destani, Bejtullah, and Jason Tomes. "Albania's Greatest Friend. Aubrey Herbert and the Making of Modern Albania". Diaries and Papers 1904 – 1923. I.B. London: Tauris, 2010.

Eickelpasch, Rolf, and Claudia Rademacher. Identität. Bielefeld: Transcript, 2004.

Enti i Statistikes se Kosoves. "Ndryshimet demografike të popullsisë së Kosovës në periudhën 1948–2006." Accessed July 28, 2019. https://ask.rks-gov.net/media/1834/ndryshimet-demografike-te-popullsise-se-kosoves-ne-periudhen-1948-2006.pdf.

Gazeta Metro. "Rada Trajkovic Lista Serpska nuk ka kredibilitet moral". Accessed August 28, 2019. https://gazetametro.net/rada-trajkovic-lista-sprska-nuk-ka-kredibilitet-moral/.

Gazeta Metro. "Rashiq: Nuk bashkëpunojmë me Listën Serbe janë instrument të Serbisë". Accessed August 29, 2019. https://gazetametro.net/rashiq-nuk-bashkepunojme-me-listen-serbe-jane-instrumente-te-serbise/.

Gazeta Periskopi. "Serbia po vazhdon të organizojë gara në Kosovë, edhe pas ankesës së FFK- së në UEFA FIFA". Accessed August 25, 2019. https://www.periskopi.com/serbia-po-vazhdon-te-organizoje-gara-ne-kosove-edhe-pas-ankeses-se-ffk-se-ne-uefa-e-fifa/.

Gazeta Periskopi. "Vuciq e shpallë tradhëtar deputetin e Kuvendit të Kosovës". Accessed August 28, 2019. https://www.periskopi.com/vuciq-e-shpalle-tradhetar-deputetin-e-kuvendit-te-kosoves/.

Gellner, Ernest. Nationalismus und Moderne. Berlin: Rotbuch, 1995.

Gerhard, Jandl. "Der Kosovokonflikt – mögliche und wahrscheinliche Verhandlungslösungen". In "Der Kosovokonflikt – Bestandsaufname und Lösungsszenarien", edited by Henriette Riegler, 7–17. Wien: Österreichisches Institut für Internationale Politik, 2000.

Haxhiaj, Serbeze. "A ka skaduar misioni i UNMIKU-ut ne Kosove". Balkan Insight. Accessed August 15, 2019. https://balkaninsight.com/2018/12/18/a-ka-skaduar-misioni-i-unmik-ut-n%C3%AB-kosov%C3%AB-12-17-2018/?lang=sq.

Ignatieff, Michael. "Die Politik der Menschenrechte". Hamburg: Europäische Verlagsanstalt, 2002.

Java News. "Rruga e gjatë dhe e përgjakshme e Kosovës, nga një vilajet osman nëpër terrorin serb te pavarësia". Accessed August 28, 2019. https://balkaninsight.com/2018/12/18/a-ka-skaduar-misioni-i-unmik-ut-n%C3%AB-kosov%C3%AB-12-17-2018/?lang=sq.

Judah, Tim. Kosovo. What Everyone Needs to Know. New York: Oxford University Press, 2008.

Judah, Tim. Kosovo: War and Revenge. New Haven: Yale University Press, 2000.

Kadare, Ismail. Identiteti evropian i shqiptarëve. Tiranë: Onufri, 2006.

KIPRED. "Administrimi dhe qeverisja në Kosovë. Mësimet e mësuara dhe ato që mbeten për tu mësuar". Accessed August 15, 2019. http://www.kipred.org/repository/docs/Rehabilitimi_i_Shoq%C3%ABrive_t%C3%AB_shkat%C3%ABrruara_nga_lufta_607584.pdf.

Kohanet. "15 vite nga trazirat e Marsit". Accessed August 14, 2019. https://www.koha.net/arberi/150981/15-vjet-nga-trazirat-e-marsit.

Kohanet. "Asistenca sociale për 25 mijë familje në Kosovë, vetëm për të mbijetuar". Accessed August 29, 2019. https://www.koha.net/arberi/180614/asistenca-sociale-per-25-mije-familje-ne-kosove-vetem-per-te-mbijetuar/.

Kohanet. "Katër vjet nga marrëveshja e pare Kosovë-Serbi në Bruksel". Accessed August 29, 2019. https://www.koha.net/arberi/12964/kater-vjet-nga-marreveshja-e-pare-kosove-serbi-ne-bruksel/.

Kosovo Agency of Statistics. Census population. Census 2011: Population by ethnic /cultural background sex and municipality 2011. Accessed August 26, 2019. https://askdata.rks-gov.net/PXWeb/pxweb/en/askdata/askdata__Census%20population/?rxid=6c75a9aa-627c-48c6-ae74-9e1b95a9c47d.

Kosovo Sever Portal. "Synod of the Serbian Orthodox Church: No Recognition and no Partition of Kosovo". Accessed June 20, 2019. https://kossev.info/synod-of-the-serbian-orthodox-church-no-recognition-and-no-partition-of-kosovo/.

Kramer, Helmut, and Vedran Dzihic. Die Kosovo Bilanz. Scheitert die international Gemeinschaft. Wien: Lit Verlag, 2005.

Krasniqi, Afrim. Sistemet politike në Shqipëri 1912-2008. Tiranë: AIPS, 2009.

Law No.03/L-149 on the Civil Service of the Republic of Kosovo, 2010. Official Gazette of the Republic of Kosovo.

Law No.04/L-125 on Healthcare, 2013. Official Gazette of the Republic of Kosovo.

Levine, David. "Why and How Population Matters". In the Oxford Handbooks of Political, edited by Robert E. Gooding and Charles Tilly, 615–624. New York: Oxford University Press Inc., 2006.

MacShane, Denis. Why Kosovo Still Matters. London: Haus Publishing Ltd., 2011.

Malcolm, Noel. Kosovo: a Short History. London: Macmillan Publishers, 1998.

Marjanovic, Vladislav. Sind Albener und Serben zum ewugen gegen seitigen haβ verurteilt?. In Aus der Geshischte Kosovas, edited by Skender Gashi, 273–278. Wien: Dardania, 1999.

Meier, Viktor. Jugoslawiens Erben: die neuen Staaten und die Politik des Westens. München: Beck, 2001.

Nohlen, Dieter. Kleines Lexikonder Politik. München: Verlag C.H. Beck, 2001.

Nurboja, Reshat. "International Civil Administration and State Building Process in Kosovo", European Scientific Journal 11, no. 13: May 2015.

Nuscheler, Franz. "Migration als Konfliktquelle und internationales Ordnungsproblem". In Friedens- und Konflikt. Eine Einführung, edited by Peter Imbusch and Ralf Zoll, 273–280. Wiesbaden: VS Verlag für Sozialwissenschaften, 2005.

Portali Shteteror i Republikes se Kosoves. "Intitucionet Qendrore". Accessed August 28, 2019. https://www.rks-gov.net/AL/f321/linqet/institucionet-qendrore.

Prorok, Christiane. Ibrahim Rugovas Leadership. Eine Anlyse der Politik des kosovarischen Präsidenten. Frankfurt am Main: Peter Lang, 2004.

Radio Evropa e Lire. "Leshohet urdher-arrest per Millan Radoiciqin". Accessed August 28, 2019. https://www.evropaelire.org/a/29728943.html.

Radio Evropa e Lire. "Shkolla me dyemra". Accessed September 01, 2019. https://www.evropaelire.org/a/1980896.html.

Radio Evropa e Lire. "Shkollat serbe në Kosovë preferojnë vetëm plan-programet e Serbisë". Accessed September 01, 2019. https://www.evropaelire.org/a/28142199.html.

Rambouillet Accords (S/1999/648). Accessed July 30, 2019 http://securitycouncilreport.org/atf/cf/%7B65BFCF9B-6D27-4E9C-8CD3-CF6E4FF96FF9%7D/Kos%20S%201999%20648.pdf.

Reiter, Erich, and Reinhard Selten. Zur Lösung des Kosovo-Konfliktes. Die Anwendung der Szenariobündelanalyse im Konfliktmanagement. Baden-Baden: Nomos, 2003.

Republic of Kosovo Ministry of Foreign Affairs. List of Recognitions. Accessed August 26, 2019. https://www.mfa-ks.net/politika%20/484/lista-e-njohjeve/484.

Security Council Resolution 1244 (1999). Accessed July 30, 2019. http://unscr.com/en/resolutions/doc/1244.

Serpska Lista Webpage. Statut. Accessed June 20, 2019. http://srpskalista.net/wp-content/uploads/2018/04/Statut-CIRILICNO-final.pdf.

Shala, Krenar. "Rajoni i Ballkanit Perëndimor dhe konteksti gjeopolitik. Ndikimi Rus". Friedrich Ebert Stiftung. Accessed July 28, 2019, http://www.fes-prishtina.org/wb/media/2015/Rajoni%20i%20Ballkanit%20Perendimor%20dhe%20konteksti%20gjeopolitik_Krenar%20Shala.pdf.

Sheehan, Michael. International Security. "An Analytical Survey". London: Lynne Rienner Publishers, 2005.

Smith, Anthony D. National Identity. Harmondsworth: Penguin, 1991.

Synovitz, Ron. "Tales from Mitrovica: Life in a Divided Kosovo Town". Radio Free Europe. Accessed June 20, 2019. https://www.rferl.org/a/kosovo-mitrovica-divided-town/24903007.html.

Të dhënat e regjistrimit të popullsisë dhe ndikimi i tyre në politikat publike, GAP Politike Analizash. Accessed August 20, 2019. https://www.institutigap.org/documents/67092_GAPanalizepertedhenateASK.pdf.

The Constitution of the Republic of Kosovo, 2008.

Therborn, Göran. "Why and How Place Matters". In the Oxford Handbooks of Political Science, edited by Robert E. Gooding and Charles Tilly, 510–516. New York: Oxford University Press Inc., 2006.

Tilly, Charles. "Why and How History Matters". In the Oxford Handbooks of Political Science, edited by Robert E. Gooding and Charles Tilly, 417–430. New York: Oxford University Press Inc., 2006.

Trautman, Reinhold. Slawisch-Baltische Quellen und Forschung. Leipzig: Verlag Market&Petters, 1937.

UNMIK. "Zyra per perkrahjen e komuniteteve". Accessed August 15, 2019. https://unmik.unmissions.org/sq/zyra-p%C3%ABr-p%C3%ABrkrahje-komuniteteve.

Viktor, Meier. Jugoslawiens Erben: die neuen Staatenund die Politik des Westens. München: Beck, 2001.

Ziegler, Jean. Globalisierung. Das Imperium der Schande. Der Kampf gegen Armut und Unterdrückung. München: C. Bertelsmann, 2005.

Zyra e Kryeministrit dhe Agjencia e Statistikave te Kosoves: Seria 5: Statistikat sociale. Statistikat e Mireqenies Sociale TM2 2019. Prishtine: Agjencia e Statistikave te Kosoves, 2019.

PART 3

Conclusion

CHAPTER 9

Social Security in the Balkans: Lessons and Recommendations

Marzena Żakowska and Dorota Domalewska

The Balkan states – Albania, Bosnia and Hercegovina, Bulgaria, Croatia, Greece, Kosovo, Montenegro, Republic of North Macedonia, Romania, and Serbia – have experienced numerous challenges resulting from the economic crisis and conflicts in the 1980s and 1990s, the transformation of political and economic systems in the move to democracy and open market economy, the 2008 economic crisis, and more recently the economic crisis caused by the COVID-19 pandemic. These challenges brought about major social problems, including a high level of unemployment, widespread poverty, brain drain, population aging, and falling birth rate, which have significantly affected the functioning of the pension and health systems, as well as the social cohesion and stability of the states. To overcome these problems, numerous and comprehensive reforms have been implemented focusing on the development of social protection mechanisms providing a broad range of social programs synchronized with a long-term strategy for economic growth, especially in the job market to ensure inclusive growth with an emphasis on equity. Nonetheless, the implementation of some reforms is still moving ahead slowly due to the complex relations between political parties and numerous lobby groups resulting in a lack of national consensus. This situation can be remedied through cooperation and strong social dialogue between the communities within the state.

The study clearly confirms that social security is a fundamental component of ensuring the stability of the state on a sustainable basis, supports development and social cohesion, affects social justice, and maintains social peace. State security is not attained by focusing solely on the political, economic, military or law enforcement domains; particularly in regions that have experienced conflict and instability. Social policy, including the welfare, pension, and health systems, is a broad security tool which the state can use to increase human capital especially when crafting an inclusive labor market policy. Thus, social policy can energise the labor market contributing to productivity growth, and the economic and socio-political development of the state.

Hence, enabling a sustainable social security system is not only a mechanism for meeting human needs and providing protection against social risks, but being grounded in citizens' rights, it is an instrument establishing peace and stability in the region. In this respect, the need for promoting social security systems has been emphasized by the EU as a fundamental part of the integration process, stressing that state development is understood as promoting political processes, enhancing economic growth, supporting access to basic services, health and education, and promoting social inclusion and cohesion. A stable social security system is one of the most crucial factors that ensures prosperity, fairness, lasting peace and, as a result, regional security. Therefore, the Balkan states should continue their path strengthening efforts directed at developing their social security systems to ensure and enhance the welfare and dignity of both individual citizens and communities.

1   Managing Social Security: Recommendations and Practical Implications

The primary goal of a social security system is to reduce social risks and protect the poor from income variability. The social protection system is integrated into national development strategies that not only provide transfers to the economically inactive poor and vulnerable individuals, but also are an instrument of supporting inclusive and sustainable development of the state. In their analyses of social security in their individual Balkan states, the authors of this three-volume publication have highlighted several important implications for improving social security policy in the welfare, pension, and healthcare systems, and labor policy. Detailed recommendations are provided by the authors in their individual chapters:

- *Volume 1* – Predrag Bejaković (Croatia); Velibor Lalić, Mile Šikman, Nevenko Vranješ (Bosnia and Herzegovina); Teuta Nunaj Kortoci, Shkëlzen Macukulli (Albania); Mirela Cristea, Graţiela Georgiana Noja (Romania); Dorota Domalewska, Irina Mindova Docheva (Bulgaria); Nikos Kourachanis, Effrosyni E. Kouskouna, Christos Koutsampelas, Aspasia Strantzalou (Greece);
- *Volume 2* – Katerina Veljanovska Blazhevska, Afet Mamuti, Katerina Mitevska Petrusheva, Kire Sharlamanov (the Republic of North Macedonia); Maja Baćović, Agata Domachowska, Tomasz Ferfecki, Natalija Perišić, Marzena Żakowska (Montenegro);
- *Volume 3* – Katarina Stanić, Gordana Matković, Maja Jandrić, Marzena Żakowska (Serbia); Dritero Arifi, Ngadhnjim Brovina, Përllumb Çollaku,

Besnik Fetahu, Remzije Istrefi, Ruzhdi Morina, Artan Mustafa, Marzena Żakowska (Kosovo).

Furthermore, the main recommendations for improving social security are summarized and outlined here:

Social protection. A serious challenge faced by the Balkan states is the reorganization of social policy to launch social programs and mechanisms enabling an optimal response to groups and individuals in need caused by social risks, to optimize vulnerable group protection, to develop mechanisms for inclusivity, equal opportunity, and the best possible level of social protection for all citizens. All Balkan states are devoted to providing social protection where economically feasible; thus, the distribution of social welfare varies across the region. A priority for social welfare is to extend and optimize cover for vulnerable groups and establish quick assistance support mechanisms.

Accordingly, policy effort should be addressed to better target groups in need as well as to provide active inclusion of beneficiaries within the policy context of minimum income protection. Specific attention should be paid to vulnerable and marginalized groups, especially those living in rural areas. Continuing reforms in this direction require supporting legislative amendments crafted to EU standards emphasizing improved effective statutory access to social protection schemes. Following this social assistance programs should place more emphasis on the promotion of gender equality including the economic empowerment of women and protection of vulnerable and marginalized groups, which will allow broader social justice.

To this end increasing the involvement of government at the local level in implementing services and dealing with poverty is vital for improving the effectiveness and responsiveness of service delivery. In this process it is extremely important to recognize the structure and dynamics of the labor market (at the local and national level), the demography of society with emphasis on population aging, and the structure of the family. This suggests further decentralization and deinstitutionalization of social security systems to improve and facilitate the distribution of social welfare to citizens of the country and the region.

Responding to the above changes requires careful management of expenditure to ensure the implementation of a fiscal consolidations strategy and introduce clear financing methods. Finally, targeting and allocation of resources needs to be improved in order to not only provide more substantial relief and thus lift more people out of poverty but also to combat corruption and protectionism. In this regard the support provided by social assistance programs should be well planned and long-term, and not reactive and a temporary response to various social pressures. Managing social challenges without a proper long-term policy for the revitalization of human and infrastructural resources may place states on the brink of financial collapse.

Pension system. The most common problem identified in the pension systems is an unsatisfactory ratio between the number of employees and the number of pensioners that leads to insufficient funding from paid contributions for mandatory pension and disability insurance. This situation raises a number of questions such as further extending the increase in retirement age, tightening early retirement criteria, changing the criteria of the pension adjustment formula (the valorization and indexation of pensions), strengthening the agricultural sector self-declaration and contribution payments, and bringing a systematic solution to the development of day-care services for the elderly.

Ensuring the long-term financial sustainability of systems requires policymakers to be cognizant of comprehensively analyzed demographic challenges (such as the aging population, the low fertility rate, the projected increase in life expectancy, depopulation due to economic migration, particularly among the young) and intergenerational fairness. Only then can they wisely craft policy and programs.

Observed intergenerational social contracts are currently heavily biased towards old age and are not favorable for the working age population and children. Retirement policies need to be encompassed in both pension schemes and a wider system of social protection benefiting all citizens especially the young. Improving cost-effectiveness enhances pension yield. Better pension individualization and the further development of voluntary pension schemes with transparent measures to protect individual citizens' accumulated pensions is the key to further promotion of the private pensions sector. A further and more challenging measure is developing a long-term strategy to reduce informal employment, and to enhance active labor market policies encouraging individuals to delay retirement (targeting the elderly).

The other matter requiring careful consideration is the scheme of social insurance and maintaining a balance between non-contributory and contributory pensions, taking into account fiscal risks resulting from demographic dynamics. Furthermore, tightening social insurance collection is necessary as numerous employers evade paying contributions, depriving governments of vital revenues needed for social and economic programs. The high social cost of pension provision requires reduction by the imposition of stricter expenditure controls and the re-evaluation of pension entitlement rules. These two measures are the key to increasing government revenue and ensuring the fairness of the system.

Health care system. The Balkan states are struggling with a number of challenges to the health care system, in particular improving the quality of medical services, accessibility to patients, decreasing out-of-pocket payments and corruption. Therefore, the reform path in this area should follow phased implementation reducing the financial burden on the state, changing the formula for cost containment, implementing private health care insurance, and improving the organization of primary health care. The COVID-19 pandemic exposed weaknesses in health systems across the region confirming the urgency for further institutional reforms, especially in primary healthcare, hospital infrastructure, service delivery, and equity of access. The effectiveness of resource allocation in local health care is now of primary importance to deliver care quality.

Social risk. The main social risks in the Balkans are poverty and unemployment. Long-term policies are required to reduce the levels of poverty across the region with emphasis on better selection and application of poverty assessment tools, and improving the governance mechanisms investing in human capital, combating corruption and protectionism. Further consideration should be given to implementing inclusive policies towards marginalized ethnic groups.

Reducing the unemployment rate and better monitoring of the labor market currently represent important priorities for economic policy in the Balkan states. An auxiliary mechanism for tackling unemployment emphasizes activation of labor market policies for the unemployed with particular reference to further developing young people for the needs of the job market especially increasing the participation of women in the workforce. A complementary challenge for the state is the creation of new jobs, which is particularly difficult in times of economic turbulence. Increasing labor market participation is the best way to reduce informal employment combating the grey economy and increasing tax revenues by broadening the tax base.

Another strategy is maximising the level of investment in human capital growth by linking education with the professional world, changing the methods and scope of teaching, and boosting public training programs for the unemployed particularly in vocational education. The introduction of these measures should reduce emigration flows and hence maintain population levels, especially among the young.

2 Structural Factors of a Sustainable Social Security System

The analysis of social security in individual Balkan countries indicates that examining a social security system requires the implementation of a set of approaches with emphasis on: (i) human needs, which are directly affected by social risk; (ii) national security approach acknowledging internal and foreign policy as well as the role and relations of social security with other security domains (e.g., political, economic, military, environmental, societal); (iii) holistic approach based on a multifaceted interplay of internal and external factors influencing the organization and development of social security. The most influential internal factors are political, societal, economic, demographic, cultural, and military, but others, such as energy and the environment, may also be considered. External factors include political actors; events and/or security threats, such as economic crises, armed conflicts, migration, and pandemics; and processes - political system transformation and EU integration. The primary factor for consideration in the Balkan region is the EU's role as a political actor in the provision of guidance and recommendations for adopting national strategies and social policies to EU accession requirements. Nevertheless, as security has a dynamic nature, the list of factors remains open-ended. These factors act and interact in various dimensions – autonomous and/or combined, which has been presented in Figure 9.1.

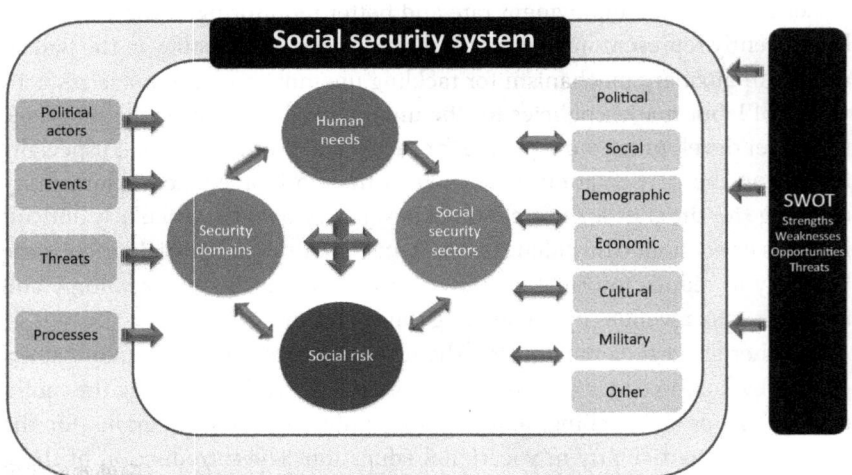

FIGURE 9.1 Factors affecting social security system
SOURCE: ELABORATION BY MARZENA ŻAKOWSKA.

The structure of the model is based on two groups of factors (a) endogenous: human needs, social risk, social security sectors, and security domains, and (b) exogenous, such as political actors, events and/or security threats, and processes. The influence of these factors on social security takes the form of complex interactions. Hence, further research is needed to fully understand the interplay of these factors; for example, the SWOT method may be used to examine the resulting strengths, weaknesses, opportunities, and threats.

3 Towards a Sustainable Social Security System in the Balkans

Social security plays a key role in securing sustainable development and social cohesion across the region. Developing social programs not only reduces risk and exposure to risk but also, through benefitting and empowering entire social groups, ensures the security and growth of the nation. Therefore, implementing social security reforms, following the recommendations presented in this three-volume monograph, is seen as an imperative to strengthening the Balkan region's role and position in European and global affairs.

This multinational study of social policy instruments of the Balkan states sheds light on national strengths and weaknesses, as well as opportunities and threats in developing effective social security strategies and reforms. Sustainable development of social security systems should be based on a comprehensive approach, including the consideration of complex factors recommended in this chapter, examination of their interaction, identification of the influence of external factors on social policy (particularly EU influence) and the close monitoring of social risks in order to adapt the social security system to the rapidly changing socio-economic context of the world (e.g., struggling with the COVID-19 pandemic).

The European integration of the Balkan states is closely bound to the implementation of the requirements of EU social policy and the development of individual states is integrally linked with the sustainable development of the Balkans as a region. Hence, more extensive research is needed to investigate national-level diversity and compare the cross-national factors shaping welfare, pensions, and healthcare systems. This will allow the further development of improved social security policies and mechanisms in the Balkan states, which will lead to enhance security of the Balkan region.

Index

absolute poverty   11–12, 34, 61–62, 67, 145
active labor market policies   117, 119
ageing   14, 101
agricultural employment   94
allowance
   care allowance   31
   child allowance   5, 31, 37–43, 45–46, 115
   disability allowance   31
   long-term care allowance   31, 35, 36, 37–38, 44, 53
anticipated pension   52, 55
arduous and unhealthy occupations   53–54
at risk of poverty or social exclusion rate   61–62

benefits
   child benefit   36–37, 144
   disability benefit   32–33, 134
   employment injury benefit   35
   in-kind benefit   83–84, 87
   long-term care benefit   35, 44
   pension benefit   32, 50–51, 53, 176–177
   social protection benefits   28–31, 35–43, 64, 136–137
   unemployment benefit   35–36, 45, 93, 114–117
birth grant   31, 36–37
budgetary transfer to PDI fund   64–65

child allowance   5, 31, 39, 45–46
childbirth-related leave   36–37
clientelistic policy   151–153
community-based services   42, 72, 74–76, 81
comprehensive security   225–227
corporatism   191
corruption   15, 215–216, 260–261

Dayton Agreement   236
decentralization   72–73, 86–87, 246, 259
deinstitutionalization   72, 87, 259
depopulation   27
disability insurance   30, 37, 51–52
disability pension   7, 32–34, 44, 51, 54, 56, 202–203

earmarked transfers   42, 75, 77–87
economic crisis   90, 92, 104, 173, 177, 182, 257

economic growth   11, 93, 181
employment
   employment elasticity   104–105
   employment policy   110–111, 117
   employment protection legislation   107–111, 117, 147
   employment rate   11–12, 91–97, 105–106, 150, 181, 197–198, 214
EPL index   110–112
ethnic Albanian   232, 234, 236, 238
European integration   2–4, 89, 189, 193–197, 207, 215–218, 246, 263
European Union   2–3, 89, 140, 190, 193–194, 207
extreme poverty   145, 210, 214

Federal Republic of Yugoslavia   127, 236–237
financial crisis of 2008   92, 104, 173, 177, 257
flat-rate pension   8, 33

German point system   51
Gini coefficient   209
grey economy   13, 43, 45, 46, 96, 261

healthcare   8–11, 260–261
healthcare reform   8–11
health insurance   30, 36, 132–135, 140, 143–144, 204, 208
hysteresis effect   108

individual pension savings insurance   167, 178
informality of the economy   13, 43, 46, 96, 261
institutional change   128–131, 136–144, 151–153
insurance
   health insurance   30, 36, 132–134, 140, 143–145, 153, 204, 208
   insurance contributions   31
   insurance fund   30, 141, 204
   pension insurance   6, 32–33, 54, 56, 67–68, 201
   social insurance   4–5, 28–36, 132, 140–144, 148–149
International Labor Organization   90, 110

Kosovo Liberation Army   127, 236

labor force   11–15, 102, 150
labor law   110–112, 147, 193
labor market   5, 14, 17, 89–90, 99–103, 104–109
labor market duality   99, 107
labor market policies
　active   17, 108, 117–119, 149, 260
　passive   35
life expectancy   62, 69
long-term care   30, 37, 206
long-term care allowance   31, 35, 36, 37, 38, 44, 53
long-term unemployment   99, 117

maternity leave   144, 149
migrants   192, 211
migration   13–14, 103, 153, 154, 181, 230–231
minimum income   7, 43, 54
minimum income benefit   45
minimum income protection   259
minimum income scheme   40
minimum pension   34, 43–44, 52, 54–55, 61

nationalism   228–229
national defined contribution   17, 179

old age pension   6–7, 32, 34, 53–65, 177–178

parental leave   36–37, 43, 144, 149
passive labor policies   35
pay-as-you-go system   17, 32, 53, 132, 134, 141
pension
　disability pension   7, 32–34, 44, 54, 56, 202–203
　early retirement pension   138, 144, 247, 260
　old-age pension   6–7, 32, 34, 53–65, 177–178
　private pensions   134–135, 148, 165, 260
　social pension   45–46, 54, 68, 201
　special pension   8
　supplementary pension   168
　survivor's pension   33, 34, 44, 46, 56
　voluntary pension   6, 135, 175, 178, 260
pension adjustment formula   260
pension and disability insurance   30, 31, 37, 51, 52, 136, 163, 260

pension reform   50–52, 141–144, 166–170
pension replacement rate   52, 56–58, 60, 65
pension system   6–8, 32–34, 43–45, 53–55, 133–135, 137–138, 162–165, 170–183, 205, 247, 260
pension system deficit   64
poverty
　absolute poverty   11, 34, 45, 46, 61–62, 210–211
　child poverty   6, 27
　poverty rate   11–13, 27, 62, 145–146, 200, 211, 214
　poverty threshold   144, 210
　relative poverty   39
poverty protection   138, 143, 144–146, 152
Private Pension Fund   165

recession   11, 90, 92, 104, 173, 177, 182, 257
reform
　healthcare reform   8–11
　insurance system reform   140–144
　pension reform   50–52, 141–144, 166–170
regional differences   100–101, 201
replacement rate   52, 56–58, 60, 65
retirement policy   7, 32, 50–55, 66, 138, 163–184, 215–216
risk of poverty and social exclusion   11–12, 27, 39, 61–62, 201
Roma population   10, 27, 29, 40, 235, 239–240, 246, 248

Security Council Resolution   1, 237
Serbian List   241–242
Serbian Orthodox Church   243–244
social assistance system   4–5, 28–36, 67, 81, 139, 144–146, 188–189, 199–201, 206–208, 214
social benefits   28–31, 35–43, 64, 136–137
social care services   41–42, 72–87, 152
social exclusion   11–12, 29, 34, 39, 61–62
social insurance   4–5, 28–36, 132, 140–144, 148–149
social insurance contributions   31
social insurance fund   30, 141
social pension   45–46, 54, 68, 201
social protection   4–5, 28–36, 81, 144–146, 188–189, 199–201, 206–208, 214
social rights   154, 193, 195, 216

social work centers   36, 74–75, 132, 138, 188, 200
Socialist Republic of Yugoslavia   131, 236
survivor's pension   33, 34, 44, 46, 56
Swiss formula   7, 51, 55, 59, 64, 65

three-pillar pension system   5, 6–8, 51, 55, 134, 165–184
trade unions   107, 170

unemployment
   long-term unemployment   99, 117
   unemployment benefits   35–36, 45, 93, 114–117

unemployment insurance   30, 31, 114
unemployment rate   91–97, 108, 109, 150, 181, 197–198
youth unemployment   14, 95, 207–208

veto points   130
veto powers   130, 151–153
voluntary Pension Fund   178
voluntary pension scheme   6, 175

welfare state   14, 27, 128, 129, 131

youth unemployment   14, 95, 207–208
Yugoslavia   127, 131, 235–237

www.ingramcontent.com/pod-product-compliance
Lightning Source LLC
Chambersburg PA
CBHW070913030426
42336CB00014BA/2394